CORNEILLE AND HIS TIMES.

CORNEILLE AND HIS TIMES.

BY M. GUIZOT.

KENNIKAT PRESS
Port Washington, N. Y./London

CORNEILLE AND HIS TIMES

First published in 1852
Reissued in 1972 by Kennikat Press
Library of Congress Catalog Card No: 76-153271
ISBN 0-8046-1569-1

Manufactured by Taylor Publishing Company   Dallas, Texas

PREFACE.

———◆———

I have reprinted, in the present Volume, one of the first works of my youth, a work published for the first time in 1813, nearly forty years ago. I have made many changes in it, and I was tempted to change much more. So many years, and such years, develope in the mind entirely new views upon all subjects, upon literature as well as life ; and no one is ignorant of the discoveries which we may make by changing our horizon, without changing our ideas. Perhaps, therefore, I ought to have re-written my work. I did not wish to do so. A book must exist and last out its time as it is. This book is, if I mistake not, a faithful image of the spirit which prevailed, forty years ago, in literature, among the men who cultivated it, and the public who loved it.

For literature was carefully cultivated and truly loved at that time, which left it so little space for its manifestation. Never had the rude hand of politics

so completely held dominion over France ; never
had force so incessantly filled years, months, and
days with its actions and hazards.   War seemed to
have become the normal state of human society,—
not war restrained within certain limits by the law
of nations and the ancient traditions of States, but
war unlimited and immense, overturning, deranging,
commingling or separating, violently and without
intermission, both governments and nations.   During
the early days of my youth, and before its termination, I beheld civilised Europe exposed to two opposite deluges of invasion and conquest, the like of
which had never been witnessed since the fall of the
Roman Empire.   During the space of ten years, I
beheld the empire of Napoleon—the most dazzling,
the most overwhelming, and the most ephemeral
meteor that ever crossed the horizon of the world—
arise, grow, extend itself, and vanish away.   And
it was not only upon the political state of nations,
the fate of crowned heads, and the lives of generals
and soldiers, that the ever-increasing weight of those
vast conflicts which were destined to prove so vain
was laid ; their influence extended throughout the
whole of society ; no existence, however independent
or insignificant it may have been, was exempted from
putting forth its share of effort and bearing its part
of the general burden ; and domestic life, in the
obscurest as well as in the most elevated regions of

society, was stricken by the same blows which over-
turned the thrones of kings and effaced the boundaries
of empires.   In 1810, the commands of absolute
power dragged from their homes sons and brothers
who had complied with all the obligations of the
law, and sent them violently to the army.   In 1814,
the rural districts were deficient in cultivators ; and,
in the towns, suspended labour and abandoned build-
ings presented an appearance of recent ruins, as
strange as it was painful to contemplate.

Such a state of things, in its glories as well as in
its disasters, is but ill-suited to the prosperity of
literature, which requires either more repose or more
liberty.   And yet, such is the intellectual vitality of
France that, even then, it did not suffer itself to be
confined or exhausted in a single career ; but it
furnished noble gratifications to the minds of men
generally, at the same time that it lavished tens of
thousands of brave and energetic soldiers to gratify
the insatiable ambition of one man.

Three literary powers (I do not here allude to
scientific men or philosophers) flourished during the
Empire, and exercised a pregnant influence both
upon authors and upon the public.   These were
the *Journal des Débats*, M. de Chateaubriand, and
Mme. de Stael.

The literary restoration of France,—-that is, a
return to the study of the ancient classics and of

our own French classics, the great writers of the
seventeenth century—was the undertaking and the
work of the *Journal des Débats*. It was a work of
re-action, often excessive and unjust, as is the case
with all re-actions ; but it was a work of good sense
and good taste, which led the public mind back to a
feeling of the truly beautiful—of that beautiful which
is at once grand and simple, eternal and national. It
was the characteristic of the seventeenth century in
France that literature was then cultivated for its own
sake, not as an instrument for the propagation of
certain systems, and for ensuring the success of particular designs. Corneille, Racine, and Boileau, and
even Molière and La Fontaine, entertained, upon the
great philosophical and political questions of the
day, either very decided opinions, or very marked
tendencies ; Pascal and La Bruyère, Bossuet and
Fénélon, made more of philosophy and polemics
than any other writers at any other period have been
able to do. But, in their literary activity, these great
men had no other pre-occupation than the beautiful
and the true, and were anxious to paint them well
and skilfully only that they might gain for them
greater admiration. They felt, for the object of
their labours, a love which was pure from every other
thought, and which was as serious as it was pure ;
for, whilst they did not assume to rule society by their
writings, they aspired to something far above the

mere amusement of mankind. A frivolous and worldly
entertainment was as far from their intentions as a
haughty or indirect propagandism. At once modest
and proud, they demanded of literature, for the public
as well as for themselves, none but intellectual enjoyments ; but they introduced and infused into these
enjoyments a profound and almost solemn feeling,
believing themselves called upon to elevate the souls
of men by charming them with the exhibition of the
beautiful, and not merely to arouse them for a
moment from their idleness or *ennui.*

And not only is this the great characteristic of the
literature of the seventeenth century, but it was by
this that the seventeenth century was essentially and
supremely a literary age. The Muses, to speak in
classic language, are jealous divinities ; they will
reign and not serve, be adored and not employed ;
and they bestow all their treasures only upon those
who seek after them solely to enjoy them, and
not to expend them upon foreign uses. It was on
this account also that the *Journal des Débats,* fifty
years ago, became a literary power. Other journals
devoted themselves, with considerable talent, to
literature ; but the *Journal des Débats* was able,
better than any other, to discern and appropriate to
itself, as it were, the truly literary idea. It reminded
literature of its own power, by referring it to the
examples of the time at which it had shone with

greatest lustre, as regarded itself, and had been animated by the purest and most independent feeling of its mission. The principal writers in the *Journal des Débats*, at the time to which I allude— MM. Geoffroy, Feletz, Dussault, Fiévée, and Hoffmann —were, in themselves, men of very distinguished mental powers ; but if they had written isolatedly, and each one had followed the bent of his own inclination, they would assuredly have obtained far less general authority and personal renown. They grouped themselves around one thought—the literary restoration of the seventeenth century ; with this object, and beneath this standard, they attacked the writers of the following century and of the age in which they lived, whether philosophers or scholars, poets or prose-writers,—men to whose influence they had long submitted, and whose tastes and ideas they frequently, at bottom, still retained. And by placing themselves thus, in the sphere of literature, at the head of the general movement of anti-revolutionary re-action, their journal became the literary journal *par excellence*, and they obtained a real sway over the public judgment and taste.

In the very midst of this dominion, and with the entire favour of the journal which wielded it, arose the boldest innovator and the most modern genius that has illustrated our contemporary literature : I mean M. de Chateaubriand, a genius as little akin to

the seventeenth century as to the eighteenth, a brilliant
interpreter of the incoherent ideas and disturbed
feelings of the nineteenth, and himself affected by
those maladies of our time which he so well understood and described, flattering and opposing them by
turns. Read once again the " Essai Historique sur
les Révolutions," "René," and the " Mémoires d'Outre-
tombe," those three works in which M. de Chateaubriand, in his youth, his mature age, and his old age,
has pourtrayed himself with such complacency ; is
there a single one of our dispositions and of our
moral infirmities which is not contained therein ? Our
vast hopes, our speedy disappointments, our changeful
temptations, our perpetual ardours, exhaustions, and
revivals, our alternating ambitions and susceptibilities,
our returns to faith and our relapses into doubt, our aspirations sometimes towards authority and sometimes
towards liberty,—that activity at once indefatigable
and uncertain, that commingling of noble passions
and of egotism, that fluctuation between the past and
the future, indeed all those variable and ill-assorted
features which, for half a century, have characterised
the state of society and of the human soul amongst
us,—of all these things M. de Chateaubriand was
conscious in his own person, and his works, like his
life, everywhere attest their influence and bear their
impress. Hence arose his popularity, which was
general, in spite of our dissensions, and continued,

notwithstanding our political and literary revolutions.
The lettered and travelled gentleman who so boldly
yielded to the exuberance of an imagination enriched
with the treasures of all ages and of all worlds, the
author who made so novel and sometimes so rash an
use of our language,—this poetical and romantic
prose-writer gained the admiration of the purest and
most rigid judges, of M. de Fontanes, of M. Bertin,
and of all the classic school of the *Journal des
Débats.* The political *émigré* and partisan of the
Bourbons, who, whenever the sovereign and definitive
question was ·proposed, invariably ranged himself on
the side of ancient recollections, has always obtained
or regained the favour of the young liberal, and even
revolutionary, generations. He was attentive and
skilful in conciliating these various suffrages; he
possessed an instinctive perception of public impressions, and could select, from his own feelings,
that which was likely to please them. But this
skilfulness would never have sufficed to gain him
such difficult and opposite successes, unless he had
been, by his merits as well as by his defects, by the
good qualities as well as by the weaknesses of his
character and genius, in harmony with his age; he
answered to inclinations and tastes which, though very
different in other respects, were equally eager after,
and delighted with, the gratifications which he offered
them. For this reason, in politics, notwithstanding

his continual reverses, he was always a formidable adversary ; and in literature, from the same cause, he exercised over the whole of the public, over those minds which distrusted him as well as over those who blindly admired or imitated him, a most prompt and remarkable influence.

Madame de Stael was not adapted thus to please so many different parties and tastes. She was a passionate and sincere person, who had her feelings and ideas seriously at heart, and she was, at the same time, a faithful representative of the eighteenth century, in its best and noblest aspirations. So true a nature, formed in the midst of so factitious a state of society, and so brilliant a mixture of the life of the soul and the life of the *salons*, of inner emotions and worldly impressions, have rarely been met with. This is the original and striking feature in Madame de Stael, and this forms her strong bond of union with the eighteenth century, although, in other and important respects, she differs widely from it. It was an age full of confusion and contradiction, of serious ambition and frivolous manners, of generosity and personality,—which became intoxicated at once with moral sentiments and with ideas destructive of all morality, which desired to attain to goodness whilst utterly disregarding its source and laws, and which led men to the gates of Hell by dreaming for them, with lively and sincere sympathy, of innocence and the happiness of Paradise. Madame de Stael retained, under the Empire, the generous sentiments of that old liberal *régime* amidst which her youth had been passed ; her mind had become elevated and purified without detriment to her faith ; and independently of their intrinsic merit, her works, whatever they might be, literature, philosophy, romance, morality or personal memoirs, received therefrom a powerful element of attraction. When a people has engaged with passionate earnestness in a great movement on behalf of a great cause, no mistakes, no disasters, no remorse, no re-action, however natural and mighty it may be, can efface from its heart the remembrance of its first days of strength and hope. The Revolution which began in 1789 has already received, and will perhaps con- tinue to receive, some harsh lessons ; it has already cost, and will perhaps continue to cost, France very dear ; the Empire, which sprang from it, disowned and maltreated it strangely ; and yet 1789 was, under the Empire, and is at the present day, and will always continue to be, a great national date, a powerful word, most dear to France. Madame de Stael was and remained attached to 1789; she clung to it by fibres ever living, even where they seemed utterly deadened. The numerous readers of her writings delighted to find in them—some their recollections and the image, manners and tone of that

old society in which they had moved, and others
their hopes, and a living faith in the principles of that
future which they had dreamed of for their country ;
for all, they contained matter either for sympathy,
for criticism, or for commentary ; and each new
work of Madame de Stael constituted, in the literary
world, in the drawing-rooms of fashion, and even
among the scattered and distant public, an intellectual
event, a theme of conversation, of discussions, of
reminiscences, or of prospects full of movement and
interest.

I am desirous to pass over no merit, and to
offend no memory : the literature of the Empire
certainly presents other names which justly occupied
public attention at that time, and which ought not
now to be forgotten. I persist, however, in my
conviction : the *Journal des Débats*, that association
of judicious restorers of the literary ideas and tastes of
the seventeenth century—M. de Chateaubriand, that
brilliant and sympathetic interpreter of the moral
and intellectual perplexities of the nineteenth—and
Madame de Stael, that noble echo of the generous
sentiments and noble aspirations of the eighteenth,
—are the three influences, the three powers, which,
under the Empire, truly acted upon our literature
and left their impress upon its history.

And all these three powers were in opposition.
The incidents of their life would teach us this even

if their writings did not exist to prove it. By an
unexampled act of confiscation, the *Journal des
Débats* was taken out of the hands of its proprietors ;
M. de Chateaubriand was excluded from the French
Academy ; and Madame de Stael spent ten years
in exile.

Absolute power is not the necessary enemy of
literature, nor is literature necessarily its enemy.
Witness Louis XIV. and his age. But for literature
to flourish under such a state of things, and to
embellish it with its splendour, absolute power must
be acknowledged by the general moral belief of the
public, and not merely accepted as a result of circumstance, in the name of necessity. It is also requisite that the possessor of absolute authority should
know how to respect the dignity of the great minds
that cultivate literature, and to leave them sufficient
liberty for the unrestrained manifestation of their
powers. France and Bossuet believed sincerely in
the sovereign right of Louis XIV. ; Molière and La
Fontaine freely ridiculed his courtiers as well as his
subjects ; and Racine, through the mouth of Joad,
addressed to the little king Joas precepts with
which the great king was not offended. When
Louis XIV., during his persecution of the Jansenists,
said to Boileau : " I am having search made for
M. Arnauld in every direction," Boileau replied :
" Your Majesty is always fortunate ; you will not

find him ;" and the king smiled at the courageous wit of the poet, without showing any symptoms of anger. On such conditions, absolute power can co-exist harmoniously with the greatest and most high-spirited minds that have ever devoted themselves to literature. But nothing of the kind was the case under the Empire. The Emperor Napoleon, who had saved France from anarchy, and was covering her with glory in Europe, was nevertheless regarded, by all clear-sighted and sensible men, merely as the sove-reign master of a temporary government, in little harmony with the general tendencies of society, and commanded by necessity rather than established in faith. He was served, and with good reason, by men of eminent minds and noble characters, for his government was necessary and great ; but beyond his government, in the regions of thought, great minds and lofty characters possessed neither inde-pendence nor dignity. Napoleon was not wise enough to leave them their part in space ; and he feared without respecting them. Perhaps he could not possibly have acted otherwise ; and perhaps this may have been a vice of his position, as much as an error of his genius. Nowhere, in no degree, and under no form, did the Empire tolerate opposition. In France, in the age in which we live, this becomes, sooner or later, even for the strongest governments, a deceitful snare and an immense danger. After

fifteen years of glorious absolute power, Napoleon
fell ; the proprietors of the *Journal des Débats*
regained possession of their property ; M. de
Chateaubriand celebrated the return of the Bourbons ; and Madame de Stael beheld the great desires
of 1789 consecrated by the Charter of Louis XVIII.
And now, after thirty-four years of that system for
which our fathers longed so ardently ! . . . . . God
gives us severe lessons, which we must comprehend
and accept, without despairing of the good cause.
After having witnessed these prodigious vicissitudes
of human affairs, we are equally cured of presumption
and of discouragement.

When, in 1813, I published this sketch of the
literature of the seventeenth century, I was aided in
my labour by a person to whom I was long indebted
for my happiness, and to whom I shall ever owe the
dearest recollections of my life. The essays on
Corneille's three contemporaries, Chapelain, Rotrou,
and Scarron, were prepared and, to a great extent,
written out by her. I have carefully revised them,
as well as the essays on Poetry in France before the
Time of Corneille, and on Corneille himself ; and
I leave them in their place as an integral part of
this work.

The Appendices annexed to the life of Corneille,
have been furnished to me by the friendship of that
learned Norman archæologist, M. Floquet, whose

researches have elucidated so many important points in our political and literary history, and who is now preparing a work on the Life and Writings of Bossuet, which is full of real discoveries. My gratitude to him, I am sure, only anticipates that of the public.

GUIZOT.

Paris : *May* 24, 1852.

CONTENTS.

✦

POETRY IN FRANCE

BEFORE THE TIME OF CORNEILLE.

LITERARY history has this advantage over general history, that it holds in actual possession, and is able to exhibit, the very objects which it desires to make known and to judge. Achilles and Priam are dead; all our knowledge of them and their actions is derived from Homer; but Homer still lives—by his poems he belongs to history, and his poems are in our hands.

To behold these creations of genius is, however, not sufficient; we must also understand them. How can we understand literary history without being acquainted with the times and the men in whose midst the monuments to which it refers were reared? and how can we become acquainted with men who were as yet unable to exercise their powers of

observation, and to gain a knowledge of themselves ?
As Milton says :—

> " For man to tell how human life began
> Is hard ;—for who himself beginning knew ? "

Literary history is, then, frequently under the
necessity of compensating, by conjecture, for the
silence of facts. But conjectures founded upon the
natural progress of the human mind fail when we
have to account for the course pursued by the literature of modern times.   Among a people whose
character is formed in a simple manner, and whose
civilisation is the result of the free and harmonious
development of the human mind, the question of the
origin of literature, although somewhat complicated
in itself, is not very difficult of solution : the answer
must be sought, and will be found, in the spontaneous expansion of our nature.   Poetry, the first
outburst of a budding imagination in the midst of a
world that is new to it, then finds, in all surrounding
objects, themes for its songs, and derives from the
simplest sights a host of sensations previously unknown.   Adam, on opening his eyes for the first
time to the light, thus describes to us his first
movements :—

> *   *   " As new waked from soundest sleep,
> Soft on the flowery herb I found me laid.
> Straight toward Heaven my wondering eyes I turned
> And gazed awhile the ample sky ; till raised
> By quick instinctive motion, up I sprung,

As thitherward endeavouring, and upright
Stood on my feet. About me round I saw
Hill, dale, and shady woods, and sunny plains,
And liquid lapse of murm'ring streams ; by these,
Creatures that lived, and moved, and walk'd or flew ;
Birds on the branches warbling : all things smiled ;
With fragrance and with joy my heart o'erflow'd.
Myself I then perused, and limb by limb
Survey'd, and sometimes went, and sometimes ran
With supple joints, as lively vigour led :
But who I was, or where, or from what cause,
Knew not : to speak I tried, and forthwith spake." [1]

Such is man at the moment when his faculties awake to the first joys of imagination ; he gazes at the ample dome of heaven—at the woods and plains ; he thinks he sees them for the first time ; around him, all things are animated and excite him ; within himself, inspiration awakes and agitates him ; his accumulated sensations demand expression ; he tries to speak, and speaks ; and poetry is born, as simple as that which man beholds, as vivid as that which he feels.   It is nature that he displays to us— nature adorned with all the wealth that its aspect has developed within man.   He wishes to describe, and he paints ; he desires to give names to what he views, and, lo !—

" His tongue obey'd, and readily could name
Whate'er he saw."

But he names everything as he perceives it—as a being filled with a life that he himself imparts to it ;

---

[1] *Milton's* Paradise Lost, book viii.

his feelings and the objects which excite them, unite
in one and the same idea :—

> "With fragrance and with joy his heart o'erflows."

His moral nature is diffused universally over the physical nature which surrounds it; and his soul peoples
space with creatures, living and sensible like himself.
The Greeks took delight in song ; and Homer sang,
—he sang the victories of his fellow-countrymen,
their quarrels and reconciliations, their games and
festivals, their business and their pleasures.   On the
shield of Achilles are displayed flocks, harvests, and
vintages ; conjugal affection gives tenderness to the
farewells of Andromache ; Priam is a father weeping
over the loss of his son ; and Achilles utters the
laments of friendship over the body of Patroclus.
Thus, the most natural feelings and the simplest
interests were what inspired the muse of the prince
of poets.   These feelings were the first that moved
the heart of man ; these interests were, at the
outset, his only interests.   Before he came into
being, they animated earth and skies ; and, in the
events of a war waged by armed barbarians to
recover a woman—in the dispute of two chieftains
who had quarrelled about a slave, Homer perceived,
and has portrayed, nature in its noblest aspects,
man in all his attributes, and the gods everywhere.
Let it not be asked how Homer was led to enter-

tain such ideas, and what combinations of customs, circumstances, and positions, concurred to form the system of his poetry ; he could have had no other. If Homer had disappeared, and it were possible to invent him, it would be said : Such a man he must have been—an exemplification of that which could not fail to be produced by the development of the happiest faculties among a people at liberty to display them all, and among whom nothing had occurred to distort their character, to disturb their harmony, or to divert their course.

Such could not be the case with regard to modern nations : when they established themselves upon the ruins of a world that had already grown old, they were ignorant and incapable of comprehending those institutions from which their coarse manners were about to receive some forms, equally rude and more incoherent. A divine religion, coming down into the midst of nations at once enlightened and corrupted by a long term of existence ; a sublime morality, based on the precepts of the Gospel, too perfect for the manners of those who were about to receive it, and yet sufficiently positive to exact their obedience ; towns and palaces, which had been conquered, and were inhabited, by savages incompetent to appreciate the skill which had erected them ; luxury, for which they acquired a taste, and to which they became habituated, before they had learned its use ; enjoyments, distinctions, and titles, which had been invented by the vanity of an effeminate world, and which were paraded by barbarian vanity rather in imitation than from necessity ; all these facts could not fail to strike these new peoples as being one of those strange and confused spectacles at which ignorant spectators cannot even manifest sufficient astonishment, because they do not perceive its hidden springs and secret workings ; all these causes necessarily led to that confusedness of ideas, to those fantastic and incomplete associations of thought, of which modern literatures, in their early essays, and even in their masterpieces, present traces which, though varying in distinctness, are everywhere visible.

The Greek, at the origin and during the progress of his civilisation, appears to us like man issuing from the hands of God, in all the simplicity and grandeur of his nature—coming into existence in a world that is ready to yield to him all the riches that his intelligence can extract from her ample stores, but which discloses those riches gradually, and in proportion to the development of his intellect. The German barbarian, transported suddenly into the midst of Roman civilisation, presents to us a type of the children of men, cast abruptly into a world formed for creatures that already possess wide experience and full development : they pass their life surrounded by objects which they will use before they have studied their properties, and which they will abuse before they have learned their use, repeating words which suggest no meaning to their minds, subject to laws the object of which they do not comprehend, and striving to employ in their service things which more enlightened generations had invented for themselves, and adapted to their own convenience.

Amidst this infancy of modern nations, how can we distinguish what belongs to a nature continually stifled beneath the pressure of a factitious position, or to an education so very unappropriate to the necessities and faculties of those who received it? In such a state of things, the reason of man could keep pace neither with his position, nor with the interests which that position involved. At the epoch which Homer depicts, when men were probably unacquainted with the use of letters, and the coinage of money; when princes and heroes themselves prepared their own meals and those of their guests; when the daughters of kings washed the garments of the household — his personages, perfectly in harmony with the manners of their time and the state of their civilisation, have simple and consistent ideas, formed with perfect good sense: but how could these qualities and this state of mind have existed among those feudal lords of the Middle

Ages, whose titles were emblazoned in characters which they could not read—who coined money and plundered travellers—who dwelt in fortified castles, and were served by a train of domestics and slaves more skilful in the art of cookery than the divine Achilles himself?

It is this complication of causes in the manners of the Middle Ages, this singular mixture of natural barbarism and acquired civilisation, of antiquated notions and novel ideas, which renders it very difficult to explain the course pursued by the various literatures that issued from these times. They came into being in the midst of a crowd of obscure and discordant circumstances which it would be necessary to distinguish and connect, in order properly to link together the chain of facts, and to discern their progressive influence. Do we believe that we have discovered some of those decisive indications which serve to explain the character and conduct of peoples? We soon perceive that even these indications do not disclose the secret of the causes which have determined the genius of literatures; for the great events of history have acted upon letters only by unknown and indirect affinities, which it is almost impossible to apprehend. On beholding Dante in Italy and Milton in England, and observing the great resemblance that exists in the genius of these two poets, though born under climates so different, and that is still more evident between the subjects of their poetry, we are disposed to seek for the reasons of this conformity in general causes, and similarity of position. We persuade ourselves that the religious controversies and civil troubles in the midst of which Dante and Milton both lived, by directing the imagination of these men to the most serious interests of life, produced the circumstances best calculated to fertilise their genius. In the grandeur of the thoughts which must have formed the subject of their meditations, in the violence of the passions which agitated their souls, we find the source of that terrible sublimity and sombre energy which are equally remarkable in the " Paradise Lost " and in the " Divina Commedia," and which are equally associated, in both poems, with that theological subtlety, that hyperbolic exaggeration, and that abuse of allegory, which are the natural defects of an imagination that has hitherto known no check, and of a mind that is dazzled by the unexpected play of its own faculties. But when we think we have thus satisfactorily accounted for these great poetical masterpieces of Italy and England, we must inquire why similar circumstances produced nothing of the kind in France ; why the disorders of the League did not bear fruit similar to that borne by the revolutions of England and the civil wars of Florence ; and why, though almost contemporary with Milton, and living at a time when literature was at least in as forward a state as when Dante wrote, Malherbe bears so little resemblance to either ? We shall look for the secret of the different effects which have resulted in the different literatures, in the special nature of the governments, in the manners of the peoples, in the particular character of the troubles which agitated them, and in the personal position in which the authors and actors of these troubles were placed ; and we shall thus be led to acknowledge the influence of those innumerable secondary causes, whose nature or power it is impossible accurately to define, and whose reality.it is sometimes even impossible to affirm.

Such are the principal difficulties encountered by the historian who is anxious to discover the causes that determined the character and direction of modern literatures, at their origin and during the epochs nearest the period of their greatest glory. Compelled to content himself with views of the subject that are seldom complete, and with researches that are rarely well-directed, he can do no more, after great study, than arrive at a few general results, and some certain affinities ; and afterwards connect with these fixed and luminous points, all the facts which seem attached to them by any bond, more or less clear and more or less remote. This is what I shall attempt to do in giving a sketch of the progress of poetry in France until the period when Corneille inaugurated the glorious age of its fullest splendour.

In their complicated and obscure position, the literary spirit was developed, among modern nations, in a very rapid and incomplete manner. We find it animated and active, even to refinement, in certain directions ; whilst, at the same time, it is inert and rude everywhere else. In the midst of the darkness of general ignorance, partial enlightenment of mind resembles those will-o'-the-wisps which deceive as regards the spot they illuminate as well as respecting those which they leave in obscurity. Too easily satisfied with what it perceives, the mind errs through ignorance, and exaggerates the importance of what it has discovered as well as the uselessness of that of which it is ignorant. Those great features of nature, those first outlines of society, which the simplicity and small number of objects allowed the ancients to catch with so much felicity and to depict with such fidelity, could not be so clearly discerned by the moderns. Sketches, frequently of a puerile character, but treated with a seriousness that increased their puerility, heralded the first efforts of that poetical spirit which taste could not accompany ; for taste is the result of a full knowledge of things, and of a just estimate of their true value. The want of truth, however, soon brought poets back to the observation of their own feelings—the only subject that they could thoroughly understand—and introduced into poetry the description of a kind of emotions almost unknown

to the poets of antiquity.   Love, which, in the form
that has been given to it by our modern manners,
is the most fruitful of all the passions in fine and delicate shades, was also best adapted to give occupation
to minds disposed to the observation of details.   In
France especially, where it had become the principal
business of an idle nobility, love was almost exclusively the subject of the earliest efforts of poetic
genius.   Often unaffected and truthful in its
sentiments, it also frequently introduced into its
inventions that subtlety, that search after ingenious
and unexpected traits of character, which has constituted the chief defect of our literature.   Raimbault de
Vaqueiras, a poet and gentleman of Provence, loved
and was tolerated by Beatrice, sister of the Marquis
of Montferrat.[1]   Beatrice, on her marriage, thought
it her duty not to continue to receive his attentions.
Raimbault, nettled at this, " because the lady had
changed her opinion, as well as to show that the
change was agreeable to himself," wrote her a farewell song, sufficiently tender in its expressions, but in
which, " at each couplet, he changed the language in
which he wrote."   The first was in Provençal, the
second in Tuscan, the third in French, the fourth in
Gascon, the fifth in Spanish, " and the last couplet

---

[1] " I' dico l'uno e l'altro Raimbaldo
       Che cantar per Beatrice in Monferrato."
                     Petrarch, " Trionfo d'Amore," cap. iv.

was a mixture of words borrowed from all these five languages ; so lively an invention," adds Pasquier, " that if it had been presented to the knights and ladies who were judges of love, I am willing to believe that they would have decided in favour of the renewal of the loves of Beatrice with this gentle poet."[1] Thus, knights and ladies, if Pasquier judges them aright, would have granted everything to the ingenuity of the poet, without giving much heed to love itself, which probably occupied only a small place in such a *gentillesse*.

Much love, therefore, was not necessary to inspire a poet ; but the little love that he really felt, he could make large enough to fill his verses, just as scruples magnify devotion and occupy life. Pierre Vidal, a troubadour of Marseilles, who loved Adelaide de Roque-Martine, the wife of the Viscount of Marseilles, was so unfortunate in his amours as to afford sport to the Viscount himself. One day the poet found the Viscountess asleep and snatched a kiss ; she awoke and was very angry. Probably Vidal annoyed her still more as a lover than he amused her as a poet ; for, delighted at having found a pretext for getting rid of a troublesome admirer, whose poetry was his only merit, she persisted so inexorably in her anger, that even her husband could not obtain Vidal's pardon. In despair, or thinking

---

[1] " Recherches de la France," lib. vii. cap. iv. vol. ii. col. 695, 696.

that he ought to be so, Vidal embarked for the Holy
Land, in the suite of King Richard. As poetical in his
bravery as in his amours, and doubtless one of those
"whose tongue," to use Petrarch's phrase, "was at once
their lance and sword, their casque and buckler,"[1] he
fancied that he had performed great exploits, and so
celebrated them in his songs. After several singular
adventures, he returned to France, still enamoured
of the Viscountess of Marseilles, although in the mean-
time he had married a wife of his own, and miserable
at not having obtained a return of the kiss which he
had snatched. What Vidal demanded was not a new
kiss, but a liberal gift of the old one : not to have
granted him this would have been very cruel. At
the request of her husband, the Viscountess yielded
at last ; Vidal was satisfied, and so well satisfied that,
after having written a song in commemoration of his
happiness, he ceased to pursue an amour which furnished no further theme for his Muse.[2]

Still more disposed than Pierre Vidal to be satisfied
with the gifts of his imagination, Geoffroy Rudel, that
troubadour of whom Petrarch said, "that he made
use of the sail and the oar to go in search of death,"
sang the praises of the Countess of Tripoli, whom he
had never seen, but with whom he had fallen in love

---

[1] *   *   *   "A cui la lingua
 Lancia e spada fù sempre, e scudo ed elmo."
                    Petrarch, "Trionfo d'Amore," cap. iv.
[2] *Millot's* "Histoire littéraire des Troubadours," vol. ii. p. 266.

from the reports which had been made to him of her
beauty by many pilgrims on their return from the
Holy Land. He sent his verses to her, and " it is
highly probable," says Pasquier, " that he was not
without the written thanks of the lady ; which was
the cause that this gentleman, commanded more and
more by love, deliberated to sail to her ; but, in
order not to serve as a laughing-stock to his friends,
he desired to cover his voyage under a pretext of
devotion, saying that he was going to visit the holy
places of Jerusalem." Falling ill on the road, Geoffroy
arrived in the port of Tripoli, in a dying state. The
Countess, hearing of his arrival, " repaired immediately to the ship, where, having taken the hand
of this poor languishing gentleman, suddenly, when
he heard that it was the Countess, his spirits began
to return to him, and it was thought that her
presence would serve as his medicine : but their joy
was short ; for when, though quite weak, he was
desirous to use beautiful language, to thank her for
the honour which he had received from her without
having deserved it, scarcely had he opened his
mouth, than his voice died out, and he rendered his
soul to the other world." [1] According to other
accounts, the Countess was more tender, and finding
Geoffroy on the point of death, kissed him. Her kiss

---

[1] "Recherches de la France," lib. vii. cap. iv. vol. ii. col. 694, 695.
Millot's "Histoire littéraire des Troubadours," vol. i. p. 85.

restored him to consciousness ; he opened his eyes and died, thanking Providence for his happiness.   Of a truth, Geoffroy was easily satisfied.

Such was poetic love in Provence, at the commencement of the thirteenth century.   A slight acquaintance with the manners of this period will suffice to convince us that it was not from real life that the poets of the time usually derived their inspiration or their subjects.   Nothing is more prone to exaggeration and subtlety than that poetry which is founded solely on the sentiments of the heart or the combinations of the mind.   In the description of an action the poet has, for judges of the veracity of his narrative, all those who know how things occur in the world beneath their eyes ; and the boldest man would not venture, without some hesitation, or without calling in the aid of some supernatural power, to give his hero strength to knock down a tower with a single blow, or to spring with a single leap over the ramparts of a town.   But who can deny to the poet the delicacy of his own thoughts, or the violence of his own inward feelings ?   Who can maintain against him, that things could not have presented themselves to his mind, or have passed through his heart, in the manner in which he represents them to have done ?   What natural and sensible fact can be exhibited before his eyes to convince him of error ?   Until the multiplicity of examples has led to comparison and reflection ; until reflection has learned to distinguish the true from the false ; until a certain poetical scale of human feelings has been established, to indicate where they must stop, even in verse,—it is impossible for the imagination not to lose itself in that field which is open on all sides to its caprices ; and nothing can better explain how our early poetry, whether Provençal or French, passes incessantly, and almost without any interval, from truthful and touching sentiments and simple and natural details, to the most fantastic ideas and the most extravagant conceptions.

Another kind of poetry, namely *Satire*, necessarily arose at an early period in France, under the influence of those habits of society and conversation which were so early cultivated, and of that semi-despotic, semi-aristocratic form of monarchy, which leaves the victims of abuses no other resource than complaint or ridicule. We meet with examples of this satire, under the name of *Sirventes*, among the Provençal troubadours of the twelfth century : [1] at that time, as at all times, complaints were made of the injustice and bad faith of men in power, of

[1] * * " Comme nos François, les premiers en Provence,
Du sonnet amoureux chantèrent l'excellence,
Devant l'Italien ils ont aussi chantés
Les satires qu'alors ils nommoient *sirventes*,
Ou *silventois*, un nom qui des *silves* Romaines
A pris son origine en nos forêts lointaines."
        La Fresnaye-Vauquelin, " Art Poètique," liv. ii.

women, of physicians, and of innkeepers.   But these
Sirventes contain nothing but personalities or vague
generalities.   The troubadours lament over the vices
of their age, but they display very little knowledge of
human nature ; they attack alternately the clergy,
the princes, and especially Charles of Anjou, whose
sovereignty in Provence was particularly odious to
them ; but these local satires exercised no influence
upon modern satire, and, at the present day, interest
only those men who make the history of that age and
country their especial study.

After the troubadours of Provence, and the
French *Trouvères,* " by small degrees our poetry,"
says Pasquier, " lost its credit, and was neglected for
a considerable time by France." [1]   It was probably
not, as Pasquier thinks, " because of that great troop
of writers, who indiscriminately took pen in hand." [2]
Some few men of real talent, by driving away the multitude from a profession which their genius had raised
above the aim of common men, might well have saved
themselves from contempt ; but poets who addressed
their songs to none but powerful nobles, and continually repeated to their patrons the same compliments and phrases, necessarily soon wearied their
listeners.   Poetry, in France, gained fresh vitality
by its diffusion among the lower classes ; without

[1] " Recherches de la France," lib. vii. cap. iii. vol. ii. col. 692.
[2] Ibid.

losing that amorous tinge which it retained from its early habits, it combined therewith a satirical and sportive character, more natural to subjects than to princes, and the germ of which might have been perceived in its first attempts. One of the oldest of French poems, the "Bible Guiot," or "Huguiot," is nothing but a long satire ; and the "Roman de la Rose," commenced during the course of the thirteenth century, by Guillaume de Lorris, is only the narrative of an amorous dream, which his continuator, Jean de Meun, used as the framework for a satire on all classes.

Satire pre-supposes the existence of determinate moral ideas ; and thus morality abounds in the satirical works of this period ; but it is less the morality which follows as a natural consequence from the narrative of human actions, than that which is the result of reflection, and which instructs the mind without animating it with any elevated and powerful sentiments. The Frenchman, from his birth a keen observer, early became proficient in penetrating into the secret motives of the conduct of men, and in casting ridicule upon vice or folly. In our old *fabliaux*, and our ancient *mémoires*, we meet with multitudes of passages which display a shrewd and often profound knowledge of the whimsicalities that mingle with our most serious thoughts, as well as with our pettiest passions. This science of man, however, was as yet neither sufficiently advanced nor sufficiently copious to furnish poetry with great and brilliant subjects ; and it was attempted to supply this deficiency by the abuse of allegory—a power which was so long dominant in French poetry, that it becomes necessary for us briefly to indicate the causes by which it was introduced and maintained.

Allegory has been regarded as the veil with which truth deemed it prudent to cover herself, that she might appear among men without giving them offence.   But in France, at this period, truth displayed herself unveiled, and satire laid no claim to delicacy.   The allegorical personages of Jean de Meun name things by their right names, and portray them under their true forms ; they continually descend from the imaginary world in which they were born, into the world of realities which constitutes the subject of their discourse ; and nothing, in these discourses, indicates any precaution or propriety which allegory had assisted to preserve.   We must look elsewhere for the reasons why this pretended poetical power was so much abused in France.

It was necessary, at any price, to introduce variety and movement into a poetry that was accustomed to deal only with sentiments and ideas ; and by means of personification, it was thought that an appearance of reality and life might be imparted to these ideas and sentiments. *Bel-Accueil, Franc-Vouloir, Male-Bouche,* and other personages of the same kind, became active beings, whose interests and doings gave animation, at least in appearance, to a stage which could not be filled by a poetry which was devoted to observations and reflections upon human nature. Thus, for instance, Huion de Mery describes a "Tournament of Antichrist," in which the Virtues combat against the Vices ; and, by the description of a real battle, endeavours to satisfy the imagination, which would not have been contented with the moral presentation of such a conflict.[1] This singular fashion, with which all modern literatures were, during a considerable period, more or less infected, had obtained such ascendency in France, that, in the first moralities that were performed in our theatres, the only actors who were introduced were such personages as *Banquet, Je bois à vous, Je pleige d'autant;* so accustomed had the public mind become to seek, in metaphysical abstractions, for that dramatic movement which the ancients had found in the representation of man and his destiny.

"At the marriage of Philibert Emanuel, Duke of Savoy, to the sister of King Henry II., a piece was performed, the action of which was purely allegorical. *Paris* appeared therein as the father of three

---

[1] *Pasquier,* "Recherches de la France," lib. vii. c. iii. col. 690.

daughters whom he desired to marry ; and these three daughters were the three principal quarters of the town of Paris, viz., the *university*, the *town* properly so called, and the *city*, which the poet had personified." [1]

And yet poetry of a much superior kind had long been known in France. I refer to the romances of chivalry, which, as pictures of manners, are as faithful as could be permitted by the system upon which they were founded. But chivalry itself, like all the primitive institutions of modern nations, leaves the imagination in great difficulty to form a clear and settled idea of its character. Fantastic enterprises and incredible adventures constitute, generally speaking, the substance of all chivalric poems ; but we, nevertheless, find therein that truthfulness of details and sentiments which is also manifested, almost without alloy, in our *fabliaux*,—a kind of narrative best adapted to the artless, sportive, and somewhat malicious character of the French mind, when left to follow the dictates of its true nature.

This character our poetry, when it had become somewhat purified and regularised, displayed in the verses of Marot, the true type of the old French style, —a mixture of grace and archness, of elegance and simplicity, of familiarity and propriety, which has not

[1] "Réflexions Critiques sur la Poésie et la Peinture," by Abbé Dubos, vol. i. sect. xxv. p. 230, edit. 1770.

been entirely lost among us, and which, perhaps, forms the most truly national characteristic of our poetical literature, and the only one for which we are indebted to ourselves alone, and in which we have never been imitated.

When we name Marot, we are not more than about sixty years distant from the birth of Corneille ; we are entering upon the commencement of that seventeenth century, which owed to him its first splendour. A revolution in poetry was in preparation ; erudition was about to force its way into its domain, not to enrich it by a free interchange of commodities upon fair and equal terms, but to invade and crush it beneath the weight of its formidable power. The narrow sphere within which the scope of French poetry was at this period confined, left abundant space for the innovations of those men who, proud of their discoveries in the field of ancient poetry, desired to transport them into modern verse, and to reign in our literature by the help of foreign aid. We then possessed no important work from which we could deduce the rules of a peculiarly French poetical system; we had nothing to put forward in defence of our nationality ; the old French spirit was constrained to yield, and to allow itself to be overwhelmed beneath the riches of antiquity, which were heaped upon it like the heterogeneous spoils of a pillaged province, rather than as the products of a friendly country, disposed to furnish us with whatever our necessities required. It would have been useless to attempt resistance against that host of poets who flourished during the reign of Francis I., and whom court favour rendered independent of the public taste ; indeed, they formed a public among themselves, most precious to poetic vanity, and far more sensible to the noise of praise than to the silence of pleasure. " Under the reign of Henry II.," says Pasquier, " the early poets made a profession of satisfying their own minds rather than the opinion of the common people." Thenceforward, that tinge of truth, which French poetry had begun to derive from the ideas and images of common life, gave place to that spirit of clanship which cannot be avoided by persons who are satisfied with hearing and pleasing each other ; thenceforward commenced the disappearance of that simplicity of language which still lent some charm to the most ridiculous inventions; and the language of poetry, becoming factitious, prepared to don those theatrical vestments which our greatest poets have never ventured, without precaution, to cast aside in order to restore the pure forms of nature and of truth.

But, at the same time, our poetry learned to array itself with a magnificence which, until then, it had not known. The treasures with which it became enriched at this period, although not derived from its native soil, largely contributed to raise it to the rank which it afterwards attained. In the hurried glance which we have cast over our old national poetry, we have seen what voids remained therein : we must now examine how they were filled up, and seek, among the men who occupied them, for the precursors of those writers of superior genius, who, through having fixed the taste of posterity, are still at the present day our contemporaries.

Let us not be astonished at the names of Ronsard, Dubartas, Jodelle, Baïf, and others : revolutions in taste, like those of empires, exert no influence upon the duration assigned to the course of human life ; and events sometimes occur with such rapidity, that one single generation may witness an entire change in the aspect of the world. The time of Marot borders so closely on the seventeenth century, that many men beheld the end of the one, and the beginning of the other. Mlle. de Gournay, the adopted daughter of Montaigne, plays a part in most of the literary anecdotes of the first twenty years of the seventeenth century. We find her, in Saint-Evremond's comedy of the " Academicians," [1] disputing against Bois-Robert and Serisay, in favour of some old words for which it appears that she felt great affection. In 1632, Chapelain wrote to Godeau, afterwards Bishop of Vence: " Luckily, we

---

[1] Act ii. scene 3. " Œuvres de Saint-Evremond," vol. i. edit. 1753.

did not find the Demoiselle de Montaigne at home, at the visit which M. Conrart and I paid her eight days ago. I pray God that this may always be the case when we call upon her ; and that, without being as insolent as Saint-Amand, we may at least be as well rid of her as he is." [1] Mlle. de Gournay was then sixty-seven years of age. The same literary quarrels and connexions which had agitated the time of Ronsard, furnished a theme for verse to Regnier, who died young in 1613 ; [2] and until 1650, or even later, the names of Ronsard, his contemporaries, and his rivals, were still the subject of general conversation : [3] their examples still served as rules, and their respective merits were still discussed, just as we might now-a-days discuss those of Corneille and Racine. Let us not, therefore, feel surprised if we sometimes see blended together, in the same picture, times which we are tempted to believe far remote from one another. At the present day, we only

[1] " Mélanges de littérature, tirés des lettres manuscrites de M. Chapelain," p. 10. Paris, 1726.

[2] Regnier, the nephew of Desportes, was a great eulogist of Ronsard, out of spite against Malherbe, who had manifested considerable contempt for his uncle's poems.

[3] See *Gueret's* " Parnasse Réformé," a curious and amusing book, written about the year 1670, and full of information upon the literary opinions of this period. At the same time that we hear of Scarron, Gombault, La Serre, and other authors of the commencement of the seventeenth century, who had then ceased to live, we find Ronsard and Malherbe disputing about their respective merits and defects, like men whose names and works were still a subject of conversation. Ménage, Balzac, La Bruyère, and the academicians generally, in their zeal for the purity of the language, treat Ronsard somewhat as an enemy.

remark the two extreme links of the uninterrupted chain which these times form between ourselves and an epoch which has become foreign to us, and we forget to cast our eyes on the short interval which connects them.

The literature of the reign of Henry II., which now appears so strange when compared with our own, stood in no less striking contrast to that which had preceded it, and the difference was not to its advantage. The most offensive defects must necessarily mark the first efforts of a poetry which, renouncing nature, seeks all its colours in a borrowed literature. Nature will one day resume her rights, but not until after they have been for some time disregarded; affectation and laboured refinement are the necessary results of studied imitation. Besides, the models which our poets then studied, together with the works of ancient writers, were not well calculated to bring them back to simplicity and naturalness. Whilst a conventional respect for old French poetry compared with the " Divina Commedia " the " Roman de la Rose," which Pasquier " would willingly have matched with all the poets of Italy," the contemporaries of this same Pasquier endeavoured to imitate the style of the Italians of the school of Marini. It was imitation of this school, and not of Dante, Ariosto, or Tasso, that formed the style of Maurice Seve, a Lyonnese poet, whom Du Bellay has

celebrated as the author of the great change which
then took place in our poetry.[1]   His chief merit was
a prodigious perplexity of thoughts, " with so obscure
and tenebrous a meaning," says Pasquier, " that,
when reading him, I should be very pleased if I
could understand him, since he desired not to be
understood." The oblivion into which Maurice Seve
has fallen proves that he was more indebted to the
age in which he lived than to the talent which he
possessed, for the happiness of beholding the success
of innovations, which he was probably not the only
person to introduce. Following the example of his
Italian masters, he devoted himself to the celebration
of the charms of a mistress who served only as a
theme for his verses ; for he taught that French
poetry should, in future, derive its inspiration from
real feelings alone ; and he employed his old age in
inventing new methods of singing the praises of love,
" seeing that in his youth he had followed in the
track of others."   Then commenced the reign of
those aerial divinities who gave their lovers no other
trouble besides that of laying the *dawn*, the *sun*,
pearls, *rubies*, and other complimentary epithets,
under contribution,—

> " Et toujours bien portant, mourir par métaphore."

---

[1] " Recherches de la France," lib. vii. cap. vi. vol. ii. col. 701.
> " Gentil esprit, ornement de la France,
> Qui, d'Apollon sainctement inspiré,
> T'es, le premier, du peuple retiré,
> Loin du chemin tracé par l'ignorance

These Platonic affections were so much in vogue during the sixteenth century, that Ronsard, after having celebrated, in his youth, two mistresses whom he had loved more "familiarly," [1] and sung in the same manner, "took the advice of the Queen for permission, or rather commands, to address himself to Hélène de Surgères, one of her ladies-in-waiting, whom he undertook to honour and praise more than to love and serve ;" such an amour being, in the Queen's opinion, more " conformable to his age and to the gravity of his learning." As it was absolutely necessary that an old poet and erudite *savant* should have a mistress,[2] it will readily be imagined that he could leave her selection to others. Ronsard was not even anxious that his fair one should possess " a pleasing countenance ;" for Mlle. de Surgères, though a lady " of very good birth," was so ugly that when,

---

[1] *Claude Binet's* " Vie de Ronsard," p. 133.

[2] Racan and Malherbe "were conversing one day of their amours, that is to say, of their intention to choose some lady of merit and quality to be the subject of their verses. Malherbe named Mme. de Rambouillet, and Racan, Mme. de Termes." Unfortunately, both these ladies rejoiced in the name of Catherine ; "and it was necessary to find some anagrams of this name, sufficiently euphonious to be introduced into verse." They spent the afternoon in this occupation, doubtless interesting enough to lovers. It was, it is true, sufficient for Malherbe, who was then about seventy years old, and so passionless that, as Bayle tells us, " numbering his stockings by the letters of the alphabet, for fear of not wearing them in pairs, he confessed one day, that he had as many as went down to the letter L." ("Dictionnaire historique et critique," sub voce *Malherbe*, note B.) Racan, who was thirty-four years younger, took the matter rather more seriously ; "he changed his poetical love into a real and legitimate affection, and made several journeys into Burgundy for this purpose." See *Racan's* " Vie de Malherbe," p. 42.

one day, after Ronsard's death, she requested Cardinal Du Perron to insert, at the commencement of the poet's works, a letter attesting that he had never loved her with any but an honourable affection, the Cardinal answered, with more frankness than politeness : " Oh ! to prove that, you need only substitute your portrait instead of the letter." [1]

It is not, however, to Ronsard's forced and obligatory amours that we must attribute his forced verses. His last and first loves equally inspired him with verses full of grace, as well as with verses of singular form,[2] remarkable for that erudite obscurity which Pasquier, his friend and admirer, is careful not to

----

[1] " Perroniana," sub tit. *Gournay.*

[2] These are the first stanzas of one of Ronsard's songs to Hélène de Surgères ; it will be seen from them that at least he had not, in his old age, forgotten his best years :—

" Plus étroit que la vigne à l'ormeau se marie,
        De bras souplement forts,
    Du lien de tes mains, maîtresse, je te prie
        Enlace-moi le corps.

En feignant de dormir, d'une mignarde face
        Sur mon front penche-toi ;
    Inspire, en me baisant, ton haleine et ta grâce,
        Et ton cœur dedans moi.

Puis appuyant ton sein sur le mien qui se pâme,
        Pour mon mal appaiser,
    Serre plus fort mon col et me redonne l'âme
        Par l'esprit d'un baiser.

Si tu me fais ce bien, par tes yeux je te jure,
        Serment qui m'est si cher,
    Que de tes bras aimés aucune autre aventure
        Ne pourra m'arracher.

compare with that of Maurice Seve, " inasmuch as it was occasioned by his learning and lofty conceptions." His is not, in fact, the obscurity of a subtle mind,

---

> Mais souffrant doucement le joug de ton empire,
> Tant soit-il rigoureux,
> Dans les Champs-Elysés une même navire
> Nous passera tous deux."

The following is a sonnet which Ronsard wrote for his first mistress, Cassandra, whose classical name had gone a great way to gain his affection :—

> " Je ne suis point, ma guerrière Cassandre,
> Ny Myrmidon, ny Dolope soudart,
> Ny cet archer dont l'homicide dart
> Tua ton frère, et mit ta ville en cendre.
>
> Un camp armé, pour esclave te rendre,
> Du camp d'Aulide en ma faveur ne part ;
> Et tu ne vois, au pied de ton rempart,
> Pour t'enlever mille barques descendre.
>
> Hélas ! je suis ce Corèbe insensé,
> Dont le cœur vit mortellement blessé,
> Non de la main du grégeois Pénélée,
>
> Mais de cent traits qu'un archerot vainqueur,
> Par une voie en mes yeux recelée,
> Sans y penser, me tira dans le cœur."

If Ronsard's Cassandra were not well acquainted with the Greek heroes and their history, as well as with the tale of Troy, she must have had some difficulty to understand this sonnet, which is, nevertheless, not the most obscure of his productions. It was to beauties of this kind that Ronsard was indebted for the commentary which the learned Muretus wrote on his works, during his lifetime, which was regarded as a mark of high honour. "Muretus, who possessed such immense erudition," says the "Menagiana," " thought Ronsard's works so excellent that he made notes upon some of them." (Vol. iii., p. 103, 3rd edition.) And Muretus himself declares, with great satisfaction, in the Preface to his Commentary on Ronsard's first book of *Amours*, "that there were some sonnets in that book which would never have been properly understood by any man, if the author had not familiarly declared their meaning to myself or some other person."

tormenting itself to create something out of nothing ;
it is that of a copious and powerful intellect, embarrassed with its own wealth, and not yet knowing how
to regulate its employment. " He is a plenteous water-
spring, it must be admitted," says Balzac ; " but he
is a troubled and muddy spring,—a spring in which
there is not only less water than mire, but so much
mire as to prevent the water from flowing freely
out." [1]   Ronsard had learned, from the perusal of
ancient authors, in what our poetry was deficient, and
he thought he possessed, in his own lofty and really
poetical imagination, ample stores to supply the deficiency.   But he did not perceive the best and truest
method of doing this.   French literature, in his
opinion, could only gain by the indiscriminate adoption of whatever he admired in the old writers.   He
did not discern, between certain forms of the Greek
and Latin languages and the character of our own
tongue, those antipathies which can only be discovered by constant observation.   Science had not,
at that time, become blended with taste, and until
her claims were brought forward, it was impossible to
distinguish clearly between what should be adopted
and what rejected.   Ronsard rejected nothing ; his
special object was to infuse richness and energy
into our language ; and encouraged by the example
of Homer, who had interwoven into his poems the

[1] " Œuvres de Balzac," 31st Entretien.

different dialects of Greece, he says, in his "Abrégé de l'Art Poétique Français :" " Thou shalt dextrously choose, and appropriate to thy work, the most significant words of the dialects of our France, when thou hast none so good nor so suitable in thine own nation; and be not careful whether the vocables be of Gascony, or Poitou, or Normandy, or Mans, or Lyons, or of any other district, provided they be good, and signify properly what thou wishest to say." Montaigne was of the same opinion : " And let Gascon step in if French will not suffice," [1] he used to say, when speaking of the little care which he took to refine his style. Ronsard carried this license so far as frequently to employ words which belonged to no country whatever ; lengthening or shortening terms as the metre of his verse required ; often changing the vowels of which his words were composed in order to adapt them to his rhyme ; and transferring bodily, into his verses, Greek words whose French termination only separated them from their own language without admitting them into any other. Thus he says to his mistress :—

" Êtes-vous pas ma seule *Entéléchie ?* "

And this word, borrowed from Aristotle's philosophy, is explained by Muretus to mean, " my sole perfection, my only soul, which causes in me all movement,

---

[1] *Montaigne's* " Essays," book i. cap. xxv.

both natural and spontaneous." We certainly, in this case, require a commentary to explain the thought as well as to elucidate the expression.

In his epitaph on Marguerite of France and Francis I., Ronsard regrets, by a rhetorical figure, that he cannot employ these three words :—

"Ocymore, Dyspotme, Oligochronien,"

and, by the expression of his regret, constitutes them into a verse.

Nor is this all : the richness and variety which the Greek language possesses by reason of the facility with which it can form words by regular associations, were a sad temptation to Ronsard. He became desirous to transfer this liberty into the French language, and so he describes—

"Du moulin *brise-grain* la pierre *rondo-plate*."

He did not perceive that the absence of roots properly belonging to the language, the deficiency of particles, and the permanence of terminations would render these aggregations impossible; and that the want of sonorous vowels would cause the connection of words, devoid alike of elegance and euphony, to result in a jingle most unpleasant to the ear.

Finally, envying the ancients the freedom of their inversions, Ronsard wished it were possible—

"Tirer avecq' la ligne, *en tremblant emporté*,
Le crédule poisson prins à l'haim empasté."

This intemperateness of ideas, this effervescence of a genius that was unable to continue in the good method of which it had caught a glimpse, drew down upon Ronsard the contempt of those writers who, in the seventeenth century, followed out, with more wisdom and good taste, the path which he had contributed to open. The men who effect revolutions are always despised by those who profit by them. That disorderliness which invariably accompanies the efforts of an ardent mind to start on a fresh track ; that confusion which it is impossible to avoid in the employment of means as yet imperfectly understood ; that incoherence which naturally subsists between the habits to which a man has long been accustomed and those which are entirely new to him,—all these causes give to the first inventions of such innovators an imperfect and monstrous appearance, in which the eyes can scarcely discern the primitive features of a beauty which time will manifest by giving polish to the work. " He is not," says Balzac of Ronsard, " he is not a poet complete ; he is the commencement and material of a poet ; in his works we perceive the nascent and semi-animated parts of a body which is in process of formation, but which is never brought to completion." [1]

This body was French poetry, such as it was when Balzac and his contemporaries began to admire it. Ronsard traced its first lineaments, full of lofty images,

[1] " Œuvres de Balzac," 31st Entretien.

mythological allusions, and a poetic spirit previously unknown. He was the first to comprehend the dignity which befits great subjects, and which gained for him during his lifetime the title of " Prince of Poets," just as a similar elevation of style procured for Corneille the cognomen of " The Great." We are probably indebted to Ronsard for the ode and the heroic poem ;[1] his odes, with all their defects, were possessed of sufficient beauties to herald the advent of the lyric muse amongst us, and were the prelude to those of Malherbe, which are our models in that style of composition. If the *Franciad* taught no one anything, the acknowledged difficulty of a French Epic may serve as an excuse for the man who first attempted to surmount it. But what Ronsard especially changed was the general tone of French poetry, to which he imparted that elevation, and that lively though somewhat studied movement, which truly constitute poetry. A single example will suffice to give some idea of the revolution which he effected in this respect ; I extract it from the commencement of one of his songs :—

> " Quand j'estois jeune, ains [2] qu'une amour nouvelle
> Ne se fust prise en ma tendre moelle,
>   Je vivois bien heureux.
> Comme à l'envy les plus accortes filles
> Se travoilloient par leurs flammes gentilles,
>   De me rendre amoureux.

---

[1] " Recherches de la France," lib. vii. cap. vi. vol. ii. col. 705.
[2] *Ains*, before.

Mais tout ainsy qu'un beau poulain farouche
Qui n'a masché le frein dedans sa bouche,
    Va seul et escarté,
N'ayant soucy, sinon d'un pied superbe,
A mille bonds, fouler les fleurs et l'herbe,
    Vivant en liberté ;

Ores il court le long d'un beau rivage ;
Ores il erre en quelque bois sauvage,
    Fuyant de saut en saut :
De toutes part les poutres [1] hennissantes
Luy font l'amour, pour néant blandissantes,[2]
    A luy qui ne s'en chaut.

Ainsy j'allois desdaignant les pucelles
Qu'on estimoit en beautés les plus belles,
    Sans répondre à leur vueil : [3]
Lors je vivois, amoureux de moi-même,
Content et gai, sans porter face blesme,
    Ny les larmes à l'œil.

J'avois escrite au plus haut de la face,
Avecq' l'honneur une agréable audace,
    Pleine d'un franc désir :
Avecq' le pied marchoit ma fantaisie
Où je voulois, sans peur ni jalousie,
    Seigneur de mon plaisir."

Marot also has developed the same idea in one of his poems :—

    "Sur le printemps de ma jeunesse folle,
    Je ressemblois l'arondelle qui vole
    Puis çà, puis là; l'âge me conduisoit
    Sans peur ne soin, où le cœur me disoit ;
    En la forest, sans la crainte des loups,
    Je m'en allois souvent cueillir le houx,
    Pour faire glus à prendre oyseaux ramages
    Tous différents de chantz et de plumages ;
    Ou me souloys, pour les prendre, entremettre
    A faire bries [4] ou caiges pour les mettre :

---

[1] *Poutres*, mares.
[2] *Blandissantes*, caressing.
[3] *Vueil*, wish, desire.
[4] *Bries*, snares to catch birds.

Ou transnouois [1] les rivières profondes,
Ou renforçois sur le genouil les fondes ; [2]
Puis d'en tirer droict et loin j'apprenois
Pour chasser loups et abattre des noix."

The difference between the two poets is striking. In Marot, all is simple and natural ; in Ronsard, all is noble and brilliant. In the last poem, the facts are such as might have been noticed by a child ; in the first, the details are such as a poet alone could have imagined : there is all the difference between a simple narrative and an animated picture—between our old poetry and our conception of poetry at the present day. Those who prefer the simple truth to all else will regret Marot and his time ; those who desire that truth should be elevated to its highest pitch, and that before coming to us it should pass through an imagination capable of exciting our own, will require that to the natural simplicity of Marot should be added the brilliant colours of Ronsard.

After the two examples which have been quoted, it is undoubtedly somewhat surprising to read this passage in La Bruyère :—" Marot, both by his turn of thought and style of composition, seems to have written subsequently to Ronsard ; between the former author and ourselves, there is only the difference of a few words. Ronsard and his contemporary authors did more injury than service to style ; they delayed it on the road to perfection ; they exposed it

---

[1] *Transnouois*, swam across.   [2] *Fondes*, leaves.

to the danger of losing its way for ever, and never regaining the right path. It is astonishing that the works of Marot, so natural and easy as they are, did not make Ronsard, who was full of poetic spirit and enthusiasm, a greater poet than either Ronsard or Marot actually were."[1]

How comes it that, after having allowed to Ronsard much " poetic spirit and enthusiasm,"—after having said that " Ronsard and Balzac, each in his own walk, possessed enough good and enough bad qualities to form after them very great writers in verse and prose,"[2] —La Bruyère totally disregards the great influence exercised by Ronsard over the lofty character of the poetry of the age of Louis XIV., and does not perceive how far distant Marot was from anything of the kind ? How was it that he did not see that, in spite of the difference of language, Ronsard's poetic spirit bordered much more closely on that of the seventeenth century, than the simple and unaffected tone of Marot ? The reason is obvious : La Bruyère, living in the midst of the magnificence of the poetry of his own time, never thought of the efforts required to raise it to that proud position ; he felt the necessity of cease- lessly combating against that want of naturalness, and that inflation of language, into which our poetry was always ready to fall ; and finding, in Ronsard, the type of these defects, and in Marot a naturalness,

---

[1] *La Bruyère's* "Characters," cap. i. vol. i. p. 116, edit. 1759.   [2] Ibid.

the somewhat naked simplicity of which he did not fear would be exaggerated by subsequent authors, he attacked what he considered excessive in the one poet, without perceiving the deficiencies of the other. Besides, a man, however superior he may be, unless he has cause to complain of the opinions of his age and of the reputation which they bestow upon himself, always shares in them to a certain extent : and we are rarely disposed to feel great enthusiasm for our immediate predecessors, whose faults we have had to correct, and whose beauties are frequently displayed to our disadvantage.   Malherbe and his school naturally despised Ronsard and returned to Marot, in whom Ronsard, on his side, as he tells us himself, had found only " vessels whence he drew, as by industrious washing, rich sediments of gold." [1]   We must allow the judgment of posterity itself to ripen, and not fear to reflect upon what it originally thought ; for it also is subject to reaction, and requires time to form a definite opinion.

La Bruyère expresses his alarm at the danger in which Ronsard involved the French language, which, he says, he might have spoiled " for ever."   Ronsard could not have done this, for he did not do it ; and in order to inflict an eternal injury, a man must possess power to prevent truth and reason from surviving him.   Whatever influence may be ascribed

----

[1] *Binet's* " Vie de Ronsard," p. 121.

to the defects of a man of talent or genius, we may
trust to his imitators to render them speedily so ridiculous that even children will point their finger at
them.   These awkward imitations at first obtain
from the public an admiration which inflames
the indignation of the wise, who strive to dis-
countenance them.   Ronsard had taught the art of
employing grand and noble imagery : and plagiarists
thought it was enough to accumulate vast ideas, to
express feeble thoughts in inflated language, and to
exaggerate those which the imagination was unable
to conceive.   Thus Du Bartas describes the world
before the creation of man, as—

> "   *   *   Une forme sans forme,
> Une pile confuse, une masse difforme,
> D'abismes un abisme, un corps mal compassé,
> Un chaos de chaos, un tas mal entassé.
> *   *   *   *   *
> La terre estoit au ciel, et le ciel en la terre ;
> Le feu, la terre, l'air se tenoient dans la mer ;
> La mer, le feu, la terre estoient logez en l'air,
> L'air, la mer et le feu dans la terre, et la terre
> Chez l'air, le feu, la mer,   *   *   * " [1]

And Pasquier, who quotes these lines, declares that
if, in the remainder of the piece, Du Bartas was supported by Ovid, he has, " in these last verses, rendered
himself inimitable." [2]

The disorder which reigned in taste called loudly
for reform.   " At length came Malherbe," and not

---

[1] *Du Bartas,* "Premier Jour de la première Semaine."
[2] "Recherches de la France," lib. vii. cap. x. vol. i. col. 722.

before his presence was needed. Wisdom, taste, and respect for propriety were required to be among the chief merits of the superior man who was destined to gain distinction for himself amidst all this license : and that providential law which, in literature as in States, produces men of genius varying according to the necessities of the times in which they appear, brought Numa into the world after Romulus, Racine after Corneille, and Malherbe after Ronsard.

Poets were then entering into a position favourable for the introduction of the change about to be wrought in literature. The Court, thenceforward fixed and undisturbed, anxious to find pleasures to fill the void which had long been occupied by public business, was about to establish another arbiter of taste than a coterie of literary men, isolated from the public, and consequently free to yield to the caprices of their own genius, without consulting the authority of common reason. Poetry in France, being generally irrelevant to the great interests of life, has taken but little part in the troubles which have agitated the nation : a people, ever disposed to external movement, and listening and reflecting only when it cannot act, has left no place for the Muses but that which it has been obliged to give to repose ; and it is perhaps permissible to attribute to the serious affairs which occupied men's minds under Francis II., Charles IX., and Henry III., that disdain which the poets felt for a public which could not yield them sufficient attention. The Court had, indeed, served as their place of refuge ; and notwithstanding the slight taste which Henry II. felt at first for Ronsard's verses, a celebrated poet is, in the eyes of his prince, a piece of property which he would be loth to lose. Charles IX., who wrote verses himself, loved poetry with the love of a poet whose taste had been formed by contemporary writers ; and his successor, Henry III. protected poetry, without having time to form an opinion upon it. The simple, practical, and somewhat illiterate rule of Henry IV. was required to dispel that superficial science, and that inflated grandiloquence which had long held sway in the realms of poesy ; and the Court, thenceforward at one with the nation, speedily resumed, over tastes, manners, and ideas, that empire which, in France, it does not easily lose. Malherbe was the poet of the Court: constantly occupied in ministering to its gratification, and in humanizing for it that literature in which it was beginning to take delight, he used frequently to say, "especially when he was blamed for not accurately following the sense of those authors whom he translated or paraphrased, that he was not preparing meat for cooks ; as much as to say, that he cared little about being praised by literary persons who understood the books which he had translated, provided he was approved by the Court." [1]

---

[1] *Racan,* "Vie de Malherbe."

The revolution which had taken place in reaction upon that attempted by Ronsard, appeared complete ; but the movements of the human mind always result in progress, and never in any but apparent retrogression. In these unfaithful but elegant translations, the simple and flowing style of which enraged Mlle. de Gournay, who called them " a ripple of clear water,"[1] the language began to acquire a precision which commerce with the learned languages could alone have imparted : and in Malherbe's verses, which are frequently adorned with beauties derived from ancient sources,[2] it preserved, from the character given it by Ronsard, a dignity and richness of style of which Marot's time had no conception, while it also became more and more subject to elegant correction.[3]

---

[1] *Bayle*, " Dictionnaire historique et critique," article *Malherbe*, note E.

[2] For example, in the *Stanzas* addressed by Malherbe to Henry IV. when he went into the Limousin, in which we find several passages successfully imitated from Virgil's fourth eclogue. The imitation is sometimes sufficiently different from the original to be able to claim the merit of invention, as in this stanza :—

> " Tu nous rendras alors nos douces destinées :
> Nous ne reverrons plus ces fâcheuses années
> Qui, pour les plus heureux, n'ont produit que des pleurs.
> Toute sortè de biens comblera nos familles ;
> La moisson de nos champs lassera les faucilles,
> Et les fruits passeront la promesse des fleurs."

[3] From among many examples that I might quote, I will select one which is not very widely known. It is a strophe from the Ode to Marie de Medici (which, notwithstanding three prosaic lines, is a beautiful poem), in which, in order to say that a king cannot justly be called *great* unless he has reigned in stormy and difficult times, he exclaims :—

> " Ce n'est point aux rives d'un fleuve,
> Où dorment les vents et les eaux,

Even the last of Ronsard's partisans, by resisting improvement, contributed to render it more complete and certain. It was not without opposition that Malherbe brought back to the true genius of the language, and to the style best adapted to the nation, a poetry which Ronsard had diverted therefrom. The poets, accustomed to draw their allusions from the obscurest fables of mythology, found it extremely difficult to speak in French of subjects calculated to interest Frenchmen. This innovation was charged against Malherbe and his school as a want of respect for antiquity; thus Gombaud, under the assumed name of Mme. Desloges, says to Racan :—

> " C'est vous dont l'audace nouvelle
> A rejeté l'antiquité   *   *
>
> *   *   *   *
>
> Vous aimez mieux croire à la mode ;
> C'est bien la foi la plus commode
> Pour ceux que le monde a charmés." [1]

And Regnier, addressing himself to Ronsard, gives vent to his irritation against—

> " *   *   Ces resveurs dont la muse insolente,
> Censurant les plus vieux, insolemment se vante

> Que fait sa véritable preuve
> L'art de conduire les vaisseaux :
> Il faut, en la plaine salée,
> Avoir lutté contre Malée,
> Et pris du naufrage dernier,
> S'être vu dessous les Pléiades,
> Eloigné de ports et de rades,
> Pour être cru bon marinier."

---

[1] " Recueil des plus belles Pièces des Poëtes Français, depuis Villon jusqu'à Benserade," vol. iii. p. 58.

De réformer les vers, non les tiens seulement,
Mais veulent déterrer les Grecs du monument,
Les Latins, les Hébreux, et toute l'antiquaille,
Et leur dire à leur nez qu'ils n'ont rien fait qui vaille." [1]

Malherbe's style, which, through seeking, sometimes without success, to avoid inflation, occasionally
fell into triviality, was also a subject of censure.
Regnier exclaims :—

" Comment ! il nous faut donq', pour faire une œuvre grande,
Qui de la calomnie et du temps se défende,
Qui trouve quelque place entre les bons autheurs,
Parler comme à Saint-Jean parlent les crocheteurs ? " [2]

Ronsard, by constituting the poets themselves the
sole arbiters of taste, had rendered it too easy for
them to write verses which were intended to please
themselves alone ; Malherbe, by familiarising the
fashionable world with poetry, made it too easy for
them to believe themselves poets, whenever they desired to be such.   But this period of the triumph, and
consequently of the decay of the new school, had not
yet arrived ; Maynard, Racan, and a few others, were
labouring, conjointly with their master, to maintain
its glory ; the victories which they still had to gain
over the ignorance of their auditors, still furnished
them with a powerful motive for studious efforts.
Malherbe used frequently to say : " Though for so
many years I have been labouring to *degasconize*
the Court, I have not yet been able to succeed ; " [3]

---

[1] *Regnier*, Satire ix.   [2] Ibid.
[3] " Œuvres de Balzac, Socrate Chrestien, Discours 10."

and this *gasconism* was the ever present foe which compelled men of letters to watch with unceasing vigilance over the purity of the language.

This Gascon Court, however, would not have tolerated an absolute want of discretion in its treatment. "To submit to tutelage," said Henry IV. to the Assembly of Notables at Rouen, "is a fancy which never lays hold on kings, greybeards, and conquerors:" he might have added, "and people of my country." Respect for the decisions of the Court, anxiety to please the Court, and conformity to the manners of the Court, became, under the most popular of our monarchs, the dominant fashion, and almost the duty of the French nation. After times of rebellion, it is usual to carry the virtue of submission beyond its ordinary bounds : Malherbe went so far as to say that "the religion of honest folks was the same as that of their prince ;"[1] and a regard for proprieties was, as it appears, the only feeling that he himself consulted in the last pious acts of his life. "At the time of his death," says Racan, "we had much trouble to induce him to confess, because, he said, he was accustomed to do so at Easter only. The person who induced him to comply was Yvrande, a gentleman who had been brought up as a page in the King's stable, and who, as well as Racan, was his scholar in poetry. What he said to

---

[1] *Racan*, "Vie de Malherbe," p. 45.

persuade him to receive the sacraments, was that, as he had always made a profession of living like other men, he should also die like them ; and Malherbe asking him what he meant, Yvrande told him that, when other men died, they confessed, communicated, and received the other sacraments of the Church. Malherbe avowed that he was right, and sent for the Vicar of Saint-Germain, who remained with him till he expired." [1]

If, therefore, when reading the poems of this period, the proprieties appear to us to have been neither very rigid, nor very strictly observed, we must not ascribe the blame to the poets : the Court required nothing more. We may discover in Malherbe a great many defects of taste, and even many grammatical inaccuracies ; [2] but he had had so many faults of this kind to correct, that, notwithstanding all his deficiencies, we are forced to admit that to him and his pupils must be ascribed the merit of having begun to introduce clearness and exactitude into our language, and elegance, sweetness, and harmony into our poetry.

In the midst of this laborious purification of the language and of poetry, appear those inconveniences which such a work must necessarily involve. Minute

---

[1] *Racan*, "Vie de Malherbe," p. 44.

[2] See *Pelisson's* report on the examination of his " Stances au Roi," by the French Academy, a short time after his death. " Histoire de l'Académie," p. 273, edit. 1653.

attention to correctness of language is not incompatible with genius ; but this correctness must not be made the chief object of its efforts, or considered the source of its most precious reward : a mind constantly bent on polishing words rises with difficulty to lofty conceptions, and the ascription of great merit to exactness of forms tends to depreciate the value set on ideas. Regnier brings it as a reproach against Malherbe and his school, that

> " *   *   leur savoir ne s'étend seulement
> Qu'à regratter un mot douteux au jugement,
> Prendre garde qu'un *qui* ne heurte une diphthongue,
> Espier des vers si la rime est brève ou longue,
> Ou bien si la voyelle à l'autre s'unissant,
> Ne rend point à l'oreille un vers trop languissant ;
> Et laissent sur le verd le noble de l'ouvrage :
> Nul esguillon divin n'eslève leur courage ;
> Ils rampent bassement, foibles d'inventions,
> Et n'osent, peu hardis, tenter les fictions." [1]

However severe these reproaches may seem, Malherbe did not entirely escape them. " Malherbe," says Saint-Evremond, " has always been considered the most excellent of our poets, but more for well-turned expressions than for invention and thought." [2] Boileau recommended that " his purity and the clearness of his happy turn " should alone be imitated. Balzac speaks of him, after his death, as " an old court pedagogue, who was formerly called the tyrant of words and syllables, who made the greatest

---

[1] *Regnier*, Satire IX.
[2] *Saint-Evremond*, " Œuvres," vol. vi. p. 17.

difference between *pas* and *point*, and treated the affair of gerunds and participles, as if it were a contest between two neighbouring nations, quarrelling about their frontiers.   *   *   Death surprised him," he adds, "while he was rounding a period, and his climacterical year arrived when he was deliberating whether *erreur* and *doute* were masculine or feminine.   With what attention did he expect to be listened to, when he was for ever dogmatising about the virtue and use of particles ? " [1]

In order to form a judgment regarding the matters about which the cleverest men then debated, we need only notice the gravity with which Pelisson relates Malherbe's dispute, about " licentious " sonnets, with his pupils Racan, Colomby, and Maynard, " the last of whom alone," says Racan, "continued to write them until his death," — defending them, says Pelisson, wherever he went, and " declaiming against the tyranny of those who opposed them." [2]   We are at first tempted to follow their example, and to feel indignant at Maynard's licentious old age ; but on enquiry, we find that " licentious " sonnets were those, the two quatrains of which were not written in the same rhyme.

The sonnet, traces and specimens of which may be

---

[1] *Balzac,* " Socrate Chrestien, Discours 10."
[2] *Pelisson,* " Histoire de l'Académie," p. 446.

found in the more ancient French poets,[1] among
others in Marot, had been brought into fashion in
France by Joachim Du Bellay, who had spent some
time at Rome ; and the taste of Catherine de Medici
for this product of her native land, had aided in
giving it vogue. The value which was then set on
the sonnet, and the pains taken to render it perfect,
explain the importance attached to it by Boileau,
whose opinion may appear singular to us at the
present day :—

> " Un sonnet sans défaut vaut seul un long poème."

On the other hand, the number of " two or three
sonnets out of a thousand," which Boileau approves
in the works of Gombaud, Maynard, and Malleville,
all three celebrated poets in their day, shows us in
what fruitless labour might be wasted the energies of
men who had consecrated their lives to poetry.

Other small poetical compositions, such as ron-
deaux, ballads, and the like, which Ronsard and his
contemporaries had desired to banish as not being
sufficiently antique, regained favour when our literature became more truly French ; epigrams and
songs also kept their place ; and the care bestowed
upon these little works, together with the imitation
of the Italian poets, employed the whole powers of

---

[1] *Sonnet* is an old French word signifying *song*.   Thibault de Champagne
calls his songs *sonnets* :—

> " S'en oz-je faire encore maint gent party,
>   Et maint *sonnet*, et mainte recordie."

the mind in seeking after delicate and ingenious
thoughts, fit to be enclosed within so narrow a
compass.   Such modes of expression were suited
only to poets whose exclusive occupation was to
please a Court not yet far advanced in literary taste,
and which they were obliged unceasingly to amuse,
either by the creation of new objects of interest, or
by the production of works that did not require
either long-continued attention, or a sensitive imagination well versed in poetical ideas.   The finest
works of poetry would not, perhaps, have contributed
to diffuse a taste for letters so much as this piecemeal
literature—this small change of wit and learning,
adapted to the commerce of the multitude.   It is not
sufficient to amuse the general public ; their pleasure
is not complete unless they also afford amusement,
and play their part in the performance which
they witness.   While restrained within the sphere
that I have indicated, literary occupations and discussions were quite within their reach ; their activity
and self-love were called into play in a degree which
sufficed the movement of their life.   " We learn
thereby, every day, the latest gallantries, and the
prettiest novelties in prose and verse ; we are told
just in the nick of time, that such an one has composed the prettiest piece in the world on such a
subject ; that some one else has written words to such
an air ; that this person has made a madrigal upon

an enjoyment, and that his friend has composed some stanzas upon an infidelity ; that Mr. So-and-so sent a *sixain* yesterday evening to Miss Such-and-such, and that she sent back an answer at eight o'clock this morning ; that one celebrated author has just sketched a plan for a new book, that another has got to the third part of his romance, and that a third is passing his works through the press."[1]   It was in this way that elegant society devoted itself to literature ; by multiplying the objects of interest offered to its tastes, it is possible to succeed in gaining its attention : literature thus became its great business, and it constituted itself its centre and its judge ; sometimes we find it split into two parties on the respective merits of two sonnets,[2] in the same way as the dispute about *licentious* sonnets had previously divided the poetical world.   Indeed, it will not always have such grave subjects of contention ; one word will keep it in suspense,[3] another will fill it

---

[1] *Molière*, " Les Précieuses Ridicules," Scene 10.

[2] That of "Job," by Benserade, and that of "Uranie," by Voiture.

[3] A great discussion arose at the Hotel de Rambouillet, on the question whether *muscadins* or *muscardins* were correct.   The case was referred to the Academy, then just established, and it is inscribed on its registers, February 1st, 1638, together with its decision in favour of *muscadins*. This was the opinion of Voiture, who wrote the following lines, in ridicule of the party who advocated *muscardins* :—

> "Au siècle des vieux palardins,
> Soit courtisans, soit citardins,
> Femmes de cour ou citardines
> Prononçoient toujours muscardins,
> Et balardins et balardines,

with admiration; it will fall into ecstacies at a *quoiqu'on die*,[1] but a homely expression will excite its disgust. The pedantry of *bons airs* will unite with that of *bel esprit*; the word *bel-esprit*[2] itself will become the title, at first honourable but afterwards ridiculous, given to those who combined the search after wit with the search after manners; and thus an easy explanation will be afforded of the existence of the Hotel de Rambouillet, at which the pretensions of the most refined elegance mingled with those of the most distinguished talent, and whose authority extended over nearly all the first half of the seventeenth century.[3]

> Mesmes l'on dit qu'en ce tems là
> Chacun disoit : rose muscarde :
> J'en dirois bien plus sur cela ;
> Mais par ma foy je suis malarde,
> Et mesme en ce moment voilà
> Que l'on m'apporte une panarde."
> > *Pelisson*, "Histoire de l'Académie," p. 270.

[1] *Molière*, " Femmes Savantes."

[2] " Le *bel esprit* est un titre fort beau,
> Quand on aime à courir de ruelle en ruelle.
> Mais ce n'est point le fait d'une sage cervelle
> De chercher à briller sur un terme nouveau.

> *   *   *   *   *   *

> Un bel esprit, si j'en sais bien juger,
> Est un diseur de bagatelles. . .
> O ciel ! diront les précieuses,
> Peut on se déchaîner contre le bel esprit ? "
> > *Saint-Evremond*, "Œuvres," vol. x., among the doubtful poems.

[3] " The celebrated Arthenice," as Pelisson calls her, " whose cabinet was always filled with the finest wits and most honourable persons at Court," was that same Marquise de Rambouillet whom old Malherbe had

There is a great difference between the influence
of the Court acting upon literature as the centre of
good taste, elegance, and distinction, and the direct
influence of the prince gathering together around his
person all that is brilliant and elevated, and making
himself the sole point towards which all converge.
A striking exemplification of this difference will be
found in a comparison of the sway of the Hotel de
Rambouillet with that of Louis XIV., who succeeded
to its influence. Henry IV. had paid but little
attention to literature ; Louis XIII. had a distaste

set himself to love, feeling quite sure that he ran no risk with a lady
whose virtue was already as well known as her wit. This disinterested
choice of the best poet that France then could boast, may lead us to consider the Marquise de Rambouillet, from that time forth, as the most
distinguished of those ladies who received the wits at their houses. The
most brilliant epoch of the Hotel de Rambouillet was during the life of
Voiture, who died in 1648. If complaints were made, at a later period, of
the judgments of the Hotel de Rambouillet, and the kind of wit that
reigned there, it was because, so long as it corresponded with the spirit of
the time, it was not thought ridiculous. When Saint-Evremond assures
us, in his poems (vol. iii. p. 294), that, during the time of the *good regency*,
viz., that of Anne of Austria :—

> " Femmes savoient sans faire les savantes :
> Molière en vain eût cherché dans la cour
> Ses ridicules affectées,"

he is speaking, in his old age, of the time of his youth ; and this becomes
indubitable when he adds that then—

> " *   *   ses *Fascheux* n'auroient pas vu le jour,
> Faute d'objets à fournir les ideés ; "

and that it would have been impossible to discover,

> " Dans le plaisant rien d'outré ni de faux."

The time of which Saint-Evremond thus speaks was the time of Scarron
and burlesque. We must not consult contemporary opinions for the dates
of revolutions in taste.

for it : the skilful and compliant vivacity of the
one, and the melancholy and feeble timidity of the
other, left their courtiers at liberty to follow their
own tastes. Thus we find that, especially under
Louis XIII., the most distinguished poets were
poets who, though undoubtedly anxious to get near
the king whenever they could, careful to boast of
the distinctions they had received at his hands, and
disposed to sing his praises whenever they thought
they could induce him to listen, nevertheless brought
under his notice works the inspiration of which
had not come from him, and which had first
sought the approval of other critics than himself.
Thus Maynard, boasting that the " ambitious
marvels" of his verses

> " N'en veulent qu'aux grands de la cour,"

may well add :—

> " Ils me font des amis au Louvre,
> Et mon grand Roi veut qu'on leur ouvre
> La porte de son cabinet."

But the inspiration of Maynard was derived neither
from " the Court grandees," nor from " his great
King ; " he only thinks of them when he has some
favour to request, or some refusal to complain of,
and if they were honoured with his best verses, it
was because he wrote against them : witness this
sonnet against Cardinal Richelieu, who not only

would not give Maynard anything, but had harshly refused him :—

> " Par vos honneurs le monde est gouverné ;
> Vos volontés font le calme et l'orage,
> Et vous riez de me voir confiné
> Loin de la cour, dans mon petit village.
>
> Cléomédon, mes désirs sont contents ;
> Je trouve beau le désert que j'habite,
> Et connois bien qu'il faut céder au temps,
> Fuir l'éclat et devenir hermite.
>
> Je suis heureux de vieillir sans employ,
> De me cacher, de viv. e tout à moy,
> D'avoir dompté la crainte et l'espérance ;
>
> Et si le ciel qui me traite si bien,
> Avoit pitié de vous et de la France,
> ·Votre bonheur seroit égal au mien."

And those well-known lines that Maynard wrote over the door of his study :—

> " Las d'espérer et de me plaindre
> Des Muses, des grands et du sort,
> C'est ici que j'attends la mort,
> Sans la désirer ni la craindre."

Under Louis XIV., it would not have been in good taste to appear dissatisfied with the Court. "There are times," says Cardinal de Retz, "in which disgrace is a kind of fire which purifies from all bad qualities, and illumines all good ones ; and there are also times in which it does not become an honest man to be disgraced."[1] Louis XIV., by the splendour with which he surrounded himself, brought favour into fashion ;

---

[1] *Cardinal de Retz*, " Mémoires," vol. i. p. 66, edit. 1719.

it was fashionable also to praise the prince, to refer
everything to him, to hold everything from him ;
the courtiers aspired to no higher title than that of
servants of their master ; and, by his patronage of
literature, Louis enrolled it among his courtiers :
from his direct protection, it desired to hold the rank
which it sought to occupy in the world ; to please
him was the object of all its efforts ; and the taste
of the prince was imposed on society, just as, thirty
years before, the taste of society had been tacitly
adopted by the prince.

It is not difficult to discern which of these two
influences is most favourable to the progress of literature and the development of poetry.   The protection
of a King is less enthralling than the familiarity of
nobles : his laws may be more severe, but his constraint is less habitual ; and poetry has perhaps less
need of liberty than of leisure.   Under Louis XIV.
Racine, Boileau, and Molière, when they had left
Versailles, lived much more amongst themselves ;
and, being much less dependent upon the opinions
of the fashionable world, they could liberate their
minds from the authority of its caprices, and even
console themselves by thinking of the influence which
those caprices sometimes exercised over their success.
Delivered from the crushing necessity of daily pleasing
a multitude of petty amateurs, they could set apart
sufficient time for the composition of those noble

works which a King, whose reign they rendered illustrious and whose Court they adorned, desired them
to complete for his glory rather than to hasten for his
amusement. Less under the necessity of seeking the
approbation of the only judges of elegance, they listened with greater freedom to their natural feeling for
the true and the beautiful ; their audience increased,
and became more enlightened as it extended ; and if
the spirit of the times still exercised over their labours
an influence that was sometimes injurious, fashion at
least no longer enslaved their taste and genius.

But, as may already have been perceived, before
this brilliant epoch in the reign of Louis XIV., during
the early years of his rule and under the government
of Louis XIII., literature was based solely upon the
mental acquirements of society. In such an order of
things, in the midst of a still unenlightened society,
how could taste be fixed upon any stable and solid
foundations ? Its natural justness would be ceaselessly warped by habits and customs, as ceaselessly
altered by fashion and the necessity of distinction
from the vulgar herd—that essential characteristic
of what is called good society. In the fashions of
the time, therefore, we must seek the source of the
character of such a literature ; and perhaps we
shall succeed in discerning, in the state of civilisation at that period, the causes of those fashions
whose influence upon literature is so evident.

At the end of the sixteenth century and the beginning of the seventeenth, some remnants of chivalry
were still maintained in existence by civil wars, in
which the pleasures of society mingled with the
dangers of battle, when the soldier still fought beneath the eyes of his *lady*, and when beauty was
frequently the prize of valour. It was in honour of the
ladies that a famous combat took place under the
walls of Paris, on the 2nd of August, 1589, between
L'Isle Marivault, a gentleman of the Royalist party,
and the Leaguer Marolles, known by the name of the
"brave Marolles." Marivault, meeting Marolles on
the edge of the trench, asked him, "if there was not
some one on his side who would break a lance for
love of the ladies." Marolles replied that he thought
it his highest glory to serve them. "You are, then,
valiant and in love," said Marivault : "I esteem you
all the more for it." A meeting having been appointed for the next day, "several princesses and
ladies dressed themselves on that day in green scarfs,
and were placed in a certain position from which, as
from a scaffold raised for the purpose, they could
behold the space which had been marked out to give
them a sight of the famous combat that was to be
fought in their honour. The fair S. S——, with
whom the Leaguer had fallen passionately in love, was
there with Mme. d'Aumale." She called Marolles
her knight ; and when he had killed Marivault,

"the ladies," says the Abbé de Marolles, "crowned his victory with their favours."[1]

Amid customs like these, at once coarse and frivolous, elegance of manners and language was not always the privilege of the most valiant, nor even of the most noble. All have heard of the coarseness of the Duke de Beaufort, *the King of the Markets*. "M. de Beaufort," says Saint-Evremond, "glories in his ignorance of delicate language.* * * He attempts neither politeness at his meals, nor cleanliness in his dress.* * * The incidents of a law-suit he calls the *accidents* of life ; if you eat meat on fast-days, he talks of informing the *politics* (the police) ; rooms hung with black he says are *lascivious,* and wanton eyes are *lugubrious.* Laval died, according to his report, of a *confusion* (contusion) of the head ; and the Chevalier de Chabot, through having been badly *japanned* (trepanned)."[2] A desire to please the ladies was, nevertheless, the habitual study even of the coarsest and most illiterate ; the ladies held sway over society, and aided in diffusing through it a taste for mental exercises, the only occupations which their weakness allows them to share with men. To the ladies, therefore, poetry addressed its chiefest homage. But, with regard to the fair sex, there is one single homage

1 "Mémoires de l'Abbé de Marolles," vol. i. p. 384.
2 *Saint-Evremond,* "Œuvres, Apologie du Duc de Beaufort," vol. vii. pp. 5—11. See also "Segraisiana," p. 11.

in which all others, when analysed, are found to be contained ; and a slight effort of mind will suffice to convince the dullest that no influence is equal to that which subjugates the heart, the desires, and the will. When speaking to the ladies, therefore, it was impossible not to tell them of love ; the worship of love besieged them on all sides ; the word *love* resounded incessantly in their ears ; and it was thought impossible to represent any great action which love had not inspired, or any extravagant deed at which love could be alarmed.   Brutus and Horatius Cocles talked of love, in the romances of Mlle. de Scudéry ; through love, Cyrus became the conqueror of Asia ; and Mandane was so utterly unable to avoid inspiring love that, in the romance of *Cyrus*, she is carried off no less than four times by four different persons ; which gave rise to this decree of the *Parnasse Réformé :* " We declare that we do not recognize as heroines, all those women who have been carried off more than once." [1]

However, either because a taste of dominion rendered the ladies less sensible to other pleasures, or because the agitation of society preserved them from the empire of the passions, this age, which told them so much about love, was the age in which love appeared to exercise the least sway over them ; for those who talked most about it, proved themselves least disposed to submit to its power.   Love was the habitual

[1] " Parnasse Réformé," article xix. p. 157.

theme of conversation at the Hotel de Rambouillet, "a true palace of honour," according to Bayle,[1] whose scepticism finds no room for doubt on this point ; and, in fact, from all their witty and tender warbling, there did not issue a single suspicion that passed the bounds of theory. "There," says Ménage, "there was gallantry alone, but no love. M. de Voiture one day giving his hand to Mlle. de Rambouillet, afterwards Mme. de Montausier, wished to take the liberty of kissing her arm ; but Mlle. de Rambouillet manifested her displeasure at his boldness in so serious a manner, that she took from him all desire of again venturing on the same liberty."[2]

Next to the ladies of that lofty rigidity which Mme. de Montausier displayed perhaps with unusual ostentation, came those more tender blue-stockings, whose hearts gave admission to love, but on conditions which imparted to it either the vagueness of objectless desire, or the refinement of desireless feeling. "These false pretenders to delicacy," says Saint-Evremond, "have robbed love of its most natural features; thinking to give it something more precious in exchange, they have transferred the seat of passion from the heart into the mind, and changed impulses into ideas. This great purification has its origin in an honest abhorrence of sensuality ; but they are not

[1] *Bayle's* "Dictionary," article *Malherbe*, note B.
[2] "Menagiana," vol. ii. p. 8.

less removed from the true nature of love than the most voluptuous ; for love has as little to do with speculations of the understanding as with brutality of the appetite." [1]

Ninon used to call blue-stockings " the Jansenists of love ;" they were, at least, its theologians.

We must, however, beware how we believe that all the women were blue-stockings, and that, as Corneille says in the " Menteur," it was no longer possible to find in Paris,

> "De ces femmes de bien qui se gouvernent mal,
> Et de qui la vertu, quand on leur fait service,
> N'est pas incompatible avec un peu de vice." [2]

In the anecdotes, and even in the history of this time, we often meet with evidences of a love less refined than that inspired by the blue-stockings ; and the collections of poems prove that the poets had not entirely forgotten it.   But this kind of love belongs to all ages ; the other is one of the particular character-istics of the epoch in which Corneille was educated ; and whether it was then more or less really adopted in the ordinary concerns of life, it became the fashionable mode of speaking in good society.   The poets were incessantly obliged to labour in seeking after *fires, ardours*, and *languors* which they took good care not to feel ; and, condemned to exaggerate

---

[1] *Saint-Evremond*, " Œuvres," vol. ii. pp. 86, 87.

[2] *Corneille*, "Le Menteur," act i. scene 1.

the language of love without expressing any of its
real sentiments, the amorous poetry of this period
was placed under the unpleasant necessity of saying
nothing that was true, and of uttering nothing that
was actually felt. Thus Maynard, when expressing
with considerable freedom, in one of his odes, his
dislike of skirts,

> " Où brille l'orgueil des clinquans,"

declares his intention to renounce all those learned
and lofty loves for which—

> " Il faut qu'une amoureuse dupe
> Se travaille quatre ou cinq ans,"

and to go to the Louvre to seek—

> " De la grâce et des compliments." [1]

To the affectation of feigned sentiment there was,
moreover, added that of borrowed wit ; imitation of
the Italian manner had been followed by that of
Spanish taste ; or, to speak more correctly, Italian
Marinism, which had been eagerly adopted in Spain,
had been transported thence into France, overloaded
with Spanish exaggeration. Gongora, a Spanish poet
who flourished at the end of the sixteenth century,
was the head of that school which is called after his
name ; and Gongora is one of the poets whom

---

[1] " Recueil des plus belles Pièces des Poètes Français," vol. iii. p. 13.

Chapelain, the great critic of the early part of the seventeenth century, recommends to careful study, as one of the good authors in Spanish literature, with whose works he was well acquainted.[1] One disciple of this school tells us that the eyes of his mistress are " as large as his grief and as black as his destiny ;" [2] another informs us that an adventure which happened to a young girl, occurred " one evening, which was a morning, since Aurora smiled, and showed white pearls in the midst of glowing carmine." [3] It will at once be perceived that Aurora was the name of the young lady ; and it is still easier to discover the origin of those comparisons with *Aurora, the Sun, the Moon,* and *the Stars,* of which Saint-Evremond found it possible to become weary, and which he considered the groundwork of our poetry,[4]—hyperbolic expressions which the French poets rendered still more ridiculous, by copying them from the Spaniards without at the same time borrowing that oriental imagination which, in Spain, clothed these phrases with a

---

[1] See the " Mélanges de Littérature tirés des Lettres manuscrites de Chapelain," p. 161.

[2] " Grandes como mi dolor,
Negros como mi ventura."

This occurs in a poem by the Portuguese Manuel de Faria y Souza. See *Bouterwek's* " History of Spanish Literature," p. 304.

[3] These are the terms employed by Felix de Arteaga, a distinguished Gongorist, in one of his songs to the fair Amaryllis. *Bouterwek*, p. 312.

[4] *Saint-Evremond,* " Œuvres," vol. iii. p. 235.

sort of reality. They became the familiar style of love poetry. When Voiture wrote

> " Je croirois d'avoir trop d'amour,
> Et de vous estre trop fidelle,
> Si vous n'estiez qu'un peu plus belle
> Que l'astre qui donne le jour,"

he probably merely intended to express, in a tone of pleasantry, one of those exaggerations from which he was no more free than others ; but it is very certain, that he did not mean to cast ridicule upon the prevailing fashion. Polite society spent a great deal of time in the serious discussion of the merits of two sonnets by Voiture and Malleville, on *La belle Matineuse;* and if a rather more graceful turn of expression, and greater poetry in the details, caused the prize to be awarded to Malleville's production, no one, during the whole of the discussion, thought of being offended by the fundamental idea of both pieces, which consisted in representing the sun, with all his magnificence, cast into the shade by the superior brilliancy of a woman.[1]

---

[1] We quote these two sonnets. Voiture's is as follows :—

> " Des portes du matin l'amante de Céphale,
> Les roses épandoit par le milieu des airs,
> Et jetoit dans les cieux nouvellement ouverts,
> Ces traits d'or et d'azur qu'en naissant elle étale,
>
> Quand la nymphe divine, à mon repos fatale,
> Apparut et brilla de tant de feux divers
> Qu'il sembloit qu'elle seule esclairoit l'univers,
> Et remplissoit de feu la rive orientale.

Although such examples as this give us an idea of
the taste of the society which held them in admiration,
they do not prove that its taste was confined to this
kind of literature only ; everything was sought after,
everything received into the gay and idle parties
of the time, which, though fond of amusement, were
no less fond of wit, and rejoiced to extend in any
direction the range of movement which varied their
existence. " M. de Nogent," says Ménage, " was an
admirable man to revive languishing conversations.
One day, being in the circle of the Queen, Anne of
Austria, and finding that the conversation had ceased,

> Le soleil, se hastant pour la gloire des cieux,
> Vint opposer sa flamme à l'éclat de ses yeux,
> Et prit tous les rayons dont l'Olympe se dore ;
>
> L'onde, la terre et l'air s'allumoient à l'entour,
> Mais auprès de Philis on le prit pour l'Aurore,
> Et l'on crut que Philis était l'astre du jour."

Malleville's sonnet runs thus :—

> " Le silence régnoit sur la terre et sur l'onde ;
> L'air devenoit serein et l'Olympe vermeil.
> Et l'amoureux Zéphir, affranchi du sommeil,
> Ressuscitoit les fleurs d'une haleine féconde.
>
> L'Aurore déployoit l'or de sa tresse blonde,
> Et semoit de rubis le chemin du soleil ;
> Enfin ce Dieu venoit au plus grand appareil
> Qu'il soit jamais venu pour éclairer le monde ;
>
> Quand la jeune Philis, au visage riant,
> Sortant de son palais plus clair que l'Orient,
> Fit voir une lumière et plus vive et plus belle.
>
> Sacré flambe du jour ! n'en soyez pas jaloux ;
> Vous parûtes alors aussi peu devant elle
> Que les feux de la nuit avoient fait devant vous."

and that for some time neither the Queen, nor the ladies (among whom was Madame de Guémenée), had spoken a word :—'Is it not, madam,' said he, breaking the silence and addressing the Queen, 'a curious whim of Nature's, that Madame de Guémenée and myself were born on the same day, and within a quarter of an hour of each other, and yet that she should be so fair and I so dark ?' "[1] If this remark really revived the conversation, and if it was for such speeches as this that M. de Nogent deserved to be quoted by Ménage as " an admirable man " for this kind of thing, we may form a tolerably correct notion of the subjects of conversation at this period, and can appreciate the eagerness with which any new topic would be welcomed. A witty rejoinder, a futile discussion, the slightest adventure, the death of a dog or cat,—all possible subjects were immediately celebrated in verses not remarkable for poetic feeling and expression, but animated by considerable facility, and by a freedom of tone which gave admission to all means of amusement. The works of Voiture, Sarrasin, and Benserade abound in pieces of this kind, which teach us how much wit may be infused into the very worst verses, and how little is required to obtain success, in fashionable society, in that kind of pleasures which their caprice has chosen.

If anything should excite our surprise, it would be

---

[1] " Menagiana," vol. i. p. 140.

that the pleasantries of this small worldly literature
were not worse, at a time when, besides that hyperbolic magnificence which did not consider the sun
sufficiently brilliant to be compared to the eyes of
Phillis, there grew and flourished, both in Court and
city, an extravagant taste for burlesque, the sublimity of which consisted in travestying *Didon* into
dondon,[1] and Venus into a *grisette.*[2] This taste,
though apparently so opposed to the excessive delicacy which seemed then to be in vogue, is, nevertheless, not at all surprising.   The courtiers of this
period, borrowing all their elegance and refinement
of mind from men of letters, resembled, for the most
part, those *parvenus*, whose tone and manners, notwithstanding the magnificence of their outward
appearance, clearly reveal their origin and habits.
Although Mlle. de Rambouillet, perhaps from haughtiness as much as virtue, took offence at the most
innocent freedoms, yet, in the general manners of
society, a modesty much less repulsive and limiting
its cares to the more essential parts of virtue, nevertheless retained a facility which at the present day
would be thought dangerous, or, at the very least,
strange.   When, in Mairet's " Sylvie," Sylvia's lover,
complaining of her rigid virtue, says :—

> " Souffre sans murmurer que ma bouche idolâtre
> Imprime ses baisers dessus ton sein d'albâtre,"

---

[1] A stout, fresh-coloured girl.   [2] See the " Virgile travesti."

Sylvia is no more scandalised at the proposition than were the spectators who witnessed these transports. The lover then exclaims :—

"O transports ! ô plaisirs du crime séparés !"

and Sylvia is really rather afraid that she will be seen, but not more than she fears being heard talking of love.[1]   This easiness of behaviour necessarily exercised great influence over the unconstraint of conversation : women who were so indulgent as to permit much, could not fail to become accustomed to hear much ; and Armande's proposition to cut off

"   *   *   *   ces syllabes infâmes
Dont on vient faire insulte à la pudeur des femmes,"[2]

proves that they thoroughly understood allusions of this kind, and that they had not yet habituated the men to show them such respect as not to indulge in such allusions.

Sentiments, then, might be pure without preventing language from being free, and ideas were still more so.   Mlle. de Rambouillet, who would not allow Voiture to kiss her hand, certainly read his verses, and pardoned the poet for implying a great deal, because he was the first who ceased to speak openly, although that also sometimes happened to

[1] " Sylvie," a pastoral melodrama, Act i. scene 5.
[2] *Molière*, " Femmes savantes."

him.[1]   This freedom, in the case of those women
who permitted it, might have been associated with
a certain innocence of imagination which, in a
pleasantry, saw nothing more than a pleasantry and
the gaiety which it occasioned ; but an innocence
capable of finding food for gaiety in such objects,
was necessarily connected with a remnant of coarseness which had not entirely disappeared before that
delicacy whose enjoyments were beginning to be
sought after.   The most chaste woman of the lower
orders may very innocently bring a blush to the
cheek of a lady of fashion, less chaste perhaps, but
more delicate.

We must not, moreover, judge of the Court and
city as a whole, at this period, by a small number
of persons who were anxious to distinguish themselves
from the rest, and in whom the fashion of wit had
found, either dispositions suited to insure its pre-
valence, or authority capable of commanding respect.
General ignorance contended against the aspirations
after wit and learning, which were struggling to gain
ground.   "Latin !" exclaimed the Commander de

---

[1] See *Voiture's* verses upon the adventure of a lady who fell from her
carriage, on her way to the country. ("Œuvres de Voiture," vol. ii. p. 32,
edit. 1665.)   Both substance and expression were much worse before his
time.   Saint-Evremond, however, speaking of the coarse freedom of the
older writers, and especially of Desportes, adds: "But since Voiture, who
had a refined mind, and lived in the best society, avoided this vulgar style
with considerable exactitude, even the stage has not allowed its authors
to write with too much freedom." ("Œuvres de Saint-Evremond," vol. ix.
p. 58.)   Thus, Molière's style was not too free for the usages of his time.

Jars, " Latin at my time ! A gentleman would have been dishonoured by learning it." [1] " I have loved war above all things," said the Maréchal de Hocquincourt to Père Canaye : " next to war I loved Mme. de Montbazon, and, such as you see me, philosophy next to Mme. de Montbazon." [2] But, taking a dislike to philosophy, because he perceived that it led him to believe nothing, the marshal gave it up. " Since then," he said, " I would willingly suffer crucifixion for the sake of religion ; not that I see any more reason in it than I saw before ; on the contrary, I think it less reasonable than ever ; but I can only tell you this, I would suffer crucifixion without knowing why." [3] Gassendi, says Segrais, " studied astronomy with a view to astrology ; " and when, having perceived the absurdity of the latter study, he attempted to disabuse the minds of other men regarding it, he repented of his endeavour, " because," he said, " whereas most people had previously studied astronomy as a preparation for becoming astrologers, many now ceased to study it at all since he had decried astrology." [4] The whole Court allowed itself to be amused, or deceived, by the tricks of an Abbé Brigalier, half a believer in what he taught, and half a quack, who had spent forty thousand crowns in an unsuccessful attempt to become a magician, and who made up for

[1] *Saint-Evremond*, " Œuvres," vol. ii. p. 81.   [2] Ibid. vol. iii. p. 56.
[3] Ibid. vol. iii. p. 60.   [4] " Segraisiana," vol. ii. p. 42.

his lack of science by his address.   One of the Court ladies gave him a piece of red stuff, that he might change its colour, which did not please her ; he returned to her a piece of green stuff ; and the strong-minded men alone, those philosophers for whom the Maréchal d' Hocquincourt had acquired such a distaste, ventured to doubt that this change was an effect of Abbé Brigalier's art.   A fowl which he caused to appear miraculously before the eyes of Monsieur, the brother of Louis XIII., by dropping it from his cassock, in which it had lain concealed, alarmed the prince so much that he drew his sword, which he returned quietly to its sheath on being told by the Abbé, with great gravity : " Do you know, my lord, that this is not a trick ? "   The fowl was increased in size by the imagination, and became, in the opinion of the Court, a " turkey-cock," that is, a new proof of the supernatural power wielded by the Abbé ; and the Queen very seriously told Mademoiselle, whose chaplain he was : " My dear cousin, you ought not to keep a chaplain who changes fowls into turkey-cocks." [1]

In that simplicity of ignorance, and that infancy of reason which is not incompatible with activity of mind, and only indicates want of reflection, it is not to be wondered at that persons to whom so many things were new and extraordinary, allowed themselves to be deceived and amused in the same way as

[1] " Segraisiana," vol. i. p. 51.

the common people. The taste of the Court, in its
diversions, did not rise above those which are now to
be seen in the public street—if, at least, we may
judge of them from the description given us by the
Abbé de Marolles of the ballets danced by the Court
of Louis XIII., and invented by the Duke de
Nemours, " who had rare ideas," says the Abbé, " in
this as in all other matters." [1] One of these ballets,
danced in 1626, represented the marriage of the
Dowager of Bilbahaut to the *Darling of Sillytown,*
" for even the names, in these matters," says Marolles,
" should have some pleasantry in them." [2] The
fertile imagination of the Duke de Nemours " furnished also the ballets of the *Fairies of the Forest
of Saint-Germain,* of the *Cups and Balls,* and of
the *Double Women,*" who were masked, on one side,
like modest young girls, and on the other, like
dissolute old women, and who acted, by turns, in
conformity to the character of these two personages ;
" until, at last, all having joined hands to dance in a
circle, it was impossible to say which was the front
or the back, so agreeably did this pretty invention
charm the imagination." [3] The same Abbé de Marolles
takes the Duke de Nemours severely to task for
having introduced into one of his ballets a personage
mounted upon a real horse, " instead of introducing

[1] "Mémoires de Michel de Marolles," vol. i. p. 114.   [2] Ibid.
[3] Ibid. vol. i. p. 134.

him upon a machine representing a horse, which is much more graceful." [1]   Thus, the essence of the royal ballets, according to the Abbé de Marolles, was the *comic* or the *pleasant*, as well as the *magnificent* and the *marvellous* ; [2] but this comicality was broad farce : we can perceive in it no trace of true comedy, which is the greatest enemy of burlesque ; and the choice of the actors in these ballets sufficiently indicates how far distant society then was from that sentiment of propriety which preserves dignity, even in amusements.

It was, then, to the most fantastic employment of the mind that the right was reserved of exciting gaiety amongst people who were as yet unaware of its true use.   The French poets had long ago set the example of that ingenious and puerile abuse of words, which, by playing with the reason more than with language, strives to impart to them, by their material arrangement, a meaning different to that which they naturally present.   We find more than one example of this in Marot ; and Pasquier himself, with a complacency which is ill-concealed beneath a slight affectation of shame, relates a multitude of these *jeux de mots*.   I shall only quote one of them, from the " Quantités" of Mathurin Cordier :—

> " *Iliades curœ quœ mala corde serunt!*
> Il y a des curés qui mal accordés seront !"

[1] " Mémoires de Michel de Marolles," vol. i. p. 133.
[2] Ibid. vol. iii. p. 119.

It was at the commencement of the seventeenth century, at the time when the fashion of burlesque universally prevailed, that *pointes* became popular in polite society. About the year 1632 or 1633, Ménage quarrelled with his father for having devolved upon him his office of King's Advocate, which he had resigned in favour of his son, but which Ménage did not wish to undertake. The bishop of Angers wrote to inquire what they had quarrelled about ; Ménage replied that it arose from his having "returned to his father a bad office,"— *de ce qu'il avait rendu à son père un mauvais office.*[1] "That was thought good at that period," said he afterwards, when quoting the joke ; "for it was then the age of *pointes.*"[2] Indeed they were so abundant at that time that Boileau thought it necessary to take notice of them, as marking one of the epochs in literature. Nothing, however serious, was entirely exempt from their insults ; they held nothing sacred :—

> " Et le docteur en chaire en orna l'Evangile."[3]

This taste at last died out, and was banished from literature :—

> " Toutefois à la cour les Turlupins restèrent,"

to amuse, at least, those persons who would have

[1] See the "Mémoires pour servir à la vie de M. Ménage," at the beginning of the first volume of "Menagiana."   [2] "Menagiana," vol. ii. p. 35.

[3] Little Père André, an Augustine Monk. See *Despreaux'* note on the "Art Poétique," c. ii. v. 122.

been greatly embarrassed by the necessity of possessing wit.

Thus everything, during the age and under the
reign of the blue-stockings, attests and explains the
existence and necessity of that coarse gaiety which
could be satisfied only by mental debauchery, and
the temporary forgetfulness of reason and propriety ;
a sort of intoxication very similar in its effects, and
sometimes in its causes, to that intoxication by wine,
sung by some of the poets of this period with more
spirit and originality than one would be led to
expect.   Brought up in good society, Voiture,
Benserade, and Sarrazin did not yield to this license,
which was too coarse for their taste, and too poetical
for their talent.   But the poets of the beginning of
this century, accustomed to live amongst themselves,
and probably glad to escape, whenever they could,
from the constraint of that elegant society in which
they were sometimes obliged to appear—since upon it
alone their success began to depend—spent their best
moments at the pot-house, and abandoned themselves
in excess to that liberty which they were not always
able to enjoy.   Though Faret has asseverated that he
owed the reputation of a debauchee, ascribed to him
by Saint-Amant, to the fact that his name rhymed
with *cabaret*,[1] Saint-Amant needed no witnesses to
prove that the thing was as familiar to him as

[1] *Pélisson*, " Histoire de l'Académie," p. 429.

the word ; for he has traced pictures of drunken-
ness which possess all the truth of a painting from
nature, and all the spirit of a poet filled with his
subject.[1] Saint-Amant, one of the most vigorous and
original writers of this kind, was, nevertheless, not
the only one ; and if proof were wanting of the vogue
then obtained by Bacchic poetry, it might be found
in the works of a strange poet of this period, Master
Adam, a carpenter, of Nevers. Unless generally
approved examples had already existed, it is no more

[1] " Qu'on m'apporte une bouteille
Qui d'une liqueur vermeille
Soit teinte jusqu'à l'orlet,
Afin que sous cette treille
Ma soif la prenne au colet.

Lacquay, fringue bien ce verre ;
Fay que l'éclat du tonnerre
Soit moins flamboyant que luy ;
Ce sera le cimeterre
Dont j'esgorgeray l'ennui.

Voyez le sang qui desgoutte ;
Il est, il est en déroute,
Ce lâche et sobre démon.

*   *   *   *   *

Hurlons comme des Ménades ;
Ces airs qu'en leurs sérénades
Les amoureux font ouïr,
Au milieu des carbonnades,
Ne sauroient nous resjouir.

Bacchus aime le désordre :
Il se plait à voir l'un mordre
L'autre braire et grimasser,

Et l'autre en fureur se tordre
Sous la rage de danser.

Il veut qu'ici de Panthée
La mort soit représentée
A la gloire du bouchon,
Et qu'au lieu de cet athée
On desmembre ce couchon.

Que dis-je ! oh ! que j'ai la vue
De jugement despourvue !
Parbleu ! c'est un marcassin
Dont la trogne résolu
Nous nargue dans ce bassin.

A voir sa gueule fumante,
Il m'est advis qu'il se vante,
En grondant mille défis,
Que du sanglier d'Erymanthe
Il descend de père en fils.

Il pourrait venir du diable,
Avec sa mine effroyable,
Si se verra-t-il chocqué,
Et d'une ardeur incroyable,
Par nous défait et mocqué."

It would be impossible for a man to abandon himself more heartily to
the extravagance of debauch. This piece is called " La Crévaille."

likely that a carpenter would have been the first to
sing of wine and the pot-house, than that a shepherd
was the first to celebrate flocks and fields in verse.
Master Adam heartily sang the praises of his barrels,
in imitation of the wits of his time, but imitated them
only feebly in his laudation of his mistress :—

> " Dont les yeux, en mourant, ostèrent à l'amour
>   Deux trônes où sa gloire étaloit tous ses charmes."

Burlesque, like bacchanalian poetry, does not originate among the lower classes of society ; the com-
monalty do not live sufficiently on a level with great
objects to see anything comic in their abasement,
and are not sufficiently well acquainted with them
to know how to render them ridiculous.   The gaiety
of the burlesque style resembles recollections of good
society, taken to the pot-house, and disfigured by
that intemperate joy, those licentious ideas, and that
unconstrained coarseness, in which topers indulge.[1]
The delicacy on which the writers of that period

---

[1] The connection between burlesque and bacchanalian poetry is so intimate, that it is not always easy to separate them ; it would be difficult to
say with any positiveness whether these stanzas of the *enamoured* Saint-
Amant were written by a toper or a burlesque poet :—

> " Parbleu, j'en tiens ; c'est tout de bon ;
>   Ma libre humeur en a dans l'aile
>   Puisque je préfère au jambon
>   Le visage d'une donzelle.
>   Je suis pris dans le doux lien
>   De l'archerot Italien ;
>   Ce dieutelet, fils de Cyprine
>   Avecques son arc mi-courbé
>   A féru ma rude poitrine
>   Et m'a fait venir à *jubé*.

were beginning to pride themselves increased the pleasantry of the contrast. More homogeneous manners would have furnished no food for gaiety of this kind. It was over the delicate and civilised poetry of Virgil that burlesque triumphed ; it failed completely against the simplicity of Homer.

It was, then, at this epoch of combined coarseness and refinement, of license and finical taste, that the hero of burlesque appropriately appeared. This hero was Scarron, whose wit and readiness had rendered him familiar with the study of literature ; who had been hurried into all kinds of debauchery by the reckless gaiety of his character, and whose infirmities threw him into good society, after having disabled him from again frequenting bad company. Bed-

> Je me fais friser tous les jours ;
> On me relève la moustache ;
> Je n'entrecoupe mes discours
> Que de rots d'ambre et de pistache.
> J'ai fait banqueroute au petun ;
> L'excès du vin m'est importun ;
> Dix pintes par jour me suffisent ;
> Encor, ô falotte beanté,
> Dont les regards me déconfisent,
> Est-ce pour boire à ta santé."

In order to become still more convinced of the resemblance, it is sufficient to read the piece entitled " La Débauche," which commences thus :—

> " Nous perdons le temps à rimer ;
> Amis, il ne faut plus chommer :
> Voici Bacchus qui nous convie
> A mener bien une autre vie——"

I dare not venture to quote more, as its gaiety is so petulant and intemperate. See the "Recueil des plus belles Pièces des Poëtes Français," vol. iii. p. 243.

ridden, but talkative, Scarron expended in pleasantry that vein of folly which had been arrested in its course by a sudden and premature old age. He infused into his books that intemperateness of imagination which had formerly served to enliven licentious parties ; but, gifted with greater discernment and good sense than is generally thought, he was careful not to cast upon persons or things any but that kind of ridicule which might, up to a certain point, fairly belong to them. Thus, Æneas *weeping like a calf* in the midst of a storm, in fear of being *devoured by soles*,[1] is only an exaggeration of that weakness which tradition attributes to the character of the pious son of Anchises ; and any man whom excess of gaiety has rendered capable, like Scarron, of stripping the sublime of those circumstances which render it earnest and imposing, will, like him, see in the *Quos ego* . . . of Neptune nothing but a *Par la mort*[2] . . . and the reticence of a well-bred man, stopping for fear of swearing too vulgar an oath.

This *Par la mort* was considered the most admirable hit of the burlesque style ; and the reputation of the " Virgile Travesti " was so firmly established that, a few years after Scarron's death, a writer ventured to represent Ovid as saying to Virgil : " By

---

[1] *Scarron,* " Virgile Travesti," vol. i. p. 28, edit. 1704.
[2] Ibid. p. 32.

his means you pass into the hands of the fair sex,
who delight to have a laugh at your expense ; and,
comparing style with style, his wanton and jocular
graces are really well worth your grave and serious
beauties.   *·   *   *   I don't think that even you
would maintain that your *Quos ego* is better than
Scarron's *Par la mort.*" Upon which, poor Virgil
answers that he does not complain that Scarron's
merit eclipses his own.[1]

But if men of taste had been the only judges of
burlesque, even though taking pleasure in it, they
would have assigned to it its true place ; and the
greatest success of a folly of this kind would have
resembled that obtained by one of those ephemeral
farces, in the performance of which those who move
in good society, and even men of talent, occasionally
seek an amusement which they would not endure in
any other quarter.   Instead of this, burlesque was
adopted at this period with all the fervour of a new
fashion ; and a fashion, as long as it lasts, carries all
before it, until, becoming denaturalised by the whimsicality or triteness of its applications, it proves distasteful even to those who, after having pertinaciously
sustained it, can no longer discern in it that grace
which had originally won their admiration.   " Did it
not appear during all these last years," says Pelisson,
" that we were playing at that game in which even

---

[1] " Parnasse Réformé," p. 27.

the winners lose ? and did not most persons think
that, in order to write reasonably in this style, it was
sufficient to say things contrary to reason and good
sense ?   All persons, of either sex, thought themselves capable of doing this—from the lords and
ladies of the Court down to the servant-maids and
valets." [1]   The booksellers would publish none but
burlesque poems, although they were satisfied if a
work were written in short verses ; so that, during
the wars of the Fronde, there was printed a *Passion
of our Lord in burlesque verses*, " a bad piece
enough," says Pelisson, " but nevertheless serious, and
whose title justly horrified those who read no
more." [2]

Such were the principal fashions that prevailed in
poetry, during the first half of the seventeenth
century.   Notwithstanding their diversity, we may
recognise in them a general character, the only one
that was suited to the whole of the literature of this
period—and that is, the absence of all true and
serious feeling, of all inspiration derived from the
objects themselves, and which transfers them completely, first into the imagination, and afterwards
into the verses of the poet.   Religious enthusiasm did
not inspire the innumerable versifiers who then
translated or paraphrased the Psalms ; love did not

---

[1] *Pelisson*, " Histoire de l'Académie," p. 171.

[2] Ibid. p. 172.   Nearly all the critics, following Naudé, have spoken of
this as a burlesque composition.

dictate a single one of the ten thousand sonnets, madrigals and ballads, into which its name was so incessantly introduced ; admiration of nature, and the aspect of her beauties, did not produce one piece that came truly from the heart or from a sincerely affected imagination. Whatever subject was chosen for a poetical composition, it was regarded merely as a *jeu d'esprit*—an opportunity for combining together in a more or less ingenious manner, words of a more or less harmonious sound, and ideas of a more or less agreeable meaning ; and no man, when writing verses, thought of looking into his soul for his true feelings and desires, fears and hopes ; of interrogating the emotions of his heart and the recollections of his life ; in short, of being a poet, and not a mere maker of verses. Some flights of a delirious imagination might be truthfully rendered ; humorous hyperbole, or malicious wit, might furnish some telling strokes for an epigram ; but nothing that related to the natural affections of man, nothing of that which is truly serious and real in his existence, appeared fit to furnish subjects or images to poets who made verses about everything ; and the impossibility of finding, in the poetical productions of half a century, a single piece really elevated, energetic, or pathetic in its tone and character, is a phenomenon which reveals to us the aspect under which poetry was regarded at an epoch when natural and powerful emotions were no more strangers to the heart of man than they have been at any other period.

Neither sentiment, nor taste, nor poetical language are compatible with that factitious wit, which takes no thought about things as they really exist. In such a system, no object is regarded in its true light, and no emotion expressed as it would naturally be felt ; and if nature seems sometimes to make her appearance, an incongruous idea or a stroke of false wit hastens to dispel the illusion, and to admonish the reader that it is not the voice of truth which he has just heard. Maynard, in his *Stanzas by a Father on the death of his Daughter*,[1] in which the force of the position described draws from him a few verses of true feeling, cannot long maintain his assumed character. This inconsolable father addresses his heart, and says :—

> " Courons, mon cœur, courons donc au naufrage
> Dans les torrens qui naissent de mes yeux."

In these two lines we meet with ridiculous imagery, false sentiment, and absurd ideas ; and nothing of the kind would have occurred to any poet who had thought that, in order to deplore such a loss, he should consult and obey the emotions of the heart. The especial deficiency of the poets of this time, is in meditation : incapable of retiring within themselves,

---

[1] See the "Recueil des plus belles Pièces des Poëtes Français," vol. iii. p. 6.

and concentrating their attention on the objects
which occupy their imagination, in order to investi-
gate their nature and discover the sentiment corresponding thereto, they pass from one to another,
and link them together without careful selection or
natural connection, and, consequently, with as little
taste as truthfulness. Saint-Amant, the frankest of
all in his manner, and who would approach most
nearly to truth if truth could be attained without
meditation, describes with considerable poetical
spirit, in his piece on *Solitude*, the inspiration which
sways him :—

> " Tantost chagrin, tantost joyeux,
> Selon que la fureur m'enflamme,
> Et que l'objet s'offre à mes yeux,
> Les propos me naissent en l'âme,
> Sans contraindre la liberté
> Du démon qui m'a transporté." [1]

This is indeed the " demon " of poetry ; but this
demon should not be a vagabond, uncertain spirit,
leading the poet from one world to another, without
giving him time to describe anything in a complete
and truthful manner. Let him resuscitate for a
moment the pagan poet, and raise him up in the
midst of the ideas and recollections of mythology—
Pan, with the nymphs and dryads, will, in his view,
people the groves ; place him under the influence of
the superstitious notions of the Middle Ages—the

---

[1] See the " Recueil des plus belles Pièces des Poëtes Français," vol. iii.
p. 242.

night will be filled with phantoms, and the sound of
a bell or the cry of a bird will be the signal for
ghostly apparitions.   But if the inspiration be real,
if it be not the vagrancy of a mind adopting con-
fusedly all the ideas that present themselves to its
notice, without possessing a definite conception of any
one of them, the poet will not group together in the
same picture Pan and the demigods climbing for
refuge, at the time of the Deluge, upon trees so
lofty—

> " Qu'en se sauvant sur leurs rameaux
> A peine virent-ils les eaux ; "

and the goblins laughing and dancing to the " funeral
cries " of the osprey,

> " Mortels augures des destins."

In order to describe the darkness of a vault, he will
not say : —

> " Que quand Phébus y descendroit
> Je pense qu'il n'y verroit goutte."

If he conduct us to the borders of a marsh so
pleasant that—

> " Les nymphes, y cherchant le frais,
> S'y viennent fournir de quenouilles,
> De pipeaux, de joncs, et de glais,"

he will not immediately add :—

> " Où l'on voit sauter les grenouilles,
> Qui de frayeur s'y vont cacher,
> Sitôt qu'on les veut approcher." [1]

---

[1] These lines are quoted from *Saint-Amant's* poem on " Solitude."   See
the " Recueil des plus belles Pièces des Poëtes Français," vol. iii. p. 236.

Truth of this kind, devoid alike of grace and interest, is not poetical truth ; for a poet, a man whose mind is deeply impressed with elevated or agreeable ideas and images, will certainly not think of the frogs that are frisking about at his feet, or, at least, will not pay so much attention to them as to describe them.

It was, nevertheless, by truth of this factitious and vulgar character, that readers, as destitute as the poets themselves of that feeling of the beautiful which is only the true placed in its right position, allowed themselves to be delighted. In Colletet's [1] *Monologue,* which serves. as the preface to the " Comédie des Tuileries," by five authors, we find these lines :—

> " La canne s'humecter de la bourbe de l'eau,
> D'une voix enrouée et d'un battement d'aile
> Animer le canard qui languit auprès d'elle." [2]

Cardinal de Richelieu, to whom Colletet read this monologue, was so enraptured with the piece, that he gave the author fifty pistoles on the spot, saying that it was a reward for these three lines only, and that " the King was not rich enough to pay for the remainder of the poem." [3]   The Cardinal merely desired that, for the sake of greater exactitude,

---

[1] The father of the Colletet mentioned by *Boileau.*

[2] See this monologue at the commencement of the " Comédie des Tuileries."   Paris, 1638.

[3] *Pelisson,* " Histoire de l'Académie," p. 182 ; and *Aubery,* " Histoire du Cardinal Duc de Richelieu," vol. ii. p. 434.

Colletet should introduce this alteration into his first line :—

" La canne *barbotter* dans la bourbe de l'eau,"

and the poet found it very difficult to avoid making the correction,[1] which, at all events, would have been in perfect keeping with the whole of the picture.[2]

Any one who reads the poets of this period will be struck most forcibly with that want of meditation which prevented their taste from becoming pure, and their sensibility from becoming profound ; they some-times pass before a great idea, but they never stop to consider it, for they have not the least suspicion of the poetry and grandeur which it contains ; in their view, it is a mere mental combination, a fleeting spark which, far from kindling a lasting fire, burns only to become extinguished speedily.   To this cold-

---

[1] On leaving the Cardinal, whom he had apparently not yet thoroughly convinced, Colletet wrote him a letter on the subject. "The Cardinal had just finished reading it," says Pelisson, " when some of his courtiers arrived, who began to compliment him about some success just achieved by the arms of the King, and said, 'that nothing could resist his Eminence.' 'You are mistaken,' answered Richelieu, laughing, 'I find even in Paris persons who resist me;' and when he was asked who these foolhardy per-sons were : 'Colletet is the man,' he replied, ' for after having fought with me yesterday about a word, he does not surrender yet, but has just written me this long letter on the subject.'" *Pelisson*, " Histoire de l'Académie," p. 182, *et seq.*

[2] The whole passage runs thus :—

" A mesme temps j'ay veu, sur le bord d'un ruisseau,
La canne s'humecter de la bourbe de l'eau,
D'une voix enrouée et d'un battement d'aisle,
Animer le canard qui languit auprès d'elle,
Pour appaiser le feu qu'ils sentent nuit et jour,
Dans cette onde plus sale encor que leur amour."

ness, which inflicts a mortal injury upon poetry, was soon added that negligence which is an essential characteristic of the grace of people of fashion, and by which they denaturalise the things which they intend to appropriate, in order to adapt them to their use. As soon as wit became fashionable, everybody wished to write verses ; and, thanks to the privilege possessed by persons of quality " of knowing everything without having learned anything," everybody wrote verses. Thenceforward it was necessary for poets, in order to be in the fashion, to write verses like persons of quality, that is, without labour—without what was called " pedantry" ; it was necessary to give them the " cavalier turn " of which that Scudéry was so proud who boasted of having " used many more matches to light arquebuses than to light candles," and of being sprung from a family which had never " worn feathers elsewhere than in the hat," and who wished to learn to write with his left hand, in order to be able to employ " the right hand more nobly." [1] " May the devil take me, if I am a poet," says one of these coxcombical wits, " and if I have the remotest conception of what enthusiasm is. I write verses, it is true, but it is to kill time ; and then they are only little gallant epistles which I compose while my hair is being

---

[1] See the Preface of " Lygdamon," addressed to the Duke de Montmorency.

dressed. I leave to professional poets all their cumbrous parade of fictions and bombastic phrases ; I deal only in tender and delicate expressions, and I think that I have succeeded in catching that court air whose sportive manner so far transcends all the wisdom of the wise." [1]   These were the persons who criticised poetry, to please whom it was written, and whose style it was indispensable to imitate in order to give them satisfaction. Malherbe was reckoned one of the " professional poets " ; and, but for the French which he had taught at Court, he would have completely lost himself in that inundation of rhymes which no one ventured to call poetry.

" I remember the time," says Saint-Evremond, " when Malherbe's poetry was considered admirable for style and justness of expression. Malherbe shortly afterwards fell into neglect, as the last of our poets ; for caprice had turned the attention of the French to enigmas, burlesque, and *bouts-rimés.*" [2]

From hence, however, were destined to issue the most brilliant epochs of our literary glory. Men of letters, by their presence and conversation, had laboured to diffuse throughout society a taste for mental occupations : this taste had possessed for themselves all the attractiveness of a novelty which men hasten to enjoy and parade ; but we soon

[1] " Parnasse Réformé," p. 65.
[2] *Saint-Evremond,* " Œuvres," vol. v. p. 18.

become accustomed to novelty; and when the good which it at first served to adorn becomes in itself a real good, capable of supplying sweet and true pleasures, we are disposed, when the novelty has passed away, to enjoy these pleasures more silently and deeply, and do not feel it necessary to parade them every day. If the public had not yet become fully enlightened, it had at least increased in numbers; and writers might hope to meet with admirers and critics beyond the limits of their own particular circle. They thus began to gain greater independence, and acquired not only more leisure for meditation, but also more liberty to follow the natural impulses of their genius. Nothing was required but favourable circumstances to guarantee this liberty, to augment this leisure, and thus to place the poets in a position to produce works of sufficient merit to guide the taste of a public which no longer required to be daily amused by their wit in order to take an interest in their labours.

The institution of the French Academy, the establishment of theatres, and, shortly afterwards, the direct protection of Louis XIV., were the principal causes which led to this great and felicitous result.

I have already alluded to the general tendency which, at the commencement of the seventeenth century, directed the attention of all minds towards literature. This tendency was not the fermentation produced by the appearance of a superior genius, whose influence is paramount and universal ; nor was it that strong and continuous warmth which results from the equal and natural development of all the faculties of a free nation : it was an intense but uncertain movement towards the light ; an irresistible impulse to action without any determinate object, in which effort after perfection was much more perceptible than vigour of invention. Fully satisfied with the wealth they already possessed, the poets appeared to be anxious only to set it in orderly array, before bringing it into use ; and, of all the deficiencies of our poetry, they were conscious only of want of regularity and want of correctness. The principal object of their labours was the purification of the language : following the example of Malherbe, "that doctor in the vulgar tongue," as Balzac calls him,[1] they believed themselves entrusted with the guardianship of its glory and prosperity, upon which, in their opinion, depended, perhaps in a greater degree than was generally believed, the prosperity of the State.[2] They devoted themselves to this task with all the assiduity that should be displayed in the discharge of a special function, and

---

[1] *Balzac,* " Socrate Chrestien."

[2] In the letter which Cardinal Richelieu desired the Academicians to write to him to request his protection, we read, " that it appeared that nothing was required to complete the felicity of the kingdom, but to rescue the language that we speak from the category of barbarian languages." *Pelisson,* " Histoire de l'Académie," p. 37.

with all the zeal that belongs to the maintenance
of superior authority. The taste for literature, which
had become diffused throughout society, rendered
the men whose province it was to explain or enforce
its laws, the chiefs of a vast and brilliant empire ;
and " grammar, which gives rules even to kings,"
could not possibly be considered, by its own ministers,
an object of slight importance. Thus, at the same
time that men of letters went into the world to enjoy
the success they had achieved, they were frequently
brought together, among themselves, by a matter of
more serious interest—the public welfare. On such
occasions, whatever might be the subject of conversation, purity and elegance of language, and choice and
propriety of terms, were observed with all the scru-
pulousness of a religious duty, and all the labour of
an imperative task. " In contradistinction to the
present practice," says Ménage, " great care was
taken to speak correctly, and not to commit mistakes
in these social conversations." [1] After one of these
meetings, Balzac being left alone with Ménage, drew
a long breath, and said : " Now that we are alone,
let us speak freely, without fear of uttering sole-
cisms." [2] Although he sneered at the custom, Balzac
observed it more strictly than most others. " He
spoke," says Ménage, " much better than he wrote.
If all those who profess to speak correctly had met

---

[1] " Menagiana," vol. i. p. 306.   [2] Ibid.

together to construct a sentence, they would not have succeeded better than he did.   *   *   *   All men of talent have been obliged to consider him as the restorer, or rather as the author, of our language, as it exists at the present day." [1]

However wearisome these conversations may have been, the fatigue they occasioned was that which results from deep and amusing interest : from the records which we possess of the letters, anecdotes, witticisms, and opinions which formed the staple of conversation at this period, it is easy to perceive how active was the circulation of ideas, though intended almost entirely for the mere ordinary interchange of daily life.   Never, perhaps, were wit and erudition so entirely devoted to the habitual routine of existence.   Literary meetings multiplied in every direction ; some were held at the houses of Mlle. de Gournay [2] and of Balzac, and afterwards at the residence of Ménage.   Others took place in the *Pays Latin*, [3] in the neighbourhood of the Colleges, at which men had begun to inquire whether it were possible to make some reasonable use of the vernacular tongue.   Pelisson relates that, on leaving college, full of contempt for the French language, he looked

---

[1] "Menagiana," vol. i. p. 311.

[2] I do not know upon what ground the Abbé de Marolles says that it was at her house that "the first idea of the French Academy was conceived." "Mémoires de Michel de Marolles," vol. iii. p. 239.

[3] See *Pelisson*, "Histoire de l'Académie," p. 356 ; and the "Mémoires de Marolles," vol. i. p. 77.

with disdain upon " the romances and other new
pieces " • that were brought under his notice, and
" returned always," he says, " to my Cicero and my
Terence, whom I found much more reasonable." At
length, he was struck by some works that fell into
his hands, amongst which was the fourth volume of
" Balzac's Letters." " Thenceforward," he says, " I
began not only no longer to despise the French
language, but even to love it passionately, to study it
with considerable care, and to believe, as I do still at
the present day, that with talent, time, and trouble,
it might be rendered capable of everything." [1] It
will at once be perceived how necessary literary
meetings were to men educated in this manner.
There were discussed all the difficulties of grammar,
and opinions were pronounced upon new works :
thither the wits of the coterie, sometimes inspired by
the ideas expressed at these conferences, and always
encouraged by the certainty of finding an attentive
audience, brought the fruits of their labours. Some
grave censors criticised these occupations, and complained that so much activity of mind was wasted
upon words ; [2] but they did not perceive therein the

---

[1] *Pelisson,* " Histoire de l'Académie," p. 481.

[2] " It was then," says Marolles, " that a young theologian, named Louis
Masson, could not refrain from expressing his astonishment, having come
upon us while we were examining certain idioms of the language ; which
he esteemed of little importance in comparison with other things in which,
in his opinion, it would have been much more proper for us to have employed
our time." " Mémoires de Marolles," vol. i. pp. 77, 78.

first indications of a more important activity, and the natural feeling of men who, feeling disposed to meet together, and desirous to act in concert, were labouring to rescue from its long-continued barbarism, that very language which was to serve as the medium of their communications,—a work which they were obliged to undertake, as none of those superior geniuses, who can make light spring from the midst of chaos, had spared them the trouble.

About the year 1629, among those who were thus brought together by a taste for literature, Chapelain, Gombaud, Godeau, Malleville, and some others, living like them in the world and engaged in business, annoyed at not being able to meet as frequently and freely as they could have wished, agreed to assemble on a certain day in each week at the house of Conrart, which was most conveniently situated for them all. This was not a literary meeting, but a company of men of kindred spirit in every respect, although similarity of mental tastes and occupations was their principal bond of union. " They conversed familiarly," says Pelisson, " as they would have done at an ordinary visit, on all sorts of subjects, business, news, literature, and the like ; and their conferences were followed, sometimes by a walk, and sometimes by a collation of which they partook together." [1] They invariably consulted each other

---

[1] *Pelisson,* " Histoire de l'Académie," pp. 9, 10.

about their respective works, and criticised only in order to advise.

Such a union of confidence and friendship admitted none but select associates ; and, in order not to be exposed to the necessity of receiving others, they resolved to keep their meeting secret. During nearly four years the secret was kept, and they passed this period in the enjoyment of a happiness which they doubtless more than once regretted in the sequel. "Even at the present day," says Pelisson, "they speak of it as of a golden age, during which, with all the innocence and freedom, of the first centuries, without noise or pomp, and with no laws but those of friendship, they enjoyed together all the sweetest and most charming pleasures which the society of cultivated minds, and a reasonable life, can afford."[1]

Perhaps, however, in proportion as their taste became more pure, and as they felt sufficient strength to maintain authority, they began to feel desirous of obtaining it : and perhaps some of them allowed themselves to instance the views of the society of which they were members, in support of their own opinions. At all events, the secret was divulged. Pelisson says that Malleville told it to Faret,[2] who immediately presented himself with a book in his hand, [3] and was admitted. Faret mentioned the

---

[1] *Pelisson*, " Histoire de l'Académie," p. 11.   [2] Ibid.
[3] Entitled " L'honnête Homme."

matter to Bois-Robert, who also solicited admission.
Bois-Robert, a creature of Cardinal Richelieu, was a
man whom it was neither easy to reject nor impolitic
to receive, and the old members seemed to feel
this. " There was no appearance," says Pelisson, " of
refusing him admittance ; for, besides that he was the
friend of most of these gentlemen, his fortune [1] gave
him some authority, and rendered him more considerable." [2]   Bois-Robert was admitted, and it was
not long before the Cardinal was informed of the
existence of the society.

Richelieu, having gained peaceable possession of the
supreme authority, was then occupied in consolidating
his power in order that he might enjoy it.   Sharing in
the taste of his time for mental amusements, he made
them subservient to his glory and policy, as well as to
his gratification.   He granted to literature an active
protection, the influence of which upon the literature
of his own time has, perhaps, been exaggerated, but
the effect of which upon succeeding generations cannot be disregarded.   " He considered the State in
reference only to his own life," said Cardinal de
Retz ; " but never did minister apply himself more
strenuously to make people believe that he was
arranging for the future." [3]   And never, perhaps, did
minister devolve more completely upon the future the

---

[1] That is, the favour in which he was held by the Cardinal.

[2] *Pelisson,* " Histoire de l'Académie," p. 13.

[3] " Memoirs of Cardinal de Retz," vol. i. p. 95.

task of displaying the grandeur of his ideas ; his own
character frequently prevented them from producing
an immediate and continuous effect ; for he repressed
from instinct that which calculation had prompted
him to elevate. Urged by a craving after dominion
and enjoyment, anxious to seize and appropriate to
himself that which he had originated, he seemed to
be ignorant that the germ, when once sown, becomes
the property of nature, whose action cannot accom-
modate itself to that of power. He desired that his
authority should regulate even the most insignificant
details ; as Cardinal de Retz well observes, " he was
a very great man, determined to be master everywhere and in all things, and carrying to a most
sovereign degree the weakness of not despising little
things." [1] He protected literature as a minister and
an amateur, and the taste of the amateur was
supported by the authority of the minister. The
sway which he exercised over men of letters was
tempered with familiarity, but it was the familiarity
of a master who gave his own ideas for inspiration, and
money for reward. When Vaugelas, whom he had
appointed to edit the " Dictionnaire de l'Académie,"
came to thank him for having restored to him an old
pension, as a recompense for his labour,—" Well !
sir," said the Cardinal, when he perceived him, " at
all events you will not forget to put the word *pension*

---

[1] " Memoirs of Cardinal de Retz," vol. i. pp. 13, 16.

into your Dictionary." " No, my lord," replied
Vaugelas, " but still less shall I forget the word
gratitude." There was more nobility in the answer
than delicacy in the joke ; but neither of them were
aware of this.[1]

Nevertheless, by rewarding men of letters by
favours almost always granted in the name of the
State, Richelieu supplied them with the means of
liberating themselves from that dependence upon
private individuals to which they were almost all
obliged to submit. During his life they could not be
otherwise than under obligations to the Cardinal ;
after his death they became the pensioners of the
Government ; and the Academy, which he had
founded merely for the sake of having a literary body
to protect and govern, became some years afterwards,
under the more liberal patronage of Louis XIV., a
literary body that was destined soon to belong to
France alone.

From the accounts given him by Bois-Robert of
the meetings held at Conrart's residence—of the
talent by which they were distinguished—of the
harmony of their opinions and the wisdom of their
decisions, Richelieu was led to contemplate the establishment of a new authority—that is to say, of a
new branch of his own authority. He inquired of
Bois-Robert whether these gentlemen would not like

---

[1] *Aubery,* " Histoire du Cardinal de Richelieu," vol. i. p. 432.

to form themselves into a body, and to meet under public authority ; and he directed him to offer them " his protection for their company, which he would have established by letters-patent, and to express to each one of them in particular his affection, which he would manifest to them on every occasion."[1] Nothing could have been less agreeable to them than such an honour ; " and when it became necessary to deter-mine what answer should be given, there was scarcely one of these gentlemen," says Pelisson, " who did not manifest the greatest dissatisfaction." [2] Some even wished to send an absolute refusal : the protection of the Cardinal would be no recommendation to them in the eyes of the public ; for the reception of his patronage gave rise to suspicions of so odious a character as to render it an object of dread to men of honour. It was believed that he maintained spies in the houses of all the powerful nobles ; and some of the future Academicians—as, for example, Serisay, the steward of the Duke de la Rochefoucauld, an enemy of the Cardinal, and Malleville, the secretary of the Marshal de Bassompierre, then in the Bastille— had great reason to fear that his protection would lose them the confidence of their masters. But a prime minister is supported by all those interests which do not act in direct opposition to him ; and Chapelain, who was in receipt of a pension from the

---

[1] *Pelisson*, " Histoire de l'Académie," pp. 16, 17.   [2] Ibid.

Cardinal, gave very plausible reasons for accepting his offer, and reminded his friends, " that as, by the laws of the realm, all kinds of meetings which were held without the permission of the prince were prohibited, it would be very easy for the Cardinal, notwithstanding all their efforts, to put a stop to theirs if he had the slightest inclination to do so." [1]   This argument was irresistible, and a letter of thanks was sent to the Cardinal, by whom, from that time forth, the " French Academy " was regarded with affection, and even treated with consideration.

Immediate steps were taken to give the new institution the form which it has since retained ; but, as had been foreseen, it became ere long a butt for sarcasm and an object of distrust.   To excite such sentiments, it was not necessary for it to have been the work of a feared and hated minister.   The Parliament, which was applied to in 1635 to register the letters-patent, did not grant this registration until 1637 ; and then only in consequence of the reiterated demands of the Cardinal himself, who threatened, in case of another refusal, to refer the matter to the decision of the Supreme Council.   Some of the magistrates, indignant at their intervention being required in an affair of such trivial importance, called to mind that, " in former times, an emperor, after having deprived the Senate of all cognizance of public affairs, had con-

---

[1] *Pelisson,* " Histoire de l'Académie," p. 21.

sulted it regarding the best sauce to be eaten with a large turbot."[1]   Others, alarmed at everything done by the Cardinal, did not know what to think of a new body created by him, and in which he appeared to take so deep an interest.   The Cardinal was obliged to write to the first President that " the intentions of the Academicians were altogether different from those which he might have been led to believe they entertained";[2] and the registration was granted at length, " on condition that the members of the said assembly and Academy shall occupy themselves only in the adornment, embellishment, and augmentation of the French language, and in taking cognizance of the books that shall be by them written, and by other persons who shall desire and wish it."[3]

Amongst the people, who, under a despotic government, give no attention to novelties except to take alarm at them, those who took notice of the Academy connected its establishment with their own special fears.   A merchant had entered into arrangements to purchase a house in the Rue des Cinq-Diamants, in which Chapelain resided, in whose apartments the Academy then met ;[4] having observed that, on

[1] *Pelisson*, " Histoire de l'Académie," pp. 103, 104.   [2] Ibid. p. 81.

[3] Ibid. p. 87.   The Platonic Academy of Florence, at the period of its re-establishment by Cosmo I., Grand Duke of Tuscany, was in like manner constrained to abandon all philosophical studies, in order to devote its attention entirely to the improvement of the Italian language. See Tiraboschi, vol. vii. part i. p. 143, edit. 1796.

[4] Conrart having married in 1634, it was thought advisable to alter the

certain days of the week, a number of carriages came
to the house, he inquired the cause, and, on being
informed, broke off his bargain, saying that he would
not live in a street in which *une cadémie de mano-
poleurs* was held every week.[1]   On the other hand,
the public were disposed to turn into ridicule a body
that assumed to subject them to their decisions.   If
one of the Academicians manifested, for any particular
words or phrases, an aversion which was common
and natural enough at a time when words were considered of so much importance, " envy and slander,"
says Pelisson, " at once set that down for an academical decision ;"[2] and Saint-Evremond's comedy of
the " Academicians,"[3] in which they are represented
as disputing and insulting one another about words
which some wish to condemn and others to absolve,
shows very clearly what was the feeling generally
entertained regarding them.   Men of letters themselves, wavering between authority and the public,

place of meeting, which was transferred first to the house of Desmarets,
and afterwards to those of several other Academicians, until, at length, at
the beginning of 1643, after the death of Cardinal Richelieu, the Chancellor
Seguier, who at the end of the same year was chosen by the Academy as
their protector, having expressed a wish that they should meet at his house,
they continued there until they were established at the Louvre. *Pelisson*,
" Histoire de l'Académie," pp. 23, 151.   [1] Ibid. p. 95.

[2] Ibid. pp. 117, 118.   Gomberville detested the word *car*; one day he
asserted that he had not used it once in his romance of " Polexandre,"
in which it was nevertheless found to occur three times ; it was assumed
from this that the Academy wished to banish *car* from the language ;
which gave rise to many witticisms and that famous letter of Voiture,
which begins with *car*.   See *Voiture*, " Lettres," vol. liii. p. 132.

[3] *Saint-Evremond*, " Œuvres," vol. i.

seemed at first to feel considerable hesitation about connecting themselves with a body respecting whose nature they did not yet possess any clearly-defined ideas ;[1] perhaps even some of those who belonged to it sometimes felt their pride wounded by the slavery to which they were subjected by the Academy, and Maynard, one of their number, wrote this quatrain on the subject :—

> " En cheveux gris il me faut donc aller,
> Comme un enfant, tous les jours à l'école ;
> Que je suis fou d'apprendre à bien parler,
> Lorsque la mort vient m'ôter la parole ! "

For two centuries, the advantages and inconveniences of such an authority have been discussed ; perhaps it would have been better first to inquire whether it were possible for an academy not to have been established, at the commencement of the seventeenth century. When, amongst a people not very numerous, and by a fortunate concurrence of moral or political circumstances, knowledge is diffused in an equable and continuous manner—when every man finds himself in a position which enables him to enjoy his rights and display his faculties, academies are

[1] Bardin, the first of the Academicians who died after its foundation, had been accused of having unconcernedly received his nomination when the Academy, at the outset, chose him for one of those selected to complete the number of forty. He afterwards declined the office. It was probably in consequence of some instances of this kind that the Academy determined to receive none who did not apply for admission. *Pelisson*, " Histoire de l'Académie," pp. 347, 348.

unnecessary, and by the natural course of things, they either are not formed or do not obtain any influence. But wherever knowledge and a taste for literature—the consequence of a special study and not of the general development of the human race—are the exclusive property of a few individuals and not the patrimony of the whole nation, men of letters will be sure to seek each other out and to unite together ; if rivalries cause temporary divisions, a more abiding interest will soon bring them back to unity ; and so long as no other obstacle exists among them but self-love, self-love will itself form the bond, which, setting aside their personal animosities, will make them feel the necessity of seeking support, in their mutual suffrages, against the ignorance and caprices of the multitude. Never had such unions been more necessary than during the first half of the seventeenth century, when society was busied with literary pursuits, without understanding what literature really was ; they naturally sprang into existence in every direction, and as naturally, that one which was most distinguished by the reputation of its members or by their position in the world, could not fail to acquire a power of opinion which it would have retained by its own strength, or would have lost only when superseded by a higher authority of the same kind. The language and taste, at that period, imperatively demanded the establishment of an authority to which recourse might be had when usage afforded only uncertain aid ; and the authority instituted in the French Academy reigned in the name of usage, which would otherwise have reigned without its guidance.

In truth, the first Academicians, in a fervour of legislation which probably consoled them for the honour which they had been compelled to receive, proposed several laws of a severity as singular as it was tyrannical. Sirmond, for example, " desired that all the Academicians should be obliged, by oath, to employ the words approved by the majority of votes in the assembly ; " so that, as Pelisson observes, " any one who failed to do so, would have committed, not a fault, but a sin." [1] This absurd proposition was rejected ; but it was determined, on the other hand, that no Academician should be allowed to place his title at the beginning of a work, unless that work had been approved by the Academy, whose book-seller swore to make no alterations in it after such approbation had been given. But the necessity of passing through this species of Chancery was too great a restraint for the Academicians, and they soon ceased to submit to it ; so that the bookseller did not find it difficult to keep his oath.[2]

Thus were gradually rejected or eluded all those

[1] *Pelisson*, " Histoire de l'Académie," pp. 57, 58.
[2] Ibid. pp. 129, 139, 140.

constraints which were based upon the caprice of
the new legislators, and not on the power of the
usages and manners of the time.   And let it not be
thought that the regulation of usage depended upon
the Academy ; it might sometimes give vogue to
mediocrity, but it could never struggle against genius.
The severity with which it condemned Chimène's
love did not prevent Boileau from extolling—

> " *   *   *   *   la douleur vertueuse
> De Phèdre malgré soi perfide, incestueuse."

The approbation of the Academy was undoubtedly
sought after ; but the works written to please it were
works which the spirit of the time commanded it to
approve.   Talent really admired by the public, could
not fail to gain access to a body which necessarily
sought all possible support from opinion, as opinion
was the sole basis of its existence.   If some few
superior men were excluded therefrom by other
obstacles than the difference of academic opinions,
that exclusion never caused the slightest diminu-
tion of their glory or their literary power.   Molière
and La Fontaine, though not of the Academy, were
not therefore less well thought of or less honoured
either by the public or by the Academicians themselves ; nor did they the less contribute to the
formation of literary taste and opinions, as they have
continued in France to the present day.

It was, then, the meeting together of men of letters which became an authority in literature. The Academy, as an academy, remained really what it was intended to be—a body appointed " to cleanse the language," and to defend it against the corruption which might be introduced into it by the vicissitudes of fashion at Court, the barbarism of the formalities of the palace, and the slang of the various professions.[1] If, when reducing the language to words commonly used and generally approved, the Academy sometimes showed excessive severity—if we are implicitly to believe in that scene in the comedy of the " Academicians," in which Mlle. de Gournay is represented as pleading ineffectually with the Academy on behalf of the word *angoisse*,[2] which custom has retained—this circumstance would teach us at the same time, that custom has frequently gained the victory. If it was decided that the Dictionary of the Academy should contain all the words in the language, the result of this decision was that the language, by extending its vocabulary, enlarged the Dictionary. Words that had become necessary, or that were of felicitous invention, soon obtained a place for themselves therein ; and, even before obtaining a place, Corneille's *invaincu* passed into poetry, where

---

[1] *Pelisson,* " Histoire de l'Académie," p. 40.

[2] " Ôtez *moult* et *jaçoit* bien que mal à propos,
Mais laissez pour le moins *blandice, angoisse,* et *los.*"
Saint-Evremond, " Œuvres," vol. i.

no one ventured to condemn it.[1] The true authority on these points, therefore, was that of our great masters, or rather of the general feeling which almost always approved them. It was as writers in possession of the means to secure a good reception from the public that the Academicians were the organs and sometimes the regulators of this feeling ; as Academicians they were only its archivists.

The direct influence of the French Academy upon literature in general was, then, only feeble and limited ; it was the representative, rather than the guide of opinion. Doubtless men of letters, by aspiring to an honourable position among an illustrious body, as a reward for their labours, sometimes sacrificed, perhaps unwittingly, somewhat of that independence which their genius would have retained, had they lived in isolation and under the influence only of their natural impulses. Poetry especially, which derives its sustenance from solitary inspirations, may have lost a little of its free, original spirit in that frequent discussion of ideas, and that daily interchange of mind, which are more conducive to the progress of reason than to the flights of the imagination ; but this influence was especially powerful over the minor poets, and though genius was not entirely free from its ascendancy, it was never either

---

[1] " Ton bras est *invaincu*, mais non pas invincible."

Corneille, " Le Cid."

stifled or subjugated by it. Every writer, in particular, may have been less free ; but literature, in
general, was more so.

Such was the direct and positive effect produced,
upon the existence of men of letters, by the
establishment of the Academy. The first moment
of hesitation was short ; and general anxiety was
soon manifested for admission into a company
protected by the Prime Minister. The Chancellor
Seguier, then Keeper of the Seals, did more than
protect it when, in 1635, he requested to be
received as a member ; and when, after the death
of Richelieu, he became its protector, he solicited
admission for his son.[1] He frequently attended the
meetings of the Academy, at which he enforced the
most scrupulous equality, not even suffering those
Academicians who belonged to his household to
call him Monseigneur. These little incidents, and
many others of a similar character, soon made the
title of Academician a distinct and honourable title,
which, when the King became protector of the Academy, was not thought beneath the ambition of any
man at Court. The two classes were thus brought
into closer connection than they had ever been before,
but their respective position had changed ; the man
of letters, certain of a good reception in society, could

---

[1] The Marquis de Coislin, who was received in 1652. Previous to the
admission of the Keeper of the Seals, M. de Servien, a Secretary of State,
had been admitted, in 1634.

now bestow upon the man of fashion a distinction all the more precious because, during more than a century and a half, the literary class, so fertile in distinguished talents of different orders, had left very little space for a display of the less academical talents of the men of the world. In proportion as, during the reign of Louis XIV., court distinctions became less honourable, distinctions of mind were more sought after, and these it was in the power of men of letters to bestow. At the beginning of the seventeenth century, they had been obliged to waste their talents in pandering to the frivolous pastimes of society : when the eighteenth century arrived, society was desirous to understand those serious ideas which formed the subject of their meditations. This revolution in manners was destined soon to become an intellectual revolution, and finally to operate a political revolution, and to change the face of the world, after having at first changed only the social relations of men of letters to men of the world. But I pause before the immense horizon and the fathomless abyss which simultaneously open before me. I merely intended to seek out the principal causes, and to sketch the original characteristics, of the state of literature, and especially of poetry, in France, at the commencement of the seventeenth century, during the period of preparation for the advent of Corneille.

I have hitherto said nothing about the fixed establishment of theatres, and the impulse which directed the taste of France towards dramatic literature. To Corneille belongs the primal glory of that literature : and with his life must be connected the history of its earliest efforts.

PIERRE CORNEILLE.

(1606-1684.)

THE progress of dramatic art is not necessarily commensurate with that made by other branches of literature. In regard to those kinds of poetry which depend for their effect upon the talent of the poet himself, in order that the influence of this talent may be properly developed, it is necessary that the taste of the public should be sufficiently cultivated to feel and admire it. The external and material means at the disposal of the dramatic author give much greater extension to his audience ; unless his self-love be very delicate, he will have slight difficulty in satisfying himself with the noisy applause of the multitude : indeed, according to all appearance, it was for the multitude that the first essays of dramatic art were everywhere intended. It was for men who were unsatisfied with merely mental gratifications that was first invented a spectacle, adapted to strike the senses :—

> " Thespis fut le premier qui, barbouillé de lie,
> Promena par les bourgs cette heureuse folie,
> Et, d'acteurs mal ornés chargeant un tombereau,
> Amusa les passants d'un spectacle nouveau."

Genius could not fail at once to appreciate and appropriate this happy invention. Poets who were accustomed to recite their verses in public, easily perceived the advantage they would derive by the employment of dialogue, and by the material representation of the objects which they formerly used only to describe. Among our Troubadours, similar causes produced analogous effects. It appears certain that these earliest of modern poets had some idea of a kind of dramatic representation, or at least of a dialogised poetry, which was recited by actors who were either the poets themselves, or persons engaged by them. During the thirteenth and fourteenth centuries, we frequently meet with theatrical pieces, of a historical or satirical character, which were represented sometimes by the orders, and at the expense, of the princes whose passions they flattered, [1] and sometimes even at the cost of the public, whom authors undertook, as at the present day, to amuse for money. [2] But the dramatic talents of those times, nurtured in Courts and amid the fantastic games of poetry, could not possibly understand either the taste of the people, or the proper character of an art which addresses

[1] Boniface, Marquis of Montferrat, the protector of the Albigenses, commanded the representation of a theatrical piece by Anselme Faydit against the Council of Lateran, entitled the "Heresy of the Fathers—*l'Heregia dels Peyres.*"

[2] This same Faydit, it is said, "not satisfied with the presents which nobles gave him for his works, erected a place suited to the performance of comedies, and received the money which the spectators gave him at the door." "Histoire du Théâtre Français," vol. i. p. 13.

itself as much to the senses as to the mind. Sprung from a soil which was not suited to their development, they bore no lasting fruits ; and, " when the Mæcenases failed," says an old author, " the poets also fell away."

The true origin of the theatre in France was popular. Every one knows how the society of the *Brethren of the Passion* originated. Pilgrims from Jerusalem, from Saint James of Compostella, and from the Holy Balm, with their minds filled with thoughts of the places they had just visited, and their imaginations excited by devotion and leisure, composed songs, which necessity taught them to adorn with every accessory that was likely to attract attention and obtain alms. To the pantomime with which they accompanied these songs they added the assistance of dialogue; and, assembling in troops in public localities, clad in their copes, covered with images of the saints, and with their staves in their hands, they edified and amused the people. Whether we are indebted to them for the first idea of theatrical representations, or whether they had themselves borrowed it from those rude performances which were employed in the churches to rekindle the piety of the faithful on the days of great festivals, [1] this idea was thought so excellent that it was speedily made use of as a means of popular amusement, and formed a part of the

---

[1] Such as the *Feast of Fools*, the *Feast of Asses*, and so forth.

games by which the city of Paris was wont to solemnise great events. Charles VI., on his entrance, " beheld with pleasure what were then called *mysteries;* that is to say, various theatrical represen- tations of entirely novel invention." On the entrance of Isabel of Bavaria, a number of young persons performed, upon different stages, " divers histories from the Old Testament." [1] These pious spectacles speedily became popular in all the provinces of the realm, and in most of the kingdoms of Christendom ; and zeal or industry soon attempted to turn them to profit. It appears probable that the first representa- tions given at Saint Maur by the Brethren, [2] were not gratuitous ; at all events it is certain that when the Provost of Paris forbade them to perform without the permission of the King, and obliged them to apply to Court for authorisation, the letters-patent which they obtained from Charles VI., in 1402, granted them permission to perform for profit. [3]

---

[1] " Histoire de la Ville de Paris," vol. xiv. pp. 686, 707.

[2] In 1398, they had hired a room at Saint Maur, in which they repre- sented the " Mysteries of the Passion of Our Lord Jesus Christ."

[3] The patent runs thus : " On which fact and mystery the said Brother- hood has paid and expended much of its property, as have also the Brethren, each only proportionally ; saying, moreover, that if they played publicly and in common (that is, before the people), that it would be to the profit of the said Brotherhood, and that they could not do so rightly without our leave and license. * * We, who desire the benefit, profit, and use- fulness of the said Brotherhood, and that its rights and revenues should be by us increased and augmented by favours and privileges, in order that each one by devotion may and ought to join himself to their company, have given and granted," &c.

Thus was instituted a theatrical performance according to the taste of the public, who, by paying for admission, obtained the right of expressing their opinion. For this, dramatic art was indebted to the Brethren of the Passion. But the public, as uncouth as the men who undertook to divert it, was not yet capable of training them ; the actors were deficient in emulation, and the spectators in comparison ; and at the end of a hundred and fifty years the last mysteries, though quite as ridiculous as the first, were distinguished only by less simplicity and good faith ; and the orders given to the Brethren, in 1548, to discontinue this kind of performance, proves that good taste and good sense had made progress, by which the mystery-mongers had not profited.

At this period, there originated a new dramatic system, perfectly independent of that of the Brethren, and independent also of the taste of the public, for whose gratification it was not designed. This system was one of the first fruits of that erudite literature which, according to the usage of pedagogues in all ages, imposed silence upon its disciples before making any effort to correct their taste. Already several Greek tragedies, among others the " Electra " and the " Hecuba," had been translated into verse, but simply as specimens of a foreign drama, and without the slightest intention of enriching our own therewith. On the other hand, the events of the fabulous history of the Greeks had been represented upon our stage, but in the form peculiar to it,[1] and without any imitation of the art of the ancients, from whom were borrowed merely subjects more rich in interest or more widely known than those that might have been supplied by our own history. Jodelle, the contemporary and friend of Ronsard, Du Bellay, Baïf and Pasquier—a man of small erudition himself, but whose mind was deeply impregnated with the atmosphere of learning by which he was surrounded, was the first who conceived the idea of introducing, into French pieces of his own composition, the dramatic forms of the ancients, or at least of Horace ; that is to say, the division into acts, the three unities, and the scrupulous exclusion from the stage of all machinery and hideous representations, especially of the devils, hell, and tortures of the damned and of martyrs, which constituted, perhaps, the most approved part of the Mysteries. Comedy depicted manners more elevated than those of the populace, tragedy was reserved for the adventures of Kings and Princes ; and the poetical coterie celebrated this invention with transports of delight. " Those who

---

[1] We have the " Mystère de la Destruction de Troyes la grant," in four days, which comprehend the whole period which elapsed from the judgment of Paris until the return of the Greeks after the capture of Troy. Paris is represented as offering *a hundred crown-pieces* to the temple of Venus, and a note informs us that Troy was forty leagues in length and eight in breadth. The writer was probably ignorant of that passage in Homer in which Achilles chases Hector thrice round the walls of Troy.

at that time were judges of such matters," says
Pasquier, " declared that Ronsard was the first of
poets, but that Jodelle was the *dæmon* of poetry
himself."[1] The unimpassioned frigidity of these
tragedies, which were composed almost entirely of
narratives and monologues, was not distasteful to
men whose minds were driven to the opposite
extreme by their contempt for the performances of
the Brethren ; and the indecency of the comedies
could not revolt an age in which *farces* were still
tolerated.

These two kinds of dramatic composition, then,
possessed in France at this period rules known and
approved by the sovereign authorities in literature ;
by the Court which, unskilful in creating pleasures
for itself, willingly accepted those which were offered
to it ; and by poets and learned men, by whom the
new pieces were written, performed, and applauded.
" ' Cleopatra, ' a tragedy, by Jodelle, and ' La
Rencontre,' a comedy, by the same author, were
performed before King Henry at Paris, at the Hotel
de Reims, with great applause from the whole
company ; and afterwards again at the College de
Boncourt, at which all the windows were crowded by
an infinity of persons of honour. * * And the actors
were all men of name, for even Remy Belleau and
Jean de la Peruse played the principal parts."[2]

---

[1] "Pasquier," book vii. p. 705.   [2] Ibid. p. 704.

Jodelle, who was young and handsome, had undertaken the part of Cleopatra.

This new form of dramatic art laid open to poets
a career which they might well judge worthy of
their talents ; the imitation or even translation of
the Greek tragedies furnished them with numerous
and fertile subjects.   In truth, they strangely changed
their nature in their imitations ; for they lived at a
time which could not conceive of grandeur without
emphasis, and when naturalness speedily degenerated
into coarseness ; the dignity of supreme rank, the
lofty character of the learned French spoken by the
personages in their tragedies, did not always preserve
them from the tone and manners of low life ; and the
lovers of antiquity were not shocked at seeing
Jodelle's Cleopatra, when Seleucus accuses her before
Augustus of having concealed a portion of her
treasures, seize Seleucus by the hair, and overwhelm
him with blows and insults.

More successful in comedy, which he based upon
the manners of the time alone, and supported perhaps by some national models of true comicality,
endemic in France, as is proved by the old farce of
" Patelin," Jodelle was also more successfully imitated.
Comedies devoid of character and probability, but
not without intrigue and gaiety, presented some more
natural productions of the French mind.   Ere long
Larivey introduced, with considerable success, upon

our stage, some imitations of Latin and Italian comedies ; and at the same time Garnier, the immediate
successor of Jodelle, whose reputation he outshone,
gave greater nobleness to the tone of tragedy.
Without clothing it with an interest and verisimi-
litude which the art of the poets of that period was
not capable of reconciling with the restraint imposed
by observance of the unities, he imparted to it greater
decency, arrayed it in a more poetical style, and
introduced a pathos of sentiment which was not what
Ronsard and his partisans had sought to imitate from
the ancients.

This progress was still confined within the narrow
sphere by which poets were then surrounded.
The Brethren of the Passion, in possession of the
exclusive privilege of offering to the public a
performance for admission to which money was to be
paid, but unable of themselves to turn this privilege
to further advantage, since they had been forbidden
to perform mysteries, leased the privilege and the
Hotel de Bourgogne to a troop of comedians, whose
aim was no longer to edify, but simply to amuse, the
spectators. It was not with poetry in Ronsard's
style, or with tragedies even more devoid of action
than laden with erudition, that the spectators at the
Hotel de Bourgogne were to be amused. Broad
farces and moralities, the subjects of which were
taken from recent and well-known occurrences—such

as, for example, the execution of a valet at the Place de Grève for having seduced his master's wife (the valet being hanged upon the stage)—were what suited the taste of the frequenters of the Théâtre des Confrères. The educated poets of the time do not appear to have ever entrusted their pieces to the comedians of the Hotel de Bourgogne. They were performed either in the colleges or at the expense of some of the nobility ; most were merely made public by means of the press, and then any one who pleased might perform them. Garnier, in the preface to his " Bradamante," informs " those who may choose to perform it " that, as there are no choruses to the piece, the acts must be separated by means of interludes ; and we learn from the " Roman Comique " that the provincial actors used to play " Bradamante."

Sometimes, when tragedies had been printed and published, the comedians of the Hotel de Bourgogne endeavoured to turn them to account ; but it is certain that they did not meet with a favourable reception from spectators who were unable to comprehend them. These performances, however, and their publication, obtained for them a kind of popularity in the semi-literary world, which increased in numbers daily. This period was inundated by a host of tragedies divided into acts ; but it must be confessed that these acts, which were sometimes seven in

number, [1] frequently include, in the same performance,
as many years and countries as the old mysteries
could have done.   Fabulous and historical ideas are
commingled therein in the strangest fashion.   In
1661, nine years after Jodelle's pieces had obtained
such brilliant success, Jacques Grevin, in the preface
to his dramatic works, complains of " the grievous
faults that are daily committed in the games of the
University of Paris, which ought to be a paragon of
perfection in all knowledge, but where, nevertheless,
they perpetrate, after the manner of tumblers, a
massacre upon a scaffold, or utter a speech of two or
three months' length." [2]   The rules of Aristotle,
which were violated as frequently as those of common
sense, were as incapable of reforming the taste of the
public as they were of satisfying it.

One fact is especially deserving of remark at this
period, and that is, the small number of comedies, as
compared with the countless host of tragedies that
were written.   Perhaps the labour of invention which
was indispensable in a kind of composition that, unlike

[1] As, for example, the " Cammate " of Jean Hays, king's advocate in the
bailiwick of Rouen, published in 1597.

[2] In the " Soltane " of Gabriel Bounyn, published in 1560, the Sultana
Rose, a witch, in order to destroy the son of her husband, the Sultan
Solyman, proposes to call in the demons to her aid, among whom she
enumerates *Vulcan with his dragoons.*   In the " Aman " of Pierre Mathieu,
Aman, whose pride drives him mad, boasts that he is *the gun of the infernal
troop.*   In the " Loyauté Trahie " of Jacques du Hamel, published in 1586,
we meet with an *Infanta of Astracan* at the court of a *King of Canada.*
These are but a few out of many thousands of similar instances.

tragedy, could not draw upon history for its subjects and materials, deterred literary men in general from devoting their talents to comedy. Thus much is certain that, in both kinds of dramatic composition, Jodelle, with his contemporaries and successors, contributed but very little to the improvement of our national drama, if we may give such a name to those crude performances with which the people of Paris and the provinces allowed themselves to be amused or bored for nearly two centuries.

It was, nevertheless, from this rude cradle that, dating from the early years of the seventeenth century, dramatic art issued to make most rapid progress. Civil war had broken up old customs ; peace and happiness, restored by the triumph of Henry IV., demanded the institution of new ones ; and the pleasures which Paris could afford, no longer satisfied its inhabitants. The contempt into which the Brethren of the Passion had fallen, encouraged men to attack their privileges. Various troops of playwrights had already unsuccessfully attempted to do so ; but at length, in the year 1600, notwithstanding the opposition of the Brethren and the decrees of the Parliament, a new troop established itself in Paris, at the Hotel d'Argent, in the Marais, on condition of paying the privileged fraternity one crown-piece for every performance. The hopes of the new company were based upon an engagement which they had

made with a man whose success is as astonishing to
us as his talents were marvellous to his contemporaries.   Hardy, the founder of the Parisian stage,
and the precursor of Corneille, was not one of those
men whose genius changes or determines the taste of
his age ; but he was the first man in France who
conceived a just idea of the nature of dramatic poetry.
He understood that a theatrical piece ought to have
a higher aim than merely to satisfy the mind and
reason of the spectators ; and he was at the same time
of opinion, that carefulness to employ their senses and
excite their imagination, should not prevent the play
from being regulated by reason and probability.
Hardy was not one of those erudite and happy poets
who were content to limit their ambition to obtaining
the suffrages of literary men and the applause of
Courts.   Though daily compelled to look to his
talents to furnish him with the means of subsistence,
he was not one of those mountebanks who are capable
merely of amusing a populace in whose ignorance
they participate.   His education had not left him
unacquainted with the literary acquirements of his
time.   His poverty had connected him with a troop
of wandering comedians, who were more at liberty to
exercise their profession in the provinces than in Paris,
whence they were banished by the monopoly possessed
by the Brethren.   Thus early accustomed to stage
plays, he endeavoured to apply to an important mode

of action the rude means of interest which those plays
could furnish. The step which he had to take, and
which he really did take, can alone explain the
success which he obtained.

Those foreign critics[1] who represent the French
drama, subsequently to Jodelle, as trammelled by the
general adherence of the public to the authority of
Aristotle's rules, either have not read Hardy, or
appreciate very imperfectly his importance in the
history of the stage in France. Hardy was irregular
enough to have been a Shakspeare, if he had possessed a Shakspeare's genius. His first dramatic
work with which we are acquainted contains the
whole romance of " Theagenes and Chariclea ;"[2] it
is divided into eight days, one for each book of the
romance, and is written in precisely the same form as
the Mysteries. To say truth, this work met with an
unfavourable reception from men of letters: " I know,
reader," says Hardy himself,[3] " that my ' Æthiopic
Story,' rendered monstrous by the faults that crept
into the first impression, produced an unfavourable
feeling with regard to my other works in the minds of
certain imitators of Aristarchus." In order for this
piece, when printed, to have been deemed worthy of

[1] Among others, M. Bouterwek, in his " History of French Literature,"
published at Gottingen, in 1809.

[2] " Les chastes et longues Amours de Théagène et Chariclée," in eight
consecutive dramatic or theatrical poems.   1600.

[3] In his preface to " Didon se Sacrifiant."

the attention of the critics, it must have obtained considerable success when performed.   Perhaps, a larger amount of success would have gained their approbation for the work.   At all events, if we judge of what the critics required by what Hardy gave them, it is evident that a very strict adherence to rules was not expected of dramatic authors, and that Aristotle's authority was not so great on the stage as it was in the schools.

After the production of the " Loves of Theagenes and Chariclea," Hardy abandoned the arrangement of his dramas into days, and divided his pieces into acts, giving them the more becoming name of tragedies and tragi-comedies.[1]   But he did not consider himself obliged, by the adoption of this new costume, to observe more rigid regularity.   In the first act of his " Alcestis," he represents Hercules at the court of Eurystheus ; in the second, third, and fifth acts, the scene is laid at the court of Admetus ; and in the fourth, we are taken to the infernal regions, whither Hercules goes to fetch Alcestis, and whence, on the same occasion, he delivers Theseus and carries off Cerberus.   In " Phraates, or the Triumph of True Lovers," the spectator travels from Thrace into Macedonia, and from Macedonia back again into

---

[1] He gives the name of a "dramatic poem," however, to his "Gigantomachia," a piece in which machinery is introduced, to represent a combat of the gods with the giants.   This piece is, nevertheless, divided into acts.

Thrace. The tragedy of "Pantheus" extends over several days; the first three acts of "Gesippus, or the Two Friends," take place at Athens, and the last two at Rome, several years afterwards. Doubtless relying very little upon affording gratification to the spectators by means of a dialogue which, though sometimes rational, was always cold, languishing and unattractive, Hardy made up for the omission of this by the introduction of action, which he employed without reserve. In " Scedasus, or Hospitality Violated," two young girls who are ravished by their hosts, defend themselves upon the stage to the last moment, and probably end by retreating behind the scenes, though this is not indicated by any interruption of the dialogue. Their ravishers afterwards put them to death upon the stage. In " Lucretia," who is certainly not Lucretia the chaste, a husband, the witness of his wife's infidelity, narrates to the spectator what is passing between the two lovers behind the scenes, and does not interrupt them until he has " seen with his own eyes " that which he requires to authorise him to put them both to death. Aristoclea, in the " Unfortunate Marriage," dies upon the stage, in consequence of the effort made by the servants of Straton, who is in love with her, to carry her off from the relatives of Callisthenes, her husband, who are naturally anxious to detain her.

In these compositions, it is difficult to discern

what constitutes the difference between tragedy and
tragi-comedy ; it certainly depends neither upon the
nature of the subject, nor upon the rank of the
personages.   " Scedasus," all the personages of which
are merely private individuals, is a tragedy, and
certainly deserves this title from its *dénouement;* but
the frightful death of Aristoclea furnishes nothing
more than a tragi-comedy.   " Dido " is a tragedy ;
but the dignity of the personages of " Alcestis," and
the pathetic character of their position, do not raise
it above the rank of a tragi-comedy.   Two subjects,
both equally tragic, derived from the Greek mythology, furnish Hardy with the tragedy of " Meleager,"
and the tragi-comedy of " Procris."   The irregularity
is the same in both kinds of composition ; and as
regards tone, that of Hardy, in general not very
lofty, scarcely allows us to perceive the shades of that
more familiar naturalness which he appears to have
wished to introduce into some scenes of his tragi-
comedies.   In " Procris," for example, Tito complains
to his confidant in very light terms of the infidelity
of his wife, and Aurora banters Cephalus with considerable freedom of speech ; and in " Alcestis," the
father and mother of Admetus, after having expressed
their grief that they cannot ransom their son's life by
the sacrifice of their own, change their mind when
informed by the oracle that it is in their power to
save him by an act of self-devotion, and unite in

declaring that they would rather live the whole time allotted to them by the Fates.

Hardy, then, was neither the successor of Jodelle and Garnier, nor the imitator of the Greeks, but a national dramatic poet, as far as it was possible to be such in a literature in which recollections of the ancients occupied so prominent a position. Hardy was not guided by their precepts, although he some-times profited by their example ; he frequently borrowed from them subjects for his dramas, but did not imitate their treatment of them ; he omitted from their rules whatever he thought unsuited to the stage and the prevailing taste of his time ; and, while he adopted the arrangement of their tragedies, he did away with the choruses, as being " superfluous to the performance, and too troublesome to recast." He remodelled, according to his own manner, the subjects which he adopted. Too sensible, and too unversed in the ways of the world, to dress up, as was done at a later period, Greek and Roman characters in the costume of the day, he was, never-theless, careful to strip them of that antique and local colouring which would greatly have astounded an entirely French audience. It was in French, moreover, although in bad French, that Hardy addressed the public. The faults of his style are neither the erudite obscurity, nor the contorted phraseology, nor the studied neologism of Ronsard ;

he is characterised by the harshness, incorrectness,
impropriety and triviality of a man whom the necessity of providing for his own subsistence and for that
of a troop of comedians, sometimes compelled to
furnish two thousand lines in twenty-four hours.
Hardy's talent knew no other shackles but those of
poverty ; fecundity was all that was expected from
him, and never was a duty better fulfilled. Six
hundred dramatic pieces,[1] all in verse, and some of
which were composed, learned, and performed within
three days,[2] served by their number, as much as by
their merit, to establish Hardy's reputation, and a
taste for dramatic works, in France. Like Hardy,
Lope de Vega composed a play in twenty-four hours;
and both these men were the founders of the drama
of their respective nations. Variety is the merit
most necessary to ensure the primary success of an
art which requires a crowd to witness its efforts :
before having formed that taste or habit which

[1] Some say eight hundred; only forty-one are now extant, including
the eight dramatic poems which relate the "Loves of Theagenes and
Chariclea." See *Gueret*, "Guerre des Auteurs," p. 161.

[2] It appears that the price of these was three crowns apiece. Mademoiselle Beaupré, the actress, who performed in the dramas of both Hardy
and Corneille, used to say : "M. Corneille has done us great injury; formerly we used to have dramas at three crowns each, which were written
for us in a night; people were used to them, and we gained a great deal by
them; now, Corneille's pieces cost us a great deal, and gain us very little."
"It is true," adds *Segrais*, who relates this remark, "that these old pieces
were wretchedly bad ; but the actors were excellent, and gained applause for
them by their admirable performance." ("Segraisiana," p. 214.) Hardy
was, it is said, the first man who received money for his pieces. Previously, the actors used to take such as they found in print, or else wrote
dramas for themselves.

enlists the attention of spectators, movement must be supplied to attract them, and curiosity alone is able to produce this movement ; but this curiosity must be continually renewed, and must incessantly recall the mind, by the expectation of novelty, towards pleasures which habit has not yet transformed into necessities. Neither the relative decency which Hardy infused into the tone of his characters, nor a certain measure of reason and probability which he endeavoured to introduce into his plans, nor the movement which he invariably imparted to his action, nor even the machinery with which he sometimes adorned his plays, would long have reconciled the spectators to pieces in which they found nothing either to satisfy a discriminating taste, or to awaken profound emotion. If, however, Hardy had employed the same time in perfecting his plays which he did in varying their subjects, some few men of taste might possibly have applauded his intentions, but the multitude would certainly have withdrawn their patronage. Cinthio, an actor belonging to an Italian troop, answered the Earl of Bristol, who found fault with him for the want of probability of the pieces which he performed : " If there were more of it, good actors would die of hunger with good comedies." And when actors die of hunger, they leave no successors, and dramatic authors, in consequence, come to an end.

Hardy's performers did not starve ; and this was then the greatest service that he could have rendered to his art.   Frequently, a thin attendance of spectators obliged the two troops to unite, and limit their exertions to a single performance at the Hotel de Bourgogne, the actors belonging to which obtained, in 1612, the title of the " King's Comedians," and a pension of twelve hundred livres ; but ever after the year 1600, there was always at least one troop of actors at Paris, and Hardy's dramas long constituted their principal stock in trade.   The moment had arrived when poets only required the establishment of a regular theatre to induce them to write for it. Hardy had rendered the stage more decent, and more worthy of their efforts.   The taste which the public was beginning to feel for mental enjoyments found only weak and chilling nutriment in the precise and formal verses of Malherbe's school.   The stage summoned to its aid all those men whom a more lively imagination, a more unfettered genius, and a more active character, urged upon a more animated career and to more boisterous success.   Théophile, a poet very deficient in taste though not wanting in talent, thus addresses Hardy :—

> " Jamais ta veine ne s'amuse
> A couler un sonnet mignard ;
> Détestant la pointe et le fard
> Qui rompt les forces à la muse

Je marque entre les beaux esprits,
Malherbe, Bertaut, et Porchères,
Dont les louanges me sont chères,
Comme j'adore leurs écrits.
Mais à l'air de tes tragédies
On verroit faillir leur poumon,
Et comme glaces du Strymon
Seroient leurs veines refroidies."

Théophile gave to the stage his " Thisbe," in which
we sometimes meet with a poetic elegance of which
Hardy never had any idea, mingled with the ridiculous
concetti of the time. Racan, whose imagination
Malherbe admired, and whose negligence he blamed,[1]
introduced into his "Bergeries" still greater elegance
and purity. The names of Mairet and Rotrou became
known by their dramatic works alone ; and Scudéry
and La Calprenède devoted themselves to the stage
with heart and soul. " After Théophile had
performed his ' Thisbe,' and Mairet his ' Sylvie,'
M. de Racan his ' Bergeries,' and M. de Gombaud his
' Amaranthe,' the stage became more celebrated, and
many persons endeavoured to give it new support.
The poets no longer made any difficulty about allowing
their names to appear on the bills of the actors ; for
formerly, no author's name had been given, but it
was simply stated that their author had written for
them a comedy of a certain name." [2] The dramatic
poet was no longer the *author* of the actors, but of

---

[1] Malherbe used to say of Racan "that he had power, but that he did
not labour enough at his verses." *Pelisson*, "Histoire de l'Académie," p. 47.

[2] *Sorel*, " Bibliothéque Française," p. 185.

the public ; the dramatic art became in literature one of the most brilliant means of achieving success, and the taste which Cardinal Richelieu felt for this kind of amusement soon made it one of the surest means of obtaining favour. French poetry was evidently turning in the direction of dramatic composition ; but there was nothing as yet to announce the impulse it was about to receive from Corneille. It is easy to conceive what must have been the condition of a drama abandoned to the caprices of an imagination that sought only to deliver itself from the yoke of the rules imposed upon other kinds of poetry,—of a drama satisfied with the applause of a public that desired nothing but novelty,—subject to the whims of fashion, and to the ambition of all those poets who were led, by beholding a new career, to believe that they possessed a new order of talent. Mairet presented himself on the stage at sixteen, and Rotrou at eighteen years of age. Scudéry wrote in Gascon, [1] and boasted of his ignorance :—" In the music of the sciences," he says, " I sing only by nature.   *   *   I have spent more years in the camp than hours in my study, and used more matches to fire arquebuses than to light candles ; so that I can arrange soldiers better than words, and square battalions better than I can round periods." [2]   The stage was just suited to

---

[1] Some say it was Norman. Scudéry was of Provençal origin, but was born at Havre, where his father was married.

[2] Preface to " Lygdamon."

Scudéry's poetical impertinence : in dramatic literature it was thought allowable to dispense with
carefulness, and even correctness of style ; an author
might mingle at his pleasure the finical with the
bombastic, or the thoughtful with the trivial ; and
extravagance of language was surpassed only by
eccentricity of ideas.   Movement, which had been
almost entirely banished from other kinds of poetry,
seemed to be the only merit required on the stage ;
and this movement, which never was allowed to
originate in the passions of the soul, was kept up by
an accumulation of romantic adventures : abductions,
combats, disguises, recognitions, infidelities,—nothing
was spared to give animation to the scene, and to
prevent the spectator from noticing the dulness and
truthlessness of those insipid romances, which were
almost invariably brought on the stage under
the convenient title of tragi-comedies ; the tragic
element in which was distinguished only by a more
singular mixture of triviality and bombast—the
comic, by a stranger disregard for propriety—and
the pastoral, by a more monstrous employment of all
available means.

Amidst this confusion, what became of the rules of
Aristotle, and the recollections of the Greeks and
Romans ?   The unities—observed by chance, or
violated without scruple, prescribed by a few men of
letters, and contemned by most others—furnished

only a subject of discussion, and were regarded with utter indifference by those who should have paid most attention to them.   The simplicity of ancient or historical subjects was thought too naked, and they had been superseded by subjects of pure imagination, in which there was nothing to trammel the eccentricity of the author's conceptions, and by innumerable imitations of the Spanish and Italian dramas, whither some men of taste advised the poets to repair in order to obtain some idea of the regularity necessary to the dramatic poem.[1]   The less-refined public gave full permission to those who undertook to cater for their amusement to select whatever means they chose to employ ; their ignorant favour was within the reach of all who took a little trouble to win it; talent might succeed in gaining it, and mediocrity might lay claim to it ; no path had been definitely marked out, but all were equally open, when Corneille appeared.

Pierre Corneille, born at Rouen on the 6th of June, 1606, of a family distinguished for magisterial services,[2] was intended for the bar, and was brought

[1] Mairet having been requested by Cardinal de la Valette to compose a pastoral in the form and taste of the Italian school, was led by study of the Italian dramatists to perceive the necessity of observing the unities, which he had not thought it necessary to do so long as he considered them inculcated only by the example of the ancients.   He composed his "Sylvanire" in 1625, in conformity with the unities ; but did not always observe them afterwards.

[2] His father was royal advocate at the marble table of Normandy, and special master of the waters and forests in the viscounty of Rouen ; his mother, Marthe le Pesant de Boisguilbert, was the daughter of a *Maître des Comptes*.   In the Appendix to this " Life of Corneille " will be found some

up to the severe studies of that learned profession. [1]
He felt his genius, however, early incline towards
occupations more in unison with that career upon
which he was urged by a vocation so well authenticated by the whole course of his life. Love dictated
his first verses, and to love has he ascribed the glory
which he achieved as a poet :—

> " Charmé de deux beaux yeux, mon vers charma la cour,
> Et ce que j'ai de mieux, je le dois à l'amour." [2]

It will, nevertheless, be difficult to believe that love
was the principal source of Corneille's genius ; and, in
order to become convinced that he was but slightly
indebted to this sentiment for his inspiration, we need
only read what he says elsewhere of his first love :—

> " Soleils, flambeaux, attraits, appas,
> Pleurs, désespoirs, tourments, trépas,
> Tout ce petit meuble de bouche
> Dont un amoureux s'escarmouche,
> Je savais bien m'en escrimer ;
> Par là je m'appris à rimer."

interesting and novel details regarding his father, and the letters of
nobility conferred upon him by Louis XIII. I am indebted for these
documents to the kindness of M. Floquet, than whom no one is better
acquainted with the political and literary history of Normandy. See
Appendix A.

[1] He pursued his studies at the Jesuits' College at Rouen, and gained a
prize either in 1618 or 1619. "I have seen," writes M. Floquet, "in the
valuable library of the late M. Villenave, the volume which was then given
to Pierre Corneille : it is a folio volume, and on the sides of the book are
embossed in gold the arms of Alphonse d'Ornano, lieutenant-general and
governor of Normandy at this period, who, in that capacity, had paid the
expense of the prizes distributed at the College. A notice of some length,
signed by the principal, indicates the number of the class, and the reason
why this reward was given to young Corneille."

[2] " Excuse à Ariste," &c.

Love taught him merely to rhyme, and to string rhymes together was a very small matter for Corneille. But, if we are to believe Fontenelle, love taught him something more than this : " Hardy was beginning to grow old, and his death would have made a great breach in the drama, when a slight event which occurred in a respectable family in a provincial town, gave him an illustrious successor. A young man took one of his friends to see a girl with whom he was in love ; the new-comer established himself upon the downfall of his introducer ; the pleasure which this adventure occasioned him made him a poet ; he wrote a comedy about it—and behold the great Corneille ! " [1]

---

[1] *Fontenelle*, "Histoire du Théâtre Français," pp. 78, 79. Such is, in reality, the subject of " Mélite," his first piece. This anecdote, however, seems to be contradicted by a note to the "Excuse à Ariste," in which we are informed that the "beautiful eyes" which so charmed Corneille belonged to Mme. de Pont, the wife of a *Maître des Comptes* at Rouen, " whom he had known as quite a little girl, whilst he was studying in the Jesuit College at Rouen."

> " Elle eut mes premiers vers, elle eut mes premiers feux,"

says Corneille ; and he repeats, in several passages of the same piece, that this love " taught him to rhyme," and that the taste of his mistress for poetry,

> " Le fit devenir poëte aussitôt qu' amoureux."

Soon after he adds :—

> " Je ne vois rien d'aimable après l'avoir aimée ;
> Aussi n'aimai-je plus, et nul objet vainqueur
> N'a possédé depuis ma veine ni mon cœur."

These lines were written in 1635 or 1636 ; therefore the object of that sole passion which occupied the first ten or eleven years of Corneille's life, and inspired the earliest efforts of his Muse, was of necessity his Mélite, if Mélite ever existed. But how can we reconcile this early *liaison* between Corneille when a student, and Mme. de Pont when quite a little girl, with

Such, at least, was the starting-point of the great Corneille ; but it contains no presage of his future glory. If, in his earliest works, we discover some

the manner in which Fontenelle introduces Corneille to Mélite, as a full-grown lawyer ? (See *Fontenelle,* "Vie de Corneille," p. 81, in the third volume of his Works.) It is equally difficult to harmonise with these various circumstances the date of the year 1625, which is indicated by Fontenelle as the period at which "Mélite" was performed. Corneille, who was born in 1606, would then have been only nineteen years old, and could hardly have completed his studies ; and it is difficult to believe that, before composing his piece, he had, as Fontenelle assures us, already appeared at the bar, although "without success." Other works place the date in 1629. Fontenelle, who wrote seventy years afterwards (about 1700), and who was born fifty years after his uncle (in 1656), may only have found confused and doubtful traditions of his great relative in a family by whom literary anecdotes of Corneille's life were probably considered less interesting than they were afterwards thought to be by a nephew who had grown rich by his fame. Those for whom they would have possessed the deepest interest, Thomas Corneille and Mme. de Fontenelle, a woman, it is said, of considerable talent, were born long after their elder brother (Thomas was born in 1625), and could have had no personal knowledge of the matter. I shall have occasion in the course of this sketch to correct several manifest errors of Fontenelle with regard to the facts of his uncle's life.

M. Taschereau, in his "Histoire de la Vie et des Ouvrages de Corneille," (Paris, 1829), has also called in question the anecdote related by Fontenelle ; and in a paper read by M. E. Gaillard before the Academy of Rouen, in 1834, which contains some curious biographical notices of Corneille, I find the following passage : " M. Taschereau has fallen into error regarding Mélite, whom he treats as an imaginary being. If he had read the ' Moréri des Normands,' a manuscript in the Library at Caen, he would have seen that *Mélite* is the anagram of *Milet ;* and Abbé Guyot, formerly Secretary of the Puy de la Conception, at Rouen, affirms that Mlle. Milet was a very pretty young lady of our town. I may add that she lived at Rouen, in the Rue aux Juifs, No. 15. This fact was attested to me by M. Dommey, formerly Chief Clerk at the *Chambre des Comptes,* a man who, if alive, would now be 120 years old, and who told me that he had this information from some very old ladies who used to live in that house, in the Rue aux Juifs, when he was a very young man. The existence of Mlle. Milet is, moreover, a tradition at Rouen. In my youth I have heard it related to octogenarians of the highest rank, one of whom, the Chevalier de Maisons, was the friend of M. de Cideville." " Précis Analytique des Travaux de l'Académie de Rouen pendant l'année 1834," pp. 165, 166.

traces of an original mind, it is not the originality of
genius, but merely of good sense beginning to discern
the absurdity of that which it condescended to imitate.
The models set up for Corneille's imitation were
adapted neither to direct, nor to fetter him.   " I had
no guide," he says, in his examination of ' Mélite,'
" but a little common sense, together with the
examples of the late M. Hardy,[1] and of a few
moderns who were then beginning to appear, but who
were not more regular than he was."   Consequently, to
use his own expression, " ' Mélite ' was not written in
conformity to the rules ; for," he adds, " I was not
then aware that there were any rules."   It was of
little consequence for him to know them ; to learn
how to confine within twenty-four hours an intrigue
which Corneille has extended over a month, was
then a progress of little importance to an art in
which everything still remained to be created, and
which it was necessary to furnish with well-selected
subjects, and true and passionate feelings, before
thinking of laying a foundation, in the void, for forms
as yet of no utility.

Reason, however, had indicated some of these
forms to Corneille.   " That common sense," he says,
" which was my only rule, taught me the use of unity
of action to set four lovers at variance by a single

---

[1] Hardy was dead when Corneille wrote his examinations ; but he was
alive when " Mélite " was performed, and did not die until two or three
years afterwards.

intrigue, and gave me sufficient aversion for that horrible irregularity which brought Paris, Rome, and Constantinople upon the same stage, to make me reduce mine to a single town."[1] But here the art of young Corneille comes to an end ; here ceases his contribution to truth of representation and probability of action. Erastus, enraged against Tircis for having supplanted him in the favour of his mistress, writes love-letters, in the name of that mistress, to Philander, who is in love with the sister of Tircis. Philander's vanity does not allow him either to doubt his good fortune, or to resist it, or to conceal it ; and this is the intrigue which sets the four lovers at variance, without either of them attempting to obtain from each other the slightest explanation. Tircis and Mélite, the hero and heroine of the piece, are ready to die of grief, without inquiring its cause. Erastus believes they are dead, is seized with remorse, and becomes mad. In his madness he imagines that he is descending to Tartarus to rescue them, and expresses his determination, if Pluto will not give them up, to carry off Proserpine. He jumps upon the shoulders of a neighbour, whom he takes for Charon, and belabours him unmercifully, in order to force him to give him a passage in his boat. He afterwards meets Philander, whom he takes for Minos, and confesses to him the trick of which he had been guilty. This was the

---

[1] Examination of "Mélite."

kind of comedy which Corneille, "though condemn-
ing it in his heart,"[1] employed as "a theatrical
ornament which never failed to please, and frequently
gained admiration."[2]   Mélite, to whom Tircis speaks
of the love which she inspires, replies :—

> "Je ne reçois d'amour et n'en donne à personne :
> Le moyen de donner ce que je n'eus jamais ?"

Instead of love, she is willing "to lend to Erastus the
coldness" of her soul ; but coldness melts away when
she is present :—

> "Et vous n'en conservez que faute de vous voir !"

Erastus gallantly replies ; to which Mélite, who is
determined to have the last word, immediately
answers—

> "Eh quoi ! tous les miroirs ont-ils de fausses glaces ?"

Such was "the natural style which truly depicted
the conversation of respectable persons" ;[3] by such
means comedy, for the first time, obtained the honour
of exciting laughter "without the introduction of
ridiculous personages, such as jesters, valets, captains
and doctors, but simply by the sportive humour
of persons superior in rank to those represented in
the comedies of Plautus and Terence."[4]   As regards
the characters, Tircis might be substituted for
Erastus, and Erastus for Tircis, without any

---

[1] Examination of "Mélite."   [2] Ibid.   [3] Ibid.   [4] Ibid.

perceptible difference. A gay, but rather cowardly lover, who is introduced in order to show off the hero of the piece, and a merry and careless girl, who is placed in contrast to the sensible Mélite, are the most salient characteristics of this comedy ; but its style, "being unexampled in any language," and its originality and merit, compelling the approbation of the public, who had at first paid little attention to the work of an unknown poet,[1] obtained such success and drew such crowds that the two troops of comedians, then united at the Hôtel de Bourgogne, separated once more. The troop of the Marais, resting the most brilliant hopes upon the new author who had made his appearance with so much distinction, resumed their former habitation ;[2] and old Hardy, who continued connected with the troop which his labours had supported, frequently had

[1] "The first three performances together were not so well attended as the least of those which took place during the same winter."—*Corneille*, "Épître dédicatoire de Mélite."

[2] See the "Histoire de la Ville de Paris," book xxix. As nearly as we can gather from the confused details which have reached us regarding the theatres of this period, it would appear that the comedians of the Hôtel de Bourgogne, faithful to their inheritance of the *Confrères* and the *Enfants de Sans-Soucy*, habitually performed farces, and that the actors of the Théâtre du Marais devoted themselves more especially to comedy and tragedy. Mondory, the most celebrated tragic actor of those times, was leader of the troop at the Marais. The taste of the regular spectators, however, by banishing farces, placed both troops at last upon the same footing. The comedians of the Hôtel de Bourgogne were frequently recruited by actors from the troop of the Marais, who were transferred therefrom by order of the government, probably at their own request. Notwithstanding these losses, the Marais troop maintained its position until 1673, when it was united to that of the Palais Royal, a third troop which had been formed under the auspices of Cardinal Richelieu.

occasion to acknowledge, at all events when the profits were divided, the superior merits of his young rival.[1]

How, then, are we to account for the astonishing success obtained by Corneille's first work ? Its merits were, a superiority of art and intrigue equalled by none of his contemporaries ; a wisdom of reason commensurate with its affluence of wit ; and last, though not least, the novelty of a first glimmering of taste, of a first effort towards truthfulness. Its style, which appears to us so very unnatural, was, nevertheless, as Corneille informs us, the language of gallantry and the common conversation of polite society. The dialogue in " Mélite " could not but appear simple and natural in comparison with that in " Sylvie," [2] " which was so much recited," says Fontenelle, " by our fathers and mothers in their pinafore days," [3] and which is entirely composed of forty or fifty distichs of this kind :—

PHILEMON.

" Arrête, mon soleil : quoi ! ma longue poursuite
Ne pourra m'obtenir le bien de te parler ?

SYLVIE.

C'est en vain que tu veux interrompre ma fuite ;
Si je suis un soleil, je dois toujours aller.

---

[1] It would appear that, besides his three crowns for every piece, his contract secured him a share in the profits of the theatre. On receiving his share of the profits of the performance of " Mélite," he used to say, " It's a good farce," perhaps to indicate that he allowed it no higher merit.

[2] A Pastoral, by *Mairet*.

[3] *Fontenelle*, " Histoire du Théâtre Français," p. 80.

PHILEMON.

Tu peux bien pour le moins, avant ma sépulture,
D'un baiser seulement ma douleur apaiser.

SYLVIE.

Sans perdre en même temps l'une ou l'autre nature,
Les glaces et les feux ne sauraient se baiser.

PHILEMON.

Oh cœur ! mais bien rocher, toujours couvert d'orages,
Où mon âme se perd avec trop de rigueur !

SYLVIE.

On touche le rocher où l'on fait le naufrage ;
Mais jamais ton amour ne m'a touché le cœur."

However careful Corneille may have been to conform to this deplorable kind of wit, a correcter reason displayed itself continually, and, as it were, in spite of his efforts, in his work. In the style of " Mélite," also, might be perceived a kind of boldness necessarily unknown to those authors who were so proud of the haste and negligence with which they composed their dramatic works. No one had as yet introduced that tone of moderate elevation which maintains the characters of a play in the same position throughout, and is equally removed from vulgarity and ridiculous pomp. [1] At length, excepting

[1] The use of the second person singular which so much shocked Voltaire and which is frequent in all Corneille's early comedies, was probably at that time not an impropriety, and was less an indication of the intimacy of two lovers, than of a sort of familiarity which was allowable with persons with regard to whom it was not thought necessary strictly to observe forms. It is thus used more frequently by women than by men, and appears to be one of the signs of that superiority which a woman assumes over a lover of whose affection she is sure. In "Cinna," Emilie addresses Cinna in the second person singular, but he does not use it in his answers. In "La Veuve," one of Corneille's earliest comedies, Clarice thees-and-thous Philiste, who, far from thinking he has any claim upon her, has not even

only in his fantastic description of the pagan madness of Erastus,[1] Corneille had attained, if not to real and complete truth, at least to a kind of relative truthfulness, on which no previous writer had bestowed a thought. Instead of figures naturally full of life and animation, he sought as yet merely to represent the artificial figures of contemporary society ; but he had felt the necessity of taking some model, and while the authors of his day were as incapable of imitation as of invention, he had at least striven to copy some characteristics of the world beneath his eyes.

Of these merits, most of which were negative and the only ones by which we can explain Corneille's first success, some were revealed to him by criticism. Having come to Paris " to witness the success of

ventured to confess his love, and maintains the deepest respect in his language towards her. He informs us that she is of higher rank than himself, and this is probably the cause of her familiarity. In the same piece, Chrysanthe, an old woman, says thee and thou to Géron, a kind of business man, who never addresses her otherwise than as *you.* In other places, we find instances of old ladies speaking in this manner to their servants. Fontenelle blames the theeing-and-thouing in Corneille's pieces only on account of its impoliteness. See his " Vie de Corneille," p. 93.

[1] In all the comedies of the time we find the same use of the language of Paganism by thoroughly modern personages. Thus, in the comedy of the " Thuilleries," a production of the " five authors," the intrigue of which actually takes place in the garden of the Tuileries, the lovers tell us that they met in the *temple,* whither they had gone *to adore the Gods* ; and Aglante relates that a hermit whom he had consulted as to whether it was allowable to marry without love, spoke to him of love as the *Master of the Gods,* and threatened him with their anger if he dared to approach his altar with irreverence. At the same time his uncle, who is vexed by this decision, ironically calls the hermit " this venerable father," and laughs at his nephew because he can—

" Au retour d'Italie, être encor scrupuleux."

'Mélite,'" he learned "that its action was not included within twenty-four hours; and this," he says, "was the only rule known at that period"; [1] although authors attached little or no importance to it. The charge of irregularity, however, was not sufficient to console them for the success of "Mélite"; they blamed it for its deficiency of events, and for its excessively natural style. "I learned," says Corneille himself, "that those of the craft found fault with it because it contained few effects, and because its style was too familiar." Fortunately for taste, Corneille had already entered the lists on its behalf. Self-respect came to the aid of reason. His firmness in the defence of truth rested complacently upon the success of his work. "To justify myself," he says, "by a sort of bravado, and to show that this kind of drama possessed the same theatrical beauties, I undertook to compose one regular piece, that is to say, extending over twenty-four hours only, full of incidents, and written in a loftier style, but which should be worth absolutely nothing,—in which I completely succeeded."

If Corneille's sole object in the composition of "Clitandre" really was to render the triumph of good taste more illustrious by a display of bad taste, never did an author sacrifice himself more entirely for the public good. A party of two couples, meeting by

---

[1] Examination of "Clitandre."

chance at the same time and place, in consequence
of a double project of assassination ; the frustration
of these projects by each other ; a man who attempts
to violate a girl upon the stage, and the girl who
defends herself by piercing his eye with the bodkin
from her hair ; combats, disguises, a tempest, the
police, a prison—all these materials did Corneille
laboriously combine, in order to furnish us in
" Clitandre " with a monstrous drama, worthy of the
public whom it was intended to please—for it is
difficult to suppose that Corneille designed solely to
instruct them.   Perhaps he believed this himself
thirty years afterwards, when he wrote an examination of this work, which he then so heartily disdained :
our present sentiments strangely modify the remembrance of our past feelings, and one of the most
common effects of evidence, when we have been once
struck by it, is to persuade us that we always were
of that opinion.   But at the time at which
" Clitandre " appeared, thus to judge and sacrifice
himself was above the taste of the author of " Mélite,"
and beyond the courage of a self-love so keenly
sensitive regarding the criticisms which had been
passed upon his work.   In the preface which he
wrote in 1632, when " Clitandre " was printed,
Corneille admits the obscurity which must result from
the multiplicity of events and the brevity of the
dialogue ; but he boasts " of having preferred to

divert the eyes rather than importune the ears," by
bringing upon the stage " what the ancients would
have introduced into the dialogue " ; and he congra-
tulates himself that, in adopting the rules, " he has
culled their beauties, without falling into those
inconveniences which the Greeks and Latins, who
also followed them, were usually unable, or at least
did not venture, to avoid." His dignity in his own
defence is not the pride of a man who can dispense
with the approbation of the public, but the confidence
of an author who is certain of obtaining it, whatever
means he may use to request it. " If I have confined
this piece," he says, " within the rule of a single day,
it is not because I repent of not having pursued the
same plan in ' Mélite,' or because I have resolved to
do so in future. At the present day, some persons
adore this rule, and many despise it ; for myself, I
am desirous only to show that, if I depart from it, it
is not for want of knowing it." [1] But he was anxious
to prove himself equal in attainments to his contemporaries, and superior to them in his manner of
employing his knowledge. " If any one should
remark coincidences in my verses," he says, "let him
not suppose them to be thefts. I have not willingly
borrowed from anybody, and I have always believed
that, however fine a thought may be, you buy it
at more than its value if it be suspected that you

---

[1] Preface to " Clitandre."

have taken it from some one else ; so that, in the state in which I lay this piece before the public, I think nothing will be found in it in common with most modern writers, except the little vanity which I display here." [1]

In the composition of " Clitandre," Corneille had not entirely renounced this vanity ; the pleasure of exhibiting his superiority to his rivals, even in a style of composition which he despised, had doubtless stimulated him not to leave any defects "wittingly " in his work, excepting those inseparable from the style itself, which he could not better disparage than by displaying enough talent to prove that, if the piece were bad, it was not the fault of the poet.　He even took care to point out the faults which he had avoided ; and thus he explains, in his Preface, why he did not indicate the place in which the scene is laid.　" I leave," he says, " the locality of my play to the choice of the reader, although it would be no trouble for me to name it here.　If my subject be true, I have reasons for not mentioning it ; if it is a fiction, why should I, in order to conform to I don't know what chorography, give a fillip to history, assign imaginary princes to a country, and attribute to them adventures of which there is no record in the chronicles of their realm ? "　Even in his irregularities, Corneille manifested a good sense which

---

[1] Preface to " Clitandre."

was quite unprecedented among his contemporaries, and by which they were not yet in a condition to profit.

After that sally of humour and self-respect which induced him to write " Clitandre," Corneille no longer allowed the taste of his time to rule solely and despotically in his works, unless it were without his knowledge ; he preferred to rely upon his own reflections, and upon the experience which he was daily acquiring of theatrical effects. The hour at which his genius was to awake had, nevertheless, not yet arrived ; for some time still, he will grope painfully for his way amidst the surrounding darkness ; but every effort will cast a ray of light upon his path, and every step will be a step in advance. Already a natural feeling of reserve had banished from Corneille's works that excessive license which was scarcely noticed by his contemporaries ; for an unsuccessful attempt at violation[1] cannot be regarded as an indecency upon a stage on which a woman was represented as receiving her lover into her bed, merely recommending him to be discreet. It is only fair to say that after this piece of advice had been given, the curtain fell. If the custom of his time led Corneille to introduce an objectionable scene into " Clitandre," and to indulge in some questionable pleasantries in " Mélite," they had so little real

[1] In " Clitandre."

connection with these pieces, that he had no difficulty in omitting them from the printed versions, and afterwards he did not find it necessary to make any further curtailments. In his early days, too, he had composed some rather gay poems, which have never been inserted in the collected edition of his works. And at the same time that he banished from the stage these singular manifestations of illegitimate or unbridled passion, he began to infuse a little more truthfulness into the language of honourable affection, and to divorce it from the jargon of gallantry. In the " Veuve," a mother, inquiring about the progress which her daughter is making in the heart of a young man whom she wishes her to marry, expresses her dissatisfaction at the tone of his declarations, which lay all the divinities of Olympus under contribution :—

> "Ses yeux, à son avis, sont autant de soleils,
>   L'enflure de son sein un double petit monde :
>   C'est le seul ornement de la machine ronde.
>   L'amour à ses regards allume son flambeau,
>   Et souvent pour la voir il ôte son bandeau.
>   Diane n'eut jamais une si belle taille ;
>   Auprès d'elle Vénus ne serait rien qui vaille :
>   Ce ne sont rien que lys et roses que son teint."

The anxious mother considers this the language of pleasantry ; but her agent reassures her :—

> " C'est un homme tout neuf, que voulez-vous qu'il fasse ?
>   Il dit ce qu'il a lu."   *   *   *   *

Corneille clearly perceived that it was not in books, nor even in the love-poems of his time, that he must

seek a language capable of awakening, within the
breasts of his audience, those sentiments which he
was desirous to describe.   In the "Galerie du Palais,"
two young people, standing in front of a bookseller's
shop, reason upon comedy, and the manner in which
love is treated therein :—

> "Il n'en faut point douter, l'amour a des tendresses
> Que nous n'apprenons point qu'auprès de nos maîtresses ;
> Tant de sortes d'appas, de doux saisissements,
> D'agréables langueurs et de ravissements,
> Jusques ou d'un bel œil peut s'étendre l'empire,
> Et mille autres secrets que l'on ne saurait dire,
> Quoique tous nos rimeurs en mettent par écrit,
> Ne se surent jamais par un effort d'esprit,
> Et je n'ai jamais vu de cervelles bien faites
> Qui traitassent l'amour comme font les poëtes :
> C'est tout un autre jeu.   Le style d'un sonnet
> Est fort extravagant dedans un cabinet ;
> Il y faut bien louer la beauté qu'on adore,
> Sans mépriser Vénus, sans médire de Flore ;
> Sans que l'éclat des lys, des roses, d'un beau jour,
> Ait rien à démêler avecque notre amour.
> O pauvre Comédie ! objet de tant de peines,
> Si tu n'es qu'un portrait des actions humaines,
> On te tire souvent sur un original,
> A qui, pour dire vrai, tu ressembles fort mal."

The natural good sense, by which Corneille was
distinguished, is sometimes productive of singular
effects by its mixture with those false habits from the
influence of which the poet had not yet escaped.   In
the "Place Royale," his fifth comedy, a young girl,
unworthily treated by the man she loves, and by
whom she believed she was loved, bursts into anger
against him; and when her perfidious admirer, who is
anxious to drive her to extremities, insolently present~

her with a mirror that she may behold therein the reasons for his indifference, she exclaims :—

> " S'il me dit des défauts autant ou plus que toi,
> Déloyal, pour le moins il n'en dit rien qu'à moi :
> C'est dedans son cristal que je les étudie ;
> Mais après il s'en tait, et moi j'y remédie ;
> Il m'en donne un avis sans me les reprocher,
> Et me les découvrant, il m'aide à les cacher."

To this very ill-timed outbreak, who would not answer in the words of Alidor, her false lover :—

> " Vous êtes en colère, et vous dites des pointes ! "

This criticism is so just, that we are surprised that the good sense which dictated it to the poet did not preserve him from incurring it ; but the first step in advance is to perceive the truth ; the second, and most difficult, is to obey it.

In the conduct of his pieces, Corneille's progress was more sure and rapid. The plot, being arranged with greater care and skill, fastens upon the curiosity ; and all the characters present themselves with a marked physiognomy which distinguishes them from each other. These distinctive features are, in truth, more the result of fancies of the imagination than of natural dispositions and real varieties of character. An Alidor wishes to desert his mistress because she is so perfect and so tender that she gives him no cause for complaint to justify him in abandoning her, and because he loves her too much to be master of his own liberty, when she is near. A Célidie[1] takes a sudden liking for a new comer, and in order to gratify her taste, strives to banish the feelings which speak within her breast on behalf of a faithful lover, to whom she has plighted her troth. These various whimsies are often rendered with a vivacity which somewhat diminishes their absurdity. Corneille's mind enlarged daily, but he had not yet discovered the legitimate and great use of his increasing powers; instead of turning his attention to that inexhaustible source, the observation of nature, he wasted his strength in efforts to make the best of the barren field which he had chosen. He daily acquired greater industry, but his art remained stationary at nearly the same point; and Corneille had as yet succeeded only in showing what he could do in a style of composition in which excellence could be attained by no one.

Six works,[2] the fruits of his earliest labours, had laid the basis of his fortune and established his reputation. The favour of Cardinal Richelieu had not overlooked his rising genius, and Corneille shared with Colletet and Bois-Robert the honour of working, under the orders, supervision, and direction of His Eminence, at those pieces which were laboriously

---

[1] In the "Galerie du Palais."

[2] These were, "Mélite," in 1629; "Clitandre," in 1632; the "Veuve," in 1633; the "Galerie du Palais" and the "Suivante," in 1634; and the "Place Royale," in 1635.

brought into being by the will of a minister, and the talents of five authors.[1]   Lauded by his competitors in the dramatic career, Corneille was still regarded by them merely as one of the partners in that literary glory which was common to them all : satisfied with their possession of bad taste, they were far from anticipating that revolution which was soon to overthrow its empire and their own.

This revolution was not inaugurated by Corneille. It is difficult, at the present day, to divine what lucky chance dictated Mairet's " Sophonisbe," the only one of his pieces in which he rises at all superior to the taste of his times.   Its merits taught nothing to its author, to whom it was nothing more than a piece of good fortune ; but there is reason to believe that it revealed to Corneille the powers of his own genius. " Sophonisbe " appeared in 1633.   Corneille, then known only as a comic poet,[2] not even knowing himself in any other character, and incapable of discerning tragedy amid that accumulated heap of whimsical and puerile inventions which he had, as it were in spite of himself, imitated in " Clitandre,"— Corneille suddenly learned that it was possible for

---

[1] These five authors were L'Etoile, Colletet, Bois-Robert, Rotrou, and Corneille, who, according to Voltaire, was " rather subordinate to the others, who exceeded him in fortune or in favour," and who were probably more docile in a work in which it was necessary to take care not to display either originality or independence.

[2] Mairet addressed to him, on the appearance of his " Veuve," some lines headed : " À Monsieur Corneille, poète comique."

another kind of tragedy to exist. In the midst of
that comic triviality from which Mairet was unable to
free either his plot, or the tone of his characters,
Corneille perceived that great interests were treated
of, and many feelings depicted with considerable
power. The sensitive chord had been touched ; his
fine native faculties, placed far above the circle within
which he was confined by habit, awoke and demanded
their manifestation. Henceforward he resolved to seek
the subjects of his pictures beyond this limited sphere :
he turned his eyes towards antiquity ; Seneca
presented himself, and in 1635, " Médée " appeared.

> " Souverains protecteurs des lois de l'Hyménée,
> Dieux garants de la foi que Jason m'a donnée !
> Vous qu'il prit à témoin d'une immortelle ardeur,
> Quand par un faux serment il vainquit ma pudeur ! " [1]

" These lines," says Voltaire, " announce the advent
of Corneille." [2] They did more—they inaugurated
tragedy in France : the tragic Muse had at length
appeared to Corneille ; and her features, though still
roughly sketched out, could no longer be mistaken.
Neither the ridiculous love of old Egeus, nor the
puerile desire manifested by Creusa to possess Medea's
robe, nor the frequently ignoble style of the time, nor
the absence of art discernible throughout the piece,
will deter from a perusal of " Médée " any person
who has had the courage to prepare for it by a

---

[1] *Corneille,* "Médée," act i, scene 4.
[2] *Voltaire,* " Commentaires."

slight acquaintance with the drama of that period.
On coming to this composition it seems as though,
after having long wandered without object, compass,
or hope, we had at last disembarked upon firm
ground, from whence we can perceive, in the distance,
a fertile and luxuriant country. Imagination and
reflection appear at last applied to objects worthy of
their notice ; important feelings assume the place of
childish mental amusements, and Corneille already
manifests his wondrous powers of expression. We
already perceive in Medea's " Moi," so far superior to
Seneca's " Medea superest," an example of that energetic conciseness to which he could reduce the expression of the loftiest and most sublime sentiments. In
the following lines, which he has not imitated from
the Latin tragedian—

> " Me peut-il bien quitter après tant de bienfaits ?
> M'ose-t-il bien quitter après tant de forfaits ? "

we are struck by the force and depth of thought that
he can include in the simplest expressions ; and, in
that scene in which Medea discusses with Creon the
reasons which he may have for expelling her from his
dominions, we acknowledge the presence of a powerful and serious reason, not often met with in the
poetry of that time, and which gained for Corneille this
eulogy from the English poet, Waller : " The others
make plenty of verses, but Corneille is the only one
who can think ! " Even thus early he displayed that

close and rigorous dialectics, which the recollection of his original studies, as much perhaps as the spirit of his time, caused too frequently to degenerate into subtilties, but which, whenever it struck fully, dealt irresistible blows.

It is of little importance to inquire whether Corneille, in "Médée," borrowed from Seneca or not; for more than a century, his predecessors and contemporaries had not been wanting in models. In a translation of Seneca's "Agamemnon," published by Rolland Brisset, less than fifty years before, Clytemnestra called Electra *a hussy;* and this line of Trissino's " Sofonisba,"—

> " E rimirando lui, penso a me stesso."

was, in 1583, about the same period, thus translated by Claude Mermet,—

> " En voyant sa ruine et perte non pareille,
> Bien m'advise qu'autant m'en peut pendre à l'oreille."

To raise to the elevation of noble sentiments, great interests, and lofty thoughts a poetical language which had never had to express anything but tender or natural feelings and ingenious or delicate ideas, was an achievement which Ronsard had commenced in reference to general poetry ; and this task Corneille first undertook for dramatic poetry, which, though regarded as a more exact representation of nature, imitated her only in those grosser forms in which she sometimes appeared amidst a state of society still sadly deficient in delicacy and respect for propriety. It was a matter of little consequence whether an idea belonged originally to Corneille or to Seneca ; but it was essential that that idea, whoever its original inventor might have been, should not be robbed of all nobleness and gravity by expressions which conveyed to the mind none but the most ridiculous images ; [1] it was essential that details of the most puerile familiarity [2] should not be allowed to occupy a stage destined for the exhibition of higher interests ; it was essential that personages supposed to move in the highest circles of society, and to be actuated by mighty passions or important designs, should not use language similar to that employed by the vulgar herd in its brutal rage ; [3] in a word, it was essential, by propriety, precision and careful choice of terms, to establish, between the style and the subject, a harmony which had previously been utterly unknown. This was

[1] In *Mairet's* "Sylvie," a prince, in despair at the death of his mistress, whom he deplores in a most tragic tone, speaks of his heart as a place --
"Où l'amour avait fait son plus beau cabinet."

[2] In *Scudéry's* "Didon," written in 1636, after Æneas and Dido, being forced by a storm to take refuge in a grotto, have given each other proofs of their mutual love, Æneas advances on the stage to look at the weather, and says to the Queen, who had remained in the grotto :--
"Madame, il ne pleut plus ; votre Majesté sorte."
Then, being requested by her to climb upon a rock to summon her sister and suite to join them, he shouts out :--
" Hola ! hi ! L'on répond ; la voix est déjà proche.
Hola ! hi ! la voicy ?   *   *   * "

[3] Syphax, in *Mairet's* "Sophonisbe," calls his wife *impudent* and *brazen-faced.* It is true that she deserved both epithets ; but they are rather beneath the dignity of tragedy.

a lesson which neither Seneca nor any other poet could teach Corneille. His genius alone raised him to a level with lofty thoughts, and he expressed them, as he had conceived them, in all their grandeur and sublimity.

" After writing 'Médée,'" says Fontenelle, " Corneille fell back again into comedy ; and if I may venture to say what I think, the fall was great." [1] I shall therefore say nothing of the " Illusion Comique," the last production of what we may call Corneille's youth, in which, taking leave of that fantastic taste which he was soon to annihilate, he gave himself up to its vagaries with a recklessness which might be charged with negligence, if Corneille's anxiety for success had ever allowed him to be negligent. This is the only one of his pieces into which he has introduced the " Matamore," a principal character in the comedies of the time, borrowed from the Spanish drama, as the name indicates,[2] and whose comicality consists in bragging of the most extravagant achievements while giving continual proofs of the basest cowardice. The amorous conquests of the Matamore are on a par with his warlike exploits ; Corneille's hero once delayed the dawn of day—Aurora was nowhere to be found, because, he says, she had gone—

" Au milieu de ma chambre à m'offrir ses beautés."

---

[1] *Fontenelle*, " Vie de Corneille," vol. iii. p. 94.
[2] " Capitan Mata-moros," Captain Moor-killer.

Scarron describes a hero of the same kind, who, for pastime, had—

> " *   *   *   Roué la fortune,
> Ecorché le hasard et brûlé le malheur."

After the production of "Médée," such eccentricities were no longer allowable in Corneille; and the "Illusion Comique" would not be deserving of mention, if, by a singular coincidence, the date of its first performance[1] did not justify us in supposing that, even while his humour was taking such fantastic flights, Corneille was already busy with the "Cid."

The genius of Corneille had at length discovered its true vocation; but, timid and modest almost to humility, although inwardly conscious of his powers, he did not yet venture to rely upon himself alone. Before bringing new beauties to light, he had need, not of a guide to direct him, but of an authority upon which he could fall back for support; and he resorted to imitation, not to reinforce his own strength, but to obtain a pledge for his success. The Court had brought into fashion the study of the Spanish language and literature, and men of taste had discovered therein beauties which we were still far from having attained. M. de Châlon, who had been secretary to the Queen-mother, Marie de Medici, had retired, in his old age, to Rouen. Corneille, emboldened by the success of his first pieces, called upon him : "Sir,"

---

[1] During the year 1635.

said the old courtier to him, after having praised him for his wit and talents, " the pursuit of comedy, which you have embraced, can only bring you fleeting renown ; you will find, in the Spanish authors, subjects which, if treated according to our taste, by such hands as yours, will produce immense effect. Learn their language ; it is easy. I will teach you all I know of it, and until you are competent to read it yourself, I will translate for you some passages from Guillermo de Castro."[1] Whether Corneille was indebted to himself or to his old friend for the choice of the subject of the " Cid," the " Cid " soon belonged to himself alone.

The success of the " Cid," in 1636, constitutes an era in our dramatic history ; it is not necessary now to explain the causes of the brilliant reception which it obtained. " Before the production of Corneille's ' Cid,' " says Voltaire, " men were unacquainted with that conflict of passions which rends the heart, and in the presence of which all other beauties of art are dull and inanimate." Neither passion, nor duty, nor tenderness, nor magnanimity had previously been introduced upon the stage ; and now, love and honour, as they may be conceived by the most exalted imagination, appeared suddenly, and for the

---

[1] This anecdote was related by Père Tournemine, one of Corneille's tutors at the Jesuit College at Rouen. See the "Recherches sur les Théâtres de la France," vol. ii. p. 157.

first time, in all their glory, before a public by whom honour was considered the first of virtues, and love the chief business of life. " Their enthusiasm was carried to the greatest transports ; they could never grow tired of beholding the piece ; nothing else was talked of in society ; everybody knew some part of it by heart ; children committed it to memory ; and in some parts of France it passed into a proverb:—
That is as fine as the Cid." [1]

Although carried away at first in the general stream, astounded at his remarkable success, and reduced to silence by their amazement, Corneille's rivals soon regained breath, and their first sign of life was an act of resistance against the torrent which threatened to sweep them into annihilation. The instinct of self-preservation gave unity to their efforts, and, with the single exception of Rotrou, the insurrection was general. A powerful auxiliary undertook to support and direct their movements.

At the distance at which we stand from these events, it is difficult to assign any cause for Cardinal Richelieu's violent participation in this struggle against public opinion. Of all the motives which have been ascribed to him, the least probable is that ridiculous jealousy which it is said that the minister entertained against the poet who laboured in his service. The literary self-love of Richelieu was certainly very

---

[1] *Pelisson*, " Histoire de l'Académie Française," p. 186.

susceptible, but his vanity as a nobleman must have served as a counterpoise to it ; and a poetical prime minister could not possibly have felt any idea of emulation, nor consequently of jealousy, for a mere professional poet. That " vast ambition " of which Fontenelle speaks,[1] and which could so easily reduce itself to the dimensions of the smallest objects, was, according to all appearance, the ambition of power rather than a craving after glory. The suffrages of public opinion lose much of their value in the eyes of men who are raised above its censure ; and a powerful minister feels great inclination to believe that obedience is approval.

Corneille was, however, unacquainted with that art which is so necessary to render obedience flattering. " At the end of 1635, a year before the performance of the ' Cid,' the Cardinal had given in the Palais-Cardinal, now called the Palais-Royal, the comedy of the ' Thuilleries,' all the scenes of which he had himself arranged. Corneille, who was more docile to his genius than subservient to the will of a prime minister, thought it necessary to make some alteration in the third act, which had been entrusted to him. This estimable liberty was ascribed to false motives by two of his colleagues, and gave great offence to the Cardinal, who told him that he must have an *esprit de suite*, by which he meant that submission

---

[1] *Fontenelle,* " Vie de Corneille," p. 97.

which blindly obeys the orders of superiors."[1] Whatever meaning may be ascribed to words spoken in an angry moment, the disposition which had dictated them was not likely to be mollified by such a success as the " Cid" had obtained without the orders of the minister. There is even reason to believe that, before achieving this insolent success, Corneille had seen marks of preference bestowed upon his associates, which he had disregarded ; and to fill up the measure of his offences he seemed to boast of not having obtained them :—

> " Mon travail sans appui monte sur le théâtre.
>   *   *   *   *   *
> Par d'illustres avis je n'éblouis personne.
>   *   *   *   *   *
> Je ne dois qu'à moi seul toute ma renommée."[2]

These lines he printed in 1636, between the appearance of " Médée " and that of the " Cid." This was doubtless a part of his crime. Astonished that any one should consider himself independent, and indignant that he should venture to declare it, Richelieu believed himself set at defiance. The enemies of Corneille, says Voltaire, " his rivals in the pursuit of glory and favour, had described him as an

---

[1] *Voltaire's* Preface to the "Cid." He adds that "this anecdote was well-known to the last princes of the house of Vendôme, the grandsons of César de Vendôme, who was present at the performance of this piece of the Cardinal's."

[2] *Corneille*, " Excuse à Ariste." It is well known that this piece gained its author a host of enemies. It was frequently quoted during the quarrel that arose about the " Cid."

upstart spirit who ventured to brave the first minister, and who looked with contempt not only upon their works, but also upon the taste of their protector." They did not neglect this opportunity of satisfying their jealousy by the basest means. As Corneille lived at Rouen, and came to Paris only to arrange for the performance of his pieces, his only weapons against their attacks were his successes, and even these were turned into arms against him. The success of the " Cid " was regarded as an insult by the resentment of a protector whom he had neglected and irritated ; and it appeared, in his eyes, the triumph of a rebel.

All arms were considered good enough to attack him ; Scudéry was thought less ridiculous, and even Claveret [1] was deemed a worthy and useful auxiliary. The Cardinal wrote, by means of Bois-Robert, to Mairet, who had praised the " Veuve," but declared against the " Cid " : " His Eminence has read with extreme pleasure all that has been written on the subject of the 'Cid,' and particularly a letter of yours which was shown to him." In this letter, Corneille's answers to the gross insults of his enemies are called *libels* ; and, though he had not read them, his Eminence, on seeing their rejoinders, " presupposed that he had been the aggressor." [2]

---

[1] The unknown author of a few dramas and other works, which are very bad even for the time at which they were written.

[2] See *Bois-Robert's* letter to Mairet, in the preface to the "Cid," and in *Abbé Granet's* " Recueil des Dissertations sur Corneille et Racine."

The bitterness of Corneille's enemies may easily be conceived by the humility of their confessions. Scudéry thus begins his attack upon the " Cid ":— " There are certain pieces, like certain animals that exist in nature, which, at a distance, look like stars, and which, on close inspection, are only worms." He then expresses his astonishment that such fantastic beauties " should have deluded wisdom as well as ignorance, and the Court as well as the citizen " ; and, begging pardon of that public whom he thinks it his duty to enlighten, he " conjures honourable persons to suspend their judgment for a little while, and not to condemn without a hearing the ' Sophonisbe,' the ' César,' [1] the ' Cléopatre,' [2] the ' Hercule,' [3] the ' Marianne,' [4] the ' Cléomedon,' [5] and a host of other illustrious heroes who have charmed them on the stage." Satisfied with this cry of distress, Corneille might well have pardoned enemies who, at the outset, confessed themselves vanquished. But even self-love has its humility, and will disdain no opponent. Such is the strange mixture of loftiness and timidity, of vigour of imagination and simplicity of judgment ! By his success alone Corneille had become aware of his talents ; but when once he knew his own powers, he became, and remained,

[1] By *Scudéry*.   [2] By *Benserade*.   [3] By *Rotrou*.   [4] By *Tristan*.
[5] By *Duryer*. Most of these pieces had been performed during the same year as the " Cid," which, as it appears, was not brought on the stage until the end of the year.

fully convinced of their extent and worth. As soon
as he felt that Corneille was a superior man, he
said so, without imagining that any one could
doubt it :—

"Je sais ce que je vaux, et crois ce qu'on m'en dit,"

he says himself in the "Excuse à Ariste ; " and, in
the same piece, he speaks thus of his genius :—

"Quittant souvent la terre, en quittant la barrière,
Puis d'un vol élevé se cachant dans les cieux,
Il rit du désespoir de tous ses envieux.
*   *   *   *   *
Je pense toutefois n'avoir point de rival,
A qui je fasse tort en le traitant d'égal."

It is not to be wondered at, that, holding this opinion
of himself, Corneille considered the first criticisms of
his works as an insult to evidence. Afterwards,
however, they caused him some anxiety, both regarding his glory, and the opinion which he had formed of
it. He was afraid to call in question that which he
had believed to be certain ; and he struggled against
such a contingency at first, with the haughtiness of
conviction, but afterwards, with the violence of fear.

At this juncture in his history, when Corneille is
about to enter personally into the lists in opposition to such powerful enemies, it is necessary that we
should obtain a complete idea of his character and
position, in order to be able rightly to judge both
of the necessity for making concessions, and of
the courage requisite for resistance. Corneille was

immediately dependent upon the Cardinal, whom, in a letter to Scudéry, he calls "your master and mine."[1] This expression shocked Voltaire ; but it was not at all at variance with the customs of Corneille's time. At a period when gentlemen of the highest birth entered the service of others more rich than themselves ;[2] when money was the natural price paid for all services,[3] and wealth a sort of suzerainty[4] which collected around itself vassals ready to pay it a kind of homage which was considered perfectly legitimate, we need not be surprised that a burgess of Rouen felt no shame in considering himself almost a domestic,[5] or,

---

[1] See the "Réponse aux observations sur le 'Cid.'" He was in receipt of a pension from the Cardinal.

[2] Cardinal de Retz, when merely Abbé de Gondi, during his travels in Italy, had in his suite "seven or eight gentlemen, four of whom were Knights of Malta." "Memoirs of De Retz," vol. i. pp. 16, 17.

[3] It appears that, independently of the prologue in verse with which authors sometimes preceded their pieces, the first performance was opened by a sort of prose prologue, in which the authors were named. Cardinal de Richelieu, feeling desirous that Chapelain should consent to have his name mentioned in the prologue to the comedy of the "Thuilleries," "besought him to lend him his name on this occasion," adding that, in return, he "would lend him his purse when he needed it." It is to be hoped, for the honour of Chapelain's taste, that he set a high price on the performance of a service of this kind.

[4] That sort of pride which maintains equality of condition under inequality of fortune, was then completely unknown. "I have never been touched with avarice," says the Abbé de Marolles, "nor of a humour to ask for anything, although presents from rich and disinterested persons would have been agreeable to me, because they require no return, except pure civilities, which give no trouble ; whereas presents from poor persons, or equals, always compel us to give greater ones." "Mémoires de Marolles," vol. ii. p. 143.

[5] *Domestic* was the title then assumed by all those who were attached to the service of powerful men. Pelisson speaks of several Academicians who were *domestics* of Chancellor Seguier. ("Histoire de l'Académie," p. 155.)

if you prefer it, a subject of an all-powerful minister, whose liberality was his mainstay, and in whose favour his hopes were centred. The increased power and diffusion of knowledge have, in our day, enhanced the worth of merit, and established a juster proportion between man and things. The honest man has learned to estimate himself at his true value, and to respect himself even when his fortunes are low ; he has learned that the reception of a benefit cannot enslave him, and has felt that he must not solicit benefits in return for which he is expected to give gratitude only, and not personal work. Quickened by that instinctive feeling of delicate pride which has been developed in us by education, and which a regard for propriety maintains even in those over whom it exercises the least influence, we shall meet with many actions and words, in the life of Corneille, utterly at variance with our ideas and habits. We shall pass with surprise from his tragedies to his dedicatory epistles ; and we shall blush to see the same hand—

"   *   *   *   La main qui crayonna
L'âme du grand Pompée et l'esprit de Cinna,"[1]

stretched forth, if we may be allowed the expression,

La Rochepot, a cousin-german and intimate friend of that Abbé de Gondi, who had four Knights of Malta in his suite, was a *domestic* of the Duke of Orleans. ("Memoires of De Retz," vol. i. p. 21.) It is not impossible that Corneille may have had the title of some office in the Cardinal's household.

[1] See the letter to Fouquet, printed at the beginning of "Œdipe," in Voltaire's edition ; and in vol. x. p. 75, of the edition of 1758.

to solicit liberalities which it did not always obtain.[1] We shall ask ourselves whether the same man could thus alternately rise to such lofty heights of genius and descend to such depths of abasement; and we shall find that, influenced sometimes by his genius and sometimes by his circumstances, he really was not the same man in both positions.

Let us first look at Corneille in his social relations. Destitute of all that distinguishes a man from his equals, he seems to be irrevocably doomed to pass unnoticed in the crowd. His appearance is common,[2] his conversation dull, his language incorrect,[3] his timidity awkward, his judgment uncertain, and his

---

[1] See his "Epître de la Poésie à la Peinture," in which he speaks of liberality as a virtue which has been so long banished from the Court that even its name has been forgotten :—

"J'en fais souvent reproche à ce climat heureux ;
Je me plains aux plus grands comme aux plus généreux ;
Par trop m'en plaindre en vain je deviens ridicule ;
Ou l'on ne m'entend pas, ou bien l'on dissimule."
                 Corneille, "Œuvres," vol. x. p. 81.

[2] "The first time I saw him, I took him for a shopkeeper," says *Vigneul Marville*, in his "Mélanges d'Histoire et de Littérature," vol. ii. p. 167. "M. Corneille was rather large and full of body, and very simple and common in appearance," says *Fontenelle*, in his "Vie de Corneille," vol. iii. p. 124. He had, however, according to Fontenelle, "a rather agreeable countenance, a large nose, a pretty mouth, eyes full of fire, an animated physiognomy, and very marked features, well-adapted to be transmitted to posterity by means of a medallion or a bust."

[3] "Another is simple and timid, very tiresome in conversation; he takes one word for another. * * He cannot recite his own pieces, nor read his own writing." *La Bruyère*, "Des Jugements," vol. ii. p. 84. "His conversation was so dull that it became burdensome, even if it lasted only a short time. He never spoke the French language very correctly." *Vigneul-Marville*, vol. ii. pp. 167, 168. "His pronunciation was not altogether clear ; he read his poems forcibly, but not with grace. In order

experience perfectly childish. If he finds himself brought into contact, either by necessity or chance, with persons whom birth or fortune have placed above him, he does not rightly appreciate the position which he occupies in respect to them, but thinks only of the one connection of protector and protected, which subsists between him and them. Of all their different titles to consideration, he regards only the claims which they may possibly have to his gratitude, and thus he will place a Montauron [1] on a level with,

---

to find out the great Corneille, it was necessary to read him." *Fontenelle*, p. 125. It was said that he was worth hearing only at the Hôtel de Bourgogne, and he was so conscious of this that he says himself, in his "Letter to Pelisson:"—

> "Et l'on peut rarement m'écouter sans ennuy,
> Que quand je me produis par la bouche d'autrui."
> *Corneille*, "Œuvres," vol. x. p. 124.

[1] The partisan Montauron, to whom Corneille dedicated "Cinna." In his dedicatory epistle he compares him to Augustus, because Augustus united clemency with liberality. M. de Montauron, who was as liberal as Augustus, must necessarily, like him, possess both virtues conjointly. It is somewhat singular that, in several editions in which this epistle is contained, the epithets *liberal* and *generous,* applied to M. de Montauron, are printed in large characters like those used for the words *Monseigneur* or *Votre Altesse*, in order to point out M. de Montauron's title to this kind of homage. It is said that the dedication of "Cinna" gained Corneille a thousand pistoles. It is added that he at first intended to dedicate this play to Cardinal Mazarin; but he preferred M. de Montauron, because he paid better. Although men were accustomed to the most inflated style of eulogy, great fault was found with Corneille for this epistle; and praises of this kind, written on such terms, were called thenceforward dedications *à la Montauron*. The eleventh article of the "Parnasse Réformé" declares: "We suppress all panegyrics *à la Montauron*." This Montauron having ruined himself, Scarron wrote:—

> "Ce n'est que maroquin perdu
> Que les livres que l'on dédie,
> Depuis que Montauron mendie."

if not above, Richelieu and Mazarin. It is always possible to determine by the nature of the homage which Corneille pays, the amount of the reward he received for it ; and the excessive character of his eulogies will never prove anything but the excess of his gratitude. Nothing in these panegyrics seems to be at all repugnant to those feelings which he had not raised above his position ; and in most of his actions, he is nothing more than what fortune made him.

" Let him elevate himself by composition ; he is not inferior to Augustus, Pompey, Nicomedes, or Heraclius. He is a king, and a great king ; he is a politician—nay more, a philosopher." [1] He has passed into a new sphere ; a new horizon has opened before him ; he has escaped from the trammels of a position which bound down his imagination to the interests of a fortune far inferior to his faculties ; he can now appreciate all the duties necessarily imposed upon generous souls, by an important existence, a lofty destiny, and the possibility and expectation of glory ; and with all the force of deep, inward conviction, he has laid upon his heroes obligations which he had not been accustomed to attach to the humble social existence of Pierre Corneille.[2]

---

[1] *La Bruyère*, " Caractères," vol. ii. p. 84.

[2] " He clothes his old heroes with all that is noble in the imagination ; and you would say that he forbids himself the use of his own property, as if he were not worthy of it." *Saint-Evremond*, " Œuvres," vol. iii. p. 246.

There is, however, one point on which he is raised by this existence above the vulgar herd—his works issued from the obscurity in which his life was spent. By his literary renown he acquired public importance ; and thenceforward, he regarded his renown as an object of duty. In his works he pays proper respect to himself ; with them were connected not only the honour of his glory, but also the dignity of his character; he would deem himself degraded if he did not acknowledge their merit with all the frankness and boldness of a champion entrusted with their defence, or if he consented to abdicate the rank in which they had placed him. "It is not your fault," he says to Scudéry, " that, from that *first rank* in which I am placed by many competent persons, I have not descended lower even than Claveret. * * * Of a truth, I should justly be reprehensible if I were incensed against you on account of a matter which has proved the accomplishment of my glory, and from which the ' Cid ' has gained this advantage, that, out of the multitude of poems which have appeared up to this time, it is the only one whose *brilliancy* has obliged envy to take up its pen." [1]

Nevertheless, even while defending himself so proudly, Corneille did not depart from the ordinary ideas and habits of his conduct, in those things which concerned him as a man, and not as a poet. He

---

[1] *Corneille,* " Réponse aux Observations de Scudéry."

evidently believed in two very distinct kinds of honour, which it appeared to him all the more ridiculous to confound together, as he made no use at all of one of them. The same man who, in the " Cid," had dilated so loftily upon the duties imposed by honour upon brave men,[1] did not think it necessary to fulfil those duties himself ; and looking at his physical courage as entirely unconcerned in the question, he thus replied to Scudéry's rhodomontades:[2] " There is no necessity for knowing how much nobler or more valiant you may be than myself, in order to judge how far superior the ' Cid ' is to the ' Amant libéral.'[3] * * I am not a fighting man ; so that, in that respect, you have nothing to fear." Corneille was no longer either a Count of Gormas, or a Don Rodrigue, but a man whose glory consisted in writing fine poetry, and not in fighting ; though bold enough to brave the resentment of a minister by defending compositions which gained him universal admiration, he would not expose himself to a sword-

---

[1] At a time when efforts were being made to abolish duelling, it was found necessary to omit as dangerous the following lines, in which the Count of Gormas replied to Don Fernand's attempts to reconcile him to Don Diègue :—

> " Les satisfactions n'appaisent point une âme ;
> Qui les reçoit n'a rien ; qui les fait se diffame ;
> Et de tous ces accords, l'effet le plus commun
> Est de déshonorer deux hommes au lieu d'un."

[2] Contained in a private letter, in which Scudéry had sent him a sort of challenge.

[3] One of Scudéry's worst comedies.

thrust, in order to establish a reputation for courage, about which no one felt any interest. He thought it marvellous that such an idea should have found its way into a literary discussion ; so he looked with equal contempt on Scudéry's challenge and his arguments, without deigning an answer to either ; and did not think himself more dishonoured by being less valiant than a practised swordsman, than he could be by refusing to appear in a character which was not his own. So strong was his conviction that the honour of Corneille did not depend upon his physical courage!

The tone, however, which these disputes assumed convinced Cardinal Richelieu of the necessity of putting a stop to them. In order to insure the triumph of the cause which he promoted, he judged it more prudent to appeal to the authority of a tribunal, than to leave the decision to the issue of a combat in which the voice of the people—which, in this case, was certainly "the voice of God"—did not seem disposed to give judgment in his favour. Silence was, therefore, imposed upon both parties, pending the decision of the Academy, which, for the second time, found itself involuntarily invested with the dangerous honours of authority.[1] In vain did it allege its well-grounded fear of making its young

---

[1] Scudéry had written to submit his case to the judgment of the Academy, and the Cardinal expressed a wish that it should pronounce upon the matter. *Pelisson,* " Histoire de l'Académie," p. 189.

existence odious by the exercise of a power which it
was not admitted to possess. The wisest of its
members said, " that it was barely tolerated, upon
the simple supposition that it claimed some authority
over the language : what would be the result if it
manifested any desire to vindicate that authority,
and undertook to exercise it over a work which had
satisfied the majority, and gained the approbation of
the people ? " [1] The Cardinal was not, however, to be
deterred from his purpose by such arguments as
these : as Pelisson says, " they appeared to him of
very little importance." But the Academy now
urged conformity to its statutes, which enacted
" that it could not judge a work without the consent
and request of the author ; " and Corneille was not
disposed to remove this obstacle. In vain did Bois-
Robert employ all the efforts of a Court friendship to
obtain the accomplishment of his master's desires.
By his residence at Court, Corneille had at least
learned those formalities by which trickery may
be frustrated. " He continually maintained," says
Pelisson, " a complimentary tone, and answered that
such an occupation was not worthy of the Academy ;
that a libel which deserved no answer was beneath
its notice ; that the consequences of giving an
opinion on the matter would be dangerous, because
it would give envy a pretext for continually

---

[1] *Pelisson,* " Histoire de l'Académie," p. 190.

appealing to their decision ; and that as soon as a fine piece had appeared on the stage, the poetasters would think themselves justified in bringing charges against its author before the members of the Academy." [1] These unanswerable reasons were urged in reply to Bois-Robert's reiterated entreaties ; and the force of these reasons, independently of all personal considerations, resisted all the insinuations of a pretended friendship. At length, it became necessary to change these insinuations into positive language, and formally to announce the wish of a minister with whom a desire was a command. Then, also, it became necessary to understand clearly and answer distinctly. After Corneille had once more repeated his usual objections, " there escaped from him," says Pelisson, " this addition : ' The gentlemen of the Academy may do as they please ; as you write that Monseigneur would be glad to have their judgment, and that it would divert his Eminence, I have nothing more to say.' " [2]

Corneille might regard these last words as a refusal,[3] but Richelieu would take them for a consent. The Academy still resisted : and authority, driven to its utmost limits, used its last resources. " Tell those

---

[1] *Pelisson*, " Histoire de l'Académie," p. 192. [2] Ibid. p. 193.

[3] See in Voltaire's edition of Corneille, vol. i. p. 159, the preface placed at the commencement of the " Cid," after the death of the Cardinal, in which he formally denies ever having "agreed on judges regarding his merit," as he would consider such a proceeding "a disgraceful blot on his reputation."

gentlemen that I desire it, and that I shall love them as they love me." These were the last words which the minister had to utter; the Academy, like Corneille, thought it had nothing more to say.

It obeyed; but the danger, nevertheless, continued. Richelieu had intended to obtain support, and not opposition, to his opinion. Angry remarks,[1] appended by him to the report of the Academy, which was always presented in fear, and received with ill-humour, testified to the irritation of his mind, which daily became more exasperated at a kind of opposition over which he felt, perhaps for the first time, that authority had no power. The report was laid before him a second time with no better success;[2] he desired that it should breathe the complaisance of submission, but he found merely the compliance of gratitude. On more than one occasion Richelieu lost his temper. " At one of the conferences which took place on this subject at the Cardinal's house, Cerisy, who had been summoned to attend, having absented himself on some pretext or another, M. Chapelain," says Pelisson, " endea-

---

[1] " At one place, where it was said that poetry would now be much less perfect than it is, but for the disputes which had arisen about the works of the most celebrated authors of the last age, such as the ' Jerusalem Delivered,' and the ' Pastor Fido,' he wrote on the margin : ' The applause and blame of the ' Cid ' lies only between the learned and the ignorant, whereas the disputes about the other two pieces occurred between men of talent.' "—*Pelisson*, " Histoire de l'Académie," p. 198.

[2] This report was rejected three times by the Cardinal; and Chapelain was appointed to prepare it for the fourth and last time.

voured, as he told me, to make excuses for M. de
Cerisy as he best could ; but he perceived at once
that that man would not be contradicted ; for he
saw him grow angry and put himself into action,
until, addressing him, he took him and held him for
some time by the button, just as you do when you
wish to speak strongly to any one and convince him
of anything." [1]   But bad temper was not sufficient ;
the Cardinal could no longer say, " I will," and the
Academy would take no hints.   Timid but perse-
vering reason at length prevailed ; and after five
months' labour, the " Sentiments of the Academy "
appeared.   " I know perfectly well," says Pelisson,
" that the Cardinal would have wished them to treat
the ' Cid ' more harshly, if they had not skilfully
given him to understand that a judge ought not to
speak as an interested party, and that, the more
passion they displayed, the less weight would be
attached to their authority." [2]

The public taste, becoming more enlightened by
the progress of reason and the contemplation of
great models, gave entire approval neither to the
censures, nor even to all the praises of the Academy.[3]
In the ideas of a literature which was in entire

---

[1] *Pelisson,* " Histoire de l'Académie," p. 202.   [2] Ibid. p. 221.

[3] As, for example, the praise bestowed upon this line :—

" Ma plus douce espérance est de perdre l'espoir,"

which it declared very fine, notwithstanding Scudéry's criticism that " it
was not far removed from balderdash." Ill-temper enlightened Scudéry's
bad taste : the bad taste of the time warped the judgment of the Academy.

conformity to the usages and decorum of society, it was impossible to learn how to appreciate the master-pieces of an art essentially popular—of an art which aimed at seeking out, from among the deepest and most independent of natural feelings, precisely those sentiments which society teaches us to restrain and conceal. Writers accustomed to discuss the merits of a sonnet, according to fixed rules, could not but feel that all these rules were thrown into confusion when applied to the most imperious movements of the human heart. Nothing in their own literature had revealed to them the truth ; and nothing in ancient authors furnished them with reliable data by which to judge of that new truth which Corneille had imparted to the portraiture of modern manners. " Corneille," said Boileau, " has invented a new kind of tragedies, unknown to Aristotle." [1] " Let us not believe," says Fontenelle, " that the truth is victorious as soon as it manifests itself ; it conquers in the end, but it requires some time to subjugate the minds of men." [2] Our minds resist the truth even after our feelings have acknowledged it ; and the reason always perplexes before it elucidates that which the heart understands at first sight. The spectators who were most affected by the beauties of the " Cid," might have been greatly

[1] *Boileau*, " Lettre à Perrault," in vol. v. p. 185 of his works.
[2] *Fontenelle*, " Vie de Corneille," in vol. iii. p. 57 of his works.

embarrassed to account for their feelings ; provided
that they had their pleasure, they consented willingly
to suppose that they had not enjoyed it in accordance
with the rules; but the Academicians, on the contrary,
had to busy themselves solely about the rules. As
members of the public they could not refrain from
admiring things which, in their quality of judges, they
were perhaps bound to condemn. Though obliged, out
of respect for propriety, to blame the first scene of the
fifth act, and to find especial fault with the line—

"Sors vainqueur d'un combat dont Chimène est le prix ; "

they could not resist the overpowering force
both of the sentiment and the expression. " This
scene," they said, " is characterized by all the
imperfections it must possess if we consider the
matter as forming an essential part of this poem ;
but, on the other hand, considering it apart and
detached from the subject, the passion which it
contains seems to us very finely pourtrayed and
admirably managed, and the expressions are worthy
of high praise." Balzac, who had retired into the
country, and took no part in the Academy's
deliberations upon the " Cid," wrote thus to Scudéry,
who had sent him a copy of his " Observations :"
" Consider, Sir, that all France sides with him (the
author of the ' Cid'), and that perhaps there is not
one of the judges whom you have agreed upon, who

has not praised that which you desire him to
condemn ; so that, even if your arguments were
unanswerable, and your adversary admitted their
force, he would still have great reason to take
glorious consolation for the loss of his cause, and to
tell you that it is far better to have delighted a
whole kingdom than to have written a regular
piece.   *   *   *   This being the case, Sir, I do not
doubt that the gentlemen of the Academy will find
themselves greatly perplexed in deciding upon your
suit, and that your reasons will influence their
minds on the one hand, and public approbation will
affect them on the other."   " The 'Cid,' " said La
Bruyère, " is one of the finest poems possible to be
written ; and the criticism of the ' Cid ' is one of the
best ever written on any subject." [1]

Independently of the formal approbation bestowed
on various parts of the work, the Academy admitted
" that even learned men must grant some indulgence
to the irregularities of a work which would not have
had the good fortune to please the community so much,
if it had not possessed uncommon beauties ;   *   *   *
and that the naturalness and vehemence of its
passions, the force and delicacy of many of its
thoughts, and that indescribable charm which mingles
with all its defects, have gained for it a high rank
among French poems of the same character."

[1] *La Bruyère*, " Caractères," vol. i. p. 113.

The "Sentiments" of the Academy were addressed to Scudéry, as his "Observations" had served as their text. Scudéry completed the absurdity of the whole affair by thanking the Academy. The Academy, however, caring little for his thanks, sent him through its Secretary an answer, the substance of which was "that its chief intention had been to hold the balance fairly, and not to turn a serious matter into a mere civility or compliment ; but that, next to this intention, its greatest care had been to express itself with moderation, and to state its reasons without wounding either party ; that it rejoiced at the justice he did it by acknowledging it to have acted justly ; and that, at some future time, it would requite his equity, and whenever it was in its power to do him a service, he should have nothing to desire from it."[1]

Scudéry perhaps affected an appearance of satisfaction ; but Corneille might reasonably think he had a right to complain, and Boileau's judgment confirmed his opinion.[2] While affecting the utmost indifference, he complained bitterly, and heaped upon the Academy those reproaches which he dared not cast upon a more exalted delinquent ; because, he said, " it has proceeded against me with so much

[1] *Pelisson*, " Histoire de l'Académie," p. 206.
[2] *Boileau*, Satire ix. 233, 234.
          " L'Académie en corps a beau le censurer,
            Le public révolté s'obstine à l'admirer."

violence, and employed so sovereign an authority to shut my mouth."[1]   But at the same time, continuing his correspondence with 'the Cardinal through Bois-Robert, Corneille received " the liberalities of His Eminence," [2] and acknowledged the wisdom of the advice given him by Bois-Robert not to prolong this affair, " considering the persons engaged in it," although his original intention had been to write an answer to the Academy, and dedicate it to the Cardinal.   " I am," he said, " rather more worldly than Heliodorus, who preferred to lose his bishopric rather than abandon his book, and I value the good graces of my master more than all the reputations upon earth." But at the same time that he held this language, he dedicated the " Cid" to the Duchess d'Aiguillon, the Cardinal's niece ; [3] and spoke of the "universal success" of the piece as having surpassed " the most ambitious hopes" of the author, and justified "the praises" with which the duchess " had honoured it."

This twofold course of procedure is very puzzling, and the mind strives vainly to gain a clear idea of the true characters of Richelieu and Corneille, in this strange contest.   We behold the " Cid " established, so to speak, in the family of its

---

[1] *Pelisson,* " Histoire de l'Académie," p. 208.

[2] His pension, which was paid him by Bois-Robert.

[3] Then Mme. de Combalet.   Voltaire assures us that, but for her, Corneille would have been disgraced.

persecutor ; we shall soon find the author himself enjoying the familiarity of that protector who had for a moment become his enemy. The dedicatory epistle of " Horace," addressed to the Cardinal, proves that Corneille read his pieces to him, and this precaution perhaps secured his approbation. The storm does not appear to have been allayed or forgotten ; it would seem never to have burst forth ; and here we must place, if we admit its truth, an incident in Corneille's life related by Fontenelle, which would prove a kindly feeling on the part of the Cardinal, by which it is not likely that he would have been actuated during the quarrel about the " Cid." " Corneille," says Fontenelle, " presented himself one day, more melancholy and thoughtful than usual, before Cardinal Richelieu, who asked him if he were working at anything. He replied that he was far from enjoying the tranquillity necessary for composition, as his head was turned upside down by love. By and bye, he came to more minute explanations, and told the Cardinal that he was passionately in love with a daughter of the Lieutenant-General of Andely, in Normandy, and that he could not obtain her in marriage from her father. The Cardinal sent orders for this obstinate father to come to Paris ; he quickly arrived in great alarm at so unexpected a summons, and returned home well satisfied at suffering no worse punishment than giving his daughter to a man who was in such high favour."[1]

It is certain that Corneille married Marie de Lampérière, daughter of the Lieutenant-General of Andely ; and it is also certain that, as Fontenelle goes on to relate, a report was spread at Paris, on the very night of his marriage, that he had died of peripneumony. Some Latin verses, written by Ménage on the occasion, give us a tolerably accurate clue to the date, as he is mentioned therein as the author of the "Cid," of "Horace," and of "Cinna."[2] So singular a circumstance would need to be supported by some less doubtful authority than that of Fontenelle, who does not even affirm it positively, although he had it, as he tells us, from one of the family ;[3] yet the very singularity of the anecdote

---

[1] *Fontenelle*, "Vie de Corneille," vol. iii. p. 122.

[2] The piece is entitled, "Petri Cornelii Epicedium," and is prefaced in these words by Ménage : "Scripseram cum falsò nunciatum Cornelium, quo die uxorem duxerat, ex peripneumoniâ decessisse." The lines which indicate the date of the occurrence are the following ;—

> " Donec Apollineo gaudebit scena cothurno
>   Ignes dicentur, pulchra Chimena, tui ;
> Quos male qui carpsit, dicam ; dolor omnia promit ;
>   Carminis Iliaci nobile carpat opus.
> Itale, testis eris ; testis qui flumina potas
>   Flava Tagi ; nec tu, docte Batave, neges ;
> Omnibus in terris per quos audita Chimena est.
>   Jamque ignes vario personat ore suos.
> Nec tu, crudelis Medea, taceberis unquam ;
>   Non Graiâ inferior, non minor Ausoniâ.
> Vos quoque tergemini, Mavortia pectora, fratres,
>   Et te, Cinna ferox, fama loquetur anus."
>   Ægidii Menagii Poemata, pp. 30—32.

At all events he is necessarily mistaken as to the date, as he refers it

will not allow us to believe that it was invented by the narrator, or that Corneille's family would have so completely forgotten the resentment of so powerful a protector as Cardinal Richelieu, unless the Cardinal himself had also forgotten it.

The lines which Corneille wrote upon the death of the Cardinal would even seem to indicate the reception of greater benefits than a mere pension, while at the same time they make us aware that the consciousness of obligation had alone imposed silence on the rancorous feelings of the poet.

> " Qu'on parle mal ou bien du fameux Cardinal,
> Ma prose ni mes vers n'en diront jamais rien :
> Il m'a fait trop de bien pour en dire du mal ;
> Il m'a fait trop de mal pour en dire du bien." [1]

It was natural enough for the poet to remember what the minister had forgotten ; and Corneille found it difficult to believe in the sincerity of a reconciliation which on his side was not complete. Before the performance of " Les Horaces," he wrote to

to Corneille's early youth : " M. Corneille," he says, " while still very young, presented himself," &c. " Cinna " appeared probably towards the end of 1639, " Horace " having come out the same year; some time must have elapsed since the performance of " Cinna ;" and Corneille could not then have been less than thirty-four years old. Perhaps Fontenelle, having only a vague impression about this event, thought it more reasonable to refer it to the period when Corneille's favour had as yet been overcast by no cloud.

[1] *Corneille,* " Œuvres," vol. x. p. 41. See, in Appendix B., a letter written to Corneille, in December 1642, by the learned Claude Sarrau, counsellor to the parliament of Paris, to request him to write a poem to the memory of the Cardinal. This letter proves that, at this period at least, Corneille's friends were far from considering the Cardinal as his enemy.

one of his friends : " Horace was condemned by the
Duumvirs, but acquitted by the people." [1]   Armed
at all points, Corneille firmly awaited the enemy, but
none appeared ; the outburst of truth had imposed
silence upon envy, and it dared not hope to renew,
with equal advantage, a warfare the ridicule attendant
upon which had been more easily borne by Richelieu
than by Scudéry. The universal cry of admiration
is all that has reached us. From that time forth,
for many years, master-pieces followed one another
in quick succession, without obstacle and almost
without interruption. We no longer have to look
for the history of the stage amidst a chaotic heap of
crude conceptions in which we vainly strive to
discover a single scintillation of genius or evidence
of improvement ; these children of darkness still
venture to show themselves for a brief period after
the dawn of day ; they may even temporarily
obtain the support of the wavering taste of a public
which is capable of admiring tinsel even after having
done homage to the splendour of pure gold ; but
such works, henceforward, leave no trace of their
existence in the history of the art, and yield to the
productions of genius all that space which they had
formerly usurped.

Until the advent of Racine, the history of the

---

[1] It is not known who was the second enemy whose opposition Corneille
feared for "Les Horaces;" contemporary documents mention him in
vague terms, as "a person of great distinction."

stage is contained in the life of Corneille ; and the biography of Corneille is wholly written in his works. Though forced for a time to stand forward in defence of the "Cid," he withdrew immediately afterwards into that personal obscurity which was most congenial to the simplicity of his manners ; and in the monuments of his genius we are alone able to trace the efforts which he made to avoid the importunate clamours of criticism, which ever lies in ambush on the path of a great man, and is constantly on the watch to reveal his slightest errors or mistakes.

"Au "Cid" persécuté "Cinna" doit sa naissance,"[1]

and already, in "Horace," Corneille, abandoning that imitation for which he had been so virulently assailed,[2] goes forward trusting to his own powers, and confident of his own resources. In the "Cid," great scandal had been occasioned by the triumph of love—a triumph so long resisted, and so imperfectly achieved ; in "Horace," love will be punished for its impotent rebellion against the most cruel laws of honour ; in "Cinna," as if in expiation of Chimène's weakness, all other considerations are sacrificed to the implacable duty of avenging a father ; and finally, in "Polyeucte," duty triumphs in all its loveliness and purity, and the sacrifices of Polyeucte, of Pauline, and of Sévère, do not cost them a single virtue. At

[1] *Boileau,* "Épître à Racine."
[2] See the various pamphlets against the "Cid."

the same time, the circle of Corneille's ideas becomes enlarged ; his style reaches an elevation commensurate with the loftiness of his thoughts, and becomes more chaste, perhaps without any care on his part ; his expressions increase in correctness and precision under the influence of clearer ideas and more energetic feelings ; and his genius, henceforth in possession of all its resources, advances easily and tranquilly in the midst of the highest conceptions.

Like the " Cid," " Polyeucte " was marked by beauties of a character previously unknown, and well calculated to astound the regularity of those supreme tribunals of good taste and *bon ton*, which, with the code of proprieties in their hand, gave the law to the passions and emotions of the soul. It seemed as though Christian ideas could not, with any decency, be introduced upon a stage of which Paganism had taken such complete possession that no one dared to utter the name of God except in the plural number. Voiture, who was appointed to convey to Corneille the opinion of the Hotel de Rambouillet, at which he had read his piece, told him that " its Christianity had especially given extreme offence." [1] A well-educated man, brutally interrupting a sacrifice at which the governor of the province and the favourite of the Emperor were present, could not fail to be thought very much at variance with polite usage, at

[1] *Fontenelle,* " Vie de Corneille," p. 103.

the Hotel de Rambouillet, and Bishop Godeau
condemned the fury of Polyeucte, less, probably,
because he was a Bishop than in his character
of "a man of honour"[1] who was aware of the
importance of the duty of behaving like the rest of
the world. Alarmed by this disapprobation, Corneille
wished to withdraw his piece, and only consented to
its performance on the entreaty of one of the actors,
" who did not play in it," says Fontenelle, " because
he was so bad a performer."[2]

"Pompée" followed "Polyeucte," and the "Menteur"
followed " Pompée." Spanish literature shared with
Corneille the honour of the first French tragedy and
comedy.[3] Genius is evidently as necessary for
selection and imitation as for invention; for although
Spanish literature was open to all the wits of the age,
Corneille alone was able to derive from it the " Cid "
and the " Menteur." It is not by the arrangement
of its plot, or by the truth of its sentiments, that the
" Menteur " is distinguished from Corneille's earlier
comedies. In many of these latter, the rules are as

---

[1] A *man of honour* (*honnête homme*) was then synonymous with a *man of
the world*. Saint-Evremond used to say : "To be a man of honour is
incompatible with good conduct."

[2] This actor was, nevertheless, a man of ability. His name was Hauteroche,
and he had written several plays ; viz., "Crispin Médecin," the "Esprit
Follet," the "Cocher Supposé," and others.

[3] The "Menteur" is an imitation of a Spanish comedy called "La
Sospechosa Verdad " (the "Suspected Truth"), ascribed by some to Lope
de Vega, by others to Pedro de Roxas, and by others to Don Juan
d'Alarcon.

carefully observed ; unity of place is more so in the
" Place Royale," and unity of time in the " Suivante ;"
but the dramatic effect of the " Menteur " arises
from the portraiture of a real, well-known character,
and Corneille once more taught the public to enjoy
the charms of truth. Before the time of Hardy,
comedy had been gay, but licentious ; after Hardy,
it was licentious and melancholy : and Corneille, by
rendering it more pure, may perhaps have made it
somewhat more sober. Deprived of the unfailing
resource of the coarse witticisms of valets and the
scandalous adventures of their masters, comedy had
sought its means of effect in the whimsical exaggeration of ridiculous characters ; and Corneille, who, in
the " Suivante," had depicted, with much wit and
nicety, the troubles of a shameful coward, afterwards
condescended, in obedience to the taste of his times,
to use the extravagant gibberish which constituted
the humour of the " Matamore." Desmarets, though
carefully preserving this character in his comedy of
the " Visionnaires," had connected with it a host of
idiots of the same description,[1] and their vagaries,
by their allusions to the current jokes of the day,
gained his piece the name of the " inimitable
comedy." It was thought that Desmarets had
disfigured these characters by falling into error as to

---

[1] A Philidan, who fancies himself in love ; a Phalante, who imagines
himself to be rich ; a Melitre, in love with Alexander the Great ; and so on.

the kind of comedy that might be derived from them. It was felt, however, that the truly comic consisted in this, and Corneille was the first to carry the idea into action.

After this attempt, which probably arose from a desire felt by Corneille to vanquish his rivals in a style of composition in which he had hitherto been only their equal, tragedy resumed possession of his genius, which had been, so to speak, formed by it and for its service ; and, with the exception of the sequel to the " Menteur,"—a piece which does not occupy a prominent position, either in the progress or decay of Corneille's dramatic life—we can discover, in his works, no beauty which does not belong to that style in which he achieved his greatest glory.[1] That glory had now arrived at its climax. "Rodogune" and "Heraclius"[2] still maintained it ; but

---

[1] " Don Sanche " is entirely in the heroic style.

[2] It is well known that the subject of this piece is the same as that of Calderon's drama, entitled, " En Esta Vida todo es Verdad, y todo Mentiza," (" In this life all is truth and all falsehood,") which was performed in Spain at a time very different from that at which " Héraclius " was performed in France. There has been much discussion as to whether Corneille or Calderon were the imitator ; but the priority must be ascribed to Calderon, according to all the probabilities, including even the absurdity of his piece, which will not allow us to suppose that he had a rational model beneath his eyes. It is easy to understand why Corneille, who is so exact in such matters, does not speak of his borrowings in this case, when we consider that he has merely adopted the idea of making Heraclius the son of Maurice, and having him brought up with a son of Phocas, so that the latter cannot distinguish one from the other; he has also copied a few lines which result from this position : in other respects there is not the slightest resemblance in the plot, or in the events of the proscenium which Corneille has taken no pains to render in agreement with history. It

between these two pieces, "Théodore" appears, and
we are thunderstruck by so great a fall after so
sudden and prodigious an elevation. His position
will, however, be retrieved by two vigorous productions; after "Andromède," in favour of which
I shall not count the success which it obtained by
the novelty of its style and the marvels of its
machinery,[1] came "Don Sanche d'Aragon," and
notwithstanding that "refusal of an illustrious
suffrage,"[2] which, in Corneille's opinion, was fatal to

might be supposed that Corneille knew nothing of Calderon's piece, except
from some extract sent into France at the time of the performance, from
which he might have derived the idea of the leading feature of the plot,
and a few distinctive lines of the dialogue. In support of this supposition,
it is said that Calderon's piece was not printed until after 1645, the time of
the performance of "Heraclius." See p. 35 of the advertisement to the
edition of Corneille's works published in 1758.

[1] This "ravishing piece," to use the expressions of the newspapers of the
time (see the "Gazette de France" for 1650), was, nevertheless, not the
first French drama, into which music and machinery were introduced,
which had been performed on the Parisian stage. Hardy had introduced
choruses into some of his tragedies, and machinery into his pastorals, and
it appears that all these accessories were combined in the "Mariage
d'Orphée et d'Eurydice, ou la grande Journée des Machines," performed
in 1640, ten years before the representation of "Andromède." Besides the
difference in merit between the two pieces (although Corneille's was bad
enough), there was certainly a great difference between the expense
incurred, for the performance of "Orphée," by the comedians of the
Marais and the Hotel de Bourgogne, and that incurred by the Court, for
whom "Andromède" had been composed, and in whose presence it was
first performed. Particular notice was taken of a great star of Venus, in
which that goddess descended upon the stage, and the brilliancy of which
illuminated the entire theatre. It appears that plays of this kind gave
great alarm at first to the devout; but their scruples were so very soon
dissipated that, as the "Gazette de France" informs us, "the most
considerable persons of this city no sooner saw the field opened to so
innocent a diversion, than there were few, of all conditions, both ecclesiastical and secular, who did not desire to enjoy it."

[2] The approbation of the Great Condé. This piece, as it appears,

the success of this drama, we feel again, when reading it, some of those proud emotions which are kindled in the soul by the magnificent poetry of the " Cid." [1]   " Nicomède," more imposing and more original, " is, perhaps," says Voltaire, " one of the strongest proofs of Corneille's genius." Never, indeed, has Corneille thrown so sustained and pathetic an interest into the mere portraiture of a great character, without any aid from external circumstances ; and never has he so strikingly manifested the power of a spring of action which he has better employed elsewhere. The failure of " Pertharite " was the first blow given to that respect with which the public were inspired by the great name

succeeded at first ; and Corneille attributes the coolness which followed its early success to the distaste which the prince manifested to " Don Sanche." " Corneille should have remembered," says Voltaire, " that the distaste and criticisms of Cardinal Richelieu, a man of more weight in literature than the great Condé, had not been able to injure the ' Cid.' " The failure of " Don Sanche " must, probably, be ascribed to its great deficiency in interest, which was at first unperceived through the splendour of the principal personage of the drama. The same cause was afterwards injurious to the success of " Nicomède."

[1] Although " Don Sanche " is nothing more than a heroic comedy, the beauties which are discernible in it, though its composition is cold and its plot undignified, are not unworthy of tragedy, at least of that chivalrous tragedy, which, being generally less imposing than the other kind in the magnitude of the interests involved, is sustained only by the loftiness of its characters. Carlos, the hero of the piece, loves the queen and is beloved by her ; but his birth does not permit him to aspire to her hand. The queen is anxious that he should at least decide her fate, and choose for her between three suitors who have asked her in marriage. She gives him the ring which is to be the mark of her choice. Carlos, despising the rage of the suitors, who are indignant at the power entrusted to him, declares that he will relinquish the ring in favour only of the most worthy :—

" Et je le garde.   *   *   *   À qui, Carlos ?—À mon vainqueur."

of Corneille, and which had even saved " Théodore "
from failure.[1] But even Corneille no longer defended
himself; in " Pertharite," no beauty concealed the
defects of an incomplete and somewhat factitious
system, the riches of which Corneille alone had
been able to utilise and parade with sufficient
magnificence to disguise its imperfections.

We have seen Corneille raise himself, so to speak,
by a single bound to that proud elevation at which he
towered above his age ; we behold him falling back
again below the standard of taste and enlightenment
for which his age was indebted to his labours and
example.   Now that his mission is finished, and he has
impressed upon the drama a movement with which he
is no longer able to keep pace, I wish to discover and
describe with precision the true character of this
movement, communicated by a man of genius to
men of genius as powerful as his own ; and the
peculiar nature of that genius, which, after having
raised its art and its audience to an equal elevation,
was unable to keep its place in the region to which
it had carried them.   How came it that Corneille,
the father of our drama, was not also its lawgiver ?
What were the causes which, after having made

---

[1] " Théodore " was not an entire failure. " The performance of this
tragedy was not very successful," says Corneille, in his Examination of
" Théodore ; " but when speaking of " Pertharite," he thus writes :—" The
success of this tragedy was so unfortunate that, to spare myself the pain
of remembering it, I shall say almost nothing about it."   See his
Examination of " Pertharite."

him so great, prevented him from becoming greater still ?

If Corneille accomplished the revolution which re-generated our drama, or rather, if he exercised that creative action which liberated our drama from its primitive chaos, it was because he introduced into his writings truth, which was then banished from all poetical compositions. That energy, that imposing majesty, those sublime soarings of genius, all those qualities which gained Corneille the title of " The Great," are personal merits which have immortalised the name of the poet, without preserving after him any dominant influence over dramatic art. Tragedy might be beautiful otherwise than as Corneille con-ceived it, and Corneille has remained great without preventing other great men from taking a place beside him. But tragedy could gain life only by repairing to that fountain of truth which Corneille was the first to discover. Before his appearance every day seemed to remove the public and the poets farther from it ; and every day buried the treasures of the human heart more deeply beneath the fantastic inventions of false wit and a disordered imagination. Corneille was the first to reveal these treasures to dramatic art, and to teach it how to use them. On this ground he is rightfully regarded as the father, and the " Cid " as the origin, of French tragedy.

But was Corneille's reason, though sufficiently strong to pierce through the dark clouds of error, strong enough to dissipate them entirely ?   Sure of always overcoming the enemy whom he attacked, was he always sufficiently enlightened to recognise his real enemy ? and did not his character too frequently render him subservient to an age over which his genius had made him so superior ?

It is impossible to imagine what Corneille's genius would have become, and to divine either the extraordinary beauties which it might have unfolded, or the flights of which it might have been guilty, if he had boldly abandoned himself to his own guidance.   As regarded his own personal knowledge, Corneille was in almost the same position as Shakspeare and Calderon ; but his age and country were more civilised than theirs, and criticism availed itself, for the instruction of the poet, of all the acquirements of his age and country. Corneille feared and braved criticism, and provoked it by his defiance ;   he would allow none of its censures, but he did all he could to avoid them. Taking warning by a first attack, he no longer ventured to hazard, for fear of Scudéry, all that France would probably have applauded.   Incapable of yielding to his adversaries, and angry at being obliged to combat them, he withdrew from the path in which he was likely to meet with them ; and though this perhaps involuntary prudence saved him from some dangerous quicksands, it undoubtedly deprived him of some precious discoveries. The success of the " Cid " did not efface, in his mind, the censure of the Academy ; in that drama, he had allowed himself to depict, with irresistible truth, the transports of passion ; but when he found Chimène's love so severely condemned, Corneille, doubtless alarmed at what he might find in the weakness of the heart, looked in future only to its strength ; he sought for the resisting element in man, and not for the yielding element, and thus became acquainted with only the half of man. And as admiration is the feeling chiefly excited by heroic resistance, it was to admiration that the dramatic genius of Corneille principally addressed itself.

Boileau did not consider admiration to be one of the tragic passions. " Corneille," he says, " has not aimed, like the poets of ancient tragedy, at moving his audience to pity or terror, but at exciting in their souls, by the sublimity of his ideas and the beauty of his sentiments, a certain admiration which many persons, and young persons especially, frequently like far better than real tragic passions." [1] Like Boileau, Voltaire and his school are of opinion that admiration is a cold feeling, very unsuited to dramatic effect. I reject this idea, not only because it deprives the drama of one of its noblest springs

---

[1] *Boileau,* " Lettre à Perrault sur les anciens et les modernes."

of action, but because it attacks the true principles of art.

It is one of the errors of our literary metaphysics to seek the source of the pleasure which we derive from the drama, and particularly from tragedy, in our own personal recollections, and in a return upon ourselves and our individual affections. According to this principle, it has been thought that the feelings most familiar to man, those which his position enables him most frequently to experience, are also those which it is most suitable to present to his attention. This principle received great confirmation from the authority of Boileau, when, in spite of all that the ancients have written, and in reliance upon an experience which was not his own, he preferred love to all other tragic passions ; [1] this principle was sustained by the brilliant genius of Voltaire and the pathetic effects which he educed from the passions most familiar to the human heart ; this same principle, in fine, other writers, led astray by the opinion of that great man, and, as they believed, by his example also, have carried out to consequences which Voltaire himself disavowed. They have imagined that heroic tragedy, the adventures of kings and princes, the great vicissitudes of fortune, being too far remote from us and the dangers to which we may be exposed,

[1] "De cette passion la sensible peinture,
Est pour aller au cœur la route la plus sûre."

can affect us only slightly ; and they have invented
the tragedy of common life, in which every man may
recognise his own household and its accessories, with
what happened to him on the previous day, and what
will happen to him on the morrow, and may thus
tremble, on his own account, at the dangers incurred
by persons who bear so striking a resemblance to
himself. If the principle were just, these writers
would be right ; and if the emotion which most
thoroughly overcomes us be the greatest pleasure that
the stage can afford, they have certainly discovered,
as regards many persons, the secret by which this
pleasure may be supplied.

But there is another source of pleasure to which
the arts should repair ; a pleasure the more desirable,
because it is more complete and prolonged, because
it develops and perfects the faculty which it
calls into play, whereas violent emotions deaden and
obliterate it. Our faculties have been given to us for
our use ; and the pleasure connected with the exercise of each one of them renders its use agreeable
to us, and holds them all in readiness to subserve our
various wants. As these wants are seldom sufficient to
give them full employment, and to develop all their
energy, these same faculties incessantly demand of us
suitable opportunities for bringing them into action ;
and, in the repose in which they are left by the
tranquillity of our life, they seek to exercise them-

selves upon objects in conformity to their nature, although foreign to the immediately useful end which it is not always incumbent upon them to attain. Thus the mind, not finding means for constant employment in attention to our own interests, yields itself to purely speculative combinations, which have no connection with our individual position ; and this exercise of the soul, being devoid of all reference to ourselves, is one of the liveliest pleasures that man can experience. With the emotions produced by our personal interests are mingled incitements of desire, fear, and hope, destined to stimulate us to action, which would become intolerable in a position with which we had nothing to do, and would absolutely destroy that lively but tranquil pleasure which we hope to find in the enjoyment of the arts. Far, therefore, from bringing us back to our own personal interests and recollections, and to our own individual position, the effect of the drama ought to be to divert our minds entirely therefrom ; far from concentrating our attention upon the narrow circle of our real existence, it should, on the contrary, make us lose sight of it in order to transport us into our possible existence, and occupy us not with what really occurs to us, but with what we may be—not with the particular circumstances which have called our faculties into operation, but with those faculties themselves, as they may be displayed when everything stimulates, and nothing checks, their development. Our enjoyment is then derived from ourselves, and we revel in the exalted feeling of our existence, of that state in which, as Mme. de Lafayette used to say, " to be happy, it is only necessary to exist ; " and this happiness is so thoroughly the result of the movement imparted to our soul, independently of the object by which it is occasioned, that any idea of reality, connected with that object, would destroy our pleasure, and change it into an entirely different feeling. If the illusion could carry us so far away as to make us believe that we really saw, in Hippolyte, that which the drama presents to us as a fiction, namely, a virtuous young man, the victim of a most infamous calumny, could we take delight in such a spectacle ? Would it not inspire us, on the contrary, with the bitterest emotion and the most cruel anguish ? Should we take pleasure in beholding Cleopatra actually planning, in our presence, the death of her two sons ? Horror-stricken, we should turn away our eyes from such a monster. When the haughty Nicomède, bound in chains by cowards, and delivered over to that Flaminius whom he has degraded in our eyes by his contempt, is sent captive to Rome, which he had so boldly defied,—when, rising superior to this humiliating reverse of fortune, he exclaims :—

" J'irai, j'irai, Seigneur, vous le voulez ainsi ;
Et j'y serai plus roi que vous n'êtes ici,"

if we could believe in the truth of what the poet represents to us, would not the pleasure which is occasioned us by the magnanimity of the hero be stifled, or at least diminished, by the anger which we should feel at his unworthy position ? But we believe nothing ; we content ourselves with feeling, without mingling anything with that impression which is sufficient to absorb our whole soul, and repel all extraneous ideas.

Just as, in bodily exercises, any insignificant object that may be presented to our aim, concentrates our entire attention upon the mere development of our physical powers ; so, in these mental games, which are solely intended to promote the exercise of our moral faculties, we engage with that vigorous satisfaction which springs from greater energy of existence. If a little pain be mingled with this satisfaction, the evil of suffering is then, nevertheless, no more contained in the movement which animates us, than the pleasure of feeling ; and this evil does not resume its true nature unless too acute a pain warn us of the presence of an enemy—unless an innocent conflict be changed into a dangerous combat, and disturb us with a consciousness of our weakness, instead of occupying us with the employment of our strength.

It is not, therefore, the conformity of the scene to our own particular destiny and personal feelings, which constitutes the true merit of tragedy ; it consists far more in its conformity to human destiny in general, and to our intellectual and sensible nature —in its agreement, not with the feelings with which we are best acquainted, but with those which we are most capable of experiencing. Tragedy may demand of man all that his heart contains ; it may excite tears of pity, the shudder of terror, the impetuosity of courage, the emotions of love, indignation against vice, maternal affection, filial piety ; all that has been given us, for our preservation or our morality, bears to dramatic art the tribute of that superabundant force which, during the course of a tranquil life, we so seldom find opportunity completely to employ.

Among these feelings there is one which is the perfection of our nature, the last degree of soul enjoyment, of an enjoyment which is the delightful proof of its noble origin and its glorious destiny. This feeling is admiration, the sentiment of the beautiful, the love of all that is great, enthusiasm for all that is virtuous ; it awakens us to emotion at the aspect of a master-piece, excites us at the narrative of a noble action, and intoxicates us with the mere idea of a virtue which is eternally separated from us by an interval of three thousand years. Will such a feeling allow the drama to be cold, and the spectator to be passionless ?   Will that be too calm a movement for tragedy which, hurrying the whole soul beyond itself, snatching it, so to speak, from earth and the bonds which chain it thereto, transports it, as with a single bound, to the loftiest regions within reach of its attainment ? Put the question to any man who has just experienced this sublime feeling, to any man who has just heard the *Qu'il mourût !* of old Horace thundered forth in all its energy. " We are," says Raymond de Saint-Marc, " at once surprised and enchanted to find ourselves so brave ; and it is certain that, if we were placed in the position of the elder Horace, and found ourselves animated for a moment by the same greatness of soul as inspired him, we could not prevent ourselves from feeling tacitly proud of a courage which we have not had the happiness to possess before." No ! we are not surprised ; we are not proud ; we feel no return upon ourselves and our habitual existence ; we live the new life into which the poet has transported us ; but this life becomes our own, and we feel it grow more animated because it has found within us faculties capable of more powerful development. It is not the grandeur or the virtue of old Horace which elevates us ; it is our own grandeur, our own virtue ; it is that feeling which, in real life, finding itself too often crushed beneath the weight of interest or of circumstances, here plays at will in the open fields of the imagination, and attains, without effort, that exaltation which is the last degree of happiness placed within our power to experience. Intoxicated with delight, we then bring the emotion which animates us to bear upon all surrounding objects ; and there is not perhaps a single man capable of fully appreciating the sublime beauties of Corneille, who has not felt this on witnessing the performance of his dramas. At the height to which he raises us, no low idea is able to reach us, no expression appears trivial in our eyes ; transported by the enthusiasm of Polyeucte even to an idea of the presence of God, imbued with a sense of His greatness and of the danger of His wrath, we are conscious of no impropriety in the line :—

" Tout beau, Pauline ; il entend vos paroles."

This expression, which would be undignified even in a familiar conversation, loses its vulgarity in a sublime dialogue ; divested of its personal character, it is nothing more than the symbol of an idea which kindles our emotion—the strong and natural expression of a deep feeling ; and so long as it conveys this powerfully to us, all other considerations are set aside. After the admirable scene between Horace and Curiace when about to engage in deadly conflict, after that simple development of the highest sentiments that can be inspired by the most extraordinary position, Camille and

Sabine stop the two warriors without shaking their resolution ; they afflict them by their powerless effort, and only delay a scene which they cannot prevent. Upon this, old Horace comes up, and exclaims :—

> " Qu'est ceci, mes enfants ? écoutez-vous vos flammes ?
> Et perdez-vous encor le temps avec des femmes ? "

We know that a combat is in prospect, that it must take place ; we almost feel conscious of the necessity of coming at once to this inevitable event ; and it is old Horace who, with the imposing authority and courageous reason of a father, steps in to determine the fatal moment ; and this moment is invested with such grandeur, that, in whatever manner he may announce its advent, it cannot detract from its inherent greatness.

But this emotion, excited in our breasts by beauties of so lofty a nature, sometimes disguises real defects which, after a calmer examination, it is impossible not to perceive. Nicomède makes us tolerate Prusias, and even the boastfulness of that singular personage is merged in the lofty feelings awakened in us by his courage. In the midst of the heat of admiration maintained in our souls by Polyeucte, Sévère, and Pauline, the baseness of Felix is only a slight cloud which disappears before it can cast a chill over us ; and all the declamations of Cornélie could not suddenly arrest the movement excited by the beauty of her grief, and by that remarkable entrance :

" César, prends garde à toi ! "

If the personage ceases to sustain our interest, our affection hastens to defend the poet against our judgment : part of the admiration with which we are inspired by the heroes of Corneille, has fastened upon Corneille himself ; his name alone moves us by powerful recollections ; and a sort of passion surrounds him with a veil of respect and love which reason itself feels great repugnance to pierce. This passion long warred in his favour against the glory of Racine ; it seemed as though men feared to divert their minds from that kind of impressions with which Corneille had filled their souls ; and the long injustice of his partisans, who felt wounded because a new enjoyment had ventured to disturb " those old admirations " in which they loved to indulge, has proved that admiration is one of those feelings which men consent least willingly to abandon even in the smallest degree.

It is also the feeling which occasions least weariness ; as we receive it without effort, we experience it without fatigue ; a prolonged succession of pathetic scenes will make us feel the necessity of repose far sooner than a series of lofty pictures, each of which, by raising our soul to a higher elevation, renders us more worthy of that which is to follow. But actions

capable of exciting our admiration are, by their very
nature, ill adapted to furnish very lengthy dramatic
scenes ; they usually consist in the triumph of power
over the obstacles which oppose personal interest,
passions, or inclinations, in the performance of an
important duty, or the accomplishment of a great
design. Now, power gives a single blow, and overthrows its enemy ; the resistance of this enemy can
alone produce the movement necessary to the duration
of the action. More conflicts of passion, and a little
more weakness, would have rendered Corneille's
heroes more constantly true and dramatic ; even
their virtue, which may often be regarded as the principal personage in the piece, would have interested
us more, if, though equally able to conquer, it had
been attacked by more potent foes, and had visibly
incurred greater dangers. All the vigour of his
noble genius was requisite to discover a sufficient
source of interest in those singular characters which
he alone could create and sustain ; he alone has
succeeded in awakening our uncertainty and curiosity
by their very inflexibility, which, as it is announced
at the outset, does not permit them to yield to the
slightest weakness, and multiplies successively around
them embarrassments which ceaselessly necessitate
greater and more extraordinary efforts. If we were
less convinced of Emilie's firmness, we should feel
less alarmed on her account, at the resolution of

Cinna to die if she will not permit him to break up the conspiracy. In such a struggle, an ordinary character should succumb, and it only remains to be seen whether it will sacrifice its love or its vengeance; but we well know that Emilie will renounce neither the one nor the other. What course, then, will she pursue? She hesitates; not as to her choice, but as to her means; what shall it be? What but this :—

> " *   *   *   *   Qu'il achève et dégage sa foi,
>   Et qu'il choisisse après de la mort ou de moi."

In order to attain to this invincible power, which will make all around it bend to its influence, a man must absolutely have separated himself from all that otherwise enters into the composition of human nature; he must have completely ceased to think of all that, in real life, occurs to alter the forms of that ideal grandeur of which the imagination can conceive no possibility except when, isolating it, so to speak, from all the other affections, it forgets that which renders its realisation so difficult and so infrequent. The imagination of Corneille had no difficulty in lending itself to this isolation; the loftiness of his inventions was sustained by his inexperience in the common affairs of life; as he introduced into his own ordinary actions none of those ideas which he employed in the creation of his heroes, so in the conception of his heroes he

introduced none of the ideas of which he made use
in ordinary life. He did not place Corneille himself in their position : the observation of nature
did not occupy his attention ; a happy inspiration frequently led him to divine it ; but his
unassisted imagination, gathering together outlines
of a far more simple character, composed for
him a sort of abstract model of a single quality, a
being without parts, if I may be allowed the
expression, capable of being set in motion by
a single impulse, and of proceeding in a single
direction.

Thus had he formed for himself an absolute idea
of force of soul, whether it be exerted for crime or
virtue, of patriotism and even of baseness, which, in
the Felix of "Polyeucte," and the Valens of
"Théodore," is no more embarrassed by scruples
of honour than the courage of Nicomède is checked
by a prudential reflection, or the patriotism of
Horace influenced by a movement of sensibility.
Thus, also, in another kind of composition, the great
things of the world present themselves to Corneille
under an abstract form, which he does not venture to analyse, and give to the man who possesses
them, a separate existence, with which the existence which he shares in common with the rest of
mankind has nothing whatever to do. Corneille
has formed all his characters in conformity with

the principle expressed in the following lines from
" Nicomède ":—

PRUSIAS.

"Je veux mettre d'accord l'amour et la nature,
Être père et mari dans cette conjoncture.

NICOMÈDE.

Seigneur, voulez-vous bien vous en fier à moi ?
Ne soyez l'un ni l'autre.

PRUSIAS.

Et que dois-je être ?

NICOMÈDE.

Roi.
Reprenez hautement ce noble caractère ;
Un véritable roi n'est ni mari ni père,
Il regarde son trône, et rien de plus. Régnez."

Corneille's kings, with the exception of Prusias, do
nothing but reign, are incapable of anything that is
not directly connected with their royal office, and
seem to be born for no other purpose than royalty :—

" Celles de ma naissance ont horreur des bassesses ;
Leur sang tout généreux craint les molles adresses,"

says Rodogune. When Charmion, in " La Mort de
Pompée," says to Cleopatra :

" L'amour certes sur vous a bien peu de puissance,"

she answers at once—

" Les princes ont cela de leur haute naissance."

At the height at which the poet considers princes, he
is able to distinguish them only by the splendour

which surrounds them ; he confounds this splendour
with their nature ; and without supposing them to
possess any other than that which belongs to their
rank, he goes so far as to regulate the virtues
according to the order of ranks, and to regard them
as attributes which a man assumes, together with
the costume of a new position in society. Rodelinde,
in " Pertharite," founds some very serious reasoning
upon the fact that—

> " Autre est l'âme d'un comte, autre est celle d'un roi."

The plot of " Agésilas " turns upon the whim of
Aglatide, who wishes to marry a king instead of a
sovereign prince who is not a king ; and when we
find Attila saying to the monarchs whom he is proud
to hold beneath his yoke,

> "Et vous, rois, suivez-moi ; "

we can hardly suppress a smile at this child's play of
the imagination of a great man.

Generally speaking, this imagination is so exclusively struck by the character or special position
which occupies its notice, that it does not allow
Corneille to pay sufficient attention to those ideas
which, by their natural connection with that position
or character, would be necessary to render its
delineation complete and faithful. Hence arises the
singularity of certain subjects which he selected
without the slightest solicitude about the odious or

ridiculous aspect under which they may appear. Without depicting to himself any of the ideas associated with the strange subject of " Théodore," he beheld and represented that virgin martyr led into an infamous place to be handed over to the populace and the soldiery ; and in his examination of this drama, he expresses some astonishment at that severity which would not tolerate, upon the stage, " a story which constitutes the chief ornament of the second book of the ' Virgins ' of Saint Ambrose. What would have been said," he adds, " if, like that great doctor of the Church, I had represented that virgin in the infamous place, if I had described the various agitations of her soul while there, and if I had depicted the uneasiness which she felt when she first beheld the entrance of Didyme ? " If Corneille had had the least suspicion of the feelings awakened by these words, he would have abandoned the idea of describing a situation, the dishonour of which is its slightest punishment ; but he saw in it merely the general idea of dishonour, stripped of all the revolting ideas which accompany such a kind of infamy ; and his Théodore, as if she were nothing but conscience, and were threatened only with the misfortune of committing a bad action, declares, with the utmost tranquillity, that—

> " Dieu tout juste et tout bon, qui lit dans nos pensées,
> N'impute pas de crime aux actions forcées."

She is equally resigned to the thought of devoting—

"Son corps à l'infamie, et sa main à l'encens,"

provided that she be able to retain

" *   *   *   D'une âme résolue,
A l'époux sans macule une épouse impollue."

Neither the poet nor the virgin seem to have the slightest notion that a modest and chaste girl has, in such a case, something more to think of than the state of her soul in the eyes of God, and of her honour in the eyes of men.

Thus it is that Corneille could never describe a mixed feeling, composed of two opposite feelings, without leaning too much sometimes on one side, and sometimes on the other. In the early acts Cinna execrates Augustus, and in the latter he adores him.[1] At first, the poet saw only his hatred, now he sees only his affection ; each of these feelings, taken separately, is entire and absolute, as though they were never intended to co-exist in the same heart, and consequently to have some weak point at which it would be possible to pass from one to the other. Pauline, when her father proposed to her to see Sévère once more, exclaimed :

"Moi ! moi ! que je revoie un si puissant vainqueur,
Et m'expose à des yeux qui me percent le cœur ! "

---

[1] " Vous me faites haïr ce que mon âme adore."
" Cinna," act iii. scene 4.

This is indeed the cry of love in all its ardour—the affright of a heart torn with its wounds, and which has gained over its weakness only the advantage of learning to fear it. We do not perceive that Pauline's fondness for her husband has as yet succeeded in allaying her fears ; and yet, when the danger of Polyeucte stimulates her to employ all means to save him, no expression of love is too strong for her to use, and she exclaims :

" Ne désespère pas une âme qui t'adore."

In the same manner, Chimène demands of the King, with excessive vehemence, the death of that same Rodrigue upon whom, in the next scene, she will lavish the strongest protestations of love ; and although " Polyeucte " and the " Cid " are the pieces in which Corneille has most ably mingled the various affections of the heart, it is very clear that in the division which he makes between love and duty, when he sets himself to delineate one of these feelings, he cannot help falling into too complete forgetfulness of the other.

This tendency is even more strikingly manifested in a poem which Corneille wrote on the Conquest of Holland. While busied in celebrating the victories of Louis XIV. and the success attendant upon his arms, he suddenly turns his thoughts to the conquered nation, the weakness of their defence, the

motives which must have animated them, and the
cowardice which led them to prove traitors to
themselves ; and, in a transport of Dutch republican
feeling, he exclaims :—

> " Misérables ! quels lieux cacheront vos misères,
>   Où vous ne trouviez pas les ombres de vos pères,
>   Qui, morts pour la patrie et pour la liberté,
>   Feront un long reproche à votre lâcheté ?
>   Cette noble valeur autrefois si connue,
>   Cette digne fierté, qu'est-elle devenue ?
>   Quand, sur terre et sur mer, vos combats obstinés
>   Brisoient les rudes fers à vos mains destinés,
>   Quand vos braves Nassau, quand Guillaume et Maurice,
>   Quand Henri vous guidoient dans cette illustre lice,
>   Quand du sceptre Danois vous paroissiez l'appui,
>   N'aviez-vous que les cœurs, que les bras d'aujourd'hui ? "

Corneille seems to have forgotten that, not long
before, in an address to Louis XIV., in which he
spoke of resistance as a crime, he had said of these
same Hollanders :—

> " C'est ce jaloux ingrat, cet insolent Batave,
>   Qui te doit ce qu'il est, et hautement te brave ; "

and exhorted the King to avenge upon them

> " L'honneur du sceptre et les droits de la foi,"

with as much energy as he now expresses his
indignation at their not having better defended their
" liberty and fatherland."

To the same cause also must be ascribed the
variableness of Corneille's maxims, though they are
always expressed with the most absolute confidence ;
and in this way we must explain how it is that his

morality is sometimes so severe and sometimes so lax—that he sometimes enunciates principles of the sternest republicanism,[1] and sometimes of the most servile obedience.[2] The fact is, that whether Corneille be contemplating the republican or the subject of a king—the hero or the politician—he abandons himself without reserve to the system, the position, or the character which he is describing, and carefully avoids all reference to general ideas that might come into conflict with the particular ideas which he is desirous of bringing upon the stage, and which vary according to the personages of the drama. This unreserved adoption of a special principle, changing with the circumstances of the piece, gained Corneille credit for great skill in representing the local colour and genius of different peoples and states; whilst this merit was denied to Racine, whose descriptions, being of a more general nature, seem too familiar to our eyes to

See all the speeches of Emilie in the fourth scene of the third act of "Cinna."

Horace asserts that when a king declares his subject to be guilty—

"C'est crime qu'envers lui se vouloir excuser.
Notre sang est son bien, il en peut disposer;
Et c'est à nous de croire, alors qu'il en dispose,
Qu'il ne s'en prive point sans une juste cause."

Livie says to Emilie, when speaking of the monarch:—

"Nous lui devons nos biens, nos jours sont en sa main."

And that same Emilie, who was a moment before so stanch a republican, expresses her entire concurrence in this sentiment, and says :—

"Aussi, dans le discours que vous venez d'entendre,
Je parlois pour l'aigrir, et non pour me défendre."

belong, by any possibility, to other times than our own. Racine's heroes were recognised at once, and claimed as Frenchmen ; but the singular physiognomy of Corneille's heroes enabled them to pass easily for Greeks or Romans. " Being once," says Segrais, " near Corneille, on the stage, at a performance of ' Bajazet,' he said to me : ' I should not venture to say so to others than yourself, because it would be said that I spoke from jealousy ; but observe, there is not a single personage in ' Bajazet ' who is animated by the feelings which ought to animate him, and which really are entertained at Constantinople ; all of them, beneath their Turkish dress, are actuated by the feelings prevalent in the midst of France.'   And he was right," adds Segrais ; " in Corneille's dramas, the Roman speaks like a Roman, the Greek like a Greek, the Indian like an Indian, and the Spaniard like a Spaniard." [1]

" Corneille," says Saint-Evremond, " makes his Greeks speak better than the Greeks of old ever spoke, his Romans than the ancient Romans, and his Carthaginians than the citizens of Carthage themselves. Corneille is almost the only man who possesses the good taste of antiquity." [2]   " The Romans," says La Bruyère, " are greater and more Roman in his verses than in their actual history." [3]

---

[1] " Segraisiana," pp. 63—65.
[2] *Saint-Evremond*, " Œuvres," vol. iii. p. 41.
[3] *La Bruyère*, " Caractères," vol. ii. p. 84.

And finally, Balzac wrote thus to Corneille, in reference to Rome : — " You are the true and faithful interpreter of its spirit and courage. I say more, sir, you are often its pedagogue, and remind it of propriety when it seems to have forgotten its decorum. You are the reformer of the old time, if it needs any embellishment or support. In those places where Rome is built of brick, you rebuild it of marble ; where you find a void, you fill it with a masterpiece ; and I have always observed that what you lend to history is invariably better than what you think of it. * * * What has antiquity produced, in the weaker sex, so vigorous and firm as to be worthy of comparison with the new heroines whom you have brought into the world — with ' Sabine ' and ' Emilie,' those Roman ladies of your conception ? " [1]

But if there are points in which men recognise, although they may not resemble, one another, it is no less true that there are other points in which they resemble, but do not recognise, each other. Certain feelings belong to the nature of all countries ; they do not characterise the Japanese or the Parisian only ; they are characteristic of man, and man everywhere will discern in them his own image. There is, on the other hand, a certain uniformity of ideas which can only belong to certain degrees and

[2] *Balzac,* " Lettre sur Cinna," at the beginning of that tragedy.

special circumstances of civilisation ; and the more
absolute and uniform these ideas become at any
time, in any country, the more markedly will they
characterise it.   All the actions and writings of the
period will bear their impress ; authors will
assimilate their fictions and harmonise their
characters therewith, whatever may be their age
and land : they will thus impress upon them a
particular physiognomy, which will be taken for
the local physiognomy, of the man and the time to
which the action refers, although it is, properly
speaking, the physiognomy of the author and the
period at which the action is represented ; this will
not, however, be recognised, because it will manifest
itself beneath a different costume.   When Emilie
spoke of the " republic and liberty," could she appear
anything but a Roman lady ?   And in the line :

"Si j'ai séduit Cinna, j'en séduirai bien d'autres :"

in the importance which she attaches to " her
favours," which are to be the price of a revolution,
which of the spectators ever thought of discerning
the pride of a romance-heroine of the seventeenth
century ?   Yet such she nevertheless was, but her
character was the less discoverable by the eyes of her
contemporaries, as she had borrowed from them
all the singularity of their own manners in order to
engraft it upon times and manners totally different.

Thus, unperceived and unintentionally, Corneille has subjected his characters to the sway of the ideas of his own time—a time at which protracted disorders had introduced into morality, which was still far from having made great progress, somewhat of that uncertainty which is engendered by party ties and the duties of position. The fewness of general ideas combined with the multitude and diversity of private interests to leave great latitude to that pseudo-morality, which is made to suit the necessities of the moment, and which the requirements of conscience transform into a State virtue. The principles of common morality seemed binding only on those persons who were not authorised by great interests to contemn them; and no one felt the slightest surprise at these words of Livie :—

> " Tous ces crimes d'Etat qu'on fait pour la couronne,
> Le ciel nous en absout alors qu'il nous la donne ;
> Et dans le sacré rang où sa faveur l'a mis,
> Le passé devient juste et l'avenir permis."

Unlimited devotion to the cause or condition which a man had embraced was a line of conduct which might not be approved, but which met with discussion rather than condemnation. Few actions were thought sufficiently culpable in themselves not to find an excuse in private motives ; and few characters were so well established as to be deemed inaccessible to the influence of such motives. Mme. de Rambouillet, the most respected woman of her time, received from Cardinal Richelieu, " who held her in great esteem," [1] a message in which he begged her, as a friend, to inform him of whatever was said about him at the meetings which were then held at her house ; and Segrais, on learning her refusal to comply with this request,[2] ascribes it to the fact " that she did not know what it was to be a partisan, and to do any one a bad turn." So, acting as the Cardinal's spy would have been nothing more than " becoming a partisan !" And who would have blamed Mme. de Rambouillet for becoming a partisan of the prime minister ? Emeri, the superintendent of the finances, once said in open council, " that good faith was a quality expected only of merchants, and that those masters of requests who alleged it as a reason in matters concerning the king, deserved to be punished." [3] It is true that, in his youth, Emeri had been condemned to be hanged ; but the greatest scoundrels never say aloud anything but what honest folks are willing to hear. Struck with wonder at a liberty which they did not feel themselves capable of attaining, these honest persons said : " He is an able statesman !" and their only conclusion was that, to

---

[1] " Segraisiana," p. 29.

[2] She told Bois-Robert, who had undertaken this friendly office, " that those who visited her were so strongly persuaded of the respect and friendship which she entertained for his Eminence, that not one of them would be bold enough to speak ill of him in her presence; and that therefore she would never have occasion to give him such information." —" Segraisiana," p. 30.   [3] *De Retz*, " Mémoires," vol. i. p. 99.

be a statesman, it was necessary to be a dishonest man.[1] Some men of superior mind, such as Cardinal de Retz, perceived in Emeri's opinions as much want of judgment as meanness of heart;[2] but this same Cardinal de Retz sought to obtain, by revolutionising the State, "not only an honest, but an illustrious"[3] mode of deserting the ecclesiastical order with which he had unwillingly been connected. At this epoch, long-continued disorders had left every man the care and the power of making his own position in society; all interests and all ambitions were incessantly in conflict, if only for the honour of gaining the victory. Upon a man's dignity devolved the task of maintaining his rank; glory dispensed with virtue, and pride might consist in believing oneself above the performance of duties.[4]

The most insignificant facts become worthy of notice when they clearly reveal and distinctly cha-

---

[1] That Photin is an Emeri, who, in the "Mort de Pompée," says:

"La justice n'est pas une vertu d'Etat,"

and who maintains that a prince should

"Fuir comme un déshonneur la vertu qui nous perd,
Et voler, sans scrupule, au crime qui le sert."

And Voltaire, who is violently indignant at the want of probability of such a statement, and declares in his Commentaries that such maxims had never been uttered, and that a man who wishes his advice to be taken would not dress it in so abominable a garb—even Voltaire had not thoroughly examined, and did not rightly understand, the time of Corneille. In proof that that period was very different from the time of Voltaire, it is only necessary to observe that, in Voltaire's time, not even an Emeri would have broached such an opinion in open council.

[2] *De Retz*, "Mémoires," vol. i. p. 99.

[3] Ibid. vol. i. p. 31.   [4] See Appendix C.

racterise the spirit of the age. M. de Luynes was
one day bantering the young Duke de Rhételois,
who was then sixteen years of age, on the care
which he took to have his hair well curled. The
Duke replied that it curled naturally; "and when
M. de Luynes, in presence of the king, affected
astonishment at this, the king inquired if what he
said were true. 'No, Sire,' replied the Duke de
Rhételois. 'Why did you not say so when I asked
you?' inquired M. de Luynes. 'Because,' answered
the Duke, 'I tell truth to the king, but to you what
I please.'"[1] This same Duke de Rhételois would
have laid his hand to his sword to answer a contradiction, for no one then suffered another man to
give him the lie; but claimed for himself alone the
right of contradicting his own statements.

Such traits of character as these were continually
occurring before the eyes of Corneille; and these
traits he has bestowed upon the Greeks and Romans,
who were thought "so like and yet so much flattered" by his fellow-countrymen, who eagerly
acknowledged the authenticity of these "illustrious
ancients," as they had no difficulty in feeling themselves to be Greeks and Romans like them. The
genius of Corneille, and the subtlety of his reasonings,
appeared to the men of his time to justify manners
which they were better able to maintain than to

[1] "Mémoires de Marolles," vol. i. p. 89.

explain ; the force of his dialectics threw strong light upon principles, of which they possessed a feeling rather than a clear and precise idea ; and his political reflections struck them with all the more force, because they led them farther than they had ever yet travelled upon a road with which they were well acquainted. When the Maréchal de Grammont said, " Corneille is the breviary of kings," it was less, I think, from a just appreciation of Cinna's noble deliberation, than from a courtier's admiration of that arrogant contempt for morality which is thought appropriate to lofty positions because it is at variance with vulgar maxims : but the true feelings and sublime impulses which a man of genius alone could derive from so strange a system were required to behold—

"Le grand Condé pleurant aux vers du grand Corneille."

The great vice of such a system is that the merit of its effects depends absolutely upon the position of its characters. Some moments may occur in the life of a man, when extraordinary circumstances render it imperative on him to be actuated only by one single feeling,—when the maxims of prudence, and even of ordinary morality, may and must be silent in presence of considerations of a probably superior order, and leave the man to the influence of a single virtue and a single interest. If that man, possessing an energetic and simple natural character, has accustomed himself to sacrifice all to the object of his desire—if, proceeding always with firm step to the execution of his designs, he has never experienced either those mental disturbances which arise from uncertainty with regard to duty, or that hesitation of will which is occasioned by the conflict of two affections,—then, when 'an imperious circumstance presents itself before him, with promptitude and firmness he sweeps away all obstacles at a blow, darts forward to the goal, and roughly seizes upon that fortunate necessity which makes him a great man. This sometimes occurs to the heroes of Corneille ; when the character with which he has endowed them becomes a virtue, that virtue subjugates and governs the whole man, both as regards his feelings and his position ; and everything bends before this character, to complete the greatness of which nothing is wanting after it has found employment for all its power.

But this power does not always find means for its worthy exercise, and the display of its strength sometimes bears a closer resemblance to the pomp of parade than to the real activity of combat.   Thus, in " Heraclius," Pulchérie exhausts herself in uttering insults against Phocas, which are not attended with sufficient difficulty and danger to be worthy of her ; she requires an opportunity in which the haughtiness of her contempt, and the inflexibility and frankness of her resentment, may be an act of courage and virtue. In the position of Nicomède, the necessity of braving and affronting all who surround him is not sufficiently evident to save his perpetual bravado from occasionally appearing out of place. Emilie's inflexibility is admirable if we only think of the position in which she has been placed by her thirst for vengeance ; but it is excessive if we weigh the motives of her passion for revenge : the errors of Augustus, from whom she has consented to receive so many benefits, no longer deserve the firmness with which she perseveres in her hatred of him ; and that " adorable fury " of Balzac's doctor,[1] though "adorable" if you please, when the position suits her character, is, in fact, nothing better than a " fury," when such is not the case.

It is impossible for their position not to frequently fail Corneille's characters, for they cannot find a suitable place elsewhere than in the most extraordinary circumstances of life. It has been urged against them that they speak too long, and talk too much of themselves. " They talk too much to make themselves known," said Vauvenargues ; but how

---

[1] " A doctor in my neighbourhood, who usually adopts the lofty style, certainly speaks of her in a strange manner ; and there is no harm in your knowing whither you have carried his mind. He was satisfied, on the first day, with saying that your Emilie was the rival of Cato and Brutus, in her passion for liberty. At this hour, however, he goes much farther : sometimes he says that she is possessed by the demon of the republic ; and sometimes he calls her the beautiful, the reasonable, the holy, and the adorable, fury."—*Balzac*, " Lettre sur Cinna."

could we know them if they did not speak ? A
single dramatic action could not possibly include
enough facts and circumstances for the display of
such characters in their entirety, and could not show,
by what they do, all that they are capable of doing.
They are not characters who limit their conduct to
the exertion of influence over the action of the
moment, or to bursting violently into a particular
passion ; they embrace and sway the whole individual ; and they would need an entire lifetime to
make themselves thoroughly known and understood.
Upon the stage, they have not enough time or space :
Nicomède cannot display thereon that military talent
on which he rests his confidence and pride ; powerless at the court of Prusias, he can neither give
evidence of that enlightened prudence which enables
him to foresee and to frustrate the designs of the
Romans, nor of that tranquil greatness of soul which
can find no surer means of escaping from power than
braving it,—

"D'estimer beaucoup Rome et ne la craindre point."

Consequently, in order to make us acquainted with
Nicomède, it becomes necessary for Prusias to draw
him momentarily from his inactive position by per-
mitting him to answer Flaminius in his stead.
Corneille was not aware of another expedient for
furnishing even Nicomède with enough words to

supply the place of those actions which befit such a character as his. In "Rodogune," Cleopatra, hampered by her position, cannot give vent to the violence of her hatred, and the unbending nature of her ambition ; time fails her to develop before us the progress of her combinations ; and she details them to us that we may know them. If the stern requirements of duty allowed Pauline to manifest in her actions the strength of her love for Sévère, as well as her persistence in sacrificing him, she would not be obliged to say so much about the great virtue involved in the sacrifice. All these characters speak when compelled to do so by the necessities of the scene, and not by the exigencies of the action ; they speak sometimes without waiting the proper opportunity for so doing ; though such a course is not in harmony with the almost exclusive empire exerted over them by their character. Character, regarded as a simple natural disposition, is manifested only when it finds itself in presence of an object adapted to bring it into play ; whereas passion, a violent movement of the soul, inclines in every direction, vents itself wherever it can, and is able to furnish much more naturally that abundance of discourse, which is necessary on the stage. When dying Cleopatra reveals to her son her crimes and dreadful projects, she is hurried on by passion ; her hatred is no longer able to act ; she has no consolation but in declaring it ; and her revelations are therefore perfectly natural. But the revelations which Cleopatra makes to Laonice in the early acts are not so, because they are simple developments of character, skilfully given by the person herself, instead of being naturally provoked by the course of events.

Not only do Corneille's heroes possess few passions which wage war against their character, but it rarely happens that their character is set in motion by the ordinary feelings of the heart, as they may exist under simple circumstances. They most frequently give expression to ideas, and almost to doctrines ; their speeches generally consist of reasonings, animated by strong conviction and pressing logic, but somewhat cold and confined within the circle of mental combinations. A principle, a general and systematic idea, holds sway and manifests itself throughout ; and on the truth or falsity of this principle the conduct of the persons of the drama invariably depends. Thus Pauline is guided by the idea of duty, and Polyeucte by that of religious faith ; and these ideas, admirably adapted to elevate the soul and exalt the imagination, develop a most passionate feeling in both personages ; but even this feeling is based upon a principle. When Polyeucte exclaims :

> " Grand Dieu ! de vos bontés il faut que je l'obtienne ;
> Elle a trop de vertu pour n'être pas chrétienne : "

it is the inflexibility of the principle "out of the church there is no salvation," which produces this extremely touching and truthful movement. It is a reasoned knowledge of the devotion which patriotism imposes on a Roman, which sustains the inflexible firmness of young Horace; and that sublime outburst—

"Quoi! vous me pleureriez mourant pour mon pays?"

is an expression of the astonishment of a man who hears a truth which he deems incontestable, called in question. Cinna says to Emilie—

"*Vous faites* des vertus au gré de votre haine;"

and she answers :

"*Je me fais* des vertus dignes d'une Romaine."

Emilie's hatred is, in fact, a virtue and not a feeling, in her own opinion; she thinks that she ought to hate Augustus, and she tells us why she hates him, rather than explains how she does so. Chimène's pertinacity in demanding the death of Rodrigue is altogether the result of reflection; whatever grief she may have felt at the death of her father, it is not grief which hurries her to the feet of the king, but the idea of what she is bound by honour to do. But the feeling which possesses her, continually diverts her attention from the idea which governs her; at the same time that she does what she thinks duty commands for

her father, she says what she feels for her lover, and
the " Cid," the only one of Corneille's tragedies in
which love ventures to display all its power, is also
the only one in which he has followed the natural
rule of giving action to character and words to
passion.

Moreover, in Corneille, absolute truth is, here as
elsewhere, superseded by relative truth; where we
cannot discover the characteristics of man in general,
we find the features of the Frenchman of the seventeenth century ; and the somewhat talkative virtue
of his heroes could not but be well received at a time
when the necessity of duly maintaining his rank in
society placed the act of asserting his own importance
among the duties, or at least among the accomplish-
ments, of a man of merit. To talk of oneself was then
a most common practice. It was Balzac's custom,
whenever he mentioned his own performances in
conversation, to take off his hat, apparently out of politeness to those who were listening to him. One day,
when he was suffering from a violent cold, Ménage
said he had caught it from the number of opportunities which he gave himself for taking off his hat !
This joke occasioned a serious quarrel between them.
" M. de la Rochefoucauld," says Segrais, "was the
most polite man in the world ; he well knew how to
observe all the proprieties, and above all things,
he never praised himself. M. de Roquelaure and

M. de Miossans were men of great talent, but they were never tired of praising themselves. They had a great many admirers. Speaking of them, M. de la Roche- foucauld used to say : " I repent of the law which I have imposed upon myself not to speak in my own praise ; if I did so, I should have many more followers. Look at MM. de Roquelaure and de Miossans, who, for two mortal hours, have been talking to twenty people about nothing but their own merits. Among those who listen to them, there are only two or three who cannot endure them ; but the other seventeen applaud them loudly, and consider them incomparable." [1]

Nevertheless, while endowing his heroes with taste and the gift of speech, Corneille does not forget to place them in positions in which they will have opportunity to act ; in his dramas, everything tends to effects of position ; and he is constantly seeking to prepare and to put forward these effects. In his " Examinations," he rarely praises himself for the expression which he has given to feelings and ideas ; but he is continually congratulating himself on the invention of this or that position, or else of the means which he had used to give likelihood and suit- ability to the position which he desired to introduce. In truth, he abuses the too easy art of creating the embarrassments which he needs ; and it is to the

"Segraisiana," p. 32.

subtleties of his age, rather than to nature, that he looks for the feelings necessary to the action which he intends to produce. Thus Rodogune, when ready to do her duty, and marry whichever of the two princes may be declared the elder, does not think herself at liberty to bestow her hand without exacting the condition that her first husband shall be avenged; that is to say, without obliging the prince she may espouse to assassinate his mother :—

> "Je me mettrai trop haut s'il faut que je me donne.
> Quoique aisément je cède aux ordres de mon roi,
> Il n'est pas bien aisé de m'obtenir de moi.
> *   *   *   *   *
> Ce cœur vous est acquis après le diadème,
> Prince, mais gardez-vous de le rendre à lui-même :
> Vous y renoncerez peut-être pour jamais
> Quand je vous aurai dit à quel prix je le mets."

This fearful proposition is merely a subtle invention, intended to act as a basis for the position of the fifth act, by placing "Rodogune herself under the necessity of prolonging the uncertainty of the two princes ;" and when this uncertainty is terminated by her confession to Antiochus, and by the renunciation of Seleucus, the facility with which Rodogune abandons her project adds greatly to the whimsicality of the idea that produced it :—

> "Votre refus est juste autant que ma demande.
> A force de respect votre amour s'est trahi.
> Je voudrois vous haïr, s'il m'avoit obéi ;
> Et je n'estime pas l'honneur d'une vengeance
> Jusqu'à vouloir d'un crime être la récompense."

Thus it was that the age in which Corneille lived taught him to treat the feelings of the heart. The unbounded devotion of this age to love is an example, among many others, of the effects of superstition upon true worship ; and the grave and simple Corneille, by his submission to the superstitious gallantries of his time, affords a striking evidence of the manner in which a man of genius may subject his reason to the caprices of the multitude, to whose advice he listens that he may obtain a hearing for himself.

The " Cid " and " Polyeucte " effectually raise Corneille above the suspicion of having disregarded those characteristics of love which render it worthy of being depicted by a man of genius, and of having looked to the romances of his time for that colouring which his imagination refused to supply. It is, however, impossible to deny that, in most of his pieces, Corneille has treated love, not as a passion that fills, agitates, and sways the soul, but as a position that imposes certain duties, prescribes a certain course of conduct, and coldly disposes of life, without lending it any charms. The author of the " Cid " and of "Polyeucte" could not have been ignorant of the nature of true love ; even if he had not experienced its full ardour and extravagance, he was certainly acquainted with that sincere and profound tenderness of heart, that perfect confidence, which brings two souls into union, although duty may call them in different, or even opposite directions—that sweet and intimate communion of two lovers, which leads one to sympathise with all the sufferings of the other, which opposes union of hearts to the misfortunes of destiny, and establishes, between two beings who are separated by all beside, secret bonds which nothing can avail to sunder. Chimène and Rodrigue converse of their common affairs, when speaking of the opposite duties imposed upon them ; and, if such an expression may be allowed, they arrange together for their performance :—

> " Tu n'as fait le devoir que d'un homme de bien ;
> Mais aussi, le faisant, tu m'as appris le mien."

There is nothing which the love of one of the two lovers would desire to wrest from the honour of the other :—

> " Va; je ne te hais point.—Tu le dois.—Je ne puis.
> —Crains-tu si peu le blâme et si peu les faux bruits ?
> Quand on saura mon crime, et que ta flamme dure,
> Que ne publieront pas l'envie et l'imposture ? "

But when Rodrigue and Chimène have become convinced that it is impossible to stifle their affection, and that they are not called upon to display their strength and virtue in this vain attempt, then, left for a moment to the unresisted influence of that love which constitutes their sole happiness in the midst of the most cruel misfortunes, they

feel, they think, they almost speak together ; the
echo of their words is that cry which escapes
simultaneously from two souls deeply affected by
the same grief :—

> " Rodrigue, qui l'eût cru ?—Chimène, qui l'eût dit ?
> Que notre heur fût si proche et si tôt se perdît ! "

And their farewell serves only to complete the union
of their destiny :—

> " Adieu ! Je vais traîner une mourante vie,
> Tant que par ta poursuite elle me soit ravie.
> —Si j'en obtiens l'effet, je te donne ma foi
> De ne respirer pas un moment après toi."

They can now separate. Rodrigue could even fight
Chimène's brother, if Chimène had a brother desirous
of avenging his father ; and Chimène can pursue
Rodrigue with hostile intentions. They have met, and
discovered their mutual sentiments ; they will now
understand each other in spite of appearances most
unintelligible in the eyes of the world, and the mys-
terious freemasonry of love will never allow either
of them to be exposed to the pain of being misunder-
stood by the adored being to whom he remains
faithful, even at the moment of sacrificing him.

Pauline, when united to Polyeucte, and determined
to endure all the sacrifices that may be imposed on
her by this tie, nevertheless does not attempt to
dissemble to Sévère those feelings with which he
was so well acquainted ; but she appeals to the love

of Sévère himself to support her in the performance
of a duty which—

> " *   *   * Moins ferme et moins sincère,
>   N'auroit pas mérité l'amour du grand Sévère ; "

and to him she still belongs even when she rejects
him in the name of her virtue.

The poet who could conceive thus of love undoubtedly possessed within himself the necessary
qualifications for describing it.   In a life least subject
to the empire of the passions, experience, when
properly used, supplies the imagination, on this point,
with more touching details than it is ever able to
employ. " Corneille's temperament," says Fontenelle,
" inclined him sufficiently to love, but never to
libertinism, and seldom to strong attachments." [1]
Strong attachments are always rare, and it is enough
to have been under the influence of one to know
what opinion to entertain on the subject ; but
Corneille often forgot his own opinion to remember
only what he had heard others say about it.   Speaking of himself, he has said :—

> " En matière d'amour je suis fort inégal ;
>   J'en écris assez bien ; je le fais assez mal."

Whether he made love well or ill, he did not always
write about it as well as he thought.   He too
frequently allowed borrowed habits to trample upon

---

[1] *Fontenelle*, " Vie de Corneille," p. 125.

the dictates of his heart and reason; and he sacrificed the feelings with which he had animated Chimène and Pauline for the insipidities which he had been taught to put into the mouths of Cæsar and Cleopatra.

At the present day, in order to judge the loves of Cæsar and Cleopatra, of Antiochus and Rodogune, as they were judged by the most talented and sensible men of the seventeeth century,[1] we must transport ourselves into the system of love generally adopted at that period, with which Corneille's characters, as it becomes well-educated persons, act in strict conformity. We must resign ourselves to behold in love neither liberty of choice, nor suitability of tastes, characters, and habits, nor any of those bonds which become all the more dear as we better appreciate them, and better understand their true motives. To the fashionable world of Corneille's time, love was nothing but an ordinance of Heaven, an influence of the stars, a fatality as inexplicable as it was inevitable. Every one knows by heart these lines of Rodogune :—

> " Il est des nœuds secrets, il est des sympathies
> Dont, par le doux rapport, les âmes assorties
> S'attachent l'une à l'autre, et se laissent piquer
> Par ces je ne sais quoi qu'on ne peut expliquer."

The following lines, from the "Suite au Menteur,"

---

[1] Among others, see Saint-Evremond's opinion in his "Discours sur l'Alexandre de Racine," in vol. iii. p. 149 of his Works.

would be even better known than the foregoing, if the piece were read as much :—

> " Quand les ordres du ciel nous ont faits l'un pour l'autre
> Lise, c'est un accord bientôt fait que le nôtre ;
> Sa main, entre les cœurs, par un secret pouvoir,
> Sème l'intelligence avant que de se voir ;
> Il prépare si bien l'amant et la maîtresse,
> Que leur âme, au seul nom, s'émeut et s'intéresse ;
> On s'estime, on se cherche, on s'aime en un moment ;
> Tout ce qu'on s'entredit persuade aisément ;
> Et sans s'inquiéter d'aucunes peurs frivoles,
> La foi semble courir au-devant des paroles."

The same idea occurs again in " Bérénice ; "[1] it is apparent in all Corneille's dramas ; and no wonder, for it was the idea of the time. A passion thus predeterminate was necessarily of instantaneous origin. Thus arose the passion of the Duke de Nemours for the Princess of Cleves, the various movements of which were afterwards observed with so much delicacy, and described with so much truthfulness. Beauty, the only charm whose full value is appreciated at a single glance, then held sway, not only with irresistible power, but with tyranny. " At forty-eight years of age," says Segrais, " Mme. de Montbazon was still so beautiful that she eclipsed Mme. de Roquelaure, who was only twenty-two years old; and one day, happening to meet together at an assembly, Mme. de Roquelaure was obliged to withdraw."[2]

---

[1] " *   *   *   Ce don fut l'effet d'une force imprévue :
De cet ordre du ciel, qui verse en nos esprits
Les principes secrets de prendre et d'être pris."

[2] "Segraisiana," pp. 133, 134.

The Memoirs of the time furnish us with many instances of ladies who were actually obliged to retire because a more beautiful rival had entered the room. It seemed as though beauty were a supreme and exclusive empire, the loss of which left the vanquished nought but shame and flight. La Bruyère himself declares that " that love which arises suddenly is longest in curing." He even seems to think that it alone deserves the name of love : " Love is born suddenly," he says, " without other reflection, from temperament or from weakness ; a glimpse of beauty transfixes and decides us. That love which grows gradually is too much like friendship to be a violent passion." [1]

Perhaps these sudden effects, these sun-strokes of love, which are now the exclusive property of our worst romance-writers, were then able to obtain the belief of a philosopher. Men and women, whose worldly life was ceaselessly occupied with ideas or intrigues of love, were naturally always susceptible, or at least thought themselves susceptible, of its influence ; and if, as La Rochefoucauld observes, " there are some people who would never have fallen in love, if they had never heard love mentioned," many persons, through hearing it talked of wherever they went, fancied they had found it where it did not exist.

[1] *La Bruyère*, "Caractères," pp. 179, 180.

Surprised at these effects of the imagination, some men endeavoured to explain them by other causes than the influence of the stars ; and these causes were generally of a most ridiculous character. In order to prove that the seat of love is in the blood, Segrais relates a story of a German gentleman whose faithless mistress, desiring to get rid of him, ran him twice through the body with a sword. He did not die of his wounds ; but, strange to say, when he had recovered, says Segrais, " he felt as much indifference for the princess as if he had never loved her, and he attributed this to his loss of blood." [1]

This amorous devotion—the consequence of a fatal destiny—was then the ideal of a *belle passion*, at least as regarded the perfect lover ; for fatality, to which the heart of his mistress was equally subject, could have no influence upon her conduct towards him. The ladies held firmly, at least in theory, by this principle, which was as favourable to their vanity as to their virtue. Solely entrusted with the care and duty of defending themselves, they felt themselves all the more powerful because so high a value was set on the happiness of a passion which accomplished the destiny of the loftiest souls. The proofs of this high price of their conquest constituted their glory ; for " a woman's glory " was then a common phrase. Madame de Sévigné, when she declared that " the

[1] " Segraisiana," p. 10.

honour of these gentlemen is quite as delicate and
tender as that of these ladies," believed she had
almost made a discovery ; and the Academy pronounced, in its " Opinions on the ' Cid,' " that if " it
had been allowable for the poet to make one of the
two lovers prefer love to duty, it may •be said that it
would have been more excusable to lay this fault on
Rodrigue than on Chimène ; as Rodrigue was a man,
and his sex—which is, as it were, entitled to shut its
eyes on all considerations in order to satisfy its love—
would have rendered his action less strange and less
unsupportable." [1]

This is the key to the almost constant superiority
of Corneille's heroines over his heroes. She who
commands both herself and others, in the most
important circumstance of life, must be, under all
circumstances, the most illustrious ; and after the
decision of the Academy, it is not surprising that
Corneille should have sacrificed the inflexibility of
Cinna to the advantage of bringing Emilie's unyielding
nature into strong relief.   But it will then be equally
evident to what frivolous interests that glory must be
attached which is based upon the petty events of a
woman's life, and judged by the caprices of her vanity.
No further astonishment will be felt at beholding
Eurydice, in " Suréna," deliver her lover to death by
her obstinacy in desiring that, as he cannot marry her,

---

[1] See the Appendix to Voltaire's edition of the " Cid," p. 392.

he should marry none but the person of her choice.
" I will," she exclaims—

> " *　*　*　*　* 　Malgré votre roi,
> Disposer d'une main qui ne peut être à moi.
> Je veux que ce grand choix soit mon dernier ouvrage,
> Qu'il tienne lieu vers moi d'un éternel hommage,
> Que mon ordre le règle, et qu'on me voie enfin
> Reine de votre cœur et de votre destin."

The same whim assists Bérénice to console herself
for the loss of Titus :—

> " Je veux donner le bien que je n'ose garder ;
> Je veux du moins, je veux ôter à ma rivale,
> Ce miracle vivant, cette âme sans égale.
> Qu'en dépit des Romains, leur digne souverain,
> S'il prend une moitié, la prenne de ma main ;
> Et pour tout dire enfin, je veux que Bérénice
> Ait une créature en leur impératrice."

Corneille's " Sophonisbe," the ill-success of which
Saint-Evremond ascribes solely to the excessive
perfection with which Corneille had retained " her
true character,"[1]—this daughter of Hasdrubal, amidst
her hatred of the Romans, and her dread of slavery,
regards the pleasure of robbing a rival of Masi-
nissa's affection as the greatest happiness of that
marriage which is to deprive her of her triumph.

---

[1] Corneille, who almost alone possesses the good taste of antiquity, has
had the misfortune of not pleasing our age, for having entered into the
genius of those nations, and preserved to the daughter of Hasdrubal her
true character. Thus, to the shame of our judgments, he who has surpassed
all our authors, and who has, perhaps, here surpassed himself, has restored
to these great names all that was due to them, and has not been able to
oblige us to render to himself all that we owe to him."—*Saint-Evremond*,
" Œuvres," vol. iii. pp. 141, 142.

The lovers of these illustrious coquettes, devotedly submissive to their whims, await, as Antiochus pleases, without rebellion and without blasphemy, whatever it may please their glory to ordain ; and tricks of vanity mingle without effort, in Corneille's latest pieces, with exaggerations of pride through which some few scintillations of genius and mementoes of greatness are discernible only at rare intervals.

Once entered upon a false train of ideas, Corneille was unable to regain the true path by using that resource which is supplied by the observation of the natural feelings ; for he had become too accustomed to seek them solely in his imagination. The imagination mingles much that is false with the truth which it presents ; it creates for the poet a kind of private world, placed between him and the real world which he no longer cares to contemplate, for he no longer even suspects its existence. Into this world of fancy which Corneille had formed for himself, swayed by the turn of mind of his contemporaries, and placing at their service the logical firmness of his imagination, he no longer received the light which the natural emotions of our soul cast upon the objects which excite them. Justice, goodness, indeed all the human virtues, were feelings before they were ideas ; who would ever have *imagined* generosity and devotement, if feelings had not first made him aware of their existence ?   By the order of these feelings, as they exist in a happy nature, properly developed by reflection, the order of our duties is regulated. Never will the most exalted soul, never will the severest virtue, sacrifice a single one of these duties, unless the sacrifice be commanded by a more important duty : and where this consciousness of a superior duty does not exist, the sacrifice is unjust, the virtue is counterfeit, and the appearance of greatness is deceptive.   Old Horace, when he believes that his son has fled, forgets his paternal love, and desires, nay more, almost commands, the death of his son ; but love of his country, the obligations imposed upon his family by the confidence of his fellow-citizens, the criminality of the coward who had betrayed that confidence, and even the advantage of his son, for whom death would be a thousand times more preferable than an infamous life,—all these are feelings so powerful, and of so exalted an order, that we are not surprised to see that they gain the victory over even paternal love, the well-known force of which only adds to the admiration inspired by the superior force which has conquered it.   But when Rosamonde, the widow of Pertharite, [1] threatened with the death of her son if she will not consent to marry Grimoald, the usurper of her husband's kingdom, declares to Grimoald that

---

[1] Or at least his supposed widow; for Pertharite is not dead, but reäppears at the end of the piece.

she will marry him only on condition that he will put
her son to death, because she hopes that so atrocious
an act, by destroying the affection felt by the people
for Grimoald's virtues, will render vengeance more
easy to herself, we feel neither admiration nor
sympathy for her conduct ; for the thirst for vengeance could never be sufficiently powerful, or appear
sufficiently legitimate, to stifle not only a mother's
love for her offspring, but also that sentiment of
justice which forbids us to sacrifice an innocent being
to the memory or even to the interests of another.
Rosamonde's proposition is, therefore, opposed to all
human and poetic truth.   Fontenelle, seeking for the
cause of the ill success of " Pertharite," attributes it
to oldness of mind, which, he says, " brings dryness and harshness in its train." [1]   But Corneille was
not old when he wrote " Pertharite " ; [2]   and he had
no more reasons for being harsh at forty-seven years
of age, when he had four sons, [3] than when he was

---

[1] *Fontenelle,* " Vie de Corneille," p. 108.

[2] He was forty-seven years old.

[3] Corneille had four sons and two daughters. His eldest son, Pierre
Corneille, was a captain of cavalry, and was wounded, in 1667, at the siege
of Douai, which was captured on the 6th of July, by Louis XIV. He was
brought back to Paris on a litter plentifully supplied with straw. On
arriving at the door of his father's house, in the Rue d'Argenteuil, the
porters, solely intent upon carrying the wounded man into his room,
scattered the straw about the street. This was during the early days of
that strict system of police established in Paris by the administration of
Louis XIV., and so strenuously enforced by D'Aubray and La Reynie. The
commissaries and inspectors rigorously executed the orders they had
received. One of them cited Pierre Corneille before the lieutenant of
police at the Châtelet, for contravening the regulations in reference to the

thirty-eight years old,[1] and just married; and certainly he still possessed many more lively and true feelings than are required to enlighten and regulate the mind. But a false system, the fruit of his submission to the ideas of his time, would not allow him to listen to his own feelings, and thus to paint nature with truthfulness; so that the nature which he reproduced was as factitious and false as the ideas of his contemporaries.

The style of Corneille varied with the vicissitudes of his genius. Astonishment has been expressed at this; but there would have been more room for astonishment had it been otherwise, and had his style not remained faithful, both in good and evil fortune, to the character of his thoughts. Writing was never anything to him but the expression of his ideas; and his contemporaries attest that carefulness of style was of no avail in effects which were entirely due to the grandeur of the subjects which he had to depict. " Corneille," says Segrais, " was not conscious of the beauty of his versification, and while writing he paid attention, not to harmony, but only to feeling." And Chapelain informs us, that " Corneille, who has

---

public thoroughfares. Corneille appeared, pleaded his own cause, and was immediately nonsuited, amidst the applause of the spectators, who conducted him home in triumph. This incident is frequently mentioned in the conversations and anecdote-books of the time, and Loret inserted an account of it in his " Muse Historique," in the form of a poetical letter to Madame ——, by Robinet. See Appendix D. I am indebted to M. Floquet for the discovery and communication of this interesting little fact.

[1] The age at which he wrote "Polyeucte."

written such noble poetry, was unacquainted with the art of versification, and it was purely nature that acted in him." [1]   An artistic style, which, at the time when Corneille appeared, constituted almost the whole merit of a fashionable poet, had very little indeed to do with the merit of a dramatic author. Corneille introduced style into the drama by introducing thoughts ; he said simply what he meant, and he therefore spoke nobly, for what he had to say was high and noble.   The expression naturally clothed itself with the sublimity of that which it was intended to convey—or rather, in the sublimity of his poetry, the expression appeared to count for nothing, for it was the thing itself.   " In Corneille's writings," says Saint-Evremond, " grandeur is self-recognised ; the figures that he employs are worthy of it, when he intends to beautify it with any ornament ; but, ordinarily, he neglects these vain shows ; he does not go to the skies to seek for something to increase the value of that which is sufficiently important upon earth ; it is enough for him to enter thoroughly into a matter, and the complete image which he gives of it forms that true impression which persons of good sense love to receive." [2]   Corneille himself would have vainly sought " in the skies" for wherewithal " to increase the value " of some of the feelings which

---

[1] " Segraisiana," pp. 76, 187.
[2] *Saint-Evremond*, " Œuvres," vol. iv. p. 16.

he presents to our view ; they are so lofty that, as nothing can exceed them, expression can add nothing to them ; and yet they are so determinate and precise that there are not two ways of expressing them.

We must not, therefore, expect to find in Corneille that poetical expression which is intended to increase the impression produced by an object, by connecting with it accessory ideas which the object would not have suggested of itself. We shall find in his writings that poetry which displays the object as it really is, and places it before our eyes endowed with life and animation, by using words that are truly adapted to describe it. The narrative given by Rodrigue, in the " Cid," presents a fine example of this :—

> " Cette obscure clarté qui tombe des étoiles
>   Enfin, avec le flux, nous fit voir trente voiles;
>   L'onde s'enfloit dessous, et, d'un commun effort,
>   Les Maures et la mer entrèrent dans le port.
>   On les laisse passer, tout leur paroît tranquille ;
>   Point de soldats au port ; point aux murs de la ville.
>   Notre profond silence abusant leurs esprits,
>   Ils n'osent plus douter de nous avoir surpris.
>   Ils abordent sans peur, ils ancrent, ils descendent,
>   Et courent se livrer aux mains qui les attendent.
>   Nous nous levons alors ; et, tous en même temps,
>   Poussons jusques au ciel mille cris éclatants.　*　*　*"

All these expressions are simple—just those which a man would use who wished to narrate the occurrences of which the Cid is speaking ; but the Cid mentions only those matters which are worth mentioning. All necessary circumstances, and these alone, he brings before our eyes, because he has seen them ; he could not fail to see them in the position in which he was placed, and into that position he transfers us. This is true poetry.

But the nature of the objects to be represented does not always admit of this, so to speak, material description. It frequently happens that the picture, being too vast to be reproduced in all its details, requires to be confined within a single image, which shall nevertheless convey an impression of the whole. The employment of figurative expressions then becomes necessary ; and this is the character of Cinna's narrative :—

> " Je leur fais des tableaux de ces tristes batailles
> Où Rome par ses mains déchiroit ses entrailles,
> Où l'aigle abattoit l'aigle, et, de chaque côté,
> Nos légions s'armoient contre leur liberté ;
> Où les meilleurs soldats et les chefs les plus braves
> Mettoient toute leur gloire à devenir esclaves :
> Où, pour mieux assurer la honte de leurs fers,
> Tous vouloient à leur chaîne attacher l'univers ;
> Et l'exécrable honneur de lui donner un maître,
> Faisant aimer à tous l'infâme nom de traître,
> Romains contre Romains, parens contre parens,
> Combattoient seulement pour le choix des tyrans.
> J'ajoute à ce tableau la peinture effroyable
> De leur concorde impie, affreuse, inexorable,
> Funeste aux gens de bien, aux riches, au sénat,
> Et pour tout dire enfin, de leur triumvirat.
> Mais je ne trouve point de couleurs assez noires
> Pour en représenter les tragiques histoires ;
> Je les peins dans le meurtre à l'envi triomphans ;
> Rome entière noyée au sang de ses enfans, *   *   * "

No details could in this case have presented before the imagination all that is here exhibited to its view, *en groupe*, by two or three fine images.   The remainder of the narrative is favourable to the introduction of details, and Cinna, resuming the simple tone of narration, ceases to paint matters figuratively, and limits his efforts to displaying them in their reality ; but at the end, when he finds it necessary to sum up his speech and to reduce the different emotions which he has awakened to a single feeling and idea, he thus proceeds :—

> " *   *   *   *   Toutes ces cruautés,
> La perte de nos biens et de nos libertés,
> Le ravage des champs, le pillage des villes,
> Et les proscriptions et les guerres civiles,
> Sont les degrés sanglants dont Auguste a fait choix
> Pour monter sur le trône et nous donner des loix.
> Mais nous pouvons changer un destin si funeste,
> Puisque de trois tyrans c'est le seul qui nous reste ;
> Et que, juste une fois, il s'est privé d'appui,
> Perdant, pour régner seul, deux méchans comme lui.
> Lui mort, nous n'avons point de vengeur ni de maître ;
> Avec la liberté Rome s'en va renaître ;
> Et nous mériterons le nom de vrais Romains,
> Si le joug qui l'accable est brisé par nos mains."

In this speech, which is one of the finest productions of his pen, Corneille, making a simple and sober use of the necessary figures, employs them to express his idea, but never to extend it beyond its natural limits.   Perhaps, among Corneille's most poetical expressions, we shall find few which do not possess this merit ; they are generally the result of a vigorous conception which clearly discerns its object, and which, far from surrounding it with accessory ideas, removes them to a distance in order to present

it in isolated distinctness to the imagination. Thus,
in these celebrated lines from " Othon :"—

> " Je les voyois tous trois se hâter sous un maître
> Qui, chargé d'un long âge, a peu de temps de l'être,
> Et tous trois à l'envi s'empresser ardemment
> A qui dévoreroit ce règne d'un moment,—"

the image of " devouring a reign " is only the
sensible expression of a fact which, in no other
manner, could be treated with as much felicity and
power ; it places the fact itself beneath our eyes,
but adds nothing to it. The same may be said of
this other line :—

> " Et monté sur le faîte il aspire à descendre."

Corneille has embellished nothing and disguised
nothing ; his style, guided by his thought, naturally
rose and fell with it ; and he appears obscure only
when an ill-conceived idea or an inopportune sentiment has failed to furnish him with a sufficiently
precise expression or a sufficiently simple turn of
phrase. He never disdains to use the trivial
language which is required by a trivial emotion
or position. In "Agésilas," for example, he puts
these words into the mouth of a lover who is
pressing his mistress to confess her love for him :—

> " Dites donc, m'aimez-vous ?"

A puerile idea is always rendered in all its puerility ;
and the description of Attila's bleeding at the nose is

worthy of the idea which suggested the adaptation of this accident to the purposes of tragedy :—

> " Le sang qu'après avoir mis ce prince[1] au tombeau,
> On lui voit chaque jour distiller du cerveau,
> Punit son parricide, et chaque jour vient faire
> Un tribut étonnant à celui de ce frère."

The word *brutal*, which is used by Pulchérie in speaking of Phocas, is in perfect accordance with the idea which she has formed of his character. In fine, the weakness of the poet's thought is manifested with as little disguise as its greatness ; and if he seeks to trick it out with a few ornaments, the abuses of mind to which he has recourse, the falsity of the images which he employs, and the vain inflation of his expressions, prove, as powerfully as the sublime simplicity of his beauties, that " art was not made for him." Corneille could not have made use of art ; and what his age failed to supply him with was a more simple nature, less overloaded by a multitude of conventionalisms and factitious habits, which he took for truth. If the state of society and the general character of ideas, at the time in which he lived, had been in greater conformity to the simplicity of his genius, perhaps, in one of our first poets, we should have also possessed a classic poet. Corneille is not a classic ; he is too deficient in that taste which is based upon a knowledge of truth, to

---

[1] His brother Bleda.

serve always as a model ; but beauties beyond all comparison have nevertheless established his rank, and after a century and a half of literary affluence and glory, no rival has deprived him of his title of " Great." Even his failures may be held to confirm his right to this name ; before the time of Corneille, " Pertharite," " Othon," " Suréna," " Attila," and even " Agésilas," would have been received with admiration by a public whom he alone had rendered critical. " Pertharite " was the first of his pieces which experienced this severe treatment. " The fall of the great Corneille," says Fontenelle, " may be numbered among the most remarkable examples of the vicissitudes of human affairs ; even Belisarius asking alms is not more striking." [1] Corneille felt this blow to be a misfortune to which he had not believed himself exposed ; and somewhat of bitterness is manifested in his preface to " Pertharite." " It is just," he says, " that after twenty years of labour, I should begin to perceive that I am growing too old to continue in vogue." Taking leave of the public, " before," he says, " they entirely took leave of him," he spent six years in perfect retirement, devoting himself to a metrical translation of the " Imitation of Jesus Christ." This work must be considered as a production of his piety rather than of his genius, although it occasionally exhibits brilliant traces of

[1] *Fontenelle*, " Vie de Corneille," p. 107.

superior talent.[1]   I shall not here refer to this poem,
or to a considerable number of pieces of verse, written
both in his youth and his old age,[2] as they only
prove that the drama was the imperious vocation of
Corneille, and the only field in which he could appear
with glory.   Of this he was personally conscious :—

> " Pour moi, qui de louer n'eus jamais le méthode,
>   J'ignore encor le tour du sonnet ou de l'ode ;
>   Mon génie au théâtre a voulu m'attacher ;
>   Il en a fait mon sort, je dois m'y retrancher :
>   Partout ailleurs je rampe et ne suis plus moi-même." [3]

" He was well acquainted with elegant literature,
history, and politics," says Fontenelle ; "but he regarded
them chiefly in their reference to the drama.   For
all the other branches of knowledge he had neither
leisure, nor curiosity, nor indeed much esteem." [4]

During these six years of retirement, also, Corneille
prepared his three discourses on Dramatic Poetry,
and wrote his Examinations of his pieces—an honourable evidence of the good faith of a great man who
was sincere enough with himself to confess his faults,
and with others, to speak without affectation of his
talents.   They furnish us with irrefragable proofs of
the uprightness and strength of his reason, which was
deficient only in experience of the world ; and with

---

[1] See Appendix E.

[2] These pieces were printed in the edition of 1758, and have been
reprinted in most subsequent editions of Corneille's works.

[3] These lines occur in the " Remerciement au Roi, pour l'avoir compris
dans la liste des gratifications faites aux gens de lettres."

[4] *Fontenelle*, "Vie de Corneille," p. 125.

lessons that will ever be useful to dramatic poets, for they will find in them all that his experience of the stage had taught Corneille regarding theatrical positions and effects, with which he was all the better acquainted because he had not studied them until after he had divined their character, just in the same way as he sought to learn the rules of Aristotle in order to justify those which his own genius had dictated.

His determination to renounce the drama was not, however, unalterable. " This," he says in the preface to " Pertharite," " will be the last importunity of this kind with which I shall trouble you ; not that I have adopted so strong a resolution that it cannot be broken, but there is great likelihood that I shall abide by it." These words would seem to indicate that Corneille entertained some hope that attempts would be made to induce him to abandon the intention he thus formally announced ; but he was not disposed to be easily satisfied with the proofs of esteem which he would require. His dedications too plainly show of what nature those proofs might be, and Boileau's severe lines on—

> " *   *   *   Ces auteurs renommés,
> Dégoûtés de gloire et d'argent affamés,"

were, it is said, merely the repetition of a saying of the great Corneille.[1] But Corneille, in the position in

---

[1] " Our author was congratulating the great Corneille on the success of his tragedies, and the glory he had gained thereby. ' Yes,' answered

which he was placed, considered money the proof of his glory, and was perhaps as much offended as grieved at the mediocrity of his fortune. Guided, in all that concerned his personal conduct, by remarkably simple and ingenuous good-sense, he had always observed that a handsome price was paid for things of value, and he felt indignant that this recompense was denied to his merit. Whatever he thought himself allowed to feel, he considered himself equally at liberty to express. When his friends found fault with him 'for not maintaining, by his conversation,

Corneille, ' I am satiated with glory, and famished for money.' " (Note by Brossette, to the " Art Poétique," canto iv., line 130.) The continual complaints of Corneille, both in prose and verse, reiterate almost in the same words the substance of this answer, which Père Tournemine indignantly denies, but without bringing any proof to the contrary. How, he asks, can such a sentiment have been attributed to Corneille, " who is known to have carried his indifference for money almost to blamable carelessness ; who never gained from his pieces anything but what the actors gave him, without making any bargains with them; who allowed a year to elapse without thanking M. Colbert for the renewal of his pension ; who lived without expense and died without property ? " (See the " Défense du grand Corneille," in vol. i. p. 81 of his Works.) A " blamable carelessness " for money is quite compatible with pressing wants, which compel a man afterwards to solicit too vehemently that which he had disdained too negligently. " M. Corneille," says Fontenelle, " had more love for money than ability or application in amassing it." No man feels greater indignation that his wants are not all supplied than he who cannot himself provide for them by prudence or activity. Much has been said of the disinterestedness and fraternal affection which, until the death of Pierre Corneille, led the two brothers to consider all they possessed common property, and united both families into one. I have no wish to deprive praiseworthy conduct of the merit of a good motive or a fine feeling, though this merit is more common than is generally believed ; but I will just observe that this disinterestedness does not in the slightest degree contradict the notion that has been transmitted to us of Corneille's neglect of his pecuniary affairs, nor, consequently, of the natural results of such neglect. See Appendix F.

the reputation he had gained by his writings, he
quietly replied : " I am not the less Pierre Corneille."
Just in the same manner, he frankly said to the
world that Pierre Corneille had a right to expect
better treatment. His wounded pride is always
uppermost in his complaints, and—

> " L'ennui de voir toujours des louanges frivoles
> Rendre à ses grands travaux paroles pour paroles,"

appeared to him to be nothing more than

> " Ce légitime ennui qu'au fond de l'âme excite
> L'excusable fierté d'un peu de vrai mérite."

Thus he explains himself in an Epistle to Fouquet,
inserted at the beginning of " Œdipe." This epistle
conveyed his thanks to the superintendent, for what
favour it is not known ; but this favour was a recollection, and, there is reason to believe, made up for
long neglect. Revived by this mark of esteem,
Corneille desired nothing more than to resume his
pen. Fouquet, " the superintendent," as he says,
" not less of literature than of the finances," [1] proposed
to him three subjects for a tragedy ; Corneille made
his choice, and, in 1659, " Œdipe " appeared. But
the simple beauties of Grecian antiquity were not
destined to arouse a genius which had achieved its
glory and perfected its growth among the ideas and
mental idiosyncracies of the seventeenth century.

[1] See Appendix G.

Corneille congratulated himself on having introduced, into the terrible subject of Œdipus, "the happy episode of the loves of Theseus and Dirce," upon which he has concentrated all the interest of the drama. "This has deprived me," he says, "of the advantage which I hoped to gain, of being frequently only the translator of those great men who have preceded me. But as I have chosen another course, I have found it impossible to fall in with them." He further informs us that he had the honour of obtaining an avowal from most of his auditors, "that he had written no dramatic piece which contained so much art as this." [1]   This unfortunate art, which is now forgotten, was then crowned with success ; at all events, "Œdipe" did not fall before the judgment of the public, and the Court, which probably only sought, by rewarding him, to adorn itself with a glory it had too long neglected, manifested its satisfaction by conferring new favours upon Corneille.[2]   In 1661, on the occasion of the marriage of Louis XIV., he wrote the "Toison d'Or," a kind of opera, preceded by a prologue, into which the peace which had just been concluded gave him an opportunity to introduce some noble lines on the misfortunes of war. In 1662, an admirable scene in "Sertorius" rekindled for a moment the hopes of Corneille's partisans. It was, it is said,

---

[1] See the Preface to " Œdipe."   [2] Ibid.

on hearing these lines, addressed by Sertorius to Pompey—

> " Si dans l'occasion je ménage un peu mieux
> L'assiette du pays et la faveur des lieux,"

that Turenne exclaimed—" Where did Corneille learn the art of war?" In 1663, "Sophonisbe" failed before the recollection of Mairet's piece of the same name, and not, as Saint-Evremond asserted, because Mairet, by depicting Sophonisbe as unfaithful to an old husband for the sake of a young lover, " had hit upon the taste of the ladies and the folks at court." [1] In 1664, " Othon" appeared ; it contained four lines which have continued celebrated, [2] and a few traces of that firmness in the treatment of political interests and court intrigues which was then to be found in Corneille alone. " We must believe," says Fontenelle, " that ' Agésilas ' [3] is by M. Corneille, because his name is attached to it, and there is one scene between Agesilaus and Lysander which could not easily have been written by any one else." [4] By the production of " Attila," Corneille, to use his nephew's expression, " braved the opinion of his age, the taste of which, he perceived, was turning entirely towards the most passionate and least heroic love." [5] Though we may not agree with Fontenelle in considering the development of this tragedy to have been

---

[1] *Saint-Evremond,* " Œuvres," vol. iii. p. 141.
[2] See p. 261.   [3] Published in 1666.
[4] *Fontenelle,* " Vie de Corneille," p. 112.   [5] Ibid. p. 116.

" one of the finest things that Corneille ever did," we
may recognise in it some traits of his peculiar vigour ;
among others that well-known line on the decay of
the Roman Empire and the commencement of the
kingdom of the Franks :—

" Un grand destin commence, un grand destin s'achève."

But the scenes between Attila and the capricious
Honorie are far more suggestive of the idea of a
quarrel between a ridiculous tutor and his unruly
pupil, than of that " noble ferocity " which Fontenelle
is pleased to attribute to the monarch of the Huns. [1]

A famous epigram by Boileau is connected with
the production of the two last-mentioned pieces ; [2] but
it has no other merit than that of expressing with
considerable correctness the feeling of sorrow universally experienced at beholding, in ". Agésilas," the
decay into which a great man might fall, and in
" Attila," how important it was to the glory of
Corneille that his efforts should there end.   His name,
nevertheless, was still powerful.   Molière chose him to
versify his " Psyche," which he had not time to complete
himself ; and Quinault, though already well-known,
was entrusted only with the interludes.   Corneille

---

[1] " There prevails throughout this piece a noble ferocity which he alone
could delineate."   *Fontenelle*, " Vie de Corneille," p. 116.

[2] " Après l'Agésilas,
                Hélas !
        Mais après l'Attila,
                Holà."

was also selected by Queen Henrietta of England
to measure his strength against that of Racine upon
a subject devoted to the description of the pangs of
love. This subject—"Bérénice," with which, it is said,
tender recollections were associated, [1]—was treated
by each poet without the knowledge of the other.
" Who will gain the victory ?—the youngest ? " says
Fontenelle, forgetting that it was the great and old
Corneille who gave the greatest empire to love and
the most weakness to a Roman, as his Titus proposes
to Berenice to renounce his kingdom for her sake [2]—
an idea which Racine's Titus disdainfully rejects. [3]
Finally, " Pulchérie " and " Suréna " appeared, notwithstanding their defects, to revive the recollection

[1] The affection which Louis XIV. and Henrietta of England had felt for
each other, and which they had sacrificed to the dictates of reason rather
than to those of virtue.

[2] " Eh bien ! Madame, il faut renoncer à ce titre
    Qui de toute la terre en vain me fait l'arbitre ;
    Allons dans vos Etats m'en donner un plus doux :
    Ma gloire la plus haute est celle d'être à vous.
    Allons où je n'aurai que vous pour souveraine,
    Où vos bras amoureux seront ma seule chaîne,
    Où l'Hymen en triomphe à jamais l'etreindra :
    Et soit de Rome esclave et maître qui voudra ! "

It is to be regretted that this last line was not introduced upon a worthier
occasion.

[3] " *   *   *   Je dois moins encore vous dire
    Que je suis près, pour vous, d'abandonner l'empire,
    De vous suivre, et d'aller, trop content de mes fers,
    Soupirer avec vous au bout de l'univers.
    Vous-même rougiriez de ma lâche conduite ;
    Vous verriez à regret marcher à votre suite
    Un indigne empereur, sans empire, sans cour,
    Vil spectacle aux humains des foiblesses d'amour."
                    Racine, " Bérénice," act v. scene 6.

of that firm and imposing grandeur which Corneille had imparted to our tragedy ; and this fine saying of Eurydice, on learning that the death of her lover has been caused by her obstinacy,

"Non, je ne pleure point, Madame, mais je meurs,"

formed a noble termination to the poet's career—

"Et son dernier soupir fut un soupir illustre."

Corneille was then nearly seventy years of age. Looking backwards, he could say with just pride, " I have finished my course ; my destiny as a superior man is accomplished ; whatever I was capable of doing I have done ; the rank that I was worthy to obtain I have obtained ; nothing more remains for me to desire." But few men can thus lay down for themselves the limits of their existence—can contemplate themselves only in the past which has so fully belonged to them, and acknowledge the justice of that dispensation of Providence which allots to each of us the time that each is to enjoy. Corneille, who had so long been in possession of undisputed superiority, could not tranquilly behold the rising glory of his successors. He regarded both Molière and Racine with dissatisfaction. " Sometimes," says Fontenelle, " he placed too little confidence in his own rare merit, and believed too easily that it was possible for him to have rivals." [1] Nevertheless, swayed more

[1] *Fontenelle,* " Vie de Corneille," p. 126.

by timidity than envy, he regretted the triumphs of
a rival less than he feared that his own triumphs
would be forgotten ; and on being told, in 1676, that
three of his plays had been performed at Court, he
exclaimed—

> " Est-il vrai, grand monarque, et puis-je me vanter
> Que tu prennes plaisir à me ressusciter ?
> Qu'au bout de quarante ans, Cinna, Pompée, Horace,
> Reviennent à la mode, et reprennent leur place?"

Corneille now began to think he might die, and
felt exceedingly anxious for a little popularity ; the
grief of his failures seemed almost to have extinguished in him the remembrance of his successes.
His feeling of the state of abandonment into which he
believed he had fallen is depicted, in a manner which
fills us with sympathy for the old age of a great man,
in some lines in which he implores the favour of
Louis XIV. for his last works :—

> " Achève : les derniers n'ont rien qui dégénère,
> Rien qui les fasse croire enfans d'un autre père ;
> Ce sont des malheureux étouffés au berceau,
> Qu'un seul de tes regards tireroit du tombeau.
>   *   *   *   *   *
> ' Agésilas ' en foule auroit des spectateurs,
> Et ' Bérénice ' enfin trouveroit des acteurs.
> Le peuple, je l'avoue, et la cour les dégradent ;
> Je foiblis, ou du moins ils se le persuadent :
> Pour bien écrire encor j'ai trop long-temps écrit,
> Et les rides du front passent jusqu'à l'esprit.
> Mais, contre cet abus, que j'aurois de suffrages
> Si tu donnois les tiens à mes derniers ouvrages !
> Que de tant de bonté l'impérieuse loi
> Raméneroit bientôt et peuple et cour vers moi !
> Tel Sophocle à cent ans charmoit encore Athènes,
> Tel bouillonnoit encor son vieux sang dans ses veines,
> Diroient-ils à l'envi.   *   *   *   *   *"

Corneille's jealousy was like that of a child who requires a smile for himself whenever any caresses are bestowed upon his brother. This weakness led him to see cause for disquietude in every event, and to regard the slightest circumstance as an object of dread. "He was melancholy," says Fontenelle, "and he required more solid subjects for hope or rejoicing, than for grief or fear. His incapacity for business was equalled only by his aversion to it ; and the most trivial affairs caused him alarm and terror." [1]

At home, "his humour was hasty, and apparently rough sometimes ; but, on the whole, he was very easy-tempered, a good father, a good husband, a good relative—tender, and full of friendship." [2] In society, he was by turns haughty and humble, proud of his genius, but incapable of deriving any authority from it. At the close of his life, this weakness of his character was greatly increased by the successive decay of his bodily organs. Corneille survived the loss of his faculties for a year, and died on the 1st of October, 1684, at the age of seventy-eight.

He was the senior member of the French Academy, into which he was admitted in 1647. He had presented himself for admission in 1644 and in 1646 ; but the statutes of the Academy had pronounced him ineligible, because he did not reside in Paris. In 1644, the Advocate-General Salomon was elected in pre-

---

[1] *Fontenelle,* "Vie de Corneille," pp. 125, 126.   [2] Ibid.

ference to him, and in 1646, Duryer, the tragic poet. "The register in this place," says Pelisson, in reference to this second nomination, " mentions the resolution which the Academy had adopted always to prefer, of two persons who each possessed the necessary qualifications, that one who was resident in Paris."[1] When Corneille had removed this obstacle by fixing his residence in Paris during a great part of the year, no rival ventured to contest his claim. Balesdens, a distinguished advocate attached to the service of Chancellor Seguier, the protector of the Academy, offered himself for admission, but on being informed that Corneille was also a candidate, " he wrote to the Academy a letter filled with compliments to it, and also to M. Corneille, whom he prayed the company to prefer to him, protesting that he deferred the honour to him as being his due by all sorts of reasons."[2]   On the death of Corneille, the Abbé de Lavau, then director of the Academy, and Racine, the director-elect, both claimed the right of paying him the honours granted by the Academy to the memory of each of its members. The Abbé's claim was allowed, and Benserade, who excelled in the art of expressing pleasant truths, said to Racine, " If any one had a right to inter M. Corneille it was you, and you have not done it." Three months afterwards, Racine made up for his disappointment by pronouncing at the

---

[1] *Pelisson*, " Histoire de l'Académie," p. 362.   [2] Ibid., p. 364.

reception of Thomas Corneille, who succeeded to his
brother's seat in the Academy, a splendid panegyric
of Pierre Corneille, equally remarkable for its subject,
its eloquence, and its orator.

Racine was Corneille's eulogist and Voltaire his
commentator. The genius of both judges is pledge
of their good faith ; but Voltaire's genius bore little
resemblance to that of Corneille, and this dissimilarity
has sometimes interfered with that justice which one
great man loves to render to another. The poet of
the tender and violent passions did not always feel
his heart open to those beauties which dry our tears ;
the favourite of the elegant world of the eighteenth
century was unable to overcome his repugnance to
the coarse incoherencies of a taste which Corneille was
the first to form ; in short, the haste of too easy and
sometimes too careless a labour has introduced, into
Voltaire's commentary, a sufficient number of errors
of fact [1] to make us presume the existence of those
errors of judgment which are, in reality, so apparent.

---

[1] I will quote only two instances :—When Felix, in " Polyeucte," has
unfolded to his confidant, Albin, the coward hopes which are kindled
within him by the dangerous position of Polyeucte, he adds :—

> " Mais que plûtot le ciel à tes yeux me foudroye
> Qu'à de pensers si bas je puisse consentir,
> Que jusque-là ma gloire ose se démentir ! "

Albin replies :—

> " Votre cœur est trop bon et votre âme trop haute."

Upon which Voltaire makes this reflection :—" Felix at least says that he
detests such base thoughts, and we can partially forgive him ; but can we
forgive Albin for saying that his soul is too lofty ? "
Can we forgive Voltaire himself for having so strangely misapprehended

By bestowing a little more attention on the work, and showing a little less complacency for petty passions, he would have given excellence to a work which, notwithstanding its frequently minute, and sometimes excessive, severity, is on the whole, by the abundance, justness, delicacy, and perspicuity of the observations which it contains, a model of literary criticism. Voltaire desired to perform an act of justice and

the meaning of this answer of Albin, who is represented throughout the piece as an honest and sensible man, who courageously defends Pauline and Polyeucte against his master, to whom he is continually showing the absurdity of his fears ? When Felix, with whom Sévère, in compliance with Pauline's entreaty, has been interceding on behalf on Polyeucte, says to his confidant :

> " Albin, as-tu bien vu la fourbe de Sévère ?
> As-tu bien vu sa haine, et vois-tu ma misère ? "

Albin replies, with the indignation of a reasonable man :

> " Je n'ai vu rien en lui qu'un rival généreux ;
> Je ne vois rien en vous qu'un père rigoureux."

A moment afterwards he adds :

> " Grâce, grâce, seigneur ! que Pauline l'obtienne."

On another occasion he represents the danger to which he will expose himself by putting Polyeucte to death, both from the people and from the Emperor. Indeed, the character which Albin displays throughout the piece is manifested in the line to which Voltaire objects ; it will be evident to those who read it, I will not say with attention, but without prejudice, that Albin's answer means simply this : " Your heart is too kind and your soul too lofty to allow you to stoop to such base cowardice ; " and it is plain that he only alludes to Felix's loftiness of soul to prevent him from stooping to too great degradation.

In " Œdipe," which, in truth, may excuse the inattention of the commentator, mention is made of a certain Phœdime, who had just died of the plague, and to whose care the son of Laius was entrusted. Voltaire, misled by the name, speaks of this person as a woman :—" Phœdime knew who this child was, but she is dead of the plague." This error would not be worthy of correction if it did not tend to prove the carelessness of the commentator. Such examples might be multiplied to almost any extent.

kindness to the name and family of Corneille ; and it is much to be deplored that, yielding to the natural weaknesses of his mind and character, he did not conceive and execute his design with sufficient care and conscientiousness to render it a monument worthy both of Corneille and of himself.

JEAN CHAPELAIN.

(1595—1674.)

AT once a poet and a critic,—admired as a poet during his lifetime, at least until the publication of the " Pucelle," and revered as a critic by his contemporaries, even after his death,—Jean Chapelain may be taken as the faithful representative of the taste of an age of which he was the oracle. Even when readers ceased to admire his poems, they did not charge them with having belied his principles, and his authority in the literary world was in no degree diminished by the disfavour with which his poetry was regarded. To his writings, therefore, we must look for information as to what was known and thought in reference to poetical art, in the early part of the seventeenth century : and as the judge of Corneille and predecessor of Boileau, Chapelain is deserving of attention.

Jean Chapelain, the son of a Paris notary, was born on the 4th or 5th of December, 1595. His father's profession would have well suited his peaceful and prudent character, and his gentle, sedate, and orderly mind; but "if his star, at his birth," had not "formed him a poet," he was, at all events, predestined to write verses. His mother was a daughter of Michel Corbière, the friend of Ronsard. Her youth had been impressed, and her imagination was still filled, with admiration for the "Prince of Poets;" she coveted the same glory for a son whose precocity of intellect was highly flattering to the hopes of her maternal pride; and if she had been satisfied with wishing her son the destiny of Ronsard, unaccompanied by his talent, her desires were fulfilled to a far greater extent than she had ventured to hope. Chapelain, "the King of Authors"[1] as long as he lived, and celebrated after his death as the model of unreadable poets, seems, like a dutiful son, to have undertaken the task of accomplishing the destiny which his mother had marked out for him. His studies were pursued with direct reference to the career for which he was intended; and one of his masters was Nicolas Bourbon, a celebrated Latin poet of that time, who entertained so profound a contempt for French verses that, when he read them, it seemed to him, he said, as if he were drinking water, —which was, in his opinion, the worst of insults.[2]

---

[1] "Comme roi des auteurs qu'on l'élève à l'empire."
　　　　　　　　　　　　　　　　Boileau, Satire ix., line 219.

[2] With all his taste for good wine and good cheer, Nicolas Bourbon was a miser; in addition to his avarice, he was tormented by continual sleeplessness; and from the union of these three dispositions, resulted a singular

Being afterwards entrusted with the education of
the two sons of the Marquis de la Trousse, Chapelain
spent the seventeen years through which their
education was continued in the study of poetics, or,
at least, of all that was then known on that subject.
An unpleasant joke confirmed him in his purely
literary taste. The Marquis de la Trousse, who
filled the office of *Prévôt de l'hôtel*, had given him,
either before, or during the time that he was engaged
in the education of his children, an appointment as
archer of the provostry.[1] This post conferred the
right, or rather the obligation, of wearing a sword,
and the sword was not at all in harmony with
Chapelain's character ; for men of letters, in those
days, did not consider themselves bound to possess
courage, and, of all men of letters, Chapelain was
the most pacific. One of his acquaintance, by way

infirmity, viz., that an invitation to dinner, given beforehand, caused him
such agitation that he was unable to sleep, so that his friends were careful
to invite him only on the day of the feast.—"Menagiana," vol. i. p. 315.

[1] An old manuscript copy of the "Chapelain décoiffé," a well-known
parody of a scene in the "Cid," contains these lines, which are quoted in
the "Menagiana," vol. ii. pp. 78, 79, but which were afterwards altered :—

CHAPELAIN.

" Tout beau ! j'étois archer, la chose n'est pas feinte ;
Mais j'étois un archer à la casaque peinte :
Mon juste-au-corps de pourpre et mon bonnet fourré
Sont encore les atours dont je me suis paré ;
Hoqueton diapré de mon maître La Trousse,
Je le suivois à pied quand il marchoit en housse.

LA SERRE.

Recors impitoyable et recors éternel,
Tu traînois au cachot le pâle criminel."

of diversion, proposed to him to act as second in a duel. Chapelain declined ; but, renouncing thenceforward an ornament which was dangerous unless useless, he laid aside his sword and resigned his office as archer, and never resumed them. As he possessed greater qualifications for employments which required probity and capacity than for those which called for resolute firmness of soul, he was entrusted with the administration of the affairs of the Marquis de la Trousse.

Whilst he was engaged in the education of the young Seigneurs de la Trousse, and was seeking for poetical talent in the study of the rules of poetry, there arrived in Paris the Chevalier Marini, with his poem the "Adone," which he intended to have printed, and upon which he was desirous of obtaining the opinions of the wits of France. Chapelain, though he had as yet produced nothing, was already highly esteemed by men of letters for his literary knowledge. Those to whom Marini applied, Malherbe among the number, wished to know his opinion ; and the Italian poet, alarmed by his criticisms, requested him to furnish a preface which might disarm further attacks on the part of the public. This preface, in the form of a letter to M. Favereau, was printed at the beginning of the "Adone,"[1] and is a curious specimen of the criticism of that period. Some few reasonable

---

[1] In the folio edition published at Paris in 1623.

ideas, taken, in the form of quotations, from the writings of the ancients, overwhelmed by a host of arbitrary divisions and sub-divisions, expressed in almost unintelligible French, the Gaulish barbarism of which was highly suggestive of the *style de notaire*, were the materials upon which Chapelain's reputation was built. This reputation, however, was sufficient to gain for him the attention and favour of Richelieu. An ode to the Cardinal bore witness at once to the gratitude of the poet and to his poetical talents; and from that time forth no further difficulty was felt about the choice of a successor to Malherbe.[1]

Since the death of Chapelain, this ode has frequently been spoken of as worthy to secure him an infinitely more honourable reputation than that which he gained by the "Pucelle." His panegyrists never mention it without expressions of admiration; and we are assured that Boileau admitted that Chapelain "had once written a rather fine ode—how I cannot tell," he used to add.[2] I am quite at a loss to account for this opinion of Boileau. Doubtless surprised that the author of the "Pucelle" could have produced any verses of average excellence,

---

[1] "M. Chapelain seemed to have succeeded to the reputation of Malherbe, after the death of that author; and it was loudly published throughout all France that he was the prince of French poets. This appears by the testimonies of various persons who observed what was said during the ministry of Cardinals Richelieu and Mazarin." *Baillet*, "Jugements des Savants," vol. v. p. 278, edit. 1722.

[2] "Menagiana," vol. iii. p. 73.

written clearly and correctly, and free from harshness or bad taste, Boileau rather exaggerated the marvellous character of this prodigy. Perhaps, also, taking the ode on the " Capture of Namur " into consideration, we may be permitted to doubt whether the author of the " Art Poétique " had a truly just and vivid feeling of that which constitutes the beauty of an ode. The most scrupulous attention has not enabled me to discover, in Chapelain's performance, the slightest trace of poetic fire, or even of that nobility of thought of which we sometimes catch a glimpse through the uncouth style of the " Pucelle." Its progress is cold and didactic ; the poet, confessing himself incapable of worthily celebrating the praises of his hero, limits his endeavours to the repetition of what is said of him :

> " Le long des rives du Permesse,
> La troupe de ses nourrissons," [1]

and this frigid conception leads to the still more frigid repetition of the words, *Ils chantent,* with which he commences six strophes in succession. Poetry is as undiscoverable in the imagery as in the ideas. Balzac bestowed great praise upon the lines in which, to tranquillise the modesty of Richelieu, who thinks he is indebted solely to the King his master for his knowledge and magnificence, the

---

[1] The entire ode is given in the " Recueil des plus belles pièces des poëtes Français," vol. iv. p. 181.

poet compares him to the pole-star, the guide of the pilot :—

> " Qui brille sur sa route et gouverne ses voiles,
> Cependant que la lune, accomplissant son tour
> Dessus un char d'argent environné d'étoiles,
> Dans le sombre univers représente le jour." [1]

The poet celebrates the "light" of the renown of Richelieu, which, he says, is "ever pure," notwithstanding the attempts of calumny to darken it :—

> "Dans un paisible mouvement
> Tu t'élèves au firmament,
> Et laisses contre toi murmurer sur la terre.
> Ainsi le haut Olympe, à son pied sablonneux,
> Laisse fumer la foudre et gronder le tonnerre
> Et garde son sommet tranquille et lumineux."

As regards the appropriateness of his ideas and his selection of subjects of praise, an example is supplied by this strophe, which is really curious when we consider that it was addressed to Cardinal Richelieu :—

> " Ton propre bonheur t'importune
> Alors qu'il fait des malheureux ;
> On voit que tu souffres pour eux,
> Et que leur peine t'est commune.
> Quand leurs efforts sont impuissans
> Contre tes acts innocens,
> Dans leur désastre encor ta bonté les révère ;
> Tu les plains dans les maux dont ils sont affligés,
> Et demandes au ciel, d'un cœur humble et sincère,
> Qu'ils veuillent seulement en être soulagés."

When flattery thus boldly assumes the character of falsehood, it becomes a conventional language, equally applicable to all men, which, not allowing the poet the choice of any feature peculiar to his

---

[1] "Menagiana," vol. iii. p. 73.

hero, casts him without resource into the common-places of adulation. Without doing too much honour to flattery, it is permissible to believe that, for it to be clever, it must at least have some slight connection with truth.

I attach no personal blame, however, to Chapelain for the singular eulogies which he has lavished on his protector. Such was then the general tone of praise, arising rather from want of taste and tact than from any baseness especially belonging to that epoch in the life of courts. A sort of unskilfulness in the treatment of falsehood, by forcing it to appear in its coarsest guise, also compelled truth to display itself occasionally under harsh and peremptory forms. Richelieu himself had to endure some sallies of this inconvenient candour ; and even men of letters, though bound to him by the ties of necessity and gratitude, rarely feared to maintain in private those opinions which they deemed reasonable, in opposition to that all-powerful minister upon whom, in public, they unhesitatingly lavished the most absurd praises. In the affair of the " Cid," Corneille and the Academy, with Chapelain at its head, courageously asserted their right of opinion against the declared will of the Cardinal : and on a less public occasion, the " most circumspect " Chapelain, as he was called by Balzac,[1] whose

---

[1] "Menagiana," vol. iii. p. 73.

temerity he had frequently censured,[1] firmly maintained his own opinion against one of those ideas to which a man of Richelieu's character would be likely to cling most tenaciously. Being appointed, together with several other literary men, to amuse the Cardinal's leisure by literary discussions, Chapelain had forwarded to Bois-Robert, the usual intermediary in correspondence of this kind, a lengthy and very reasonable criticism of Cardinal Bentivoglio's "History of the Wars of Flanders." In this letter, remarkable for a liberality of ideas which was rare for his time, but which would, perhaps, have been even more bold and extraordinary fifty years later, Chapelain insisted strongly upon the impartiality which a historian ought to maintain in reference to the various religious creeds. " Vice and virtue," he says, " are two foundations upon which all are agreed, and which admit of no contradiction. The true religion, which ought much rather to possess this privilege, is not so fortunate ; each man calls his own the best ; and you prove nothing to an enemy of different creed when you derive your arguments and means of attack from the falsity of that which he believes. This is why I hold that the judicious historian, who wishes to be of service to the public, should not take his reasons from such sources, because they are sure

---

[1] See the " Mélanges de Littérature, tirés des lettres manuscrites de M. Chapelain," p. 63, 64, edit. 1726.

not to meet with general approbation."[1] He also
blamed Cardinal Bentivoglio for his partiality
towards the Spaniards, the oppressors of the
Netherlands. Richelieu expressed himself satisfied
with this letter, but declared against its author's
opinion that "the historian ought to have nothing to
do with judging the facts which he relates."[2] As
firm on a point of literary criticism as any great
scholar would be on a point of erudition, Chapelain
replied to Bois-Robert :—" I esteem myself very
unfortunate in not being as completely of his
Eminence's opinion on this subject, as I am and
always wish to be in all things ; " and after making
suitable apologies, he declares himself as positively
for the affirmative as the Cardinal for the negative,
and developes his views at considerable length,
basing them upon very sound reasons. The most
singular circumstance in connection with the matter,
is that, during the whole course of the discussion,.
Chapelain looks solely to the interest which the
Cardinal took in the question as a mere reader of
history, and never at that which he would be likely
to feel in it as an historical personage. Flattery,
which might here have found a fine field for display,
alludes only to the angelic constitution of Monseigneur's mind,[3] which rendered useless to him that

[1] See the "Mélanges de Littérature, tirés des lettres manuscrites de
M. Chapelain," pp. 101—116.
[2] Ibid. p. 123, *et seq.*   [3] Ibid. p. 133.

assistance and information with which the weakness of the vulgar could not dispense. Was this the simplicity of a man of letters, or the address of a consummate courtier ?   We are too far distant both from the man and the time to decide.

In the performance of his duties as critic to the Cardinal, in which office he was associated with several other men of letters, Chapelain, who was really erudite and as judicious as the circumspect frigidity of his imagination could allow, naturally proved superior to all his colleagues ; and he therefore soon exceeded them in favour.   It was not, however, until the administration of Colbert that he was entrusted with that special mission which established his sway, if not over literature, at least over men of letters : but, under the government of Richelieu, the favour which he enjoyed was sufficiently great to induce them to attach considerable weight to his authority; and, even including Boileau, who complained of it only as a man of taste, his dominion over the literary world was generally acknowledged.

In the year 1632, he had refused to accompany the Duke de Noailles to Rome, in the capacity of secretary of legation.   Thenceforward, attached to the service of the Cardinal,[1] from whom he received

His first letter, on Cardinal Bentivoglio's book, is dated December 10, 1631 ; and it is rather singular that the second is dated only on the 9th of June, 1633.   Probably Bois-Robert, the intermediary through whom this correspondence passed, only communicated the letters to the Cardinal when a good opportunity occurred.

a pension of a thousand crowns,[1] Chapelain naturally
preferred, to the labour of a subordinate position,
that kind of independence which, in the opinion of a
literary man, specially consists in liberty to dispose of
his time as he pleases.   From this leisure, after long
and painful efforts, resulted the "Pucelle."   The
success of his preface to the "Adone" had convinced Chapelain of the infallibility of his literary
knowledge ; he never suspected that the composition
of a poem required something more than a perfect
acquaintance with the rules of poetry, and few
persons were then to be found who were any wiser
than himself on this point.   After mature thought,
he considered himself called upon, when nearly
forty years of age, to write an epic poem.   He spent
five years in the arrangement of its plan ; but we
have not been informed how much time he devoted
to the choice of his subject.   This choice was
certainly the happiest circumstance of his undertaking.   The Duke de Longueville, a descendant of

---

[1] See the life of Chapelain in *Lambert*, "Histoire littéraire du Siècle de
Louis XIV.," vol. ii. p. 361.   The sum appears rather large.   In 1663,
Chapelain was appointed by Colbert to draw up a list of the literary men
whom he deemed worthy to receive the benefits of the king, and received
a pension of a thousand crowns from that minister.   This distinction gave
rise to the famous parody of " Chapelain décoiffé," and was considered
very extraordinary.   (See the " Chapelain décoiffé," in the "Œuvres de
Boileau," vol. iii. p. 193, edit. 1772).   Ménage, speaking of the pension of
two thousand livres granted to Chapelain by the Duke de Longueville,
mentions it as "a great pension ; " and Pelisson (" Histoire de l'Académie,"
p. 20,) simply tells us that the Cardinal had manifested his esteem for
Chapelain by giving him a pension.   Lambert, a careless writer, may have
confounded the two dates.

Dunois, the bastard of Orleans, thought too much encouragement could not be bestowed upon a work which would add, to the glory of his family, all the renown that could be derived from the name and talents of such a man as Chapelain ; and a pension of two thousand livres,[1] to last until the composition of the poem should be completed, contributed largely to the anticipative celebrity of a work so well remunerated.

The twenty years spent by Chapelain in the composition of the first twelve cantos of his work, were twenty years of unmixed glory. The reputation of the poet ; the prestige derived from reading isolated passages, a sure means for an author to interest in his success those whom he appears to have chosen as his judges ; the lively curiosity always felt regarding that which is known only in part or by hearsay,—all united to concentrate universal interest upon this poem, which, though ever promised and incessantly shown in parts, seemed likely never to be given entire. The Duchess de Longueville alone, carried away by the general opinion, but enlightened

---

[1] " Menagiana," vol. i. p. 123. In a remark upon the 218th line of Boileau's 9th Satire :—

" Qu'il soit le mieux renté de tous les beaux-esprits,"

Brossette, one of the editors of Boileau's works, tells us that this pension from M. de Longueville amounted to four thousand livres, and that it had then been doubled ; which agrees with what Ménage says about the original pension. Lambert raises it to a thousand crowns, like that granted by the Cardinal.

by an instinct which did not incline her usually to coincide with her husband's tastes, said in reference to those readings, which probably occupied more of her attention than she was willing to bestow upon them : " The poem is perfectly beautiful, but it is very tiresome." [1]

No great importance was attached to this isolated opinion of a lady devoted to interests very different from those of literature, and whose taste might even be regarded with suspicion ; for in the famous duel of the sonnets, she had been almost alone in favour of Voiture's " Uranie " against Benserade's " Job." For twenty years, nothing occurred to interrupt the pleasant security of the poet, or his expectation of the brilliant success which he believed himself destined to achieve.   The desire to receive for a longer period the emoluments attached to his labour [2] induced him, it is said, to delay the enjoyments of publication and success ; but even this unfavourable judgment of Chapelain's probity allows the merit of rare moderation to his self-love.

At length, he determined to enter the lists which he considered so little to be feared.   In 1656, the

---

[1] See the note on these lines of *Boileau's* third Satire :—

"La *Pucelle* est encore une œuvre bien galante,
Et je ne sais pourquoi je bâille en la lisant."

[2] "M. Chapelain," says *Ménage*, "was so long in bringing out his 'Pucelle' only because he was paid a large pension by M. de Longueville. He feared that the prince would no longer care about him after he had published his work." "Menagiana," vol. i. p. 123.

first twelve cantos of the " Pucelle " were published. Issuing at length from that limited circle which was formed around it by the literate few, and from which isolated rays of its glory had alone hitherto proceeded, it sought the suffrages of the general public. All might now judge what a few had pronounced worthy of unmingled admiration ; and probably gaining encouragement from the presence of the public, men of letters ventured for the first time to express an opinion which they had been afraid to pronounce so long as they were the only persons to support it.[1] The promptitude of the attack justifies the presumption that it was premeditated. " Three days after this so much extolled poem had been made public," says Vigneul-Marville, " a criticism of very small merit [2] having given it the first scratch, every one fell upon it, and the whole reputation of both the poem and the poet fell to the ground—a fall," adds Vigneul-Marville, " the greatest and most deplorable that has ever occurred, in the memory of man, from the top of Parnassus to the bottom." [3]

[1] He nevertheless had fervent admirers among the literary class. Sarrasin and Maynard had eulogised him in their poems ; and Godeau, the bishop of Vence, said to a man who was urging him to write an epic, that his voice was not strong enough to do so, "and that the bishop, on this occasion, yielded the supremacy to Chapelain." " Menagiana," vol. i. p. 31.

[2] I have been unable to discover this criticism, the obscurity of which is sufficiently evident from what Vigneul-Marville says of it. Segrais asserts that Despréaux was the first who shook off the yoke by his " Chapelain décoiffé ;" but this poem is dated in 1664, and Chapelain had not to wait so long for epigrams.

[3] *Vigneul-Marville*, " Mélanges," vol. ii. p. 5.

The event, however, was not quite so dramatic as it is represented to have been by the imaginative author of the " Mélanges." The sale of six editions of these first twelve cantos in eighteen months, proved that considerable time was required for the demolition of a reputation which had been so long accumulating. But all parties united in the attack ; entire collections of epigrams[1] were published against the " Pucelle," and it became the usual butt for conversational witticisms. It was said that the " Pucelle," as long as she was kept by a great prince, had retained a sort of reputation, but that she had entirely lost it since she had become public property.[2] The respect attached to the name of Chapelain disappeared, at least among men of letters; and Furetière remarking him by the side of Patru, said : " *Voilà un auteur pauvre et un pauvre auteur.*"[3]

Chapelain's friends did not desert him in these trying circumstances. They felt it incumbent upon them to maintain the honour of their approbation, and the Duke de Longueville was especially earnest in the work. He doubled the pension which he had bestowed on Chapelain ; and the avarice ascribed to the poet gives us reason to believe that so valuable

---

[1] " Menagiana," vol. i. p. 125.
[2] Ibid. vol. i. p. 123. This saying was thus versified :—

> " Depuis qu'elle paroît et se fait voir au jour,
> Que chacun la prise à son tour,
> La Pucelle n'est plus qu'une fille publique."

[3] " Menagiana," vol. i. p. 126.

a mark of esteem must have consoled him for many criticisms. Others supported him with their pens and voices ; but, it must be confessed, the vigour of their defence was greatly modified by the astonishment into which they had been thrown by so unexpected a failure. Huet, the bishop of Avranches, the most intrepid of them all, merely asked that before judgment was pronounced, time should be allowed for the publication of the entire poem ; and he therefore thought that the poet had done wrong to publish separately the first part, which was so ill calculated to ensure a favourable reception for the remainder. Saint-Pavin declared that the " Pucelle " contained faults of so much beauty that its enemies would have been proud to commit them ; but, at the same time, he wrote this sonnet :—

> " Je vous dirai sincèrement
> Mon sentiment sur la *Pucelle* ;
> L'air et la grâce naturelle
> S'y rencontrent également.
>
> Elle s'explique fortement,
> Ne dit jamais de bagatelle,
> Et toute sa conduite est telle
> Qu'il faut la louer hautement.
>
> Elle est pompeuse, elle est parée ;
> Sa beauté sera de durée ;
> Son éclat peut nous éblouir ;
>
> Mais enfin, quoiqu'elle soit telle,
> Rarement on ira chez elle
> Quand on voudra se réjouir." [1]

---

[1] " Recueil des plus belles pièces des poètes Français," vol. iv. p. 176. and vol. v. p. 152.

This is a mere paraphrase of that saying of Mme. de Longueville which has been already quoted. Segrais, who, though but slightly disposed in Chapelain's favour, was sufficiently addicted to admiration to discover inimitable passages in the " Pucelle," nevertheless confessed that it was not a good heroic poem. "But," he added, "have we any better ? Does any one read the ' Clovis,' [1] or the ' Saint-Louis,' [2] or others of the same kind ?" [3] No one dared to defend its style, and Chapelain himself confessed that he was not a good hand at writing verses ; [4] but he made this confession haughtily, considering so small a merit quite unworthy of his attention and of the notice of his judges. " As to versification and language," he says in his preface to his last twelve cantos, [5] " they are instruments of so little importance in the epic, that they do not merit the consideration of such great judges ; they are abandoned to the fury of the grammarian tribe, without gaining greater or less esteem by the approbation which they may receive from it, or by the hard blows which it may give them." He then goes on to declare that, " strictly considered, the poem would not be less a poem if it

---

[1] By *Saint-Amant*.   [2] By *Père Lemoine*.   [3] " Segraisiana," p. 5.

[4] *Vigneul-Marville*, " Mélanges," vol. ii. p. 5.

[5] I have read this second part, which has never been printed, and which together with the Preface, exists in MS. in the National Library at Paris.

were not written in verse ; " which seems to imply that it is none the worse for being written in bad verse.

Chapelain, influenced by the first emotions of paternity, was desirous, it is said,[1] to rush to the assistance of his offspring when thus violently attacked, and at all events to protect, by his talent as a critic, a work which his talent as a poet had failed to render capable of defending itself. Second thoughts probably made him sensible that such aid would most likely be more dangerous than useful ; so he satisfied himself with labouring in silence at the continuation of his work, and reserved all his animadversions for that preface which I have already quoted, and in which—with the dignity of persecuted genius, challenging alike his friends and his enemies— he declares that " he takes nothing less than the universe for his stage, and eternity for his spectatress."

Chapelain's eternity was of short duration, and the universe has not cared to liberate the last productions of his genius from the obscurity in which he himself allowed them to languish. Neither the last twelve books of the " Pucelle," nor their haughty preface, have ever been printed. Scarcely any one has even inquired about their existence ; and, within a few months, this unfortunate work

---

[1] *Vigneul-Marville,* " Mélanges," vol. ii. p. 5.

verified the horoscope drawn of it by Linière a few
days before its appearance :—

> " Nous attendons de Chapelain,
> Ce noble et fameux écrivain,
> Une incomparable *Pucelle*.
> La cabale en dit force bien :
> Depuis vingt ans on parle d'elle ;
> Dans six mois on n'en dira rien." [1]

Few persons have felt sufficient interest in this
literary event, which has left so few traces of its
existence, to look to the work itself for the explanation of the double phenomenon of its astonishing
reputation and its fearful fall ; and if any persons
have had the courage to attempt this examination,
they have derived little pleasure from it. All
popular favour is a fashion, and the empire of any
particular fashion is as difficult of explanation as the
wind, which blows in one direction to-day, but will
change to-morrow.   Perhaps, however, curious minds
may take pleasure in learning from Chapelain's work
the limit of the taste of a reasonable, erudite, and
judicious man (for such was the author of the
" Pucelle "), when the way has not been opened to
him by the taste of his contemporaries; and when he
does not possess, in order to precede his age, that
inspiration which rises to truth by roads whose
existence was not even suspected by the vulgar,
until genius had revealed them to their eyes.   We

[1] " Menagiana," vol. i. p. 124.

may learn from the " Pucelle," how necessary
imagination is even to reason, when reason attempts
to transgress the bounds of simple common sense ;
and how indispensable it is to see far and quickly,
in order to see always clearly and justly.

Charles VII., the Maid of Orleans, Dunois, Agnes
Sorel, the Duke of Burgundy and Bedford are the
principal personages of Chapelain's poem.   God and
the angels, whom he employs to ensure success for the
projects of the Maid, and frustrate the devil and his
artifices in favour of the English—are the principal
springs of the action. Charles VII. is certainly the least
epic and least dramatic character that it would be possible to imagine. Ever boasting of his warlike ardour,
but never fighting ; getting angry with those who
oppose his will, but never having a will of his own ;
sometimes the very humble servant of the Maid, who
leads him like a child ; sometimes the dupe of his
favourite, the unworthy Amaury, who cheats him
like a fool ; in love with Agnes when he sees her,
and forgetting her as soon as she is out of his sight,
—he incessantly changes his feelings and resolutions,
and passes from weakness to vigour, or from wrath to
submission : so that nothing in his character excites
the slightest curiosity in reference to the consequences
of a position which a new display of weakness will
change as soon as it becomes too difficult to treat.
The Maid, always impassible and always inspired,

sustains tolerably well the character ascribed to
her ; but this character is a perpetual miracle : all
her prayers are heard, and every one of her words is
a decree from heaven, which overthrows all obstacles
and dissipates all resistance. Sent by God, at the
beginning of the poem, to the assistance of Orleans,
which is already reduced to the last extremities, she
leaves her native woods, arrives at the camp of the
king, is listened to with respect, finds the army at
her orders, and the court at her feet ; and all this
is effected by the utterance of a few words. Orleans
is delivered. The heroine flies from combat to
combat, and always at a given point an angel comes
down to decide in her favour a victory which the
ever-defeated demon unceasingly attempts to gain
over her. Amaury, a true terrestrial demon, enraged
at the influence which the Maid has obtained, and
fearful for the loss of his own, determines to recall,
as an opponent to his formidable enemy, Agnes
Sorel, whom the same jealousy of power had
induced him to remove by his intrigues. On the
invitation of Amaury, Agnes returns ; a look will
restore to her her empire over the feeble Charles ;
but the Maid appears, and utters a few stern words
against Agnes ; upon which Charles casts down his
eyes and turns away his head, and Agnes departs in
indignation. When her first victories have opened
the road to Rheims, the Maid desires to conduct

the king thither to be consecrated. The demon, ever on the watch, endeavours to disturb this triumphal march by inspiring " the soldiers with libidinous thoughts for shameless girls ;" but the Maid no sooner becomes aware of this than, passing from rank to rank, she—

" Ecarte d'un clin-d'œil ces criminels objets ;"

and twenty-two lines contain the entire narrative of this incident, the arrangement of which had exhausted all the genius and malice of the devil. With equal facility revolts are overcome, and the envious confounded. Nowhere does this marvellous girl find neither passions to repress nor obstinacy to conquer ; and the passions which she inspires give her no more trouble than those which rise in opposition against her. God, who here performs a part similar to that of Venus in the " Æneid," ordains that, in order better to help his favourite, all the leaders of Charles's army should fall in love with her—an idea all the more unfortunate as it exercises no influence whatever over the progress of the poem. Of all these amours, the only one which the poet has invested with any importance is that of Dunois ; but his respectful and reserved affection very properly *"poco spera, nulla chiede,"* [1] and perhaps even does not desire much ; so that, forgotten almost

---

[1] " Hopes little, asks nothing." *Tasso,* " Gerusalemme liberata," Canto ii. stanza 15.

as soon as it arose, it produces no other effect
than to cause deep affliction to poor Marie, a rather
interesting personage, but whose resignation and
reserve cannot heat the chilly atmosphere by which
she is surrounded. The ambitious and coquettish
Agnes, casting herself into the arms of the Duke of
Burgundy, whom she detests, in revenge for the
indifference of Charles, whom she loves ; and the
Duke of Burgundy, divided between his love for
Agnes, his hatred of Charles, and his indignation
against his humiliation by English tyranny—would
seem to promise some agitation, some strife of
passion : but these conflicts are of such short
duration, and the resolutions which terminate them
are so soon taken, that the imagination of the reader
finds nothing in them to rest upon, and to break the
series of battles, marches, and counter-marches, all
producing similar results, and all related in the same
tone, which, with the incidents already mentioned,
fill up the first twelve books of the poem. At the
end of the twelfth book, Dunois, who at the assault
of Paris has leaped over the ramparts without being
followed by his men, is taken prisoner by the
English. At the same moment the demon turns
against Amaury the arrow which the Maid had
just shot against the enemy. Amaury dies of the
wound ; and, after an inspection of the arrow,
Charles, convinced that the Maid has killed his

favourite, bursts into violent anger and pronounces sentence of banishment against her, which terminates her mission and deprives her of her powers, which she may no longer employ in the service of a prince abandoned by God. Grieved, but resigned, she retires to the woods of Compiègne, but is soon forced, by the approach of the English, to take refuge in the town. The English then lay siege to Compiègne. Constrained by the prayers of the inhabitants, who reproach her with deserting them, after having attracted the English forces into their neighbourhood, the Maid resumes her arms, notwithstanding her repugnance to do so, and attempts a sortie, in which, though unsupported from on high, the recollection of her former prowess maintains her advantage for some time ; but at length the artifices of the demon induce those whom she is defending to abandon her, that they may save themselves ; and she is made prisoner and taken to Rouen. At this point Chapelain halts, for the first time, in his laborious career.

The twelve cantos which follow, and which I have read in the manuscript, seem to indicate the fatigue occasioned by the violent efforts which presided over the production of the first part. The action, by being less closely compacted together, and less crowded with events, though not more rich in development, gives breathing-time, and even sleeping-time, to the characters, whom the first part of the poem kept constantly on the alert. The Maid remains quietly confined in her prison, and nothing is said about her. Dunois is even more fortunate in his dungeon, where Marie has taken him under her care, and—

> " De son long étendu sur de mollets coussins,
> N'est ni vu ni servi que de ses médecins,"

and by Marie, "his physician as well as his lover." When his cure is effected, he is exchanged by the intervention of Bedford, who seeks to separate him from Marie, as he desires that she should marry his son Edward. The French hero now passes an idle life in a camp where there is no more fighting to be done, and which Agnes, who again appears as the principal personage at Court, as well as of the poem, has rendered a scene of love and amusement. Upon a new-comer devolves almost exclusively the task of giving movement to the action. This is Edward, the son of Bedford, just arrived from London. By a singular coincidence, Edward has exactly the same features and appearance as Rodolphe, the brother of the Maid, and her fellow-prisoner. Pretending that this young warrior has been miraculously delivered from prison, he presents himself to Charles under his name, and succeeds in obtaining the confidence of the king, whom he rules, as others have done, by making use of Agnes Sorel. He deceives Charles, betrays him, thwarts all his plans, and finally attempts to poison him. For this purpose he prepares an apple of monstrous size, of the same kind as those—

"Qu'en langage fruitier *calleville* on appelle."

The king thinks it so beautiful that he desires Agnes to eat it—

"Et de sucre en poussière un nuage y répand."

Both sugar and apple are poisoned; so Agnes dies. The king at first wished to die with her, but suddenly took consolation, according to his custom, being influenced by the advice of an angel, who even induced him to do penance for his amour. The demon, on his side, has at last succeeded in persuading the English to put the Maid to death, instead of adopting the opinion of Bedford, who wished to keep her as a hostage for the safety of his son. She, whose whole joy consists in the hope of martyrdom, guesses that the fatal moment is drawing near—

"Et conçoit de sa mort un aimable soupçon."

Her trial occupies thirty lines, and her death, which is narrated with a little more detail, is as glorious as her life. Meanwhile the true Rodolphe really escapes from prison, comes to the Court of Charles to reclaim his name, and challenges and kills the traitor Edward in a duel. Dunois defeats and drives out the English :—

"Et le combat finit faute de combattans."

I pass over many incidents mentioned in the second

part of the poem, such as the enumeration of the fleet
brought from England by the brave Talbot; the
long account of the naval victory gained by the
English over the French, who endeavour to oppose
their disembarkation ; the arrival in Paris of Henry,
the young king of England ; his coronation and duel
with Charles, which is interrupted by the traitorous
interference of the English, when they behold their
king about to fall ; the escape of the princess Marie
whom Bedford wishes to force to marry his son ; and
so forth.   Nor shall I linger to explain the allegorical
meaning which Chapelain claims to have given to his
poem, "according to the precepts."[1] It is of little
consequence to the opinion which may be formed of
the talent of the poet that, in his work, France is
supposed to represent " the soul of man, Charles
the will, Agnes concupiscence, Dunois virtue, Joan
of Arc divine grace," and so on.   Chapelain had too
much good sense for us to suppose, whatever he may
say about it, that these fine allegories were really
the object of his work, and he had more than enough
wit to discover them afterwards ; they consequently
exert no influence whatever upon the progress of the
poem ; and, with the exception of a few romanesque
springs of action, the general plan is reasonable

---

[1] He praises himself, in his Preface, for the care he has taken " to reduce
his action to the universal, according to the precepts, and not to deprive
it of allegorical meaning, by which poetry is made one of the chief
instruments of architectonics." See the Preface to the first part of his
poem.

enough. The sentiments scattered through the work would appear sufficiently natural if, through not giving them enough development, the poet did not constantly manifest them as far too weak to occasion the results which they effect. We might praise the unity of subject, which Chapelain has scrupulously observed, if he had added to it simplicity of action : but incapable, on account of the barrenness of his imagination, of deriving from the incidents which he brings on the stage, all the means of interest and effect with which they might be made to furnish him, he is obliged to multiply both means and incidents ; and, as he is equally incapable of giving them variety, he incessantly repeats the same ideas and the same details, and thus falls into confusion without avoiding monotony.

It is in details especially that we discern how deficient the reason and taste of Chapelain were in imagination. There are two kinds of truths ; one, by which the poet ought to be sufficiently struck to select and render it ; the other, with which he ought to be sufficiently acquainted to take care to avoid it. Both kinds may sometimes happen to unite in the same objects: thus Racine, describing the ruin and desolation of Jerusalem, says :—

> " Et de Jérusalem l'herbe cache les murs ;
> Sion, repaire affreux de reptiles impurs,
> Voit de son temple saint les pierres dispersées." [1]

---

[1] *Racine,* " Esther," act i. scene 4.

Saint-Amant, on the other hand, gives the following
representation of a building in ruins :—

> " Le plancher du lieu le plus haut
> Est tombé jusque dans la cave,
> Que la limace et le crapaud
> Souillent de venin et de bave." [1]

In both descriptions the objects are the same ; the
only difference is in the circumstances chosen by the
two poets.   Chapelain will not, like Saint-Amant,
select a disagreeable or ridiculous truth in order to
present it under a striking form ; but his perception
of it will not be sufficiently clear to enable him to
avoid it.   He will not perceive, in his own inventions,
all that other persons may discover in them ; and
even the models which he imitates will not enlighten
him.   When Tasso represents the angel Gabriel
preparing to appear before the eyes of Godfrey de
Bouillon, he thus describes the operation by which
the celestial spirit rendered himself visible to earthly
eyes :—

> " La sua forma invisibil d'aria cinse
> Ed al senso mortal la sottopose ;
> Umane membra, aspetto uman si finse ;
> Ma di celeste maestà il compose,
> Tra giovane e fanciullo età confine
> Prese, ed orno di raggi il biondo crine." [2]

---

[1] " Recueil des plus belles pièces des Poëtes Français," vol. iii. p. 289.
[2] Fairfax's translation is as follows :—

> " In form of airy members fair embar'd,
>   His spirits pure were subject to our sight ;
> Like to a man in show and shape he far'd,
>   But full of heav'nly majesty and might,
> A stripling seem'd he thrice five winters old,
> And radiant beams adorn'd his locks of gold."

The same idea is thus treated by Chapelain. The Archangel Michael resolves to appear to Charles in the form of weeping France ; he descends from heaven, and —

> " De la plus haute sphère aux plages les plus basses
> Vient fixer l'air mobile, en assembler des masses,
> Les mêler, les unir et s'en former un corps
> Vuide par le dedans, et solide au dehors.
> De la France abattue il lui donne l'image,
> Il lui donne son air, lui donne son corsage,
> Et dans son cave sein luy-même s'enfermant,
> A ses membres divers donne le mouvement." [1]

If we consider only the effect of these two pictures, who could believe that one was an imitation of the other ? Remark with what care and delicacy the Italian poet has retained, in his description, the vagueness necessary to a sketch which could not become too palpable without being altogether false. Is it the angel himself, or simply the form which he has assumed, which is about to become visible to us ? Tasso does not tell us ; this appearance does not belong to the angel, and yet it is not distinct from himself ; insensibly our imagination confounds the one with the other, and soon it will be not merely the figure, but the angel himself who will appear to us, and whose delicate features and floating locks we shall plainly recognise. Nothing of this would be positive enough for Chapelain ; he requires something more sensible and determinate ; and therefore,

---

[1] *Chapelain,* " La Pucelle," Canto vi. p. 190.

separating very distinctly what Tasso has taken care
to commingle, he makes his figure of France a large
doll inside which the angel conceals himself, just as
in an operatic transformation, and which he will put
in motion with almost as much grace and naturalness
as Punch displays under the influence of the strings
held by his hidden director.   That imagination must
indeed be   very   insensible   to   truth   and   very
inaccessible to ridicule, which is not at once struck
with the falsity and absurdity of this image.

Chapelain is equally unaware of the impropriety
of certain clevernesses by which he attemps to
disguise too palpable truths.   Queen Christina of
Sweden, displeased at his having censured, as too
free, some lines which she had considered pretty,
exclaimed : " Your M. Chapelain is a poor fellow ;
he would wish everything to be maiden."[1]   It is
singular enough that he carried out this fancy even
in reference to Agnes Sorel ; but far more singular
are the means by which the poet has attempted to
dispel all the injurious thoughts that the reader
might entertain with regard to the *liaisons* of Agnes
with Charles VII. and the Duke of Burgundy.
When recalled by Amaury, she presents herself to
Charles with the sole purpose of offering him " her
arm and her courage ; "   and   when   Amaury
afterwards finds fault with the Maid for having

[1] "Menagiana," vol. i. p. 140.

procured the dismissal of Agnes, he alleges as the
ground of his complaint that she might have assisted
the king " with her arms."   When Agnes betakes
herself to the Duke of Burgundy, she tells him :—

> " Mon bras vient contre tous embrasser la querelle,
> Vient combattre Bedford, Charles et la Pucelle."

But, on the other hand, no explanation whatever is
given of the grounds for the confidence reposed " in the
arm of Agnes," and in the force of " her arms ; " all
her military preparations, when she is about to rejoin
King Charles, consist in looking at herself in the
mirrors which adorn her gilded chamber :—

> " À voir hors des deux bouts de ses deux courtes manches,
> Sortir à découvert deux mains longues et blanches
> Dont les doigts inégaux, mais tout ronds et menus,
> Imitent l'embonpoint des bras ronds et charnus.
>   *   *   *   *   *   *
> À remarquer surtout l'inimitable grâce
> Qui, dans ce bel amas, les beaux rayons semant,
> En rend beau l'assemblage et le lustre charmant."

Moreover, when Agnes meets the Duke of Burgundy,
who wishes to throw himself at her feet, she " clasps
him in both her arms," assures him of her " true
love," makes him sit down by her side, and takes up
her residence with him *sans façon* in his " solitary
palace " of Fontainebleau ; and the author, who tells
us nothing more, imagines that he has thus saved the
modesty, if not the virtue, of Agnes ; for the king,
when she returns to him, does not manifest the
slightest displeasure at the levity of her conduct.

Bad taste is the necessary result of this facility for dispensing with truth : and the author will not hesitate to carry hyperbole to that point at which, though given as the real image of an object, it becomes its falsest representation. Thus, on her arrival at the palace of the Duke of Burgundy, when—

> " *   *   * Déjà l'ombre vaine occupe l'hemisphère,
> Agnès lance partout des rayons et des feux,
> Et son corps parmi l'ombre est un corps lumineux."

It will cost him nothing to connect with the objects he describes, effects that are absolutely contrary to their nature. Thus, he depicts the Maid of Orleans to us as entirely "shaded by a celestial fire ; " and instead of flying from heaven to earth, the luminous angel whom the Almighty sends to the Maid, to reveal to her her mission,—

> " *   *   * Tombe sur le bois où la fille médite ;
> L'ombrage s'en éloigne et ces flammes évite."

In the same manner we shall see the Loire—

> " Murmurer en son cours de voir les matelots,
> Pour avancer le leur, battre ses vites eaux."

As we advance towards the mouth of the river, we shall behold " its wave drowning itself " in an ampler bed. If we would take the trouble to seek them out, we might easily find a hundred instances of similar absurdity : but we must here repeat, lest it should be forgotten, that Chapelain was, notwithstanding all his faults, a man of sense, convinced of the necessity of adhering to the truth, and determined, as he tells us in his first preface, to avoid "the affected and immoderate ingeniosity" of Lucan—who was so highly esteemed by the "vulgar" of his age—and "to follow in the footsteps" of Virgil.

Chapelain is, therefore, always in pursuit of that truth which so often eludes his grasp. Sometimes even he meets with it, but then he falls into another misfortune : the truth which presents itself to his observation is seldom or never noble, elegant, and poetic truth, such as the imagination can conceive in its happiest moments, but common truth, trivial circumstances which strike the eye when contemplating the most ordinary objects. His pictures are almost always descriptions, and his descriptions rarely consist of really interesting features of the object which he desires to represent. When narrating the death of the Maid of Orleans, and the cruel care with which the people prepared her funeral pile, Chapelain does not omit to mention a single faggot. After plastering the first layer of sticks with pitch :—

> "Il met sur cette couche une seconde couche,
> Et la souche d'en haut croise la basse souche ;
> Mais, pour donner au feu plus de force et plus d'air,
> Le bois en chaque couche est demi-large et clair.
> À la couche seconde une troisième est jointe
> Qui, plus courte, la croise et commence la pointe ;
> Plusieurs de suite en suite à ces trois s'ajoutant,
> Toujours de plus en plus vont en pointe montant."

He will not suffer us to lose a single item of the

preparations for the consecration of the king at
Rheims ; and begins by—

> "Dresser en échafaud un plancher de solives,"

the "long planks" of which are afterwards covered—

> "D'un tapis à fond d'or semé de roses blanches."

After a victory gained by the French over the
English, he represents to us the hungry conquerors,—

> "*   *   *   *   Le couteau dans la main,
> Sur les vivres tranchés assouvissant leur faim."

Roger, the brother of Agnes Sorel, explains to some
holy bishops the subjects of the pictures which adorn
the gallery of Fontainebleau ; and nothing can be
more natural than his gestures :—

> "Roger lève la canne et la voix à la fois ;
> L'œil s'attache à la canne et l'oreille à la voix."

But Roger cannot be always speaking and walking ;
when they reach the end of the gallery :—

> "On s'assied, on respire, et soudain on se lève."

And then the poet suddenly displays all his poetic
fire in the aggrandisement of the smallest objects :—

> "Ainsi quand l'Océan s'ébranle vers la grève,
> Et par un flux réglé, sans le secours des vents,
> Se roule toujours plus sur les sables mouvants ;
> Contre mont, flot sur flot, l'onde vive élevée,
> Aux bornes de son cours à peine est arrivée,
> Que sa masse écumeuse, en se rengloutissant,
> Dans le sein de l'abîme aussitôt redescend.
> Sur ses pas on retourne, et Roger continue."

How grand a climax—how happy a simile is this!
a page and two bishops walking up and down
a gallery, compared to the ebb and flow of
the ocean! Was it such *tours de force* as these
which led M. Gaillard to say that " Chapelain
was born a greater poet than Boileau ? " [1] Was
it this passage which induced him to declare that
his companions were always well-chosen and "well-
placed " ?

Were it not for the example which I have just
quoted, it would be difficult for me to coincide in
M. Gaillard's opinion with regard to comparisons which
recur at almost regular intervals, which are placed
with even greater regularity at the commencement of
the line, like borrowed ornaments,[2] and which invariably begin with *Ainsi, Comme, Tel,* or *Tel que.* I
am, nevertheless, willing to admit that the reader who
has courage enough to examine closely the unpub-
lished part of the poem will find it to be characterised
by a nobler, less obscure, and more elaborate style
than the rest of the work ; he will even meet with
well-chosen dashes of truth and scintillations of
genius, some examples of which I would gladly
quote, if Chapelain's talent were sufficiently sustained

---

[1] " If it were allowable to say that Chapelain was born a greater poet
than Boileau, truth would gain by this paradox." See p. 125 of a small
volume of "Mélanges Littéraires," printed at Amsterdam in 1756, without
the author's name.

[2] " Et ses froids ornements à la ligne plantés."

Boileau, Satire iv. line 100.

to furnish an entire citation.   But his happiness is of
short duration :—

> " Un vers noble, quoique dur
> Peut briller dans la *Pucelle*,"

says Boileau ;[1] but when this is the case, it either
shines in solitary splendour, or is so miserably
accompanied, that it can never be divested of the
vulgar associations by which it is surrounded.   Thus
Chapelain will express with honest energy the
indignation with which he is inspired by the
enormities committed by the French in the suburbs
of Paris, which they have carried by storm : he
describes them as slaying the vanquished in cold
blood ; henceforward—

> " Le combat est infâme et la victoire est triste.
> L'honneur ne peut souffrir tant de lâches rigueurs :
> La peine est aux vaincus, la honte est aux vainqueurs."

This last line is fine.   There is also considerable
nobleness in this portrait of the Maid, which bears
some resemblance to that of Tasso's Sophronia :—

> " Les douceurs, les souris, les attraits ni les charmes,
> De ce visage altier ne forment point les armes ;
> Il est beau de lui-même ; il dompte sans charmer ;
> Et fait qu'on le révère et qu'on n'ose l'aimer.
> Pour tous soins, une fière et sainte négligence
> De sa mâle beauté rehausse l'excellence."

But, a few lines before, we should behold " her
severe aspect : "—

> " Des moins respectueux attirer le respect."

---

[1] *Boileau*, " Œuvres," vol. iii. p. 175, parody of the first Pindaric Ode.

And, a few lines afterwards, we should find that—

> " *   *   *   *   Ses regards flamboyans
> Percent et brûlent tout de leurs traits foudroyans."

I cannot refrain from quoting some eloquent passages from the speech delivered by the Maid to her rebellious army, whom her aspect has stricken with shame and stupor. She arrives in the camp, and pretending that she cannot recognise it, inquires what has become of it :—

> " Leurs mains contre Bedford sont sans doute occupées,
> Et de rebelle sang font rougir leurs épées ;
> Car ces fronts étonnés, ses visages blêmis,
> Sont ceux qu'en me voyant prennent mes ennemis ;
> C'est là du Bourguignon la morne contenance ;
> C'est ainsi que l'Anglois se trouble en ma présence."

Here I must stop ; for the poet, who, unfortunately, did not know when he should have stopped, spoils this idea by extending it through the two following lines.

Chapelain also gives a graceful picture of Marie, timidly busied in tending Dunois ; and who, without venturing to remind him of his love for the Maid, tries in what way she may resemble her rival. On one occasion, she dons the cuirass and helmet of her lover :—

> " Cher Dunois, lui dit-elle, ils ne me pèsent pas,
> Et je pourrois sous eux affronter le trépas:
> Pour te suivre partout où la gloire te porte,
> Mon amitié du moins me rendroit assez forte :
> Et ce valeureux fer redouté des humains,
> Se pourroit signaler entre mes foibles mains."

These lines, although an imitation of Armida's speech to Rinaldo,[1] justly belong to Chapelain, who has used the same idea in a different manner; and, perhaps, the reserve of Marie will be deemed as touching as the passion of Armida. This reserve, however, is carried too far when Marie adds that "modesty" alone prevents her from following Dunois to the fight; the effect of the movement is thus entirely destroyed, and Chapelain re-appears in his true character.

I will, however, endeavour to quote one or two comparisons in which the truth, when conceived in a really striking and poetical manner, is not spoiled by the expression. In the following extract the poet alludes to young Lionel, the son of Talbot, whom an unrequited passion for Marie has reduced almost to death, and whose physical powers can scarcely recover the shock :—

> " Tel un lys orgueilleux, sur qui d'un gros nuage,
> Durant la fraîche nuit, s'est déchargé l'orage,
> Et qui sous cet effort coup sur coup redoublé,
> Et s'abat et languit de la grêle accablé;
> Bien qu'aux puissans rayons du Dieu.de la lumière
> Il reprenne l'éclat de sa beauté première,
> Qu'il se relève enfin de son abattement,
> S'il revient de sa chute, il revient lentement."

---

[1] " Animo ho bene, ho ben vigor che baste
A condurti i cavalli, à portar l'aste : "
which Fairfax thus translates :—

> " Courage I have and strength enough, perchance,
> To lead thy courser spare and bear thy lance."
>   *Tasso*, " Gerusalemme liberata," book xvi. stanza 48.

Although the first lines are rather strained, the image, as a whole, is agreeable and well expressed.

In another place, the brave Talbot himself, surrounded by enemies, gives himself up for lost ; but his courage does not fail him :—

> " Il est désespéré, mais non pas abattu,
> Et médite un trépas digne de sa vertu ;
> Tel est un grand lion, roi des monts de Cyrène,
> Lorsque de tout un peuple entouré sur l'arène,
> Contre sa noble vie il voit de toutes parts,
> Unis et conjurés les épieux et les dards.
> Reconnaissant pour lui la mort inévitable,
> Il résout à la mort son courage indomptable ;
> Il y va sans faiblesse, il y va sans effroi,
> Et la devant souffrir, la veut souffrir en roi."

Having thus endeavoured to point out the excellencies of Chapelain's style, shall I now have the courage to revert to its habitual defects ? Shall I insist upon that triviality of expression which is not only connected with triviality of imagery, but which frequently imparts meanness to that which would otherwise be merely simple : as, for example, when the poet makes his combatants " take a rude leap," or fall " with their legs upward and their head hanging down," or represents the Maid of Orleans as bearing, " upon her back," the whole weight of the war ? Shall I speak of those obscurities which a vicious construction accumulates upon the existing obscurity of the idea, as in these lines :—

> " La grandeur du Très-Haut est *son* objet unique :
> Elle en repaît le feu de *son* amour pudique,
> Et par les vifs élans de *sa* dévote ardeur
> Monte jusqu'à *sa* gloire, et soutient *sa* splendeur."

Shall I quote instances of those affected repetitions, equally devoid of gracefulness and meaning, or of those strange analogies of sound, which Chapelain is constantly striving to introduce, although it is impossible to divine what effect he intends them to produce ; as when he says of Joan of Arc :—

> " L'Anglois sur elle tonne, et tonne à grands éclat.
> Mais pour tonner sur elle, il ne l'étonne pas."

Has not Boileau done ample justice to those " harsh lines of inflated epithets," to those lines—

> "*   *   *   Et sans force et sans grâces
> Montés sur deux grands mots comme sur des échasses,"

and to—

> " Ces termes sans raison l'un de l'autre écartés," [1]

to those exaggerated expressions, and generally to all the faults of that uncouth style, which was so constantly the object of his animadversion that he never seems to have thought of bringing any other charge against the author of the " Pucelle " ?

Style is, in fact, that in which Chapelain is particularly deficient, even more so than most of his contemporaries ; to whom, notwithstanding all I have said, the author of the " Pucelle " is superior in the justness and even nobleness of his ideas, feelings and images, in the arrangement of his plan, and in the observance of the proprieties. He has done all that study and reflection could effect, at the time in which

[1] *Boileau*, Satire iv. lines 91, 96, 97, 99.

he lived ; but genius alone could supply the deficiencies of a language which was as yet equally destitute of forms and rules.   An extensive acquaintance
with the ancient authors was useless to a man who
was unable to find words in which to express their
thoughts ; and Chapelain, who aimed at following in
the footsteps of Virgil, did not know enough French
fully to appreciate the beauties of the Latin poet.

It is less, however, in consequence of his
deficiencies than of his lofty pretensions to merit, that
Chapelain has obtained the unenviable distinction
of beholding the ridicule cast upon his poems handed
down to our times.   Most of his contemporaries
have obtained the privilege of enjoying perfect
obscurity, though far more ridiculous than he was :—

> " Le *Jonas* inconnu sèche dans la poussière,
> Le *David* imprimé n'a point vu la lumière,
> Le *Moyse* commence à moisir par les bords ;
> Quel mal cela fait-il ?   Ceux qui sont morts sont morts." [1]

Chapelain was never " dead " enough to grant repose
to the vigilant anxiety of Boileau, and to calm the
indignation of the great critic against the most
illustrious example of the bad taste of his age.   Even
after his miserable failure as a poet, Chapelain's
reputation as a man of letters had continued
unimpaired.   In 1663, he was appointed by Colbert
to distribute the pensions bestowed by the King upon
authors of merit ; and the submissive respect which

---

[1] *Boileau*, Satire ix., lines 191-194.

this office inspired for the man who filled it was, to a certain extent, justified by the manner in which he exercised it.   I do not mean to affirm that Chapelain altogether resisted the seductions of almost arbitrary power, and that the self-love of the man of letters did not sometimes influence the justice of the judge. Gronovius, a learned Dutchman, complained of not having been included in the list of pensions ; and Chapelain confesses, in one of his letters, "that he had not insisted strongly upon his merit, because of the little eagerness with which he had met his advances." [1]   The success with which flattery was attended when addressed to him is demonstrated by the liberal use which was made of it.   Those who placed the " Pucelle " above the Æneid were sure to be well received by him ;[2] and of the different methods of paying court to him, the slander of his enemies seems to have been not the least effective.

> " *   *   *   Pour flatter ce rimeur tutélaire,
> Le frère en un besoin va renier son frère," [3]

---

[1] *Chapelain,* "Mélanges de Littérature," p. 41.

[2] See, in Saint-Marc's edition of *Boileau's* Works, the note on these lines of his fourth satire :—

> " Lui-même il s'applaudit, et, d'un esprit tranquille,
> Prend le pas au Parnasse au-dessus de Virgile."

Chapelain, in the Preface to his last twelve books, leaves his readers to judge "whether the address of the Legates to Bedford, Charles and Philip, does or does not prevail over that of Nestor and Venus to Achilles and Diomede."

[3] These lines, quoted in the note to the 94th line of the 1st satire, were suppressed in the edition of 1674, and have appeared in no subsequent impression.

said Boileau, whose brother Gilles Boileau, who did not love him, spoke of him in less friendly terms to Chapelain than to other persons. We also learn the value which he set upon the deference of an author, from the notes which he addressed to Colbert : one of the recommendations of D'Ablancourt is, "that he would receive the advice that was given him ;" Mézerai's great deficiency is, that " he cannot behave with docility ;" Furetière would be capable of great things, " if he would allow himself to be guided ;" there would be reason to hope much of Silhon, "if he would allow himself to be advised ;" and Le Clerc, in his mediocrity, at least possesses all the merit of a man " who will take good advice." [1] All this indicates, as his whole life had fostered, in the author of the " Pucelle," that necessity for pre-eminence which, according to Segrais, led him to bestow no praise " on those who he thought might cast him into the shade, if their merit came to be known, and who were actually residing in Paris or at the Court ;" and to honour with his esteem "those only who were far distant, in some obscure corner of a remote province." [2] There is, however, no reason to believe that this distrustful self-love corrupted Chapelain's fidelity in the important and delicate employment which he had been appointed to discharge. Whether

[1] *Chapelain,* "Mélanges de Littérature," pp. 239, 242, 246, 247.
[2] " Segraisiana," p. 227.

he held the balance fairly between Charpentier, Silhon, Le Clerc, Sorbières, Boyer, the Abbé de la Pure, and others, is a matter upon which I will not venture to decide. Ill-temper may have rendered him unjust towards Ménage, with whom he had quarrelled;[1] but Segrais, Patru, and D'Ablancourt had no reason to complain of his judgment concerning them.[2] He rendered full justice to Corneille;[3] and, in the strange dryness of his note upon Molière,[4] we merely recognise the first effect produced by too novel and original a genius upon an age which he had not yet taught to admire him.

Chapelain's contemporaries have generally borne testimony to his probity and sincerity, to the affability of his manners, and his easiness of access; but we must not expect to find, in a circumspect character like his, the free and generous virtues of an exalted nature. "He is a man," he says of himself, in his memorial to Colbert, "who makes an *exact*

---

[1] See the note on Ménage, in the "Mélanges," p. 186 *et seq.*; and also what Chapelain says of him elsewhere, in a letter to Heinsius, p. 95. This last passage will suffice to explain the other. Segrais, in his account of the quarrel, attributes the blame to Chapelain, whom he disliked, and who had refused him his vote at the Academy, to give it to Le Clerc, although he had addressed him in an ode, "which is not," he says, "the least excellent of my poems."

[2] See the "Mélanges de Littérature."

[3] "He is a prodigy of wit, and the ornament of the French drama." "Mélanges de Littérature," p. 250.

[4] "He is well acquainted with the character of comedy, and executes it naturally: the plot of his best pieces is borrowed, but judiciously; his morality is good, and he needs only to guard against scurrility."—*Chapelain*, "Mélanges de Littérature," p. 192.

profession of loving virtue disinterestedly." [1] " Exact indeed he was," says Ménage, " very punctual, and a formalist in all his actions ;" [2] he had studied virtue as he had studied poetics, and he observed its rules with equal precision, as far as the limits of his knowledge and character would allow him to do so. He was well aware of the duties of friendship, and always manifested the utmost carefulness to fulfil them ; " nevertheless," says Segrais, " his friendship was the friendship of a coward : he wished to keep on good terms with both goat and wolf." [3] Without admitting Segrais' opinion and expression in all their severity, we shall, at all events, find in Chapelain's letters abundant proofs of his unwillingness to commit himself in the disputes between his friends and acquaintance. [4] Acts of virtue, when carried beyond what would be advised by ordinary prudence, were not sure to receive his approbation. Heinsius, when appointed Secretary of the United Provinces, had to share this office with one of his relatives, who had previously held sole possession of it, and he therefore wished to leave him all its emoluments. " Although this betokens a noble feeling on your part," wrote Chapelain to him, " I do not know that it is altogether reasonable." [5] Le Fèvre, the father

---

[1] *Chapelain,* " Mélanges de Littérature," p. 233.

[2] " Menagiana," vol. iii. p. 73.   [3] " Segraisiana," p. 222.

[4] See in the " Mélanges," p. 137, his letter to Huyghens, on the quarrel between Gilles Boileau and Ménage.

[5] *Chapelain,* " Mélanges de Littérature," p. 83.

of Madame Dacier, whom Pelisson had benefitted with the utmost delicacy, dedicated a book to him during his confinement in the Bastille ; and " some persons," says Ménage, " among whom was M. Chapelain, found fault with him for so doing." [1] Although he was always willing to be of service to men of letters, there was one kind of service which they never obtained from Chapelain ; the word " give," it would appear, was as little used by him as by Harpagon. One day, however, he allowed his feelings to carry him away so far as to relieve the pressing necessities of one of his friends by the magnificent gift of a crown-piece : he thought he might justly take credit to himself for this effort of generosity ; and when he mentioned the affair, he used to say : " We ought to succour our friends in their necessities ; but we ought not to contribute to their luxury." [2] In Chapelain's opinion, luxury corresponded with what people of the simplest habits consider to be necessaries. Possessing an annual income of thirteen thousand livres, [3] which was then equivalent to more than twenty-five thousand francs at the present day, " he contented himself with a little ordinary, which was prepared for him by a female relative, to whom he paid a regular stipend ;" and on those days on which he dined out, his relative made him an allowance for

<hr/>

[1] " Ménagiana," vol. ii. p. 17.   [2] " Segraisiana," p. 225.   [3] Ibid. p. 226.

his dinner. [1] His correspondence was very extensive ; but, anxious to save himself the expense of postage, he was careful to request his friends to write to him only by private hands ; [2] and he frequently used, for his answers, the envelopes of the letters which he had received. [3] All the details of his life corresponded with this excess of economy ; and Ménage, on paying him a visit for the first time after twelve years of separation, declared that the same logs were burning on the hearth which he had seen there twelve years before. [4]

Chapelain's avarice was a perpetual subject of diversion to his friends and acquaintance. As he had no wife or children, no one could imagine why he should be so desirous to hoard his wealth. " The wags said that it was in order to marry his Maid [5] to some young fellow of good family ; and the pious declared that it was in order to obtain canonisation." [6] His colleagues at the French Academy derived much amusement from his fear of being appointed its director, and the care which he took to avoid this honour, which, in case of the death of one of the Academicians, would have put him to the expense of twenty livres for the performance of a funeral service in the Eglise des Billettes. One of their

---

[1] "Segraisiana," p. 231.   [2] Ibid.
[3] *Vigneul-Marville*, "Mélanges," vol. ii. p. 7.
[4] " Ménagiana," vol. ii. p. 31.   [5] The " Pucelle."
[6] *Vigneul-Marville*, "Mélanges," vol. ii. p. 7.

number, Chancellor Seguier, the protector of the
Academy, being eighty-four years of age, was a
threat perpetually hanging over his head. At length
the Chancellor fell ill ; the post of director became
vacant, and, either by chance, or by the intention
of those who knew his character, Chapelain was
appointed. His anguish may be more readily
imagined than described. Nevertheless, the three
months of his directorship passed by, and the
Chancellor still lived ; but he could not survive
long, and Chapelain became desirous to resign his
office. Unfortunately, on the day of their session,
the number of Academicians was not complete, and
the nomination of his successor was deferred to
another day. During the interval, the Chancellor
died. Chapelain was in despair. " I am ruined,"
he said ; " my property will not be sufficient : if
it were a simple Academician, it would be less
grievous ; but the Protector ! This expense will
reduce me to beggary !" " Good," said Patru, " the
Cardinal was at least worth as much as the Chancellor. I was director when he died ; I had his
service performed entirely at my own expense ; it
merely cost me two pistoles more, and the matter was
managed very well." Two pistoles were a great
deal too much for Chapelain ; and he therefore
declared that it was not enough for the Chancellor,
pretended that he was not rich enough to act in a

manner becoming the importance of the occasion, and at last induced every Academician to contribute according to his means and will. As he collected the contributions, he may have abstained from paying his own quota ; and it was even suspected that he made a profit by the transaction.[1]

It will readily be imagined that Chapelain did not reject the advantages to be derived from assiduous attendance at the Academy ; and, in this particular, his avarice gave confirmation to his natural exactitude. He was proceeding thither one day, after some heavy rain, and, on arriving in the Rue St. Honoré, he found the stream so wide that he could not step across. A plank had been provided for the accommodation of passengers, but a small fee was required to be paid for its use ; so Chapelain preferred to wait until the water had flowed away. Meanwhile three o'clock drew near ; in a few minutes more he would be too late, and would lose his fee. Chapelain decided at once ; plunged into the water nearly up to his knees ; arrived in time at the Academy ; and, instead of going near the fire, carefully concealed his legs under the table, for fear any one should perceive his misadventure. Chapelain was then more than seventy-nine years old : the cold seized upon him, settled in his chest, and he died a few days afterwards,[2] on the 22nd of February,

---

[1] " Segraisiana," p. 223 *et seq.*   [2] Ibid. pp. 226, 227.

1674, leaving to his heirs, according to some statements, a fortune of one hundred thousand crowns, [1]
and, according to others, four hundred thousand
livres, more than two hundred thousand of which
were in ready money. [2]

A paraphrase of the " Miserere," and three or
four small poems, compose, with the " Pucelle," the
whole of Chapelain's productions in verse. His
preface to the " Adone," and a few passages from
his letters, inserted in the " Mélanges de Littérature,"
are the only monuments which remain to us of his
talents as a critic.

[1] *Vigneul-Marville*, "Mélanges," vol. ii. p. 7.
[2] " Segraisiana," pp. 225, 226.

JEAN ROTROU.

(1609—1650.)

A MAN of genius has two classes of disciples.
One class is composed of mere imitators, who strive
only to reproduce the manner of their master, catch
with tolerable exactness the forms of his style,
devote their attention to the kind of subjects which
he treated and the ideas which he preferred, and
may even furnish us with that inferior gratification
which a poor copy affords, by reviving our
recollection of the impressions produced by the
contemplation of a splendid original. Duryer certainly had " Cinna " constantly before his eyes while
he was writing his tragedy of " Scévole." Junia,
the daughter of Brutus, and mistress of Scævola, is
a prisoner in the camp of Porsenna. She is told
that Scævola has been seen in the camp, disguised
as an Etrurian soldier ; and her informant adds, that
he has assumed this disguise in order to escape ;
upon which she exclaims :—

"Pour se sauver, dis-tu ? tu n'as point vu Scévole !"

In his tragedy of " Saul," that monarch, smitten by

the hand of God, trembles before the army of
the Philistines ; and Jonathan thus endeavours to
rekindle his father's courage :—

> " Est-il donc en état de donner de l'effroi ?
> A-t-il appris à vaincre en fuyant devant moi ?
>
> *   *   *   *   *   *
>
> Laissez voler la crainte où l'ennemi s'assemble ;
> Un roi n'est pas troublé que son trône ne tremble ;
> Mais il connoît trop tard, quand il a succombé,
> Que le trône qui tremble est à demi-tombé.
> Croyez en vos enfans, croyez en leur courage,
> D'un triomphe immortel l'infaillible présage ;
> Dans le sein de la gloire ils ont toujours vécu ;
> Enfin, je suis le moindre, et j'ai toujours vaincu."

Who cannot recognise, in these lines, the model
which Duryer had constantly before his eyes ?   Who
does not feel, when perusing them, something of
that emotion with which we are inspired by the
magnificent verses of Corneille ?

The other class of disciples pay less attention to
the examples furnished them by their master than
to the emotion which those examples originate in
their souls.   They feel that faculties are awakened
within them by the voice of genius, which, but for
its summons, would have lain dormant within their
breasts, but which are, nevertheless, their own
individual and natural faculties.   They have received
the impulse, but they direct it according to their
own judgment ; and if their productions do not
exhibit the sustained energy of those spontaneous
outbursts which are the unfettered fruits of the

ascendancy of an imperious nature, they, at least, possess a certain measure of originality, and even of life-giving fecundity. "Venceslas" is one of those original works which owe their existence to an extraneous impulse. Rotrou, who had long been a dramatic author utterly destitute of all inspiration, proved himself a poet after he had heard Corneille.

Jean Rotrou was born at Dreux, on the 19th of August, 1609, of an ancient and honourable family, which, both before and after his lifetime, held high magisterial offices in that town.[1] It appears, however, that Rotrou's father, satisfied with the competency which he derived from the possession of a moderate fortune, lived on his property without engaging in any profession. We do not know whether the son was intended to pursue a similar course ; and we are equally ignorant of the obstacles or facilities which he encountered in following his taste for a dramatic career, and of the circumstances which led to the formation of that taste. The life of Rotrou, revealed to posterity by a fine poem and a virtuous action, has, in other respects, remained entirely unknown. The first fact which I have been able to

[1] Pierre Rotrou was lieutenant-general of the bailiwick of Dreux in 1561. At the end of the seventeenth century and beginning of the eighteenth, Eustache de Rotrou was a royal councillor, president, and civil and criminal lieutenant-general of the bailiwick. M. de Rotrou de Sodreville, the grand-nephew of the poet (see *Titon du Tillet*, "Parnasse Français," p. 236, edit. 1732), was appointed a councillor of the Great Council in 1728, and his sister married the Marquis de Rambuteau. See *Lambert*, "Histoire Littéraire du Siècle de Louis XIV.," vol. ii. p. 299.

discover regarding him bears the date of 1632.
Rotrou, who was then twenty-three years of age,
and known as the author of seven or eight theatrical
pieces,—such as the "Hypocondriaque," the "Bague
de l'Oubli," "Cléagenor et Doristée," the "Diane," the
"Occasions Perdues," and perhaps the "Ménechmes"
and the "Hercule Mourant,"—was introduced by
the Count de Fiesque to Chapelain, who, in a letter
to Godeau, dated October 30th, 1632, gives an
account of his visit, and adds : "It is a pity that a
young man of such fine natural talent should have
submitted to so disgraceful a servitude ; but it will
not be my fault if we do not soon emancipate him."[1]
No explanation can be given of these words of
Chapelain. What could have been the nature of
that servitude which was considered disgraceful at
a time when men held such very lax notions on this
point ? The comedy of the "Hypocondriaque" is
dedicated to the Count de Soissons, of whom Rotrou
styles himself "the very humble subject." But this
title, which may lead us to suppose that Rotrou
considered himself dependent upon some appanage
of the Count de Soissons, indicates no domestic
servitude. Was he attached to the household of the
Count de Fiesque ? But, even supposing this to
have been the case, it could not have been regarded
as a disgrace by Chapelain, who had been so long in

---

[1] *Chapelain*, "Mélanges de Littérature," p. 4.

the service of the Marquis de la Trousse. I should, therefore, be rather inclined to suppose that he was engaged as author to a troop of comedians ; an engagement common enough at that time, and of which Hardy had been the first to set the example. The protection of the Count de Fiesque, who was held in high esteem by the comedians, to whom he had frequently rendered essential service,[1] might give greater probability to this supposition ; and it only remains for us to reconcile the idea which Chapelain gives us of Rotrou's position with what we know regarding the wealth and distinction of his family. Some peculiarities of Rotrou's character, which have been handed down to our times, furnish a plausible explanation of this enigma. Exalted feelings, and an upright and generous disposition, are not sufficient to guard a man against falling into errors, even of the most ignoble kind. Rotrou was fond of play ; and this passion, which was probably not the only passion of his youth, so violently overcame all his resolutions, that, as he tells us himself,[2] the only way in which he was able to preserve himself from the consequences of his own folly was by throwing his money

---

[1] "When it was proposed to induce the comedians to admit, or to secure the observance, on the stage, of the rule of twenty-four hours, Chapelain, who was very anxious for the adoption of this rule, which, it is said, he was one of the first to suggest to the authors of his time, persuaded the Count de Fiesque to undertake the negotiation, because his influence over the comedians was well known." "Segraisiana," p. 160.

[2] *Lambert*, "Histoire Littéraire du Siècle de Louis XIV.," vol. ii. p. 302.

into a heap of faggots—rather a singular kind of strong-box—from which it was so difficult to extract it, that his impatience allowed it to lie there for a much longer period than his weakness would have permitted it to remain in his purse. The heap of faggots, however, did not always so faithfully retain its deposit as to be never empty. Want of funds sometimes reduced the poet to painful extremities. Just as he had finished "Venceslas," Rotrou was arrested for a trifling debt, which he was utterly unable to pay. In this state of distress any bargain was good which would relieve the poet from his difficulty; and "Venceslas" was offered to the comedians, and sold for twenty pistoles.[1] There is no great injustice in supposing that a man, who, at thirty-eight years of age, exposed himself to such adventures, might, when only eighteen, have found himself compelled, by some youthful extravagance, to embrace the aid of resources quite inconsistent with the position which he was born to occupy in society. Undoubtedly, Chapelain's good-will was not useless in enabling Rotrou to escape from the unsuitable position in which he found himself placed. We soon find him figuring as one of the five authors who were pensioned to compose dramas, under the directions of the prime minister; and this new

---

[1] To this sum, after the success of "Venceslas," they thought it right to add a present. We do not know whether Rotrou accepted it or not. See the "Histoire du Théâtre Français," vol. viii. p. 189.

servitude, being more liberally paid than the other, must, on that ground alone, have appeared much more honourable. It is unknown at what period he received from the king a pension of a thousand livres.[1]

Associated, in the confidence of the Cardinal, with Colletet, Bois-Robert, and Corneille, it is not easy to perceive by what kind of services Rotrou could have obtained over the last-named poet that sort of superiority which the author of the "Cid" seemed, it is said, to acknowledge all through his life, by giving the title of *father* to a colleague who was younger and probably less serious than himself. Those who have handed down this anecdote to us assure us that it was from Rotrou that Corneille had learned the principles of dramatic art ; but what were those principles which were known to Rotrou and unknown to Corneille ? The "Hypocondriaque," which preceded "Mélite" by a year at most,[2] is rather less in accordance with the rules than the latter piece ; for Corneille has at least observed unity of place, which Rotrou has, like most of his contemporaries, utterly disregarded ; and as for good sense and probability, the "Hypocondriaque" cannot assuredly boast any superiority in either of these respects. The plot of "Mélite" is a model of

---

[1] *Titon du Tillet,* "Parnasse Française," p. 235.

[2] The "Histoire du Théâtre Français" gives 1628 as the date of its performance.

reasonableness in comparison with the adventures of Cloridan, " a young nobleman of Greece," who, on his way to the Court at Corinth, " the capital city of Greece," [1] goes mad on being told that his mistress is dead, pretends to be dead himself, takes up his residence in a coffin, and only recovers from his insanity on beholding the resuscitation of sham corpses by the sounds of music, by which he is led to believe that he cannot be dead, as the music produces no corresponding effect upon himself. It is true that Rotrou afterwards made honourable amends for the defects of this work ; and with greater modesty than most of his colleagues, he confesses in the argument to this piece, which was printed in 1631, three years after the presumed date of its performance, " that there are many excellent poets, but not at twenty years of age." [2]   But, at the very time that he printed this confession, Rotrou was bringing on the stage the " Heureuse Constance," one scene of which is laid in Hungary and the next in Dalmatia ; when twenty-five years old, he produced the " Belle Alphrède," the action of which occurs partly at Oran, and partly in London ; and in 1635 we find, in his " Innocente Infidélité," some courtiers of a king of Epirus fighting with pistols. This last piece was

---

[1] See the argument at the beginning of the " Hypocondriaque."

[2] This saying of Rotrou, who surely did not wish to diminish his claims to indulgence, would place the date of the composition of the " Hypocondriaque " in the year 1629.

performed during the year in which Corneille produced " Médée."

Compelled as we are to proceed from conjecture to conjecture, may we not suppose that Rotrou's more energetic and decided character had afforded him, on several occasions, the means of protecting the timid simplicity of a great man, whose rival his just modesty did not allow him to think of becoming? Among the wits who then laid claim to some reputation, Rotrou was almost the only one who was not alarmed at the glory obtained by the " Cid ; " and he doubtless dared to defend that which he was worthy to admire. The continually-increasing splendour of that poetical renown which thenceforward eclipsed the fame of all competitors, only inspired Rotrou with a keener admiration of the beauties which he beheld so lavishly displayed before his eyes. He expressed this in a remarkable manner in the " Saint-Genest," a commonplace work enough in other respects (especially as it appeared several years after " Polyeucte "[1]), the subject of which is the martyrdom of the actor Genest, who was converted, on the stage, by an angel who appeared to him while he was performing, in presence of Diocletian, a piece against

---

[1] The performance of the " Véritable Saint-Genest," by Rotrou, is placed in the " Histoire du Théâtre Français," in the year 1646. In 1645, appeared another " Saint-Genest," by Desfontaines, which is not quite so bad as Rotrou's piece, because the author has more closely imitated " Polyeucte." This " Saint-Genest" has been inserted by mistake in the collection of Rotrou's dramas in the National Library at Paris, 5 vols., 4to., No. 5509.

the Christians. Rotrou represents Diocletian as
questioning Genest upon the state of the drama ;
and he inquires :—

> " Quelle plume est en règne, et quel fameux esprit
> S'est acquis, dans le cirque, un plus juste crédit ? "

Genest replies :—

> " Nos plus nouveaux sujets, les plus dignes de Rome,
> Et les plus grands efforts des veilles d'un grand homme,
> A qui les rares fruits que sa Muse a produit,
> Ont acquis dans la scène un légitime bruit,
> Et de qui certes l'art comme l'estime est juste,
> Portent les noms fameux de Pompée et d'Auguste.
> Ces poëmes sans prix, où son illustre main
> D'un pinceau sans pareil a peint l'esprit Romain,
> Rendront de leurs beautés votre oreille idolâtre,
> Et sont aujourd'hui l'âme et l'amour du théâtre."

Though this eulogium is neither well placed nor
well expressed, it is, at least, very candid. Nothing
could trammel the movements of Rotrou's just and
generous character. His excessive facility, which is
at once proved and explained to us by the thirty-five
dramas [1] which have come down to us from his pen,

---

[1] The following is a list of them :—The " Hypocondriaque, ou le Mort
Amoureux," a tragi-comedy, 1628 ; the " Bague de l'Oubli," a comedy,
1628 ; " Cléagenor et Doristée," a tragi-comedy, 1630 ; " La Diane," a
comedy, 1630 ; " Les Occasions Perdues," a tragi-comedy, 1631 ; " Les
Ménechmes," a comedy, 1632 ; " Hercule Mourant," a tragedy, 1632 ; "La
Célimène," * a comedy, 1633 ; " La Belle Alphrède," a comedy, 1634 ; "La

---

* Rotrou, when sketching the plan of this piece, intended to make it a
pastoral, under the name of " Amaryllis " ; but, having afterwards changed
his opinion, he made it a comedy. Some of his friends, after his death,
found the sketch of this pastoral, and gave it to Tristan, who finished it,
and had it performed, in 1652, at the Hôtel de Bourgogne, under the
names of Rotrou and himself. (See the notice at the beginning of the

the unrestraint of his character, and his fondness for
pleasures, probably allowed his interests as a poet
only a moderate share in a life which was animated
by tastes and feelings of another kind. His name
does not occur in connection with any of the literary
events of his time ; and we very seldom meet with
it in those anecdotical collections in which several of
his contemporaries, and particularly Ménage and
Segrais, have so carefully embalmed a multitude of
facts and names which seemed destined, by their insig-
nificance, to immediate and complete oblivion. We

Pélerine Amoureuse," a tragi-comedy, 1634 ; " Le Filandre," a comedy,
1635 ; "Agésilas de Colchos," a tragi-comedy, 1635 ; " L'Innocente
Infidélité," a tragi-comedy, 1636 ; " La Clorinde," a comedy, 1635 ;
" Amélie," a tragi-comedy, 1636 ; " Les Sosies," a comedy, 1636 ; " Les
Deux Pucelles," a tragi-comedy, 1636 ; " Laure persécutée," a tragi-comedy,
1637 ; " Antigone," a tragedy, 1638 ; " Les Captifs de Plaute, ou les
Esclaves," a comedy, 1638 ; " Crisante," a tragedy, 1639 ; " Iphigénie en
Aulide," a tragedy, 1640 ; " Clarice, ou l'Amour Constant," a comedy, 1641 ;
" Bélisaire," a tragedy, 1643 ; " Célie, ou le Vice-Roi de Naples," a comedy,
1645 ; " La Sœur," a comedy, 1645 ; " Le Véritable Saint-Genest," a
tragedy, 1646 ; " Dom Bernard de Cabrère," a tragi-comedy, 1647 ; " Venceslas," a tragi-comedy, 1647 ; " Cosroës," a tragedy, 1648 ; " La Florimonde," a comedy, 1649 ; and " Dom Lope de Cardonne," a tragi-comedy,
1649.

We have also the sketch of the poetical part of a drama on the " Birth of
Hercules," Rotrou's last work, which was performed at the Théâtre du
Marais, and printed in 1649. It is probably a ballet of " Amphitryon."
Several other works, which were never either performed or printed, have
without authority been ascribed to him. The list which I have adopted
is that given in the " Histoire du Théâtre Français," vol. iv. p. 410, et seq.

"Amaryllis," and the "Histoire du Théâtre Français," vol. vii. p. 328.) Père
Niceron includes " Amaryllis " among Rotrou's Works, which raises their
number to thirty-six, instead of thirty-five. See the " Mémoires pour
servir à l'Histoire des Hommes illustres dans la République des Lettres,"
vol. xvi. p. 93, et seq.

possess upon Rotrou none of those eulogistic or epigrammatic poems which ordinarily result from the friendship of men of letters, and in which this period was more abundant than any other. All we know of him leads us to believe that, living in peace and indifference among his colleagues, Rotrou enjoyed undisturbed a reputation which he took no pains to cultivate, and regarding which the general silence might render us sceptical, if the success which Rotrou's dramas achieved were not attested by this saying of Corneille : " M. Rotrou and I could gain a subsistence even for mountebanks." [1] Whatever power friendship and gratitude may have exercised over Corneille, it is certain that nothing but the force of truth could have led him to say : " M. Rotrou and I."

In order to justify this distinction, we must not expect to find in Rotrou's works, with the exception of " Venceslas," those novel views, and that particular turn of mind which were manifested even in Corneille's earliest works, and announced the advent of an original genius, whose vigour would make way for itself in spite of the routine formalism of the time. All that romantic balderdash which then filled the stage —abductions, combats, recognitions, and imaginary

[1] " To indicate," adds Ménage, " that the public would not have failed to come to the performance of their pieces, even if they had been badly performed." "Menagiana," vol. iii. p. 306.   This is the only place in which he mentions Rotrou.

kingdoms [1]—accidental loves which spring up precisely when it is necessary to embarrass the scene,
and cease as soon as it is convenient to bring matters to a conclusion—innumerable and immeasurable
kisses, requested, given, and returned upon the stage,
sometimes accompanied by even more passionate
caresses, [2] and followed by assignations, the intention
of which is not in the slightest degree dissembled, [3]
—heroines embarrassed by the consequences of their
weakness, and running all over the world in search of
the perfidious lover who has robbed them of their
honour, —these are the leading characteristics of most
of Rotrou's plays ;—these are the ordinary inspirations of that Muse whom he boasted of having
rendered so modest that " she had laid aside her
profanity, and become as pious as a nun." [4]   Corneille alone had had the wisdom to banish these
monotonous enormities from his works.   Accordingly,
most of Rotrou's productions must be classed among
those ephemeral essays to which art is indebted
neither for discoveries nor progress ; but, in his time,
they may have been remarkable, among those
honoured with constant applause, for greater truthfulness of tone, less dulness of invention, and a more

---

[1] See the " Heureuse Constance," in which a Queen of Dalmatia is
introduced.

[2] See " La Céliane."

[3] See " Les Occasions Perdues."

[4] See the Dedicatory Epistle of the " Bague de l'Oubli."

witty and elevated style. True comic power is sometimes perceptible in them, at least in the dialogues.
One of Rotrou's pieces, "La Sœur," contains a scene
almost exactly similar to one in the "Fourberies de
Scapin," and furnished Molière with several of the
ideas which he has introduced into his "Bourgeois
Gentilhomme,"—if Molière and Rotrou were not both
equally indebted for them to some Italian play, as we
may suppose from the scene of the action being laid
at Nola, in Campania, from most of the names being
Italian, from the style of the plot, and especially from
the gaiety of several scenes—a gaiety which Rotrou
never attained except in his imitations. Anselme, the
old dupe, has been engaged for fifteen years in search-
ing for his wife and daughter, who had been captured
at sea by a corsair ; and learning that they have
been sold into slavery at Constantinople, he sends his
son Lelio thither with money to ransom them. On the
road, Lelio falls in love with a pretty maid-servant at
an inn ; and, instead of continuing his journey, marries
his mistress, takes her home with him and introduces
her to his father as his sister, declaring at the same
time that his mother is dead. Anselme, displeased at
the excessive affection which the brother and sister
manifest for each other, complains of it to the valet,
who throws the whole blame on the journey to
Turkey, which, he says, is a most dangerous country
for young folks to visit :—

"Car les Turcs, comme on sait, sont fort mauvais chrétiens ;
Les livres en ce lieu n'entrent point en commerce ;
En aucun art illustre aucun d'eux ne s'exerce ;
Et l'on y tient quiconque est autre qu'ignorant,
Pour *Catalaméchis,* qui sont gens de néant.

ANSELME.

Plus jaloux de sa sœur qu'on n'est d'une maîtresse,
Jamais il ne la quitte ; ils se parlent sans cesse,
Me raillent, se font signe, et se moquant de moi,
Ne s'aperçoivent pas que je m'en aperçois.

ERGASTE.

Là, chacun à gausser librement se dispense ;
La raillerie est libre et n'est point une offense ;
Et, si je m'en souviens, on appelle en ces lieux
Urchec, ou gens d'esprit, ceux qui raillent le mieux.

ANSELME.

Ils en usent pour Nole avec trop de licence ;
Et quoique leur amour ait beaucoup d'innocence,
Je ne puis approuver ces baisers assidus
D'une ardeur mutuelle et donnés et rendus,
Ces discours à l'oreille, et ces tendres caresses,
Plus dignes passe-temps d'amans et de maîtresses,
Qu'ils ne sont en effet d'un frère et d'une sœur.

ERGASTE.

La loi de Mahomet, par une charge expresse,
Enjoint ces sentiments d'amour et de tendresse,
Que le sang justifie et semble autoriser ;
Mais le temps les pourra démahométiser.
Ils appellent *tubalch* cette ardeur fraternelle,
Ou *boram,* qui veut dire intime et mutuelle."

This impudence on the part of a knavish valet
is quite in the style of Molière's Scapin. The idea
of the scene in the "Bourgeois Gentilhomme" is
precisely identical with that in which the valet
Ergaste, whose falsehoods are beginning to be
discovered, calls, as a witness to the truth of all he

has said, a young man, who, having been brought up at Constantinople, knows no other language than real Turkish :—

"Il n'entend pas la langue et ne peut te répondre,"

says Anselme. "I'll speak to him in Turkish," says Ergaste; and he begins to repeat his counterfeit Turkish. The young man, who cannot understand a word he says, expresses his embarrassment in answers, which Anselme does not comprehend, but which Ergaste does not fail to interpret to him in a most satisfactory manner. One of these answers contains only two words—*vare-hece*; Ergaste pretends that they are equivalent in meaning to a long phrase, with which he finds it necessary to terminate the conversation :—

"T'en a-t-il pu tant dire en si peu de propos ?"

Anselme inquires ; and Ergaste coolly replies :—

"Oui, le langage turc dit beaucoup en deux mots."[1]

The *vare-hece* in this passage is clearly the *bel-men* of Molière. [2]

The author of the "Métromanie" may also have

[1] *Rotrou,* "La Sœur," act iii. scene 5.
[2] See the "Bourgeois Gentilhomme," act iv. scene 6.
"CLEANTE.—*Bel-men.*
"COVIELLE.—He says you must go quickly with him to prepare yourself for the ceremony, in order to see your daughter afterwards, and to conclude the marriage.
"M. JOURDAIN.—Did he say all that in two words?
"COVIELLE.—Yes; it is a peculiarity of the Turkish language, that it expresses a great deal in few words."

borrowed somewhat from the scene in which Anselme's wife, on her return from Constantinople, being informed, before she has seen her husband, of the state of her son's affections, promises to promote his wishes by feigning to recognise as her daughter the young girl whom Lelio has passed off as his sister. Indeed, when that young lady is presented to her, her transports of delight are so exceedingly natural that Lelio and his valet, surprised at the talent with which she has performed her part, pay her almost the same compliments as Francaleu pays to Baliveau, in the "Métromanie."

"Je n'en fais point le fin, j'en prendrois des leçons,"[1]

says Ergaste ; and Constance puts an end to their admiration only by informing them that her transports of joy and surprise were real, and that Lelio's wife is actually her daughter, whom she believed lost. The author, as will readily be imagined, does not fail to set things in order by means of further explanations ; and Lelio is saved the misfortune of an incestuous love and marriage. The plot of this

[1] *Rotrou*, "La Sœur," act iv. scene 5. Francaleu, astonished in a similar manner at the expression of surprise manifested on Baliveau's countenance when he unexpectedly meets his nephew, says to Damis :—

"Monsieur l'homme accompli, qui du moins croyez l'être,
Prenez, prenez leçon, car voilà votre maître."

But in the "Métromanie," the effect, which is prepared beforehand by the knowledge possessed by the audience of the respective positions of the characters, is far more complete and comic.

piece is as bad as its details are sometimes humorous ; but it is difficult to believe that these details
rightfully belong to the author of " Célimène,"
" Céliane," " Clorinde," and a host of other pieces
equally dull.

Rotrou was always more successful in his imitations
than in his original works.   He had the good taste
to seek occasional models among the ancient writers,
whose merits he appreciated, even if he were not
fully conscious of the whole advantage that might be
derived from them by men of genius superior to his
own.   I would not vouch for it that he always went
back to these models themselves ; for it is difficult to
believe in the classic erudition of a man who, in
" Iphigénie en Aulide," represents Ulysses challenging
Achilles to fight a duel, [1] and whose other works give
proof of even stranger ignorance. [2]   The dramatic
poets of antiquity had already been translated into
French, and Sforza d'Oddi, an Italian author, from
whom Rotrou has imitated a comedy, [3] and whom he
praises for his imitations of " Plautus, [4] might probably

---

[1] "ACHILLE. S'agissant de se battre, Ulysse est toujours lent.
    ULYSSE. Vous ne m'en prirez point que je n'y satisfasse.
    ACHILLE. Demeurons donc d'accord de l'heure et de la place."—
                                        Rotrou, "Iphigénie," act v. scene 3.

[2] Thus, in "La Sœur," old Géronte, returning from his captivity among
the Turks at Constantinople, speaks to Anselme about the Church of Saint-
Sophia,—
         " *   *   *   où les Chrétiens s'assemblent,
         Pour l'office divin qui s'y fait avec soin."

[3] His comedy of " Clarice."   [4] See the Preface to " Clarice."

have assisted him in the production of the " Sosies "
and the "Ménechmes."

Much has been said of the obligations which
Molière's " Amphitryon " was under to Rotrou's
" Sosies ;" but little attention has been given to the
fact that the leading features of resemblance between
the two works are all to be found in the original of
Plautus. That which Molière may have borrowed
from Rotrou, or, like him, from some more modern
author, is contained within the limits of two or three
lines,[1] and the idea of the scene in which Mercury
drives Sosie out of the house, when he comes in to
dine. In the remainder of the piece Rotrou implicitly follows the Latin poet, omitting some details
which would be uninteresting to modern ears, and
rendering, in a very humorous manner, those parts

[1] Such as this line from " Les Sosies," act iv. scene 2 :—
    " Si l'on mangeait des yeux, il m'auroit dévoré."
Which Molière thus renders, in his " Amphitryon," act iii. scene 2 :—
    " Si des regards on pouvait mordre,
    Il m'auroit déjà dévoré."
And this line, which Rotrou puts in the mouth of one of the captains
invited by Jupiter in the name of Amphitryon :—
    " Point, point d'Amphitryon où l'on ne dîne point,"
is placed by Molière much more suitably in the mouth of Sosie :—
    " Le véritable Amphitryon
    Est l'Amphitryon où l'on dîne."
This reflection of Molière's Sosie :—
    " Le seigneur Jupiter sait dorer la pilule,"
is also imitated from the following remark of Rotrou's Sosie, as it does
not occur in Plautus :—
    " On appelle cela lui sucrer le breuvage."

which were likely to suit an audience in the seventeenth century. But he does not, like Molière, make
them his own by that lively and natural style of
wit, and those happy additions, which have raised
" Amphitryon " to the rank of an original work,
and assigned it a permanent position in the French
drama. Rotrou was satisfied with translating with
considerable taste that which Molière afterwards
imitated with consummate genius.

The translated comedy of the " Ménechmes," in
which Rotrou has transformed the courtesan Erotime
into a coquettish, but virtuous young widow, leads
us, less even than the " Sosies," to anticipate all that
Regnard derived at a later period from such a subject.

The ancient tragedies which were imitated by
Rotrou indicate, like his comedies, that he possessed
talent which stood in need of support, but which, at
all events, could make the best use of the helps to
which it had recourse. We must not expect to find
them characterised by the art of composition—an art
which, at that period, was understood by Corneille
alone. Rotrou's " Iphigénie en Aulide " is, with the
exception of a few scenes, an exact imitation of
Euripides' play of the same name. His " Hercule
Mourant " is the " Hercules Œtœus " of Seneca, to
which Rotrou has merely added the episode of
the loves of Iole and a young prince named
Arcas, which forms the subject of the fifth act.

And his "Antigone," which is composed from the "Phœnissæ" of Euripides, the "Thebais" of Seneca, and the "Antigone" of Sophocles, contains two tragedies within the space of one. But, in these three works, Rotrou is entitled to the merit of not having excessively disfigured the ancients by that triviality of language which his contemporaries mingled with the most ridiculous pomposity. If he has not very successfully imitated the simplicity of Sophocles, he has at least frequently diminished the inflation of Seneca : and several passages which have been most happily rendered, place Rotrou above the ordinary level of the authors of his time. In Seneca's "Hercules Œtœus" the hero, overcome by pain, implores the aid of Jupiter for the first time; and thus begs him to grant him death :—

> " *   *   *   Tot feras vici horridas,
> Reges, tyrannos; non tamen vultus meos
> In astra torsi ; semper hæc nobis manus
> Votum spopondit; nulla, propter me, sacro
> Micuêre cœlo fulmina   *   *   *." [1]

Rotrou extends this idea as follows :

> "J'ai toujours dû ma vie à ma seule défense,
> Et je n'ai point encore imploré ta puissance ;
> Quand les têtes de l'hydre ont fait entre mes bras
> Cent replis tortueux, je ne te priois pas ;
> Quand j'ai dans les enfers affronté la Mort même,
> Je n'ai point réclamé ta puissance suprême ;[2]

---

[1] *Seneca*, "Hercules Œtœus," lines 1295—1299.

[2] *Racine*, in "Phèdre," act iv. scene 2, has imitated this piece, and particularly these two lines of Rotrou :—

> " Dans les longues rigueurs d'une prison cruelle,
> Je n'ai point imploré ta puissance immortelle."

> J'ai de monstres divers purgé chaque élément
> Sans jeter vers le ciel un regard seulement ;
> Mon bras fut mon secours ; et jamais le tonnerre
> N'a, quand j'ai combattu, grondé contre la terre." [1]

By slightly diminishing the quickness of Seneca's movement, Rotrou has introduced into the piece some fine imagery.

In the " Antigone," that princess beholds from the ramparts of the town her brother Polynices, from whom she has been separated for a year, and thus addresses him :—

> " Polynice, avancez, portez ici la vue ;
> Souffrez qu'après un an votre sœur vous salue ;
> Malheureuse ! et pourquoi ne le puis-je autrement ?
> Quel destin entre nous met cet éloignement ?
> Après un si long temps la sœur revoit son frère,
> Et ne peut lui donner le salut ordinaire ;
> Un seul embrassement ne nous est pas permis ;
> Nous parlons séparés comme deux ennemis." [2]

This touching passage is not an imitation.

The " Iphigénie " also contains some ideas which properly belong to Rotrou, and which Racine has not disdained to imitate. [3] We do not, however, yet

---

[1] *Rotrou,* "Hercule Mourant," act iii. scene 2.

[2] *Rotrou,* "Antigone," act ii. scene 2.

[3] Among others, these lines, which do not occur in Euripides, in whose tragedy Clytemnestra speaks only with respect of the blood of Atreus :—

> " Va, père indigne d'elle, et digne fils d'Atrée,
> Par qui la loi du sang fut si peu révérée,
> Et qui crut comme toi faire un exploit fameux,
> Au repas qu'il dressa des corps de ses neveux."—
>   *Rotrou,* "Iphigénie en Aulide," act iv. scene 4.

> " Vous ne démentez point une race funeste ;
> Oui, vous êtes du sang d'Atrée et de Thyeste :

discover the presence of that talent which leaves traces of itself, because it follows in no one's footsteps ; and Rotrou was not yet aware of the style of composition best suited for the display of his powers. "Bélisaire," a drama in which he had attempted to impart to tragedy the tone assigned to it by Corneille, is perhaps one of his worst works. At length, however, he met with the subject of " Venceslas."

This subject does not belong to him ; he borrowed it of Don Francisco de Roxas,[1] just as Corneille had borrowed the " Cid " from Guillen de Castro. We consequently find in " Venceslas," as in the " Cid," a considerable number of fine lines which have been copied from the Spanish original. We find even more than this; for whole passages, and the arrangement of the scenes, are exactly the same in each. The entrance is the same, and so is the *dénouement*, except that, in the Spanish piece, Ladislas says nothing more about his love for Cassandra, who requests and obtains permission to retire to her

Bourreau de votre fille, il ne vous reste enfin
Que d'en faire à sa mère un horrible festin."
        Racine, " Iphigénie," act iv. scene 4.

The equivocal and ironical answers which Racine puts at first into the mouth of Clytemnestra, when Agamemnon demands of her her daughter, are not copied from Euripides. In Rotrou, it is Iphigenia who begins the scene with her father by a dialogue of this kind; which is much less becoming.—See *Rotrou*, " Iphigénie," act iv. scene 2 ; and *Racine*, " Iphigénie," act iv. scenes 3, 4.

[1] The original piece by Francisco de Roxas is to be found in the National Library at Paris, No. 6380, B. Its title is :—" No ay ser Padre siendo Re," the literal translation of which is, *There is no being a Father, while you are a King*.

estates. Rotrou, led astray by the *dénouement* of the " Cid," did not remark the difference of the circumstances in the two dramas. He did not feel that the spectator, though delighted to behold, at least in hope, Rodrigue's innocent and reciprocated affection crowned with success, is, on the contrary, revolted by the idea that the guilty Ladislas may one day obtain, as the reward of his furious passion, the hand of a woman who hates him, and whom he has just given so many fresh causes to detest him. [1]

---

[1] Marmontel, among other corrections which he introduced into Rotrou's tragedy, was desirous to alter the *dénouement*; in the last scene, therefore, when Ladislas said to Cassandra:—

> " Ma grâce est en vos mains."————————
> ————————————" Voilà donc ton supplice ! "

she immediately replied, stabbing him to the heart. This *dénouement*, which is in greater conformity to theatrical effect than to truth, is out of all harmony with the modern tone which prevails throughout the piece. Nevertheless, Marmontel's corrections were approved by the Maréchal de Duras, one of the gentlemen of the bedchamber, and as such entrusted with the theatrical arrangements of the Court. He wished to have this corrected edition of " Venceslas " performed at Versailles, and ordered Lekain to learn his part according to the new arrangement. Lekain, who did not like Marmontel, made as many objections as he dared ; but the Marshal spoke so positively that he was forced at least to feign submission. He, however, applied secretly to Colardeau for other corrections, which he substituted in the place of those by Marmontel. " Venceslas," thus performed, met with great success at Court ; and the Marshal, who had not perceived the substitution, was highly delighted at the happy result of his firmness. There is reason, however, to believe that the trick was speedily discovered. Marmontel himself informs us that his " Venceslas " was performed at Court and in Paris, but that the Court alone approved of the new *dénouement*, whereas it displeased the Parisian public; which obliged him to abandon it and return to the old one. See the " Chefs-d'œuvres dramatiques," Examination of " Venceslas :" Paris, 1773. All the corrections have since been abandoned, and, with the exception of a few expressions, the " Venceslas " performed at the present day is entirely Rotrou's own.

Reflection had not yet taught dramatic authors how greatly difference of feeling changes the moral effect of two actions apparently similar. With this exception, the Spanish piece contains the principal features of the last act of " Venceslas ; "[1] and it is only in the plot of the drama, and in the circumstances which lead to the catastrophe, that Rotrou has departed to any great extent from his original. In the work of Roxas, Prince Roger (the Ladislas of the French piece) does not appear to have any intention to marry Cassandra ; but feeling great love for her, and correspondingly great jealousy of the duke, whom he regards as his rival, he is not very delicate as to the means which he employs to rob him of his mistress. Those dishonourable attempts which Rotrou has placed in the introduction to his play, although Cassandra reminds us of them rather too frequently and too energetically,[2] are put into practice by the Spanish author. Roger forms a plan for introducing himself by night into the chamber

---

[1] With the exception only of a few, among which is this fine line of Venceslas, when he learns that the revolted populace intend to force him to revoke the sentence of Ladislas :—

"Et me vouloir injuste est ne me vouloir plus."

There will also be observed, in the French imitation, a livelier and closer turn of style than in the Spanish author. The piece is, on the whole, better adapted to produce an effect upon the French stage, the spectators of which like to see a thought included within a single line.

[2] "Foul desires," "unclean pleasures," "free conversations," "infamous messages," are expressions used far too familiarly by Cassandra, and which are now omitted in the performance of the piece.

of his mistress; but Cassandra, being informed of this design, communicates it to the king, that his authority may deliver her from Roger's persecutions. When Roger arrives, he finds Cassandra alone in a room, and before she is able to recognise him, he puts out the light, and prepares to use any violence that may be necessary for the accomplishment of his desires. But Cassandra in alarm has escaped from the room under favour of the darkness, and left the prince *tête-à-tête* with the chair on which she had been sitting, and where he is greatly astonished to find her no longer. Whilst he is looking for her, arrives Prince Alexander,[1] who is secretly married to Cassandra, and who, having been absent from Court for a whole month, in consequence of a quarrel with his brother, has come, under cover of night, to see his wife. The two brothers meet; the king arrives; they conceal themselves; and this adventure produces an imbroglio, the result of which is to persuade the prince that the duke is the husband of Cassandra. Furious with rage, he introduces himself a second time into her chamber, finds her asleep in the arms of Alexander, whom he kills without recognising him or waking him from his sleep. Cassandra, on opening her eyes, finds her husband dead, and the dagger left in the wound reveals to her

---

[1] Whom the Spanish author, and Rotrou after him, call the *Infante* Alexander. Rotrou also introduced an Infante Théodore into this play.

the name of the murderer.   Such are the incidents
upon which the Spanish play is founded, eked out by
the witticisms of some valets and the bombastic
descriptions of the prince.

Corneille had taught the poets of France that such
means were not admissible into true tragedy.   Those
devised by Rotrou are not much better ; and the
idea upon which the whole plot of the piece hangs,
namely the promise which the king has made to the
duke to grant him the first favour he may ask, whatever that may be, is a very bad spring of action.[1]   It
may also be said that the fury of Ladislas, who twice
silences the duke just when he was about to declare
his love for the Princess Théodore, is a very puerile
trick to prolong the misunderstanding which leads to
the catastrophe.

If Rotrou could lay claim, in " Venceslas," to
nothing more than these puerile inventions, it would
not be worth our while to inquire how far they may
be said to belong to him ; but the character of
Ladislas—so fiery and impetuous, so interesting even
on account of the violence of those passions which
render it dangerous and criminal—Rotrou has appro-
priated to himself by developing it in its full propor-
tions.   The Spanish author has exhibited Roger's

---

[1] The same idea is employed in "Don Lope de Cardonne," Rotrou's last
work, which is very similar in other respects to " Venceslas ; " which
similarity leads me to believe that Rotrou borrowed this romantic invention
also from the Spanish drama.

pride only in his hatred of the duke and of his
brother ; he has manifested the vehemence of his
love only by the impetuosity of his desires, and the
fury of his jealousy by the crime which it leads him
to commit ; he has also represented him as much
more harsh in his treatment of his father, and has
never displayed in him anything but the ferocity of
an indomitable character, without mingling with it
that tenderness of passion which supplies the means
of moderating its violence, and, to use the expression
of Venceslas,

> " Malgré tous ses défauts le rend encore aimable."

Rotrou was fully aware of the storms and conflicts
which a despised and jealous love could not fail to
excite in so haughty, so brilliant, and so imperious a
nature ; and he has represented its transports, weaknesses, and vicissitudes with a truthfulness previously
unknown to our drama.   Corneille had depicted love
in conflict with duty ; but love had not yet been seen
in conflict with itself, tormented by its own violence,
alternately suppliant and furious, and manifesting
itself as. much by excess of anger as by excess of
tenderness.   Granting some slight indulgence to those
deficiencies in propriety and faults of style which are
characteristic of the authors of this period, where
shall we find a more faithful picture of the vicissitudes
of passion than in the scene in which Ladislas, stung

to the quick by Cassandra's contempt, swears that his
love for her is changing into hatred ?

> "Allez, indigne objet de mon inquiétude ;
> J'ai trop longtemps souffert de votre ingratitude ;
> Je devois vous connoître, et ne m'engager pas
> Aux trompeuses douceurs de vos cruels appas.
>   *   *   *   *   *
> De vos superbes lois ma raison dégagée
> A guéri mon amour, et croit l'avoir songée.
> De l'indigne brâsier qui consumoit mon cœur,
> *Il ne me reste plus que la seule rougeur,*
> Que la honte et l'horreur de vous avoir aimée
> Laisseront à jamais sur ce front imprimée.
> Oui, je rougis, ingrate, et mon propre courroux
> Ne me peut pardonner ce que j'ai fait pour vous.
> Je veux que la mémoire efface de ma vie
> Le souvenir du temps que je vous ai servie.
> J'étois mòrt pour la gloire, et je n'ai pas vécu
> Tant que ce lâche cœur s'est dit votre vaincu.
> Ce n'est que d'aujourd'hui qu'il vit et qu'il respire,
> D'aujourd'hui qu'il renonce au joug de votre empire,
> Et qu'avec ma raison, mes yeux et lui d'accord
> Détestent votre vue à l'égal de la mort."

After a haughty reply, Cassandra retires ; upon
which Ladislas, in despair, conjures his sister to call
her back :—

> "Ma sœur, au nom d'amour, et par pitié des larmes
> Que ce cœur enchanté donne encore à ses charmes,
> Si vous voulez d'un frère empêcher le trépas,
> Suivez cette insensible et retenez ses pas.

> THÉODORE.
> La retenir, mon frère, après l'avoir bannie ?

> LADISLAS.
> Ah ! contre ma raison servez sa tyrannie !
> Je veux désavouer ce cœur séditieux,
> La servir, l'adorer, et mourir à ses yeux.
>   *   *   *   *   *
> Que je la voie au moins si je ne la possède ;
> Mon mal chérit sa cause et voit peu son remède.

Quand mon cœur à ma voix a feint de consentir,
Il en étoit charmé ; je l'en veux démentir ;
Je mourois, je brûlois, je l'adorois dans l'âme,
Et le ciel a pour moi fait un sort tout de flamme."

His sister, in compliance with his request, is about
to go in search of Cassandra, when he exclaims—

" Me laissez-vous, ma sœur, en ce désordre extrême ?

THÉODORE.

J'allois la retenir.

LADISLAS.

Eh ! ne voyez-vous pas
Quel arrogant mépris précipite ses pas ?
Avec combien d'orgueil elle s'est retirée ?
Quel implacable haine elle m'a déclarée ? "

When at last his vexation has gained the ascendancy ; when Ladislas has determined to subdue his
own feelings even so far as to promote the interests
of the duke with his mistress ; when he has encouraged him to explain to the king the nature of
the favour to which he aspires, and which, in the
opinion of Ladislas, can be nothing else than the
hand of Cassandra,—at the very moment when the
fatal name is about to be pronounced, incapable of
further self-restraint, and falling once more under
the sway of his love and jealousy, Ladislas gives
utterance at length to the transports which he
had vainly attempted to repress, and, interrupting
the duke for the second time, forces him to resume that silence which he had previously urged

him so strenuously to break. As I have already
observed, this repeated interruption is only a defective
means of prolonging a necessary misapprehension. It
is undoubtedly of great importance to Ladislas. that
the duke should not prefer his request, as the king
would at once grant that which he besought ; but
this romantic combination cannot be sufficiently kept
in mind by the spectator, nor is it likely to strike
him so forcibly as to lead him to excuse the puerility,
and at the same time, the brutality of the movement.
This movement is nevertheless brought about in a
very natural manner ; and if the passion of Ladislas
had only been pourtrayed under another form, it
would most certainly have produced a very powerful
effect.

Other deficiencies are also observable in the execution of this admirably-conceived character. The
manner in which Ladislas expresses to Cassandra
the hatred and contempt which he fancies he feels
for her, too often justifies that ironical exclama-
tion of the duchess : " O ! what noble rage." It is
not pleasing to hear a prince call a lady of his court
" insolent," telling her coarsely that he might desire
to have her as his mistress, but not as his wife, and
that he would very soon have overcome her disdain
if he had thought it worth while to employ violence.
Rotrou has been justly blamed for casting odium
upon a prince whom he intends to crown with honour

at the end of the piece, by telling him, through his father, in the first act :—

> " S'il faut qu'à cent rapports ma créance réponde,
> Rarement le soleil rend sa lumière au monde
> Que le premier rayon qu'il répand ici-bas
> N'y découvre quelqu'un de vos assassinats." [1]

So great was the want of delicacy of a time when taste had not yet learned to measure things aright, when talent, and sometimes even genius, felt a strong inclination to exaggerate both means and effects, when force was synonymous with violence, when violence was manifested by ferocity, when frankness was carried to brutality, and politeness degraded into flattery. But, beneath this offensive mode of expression and this repulsive exaggeration, we shall everywhere meet with indications of nature,—a strong, vehement, passionate nature ; and we shall ever feel convinced that Rotrou was able both to imagine and to pourtray it in all its forms.

Nor is " Venceslas " the only proof that he possessed an original talent, which did not derive its

---

[1] The Spanish author says even more than this :—

> " En essas calles y plaças,
> Siempre que el aurora argenta,
> Quando ha de adorar con rayos
> El padre de las estrellas,
> Se hallan muertas mil personas."

" In the streets and public places, whenever Aurora enlightens them, when she comes to worship the father of the stars with her rays, a thousand persons are found dead."

inspiration from the spirit and habits of his time. Another of Rotrou's works, "Laure Persécutée," which has fallen into that oblivion in which, in many respects, it deserves to remain, nevertheless contains a scene worthy to take rank with the best scenes of "Venceslas," and which, if purged of a few defects in taste, would not do discredit to many master-pieces of a higher order of perfection. Orontée, Prince of Hungary, loves and is beloved by Laura, a young girl of inferior rank. His friends have succeeded in persuading him that his mistress is unfaithful to him. In rage and despair, he demands the restoration of his letters, which Laura returns to him with touching gentleness and tenderness ; and Orontée swears never to see her again. His confidant, Octave, nevertheless, when in search of him, suspects that he will find him at Laura's door, and there, in fact, he finds him, lying on the threshold, weeping.

OCTAVE.

" *   *   Quoi ! Seigneur, et si tard et sans suite ?

ORONTÉE.

Que veux-tu ? sans dessein, sans conseil, sans conduite,
Mon cœur, sollicité d'un invincible effort,
Se laisse aveuglément attirer à son sort ;
Pour n'être pas témoin de ma folie extrême,
Moi-même je voudrois être ici sans moi-même.
Qu'un favorable soin t'amène sur mes pas !
Saisi, troublé, confus, je ne me connois pas :
Et ta seule présence, en ce besoin offerte,
Arrête mon esprit sur le point de sa perte."

Octave, who is a party to the deception which has

been practised upon Orontée, and who, if the prince sees Laura, dreads that his perfidy will be unmasked, tries to animate him to firmness of conduct, and says :—

" Il faut payer de force en semblables combats :
Qui combat mollement veut bien ne vaincre pas.

ORONTÉE.

Je l'avoue à toi seul, oui, je l'avoue, Octave,
En cessant d'être amant je deviens moins qu'esclave ;
Et si je la voyois, je crois qu'à son aspect,
Tu me verrois mourir de crainte et de respect.
Je ne sais par quel sort ou quelle frénésie
Mon amour peut durer avec ma jalousie ;
Mais je sens en effet que, malgré cet affront,
Dont la marque si fraîche est encor sur mon front,
Le dépit ne sauroit l'emporter sur la flamme,
Et toute mon amour est encor dans mon âme."

Octave, in greater alarm than ever, endeavours to overcome his weakness by representing its probable consequences, and says :—

" Laure, en un mot, Seigneur, n'est pas loin de la paix.

ORONTÉE.

Moi ! que je souffre Laure et lui parle jamais !
Que jamais je m'arrête, et jamais je me montre
Où Laure doive aller, où Laure se rencontre !
Que je visite Laure et la caresse un jour !
Que Laure puisse encor me donner de l'amour !"

The conversation continues in this way between the prince and his confidant for some time, and whenever it is not animated by passion, it is laden with subtleties and plays upon words which are too common in works of this period, for it to be necessary

for me to quote any examples.[1]   But suddenly the
prince interrupts the dialogue, and, without giving
any answer to Octave, exclaims :—

> " Qu'on m'a fait un plaisir et triste et déplaisant,
> Et qu'on m'a mis en peine en me désabusant !
> Qu'on a blessé mon cœur en guérissant ma vue !
> Car enfin mon erreur me plaisoit inconnue :
> D'aucun trouble d'esprit je n'étois agité,
> Et l'abus me servoit plus que la vérité.
> Moi ! que du choix de Laure enfin je me repente !
> Que jamais à mes yeux Laure ne se présente !
> Que Laure ne soit plus dedans mon souvenir !
> Que de Laure mon cœur n'ose m'entretenir !
> Que pour Laure mon sein n'enferme qu'une roche !
> Que je ne touche à Laure et jamais ne l'approche !
> Que pour Laure mes vœux aient été superflus !
> Que je n'entende Laure et ne lui parle plus !
> Frappe, je veux la voir.

OCTAVE.

Seigneur.

ORONTÉE.

Frappe, te dis-je.

OCTAVE.

Mais songez-vous à quoi votre transport m'oblige ?

ORONTÉE.

Ne me conteste point.

OCTAVE.

Quel est votre dessein ?

ORONTÉE.

Fay tôt, ou je te mets ce poignard dans le sein.

OCTAVE.

Eh bien ! je vais heurter.

---

[1] " Que veux-tu ? mon attente étoit une chimère
    Qui porta des enfans semblables à leur mère :
    Comme je bâtissois sur un sable mouvant,
    J'ai produit des soupirs qui ne sont que du vent."

ORONTÉE.

     Non ! n'en fais rien, arrête ;
Mon honneur me retient quand mon amour est prête,
Et l'une m'aveuglant, l'autre m'ouvre les yeux.

OCTAVE.

L'honneur, assurément, vous conseille le mieux.
Retirons-nous.

ORONTÉE.

    Attends que ce transport se passe.
Approche cependant ; sieds-toi, prends cette place ;
Et pour me divertir, cherche en ton souvenir
Quelque histoire d'amour de quoi m'entretenir.

OCTAVE.

Ecoutez donc : Un jour . . . .

ORONTÉE *rêvant.*

     Un jour cette infidelle
M'a vu l'aimer au point d'oublier tout pour elle ;
Un jour j'ai vu son cœur répondre à mon amour ;
J'ai cru qu'un chaste hymen nous uniroit un jour ;
Un jour je me suis vu comblé d'aise et de gloire . . .
Mais ce jour-là n'est plus . . . Achève ton histoire.

OCTAVE.

Un jour donc dans un bal un seigneur . . . .

ORONTÉE.

       Fut-ce moi ?
Car ce fut dans un bal qu'elle reçut ma foi ;
Que mes yeux éblouis de sa première vue
Adorèrent d'abord cette belle inconnue,
Qu'ils livrèrent mon cœur à l'empire des siens,
Et que j'offris mes bras à mes premiers liens.
Mais quelle tyrannie ai-je enfin éprouvée !
Octave, c'est assez, l'histoire est achevée."

Passing over a few improprieties, and affected
repetitions, we fearlessly ask, are not these emotions the same as we find afterwards displayed by
Pyrrhus, Orosmane, and Vendôme ? Is not this
love in all its power and all its weakness ?

It would be difficult to say whether this scene belongs entirely to Rotrou ; the energy of its last characteristic, in particular, is marked by a singularity which would seem to belong to Shakespeare and Othello, rather than to a Frenchman of the seventeenth century. The sources from which Rotrou derived his materials were so numerous and varied, and the originals that he imitated have become so foreign to our knowledge, that we cannot pretend to have discovered them all, or to distinguish, in the works of the French poet, that which really belongs to him ; but, as regards that which he borrowed, he is entitled to the merit of having discovered, felt, and rendered it. He is equally capable sometimes of discerning and expressing, with great keenness of observation, those gentler and more reserved emotions, the description of which, though they belong to nature, enters more into the province of comedy. In "La Sœur," a young girl, alarmed at not having seen her lover during the day, is anxious to find some means of bringing him to her side without compromising herself, so she orders her servant to go to him, with these instructions : —

> " Confesse-lui ma crainte et dis-lui mon martyre ;
> Que l'accès qu'un mari lui donne en sa maison
> Me le rend, en un mot, suspect de trahison.
> Mais non, ne touche rien de ce jaloux ombrage ;
> C'est à sa vanité donner trop d'avantage ;
> Dis lui que puisqu'il m'aime, et qu'il sait qu'aux amans
> Une heure sans se voir est un an de tourmens,

Il m'afflige aujourd'hui d'une trop longue absence.
Non, il me voudroit voir avec trop de licence.
Dis-lui que dans le doute où me tient sa santé . . .
Mais puisque tu l'as vu, puis-je en avoir douté ?
Flattant trop un amant, une amante inexperte
Par ses soins superflus en hasarde la perte.
Va, Lydie, et dis-lui ce que, pour mon repos,
Tu crois de plus séant et de plus à propos ;
Va, rends-moi l'espérance, ou fais que j'y renonce ;
Ne dis rien si tu veux ; mais j'attends sa réponse."

This last line is charming.

After reading these examples, it is impossible not to admit that Rotrou possessed a rare and delicate talent for depicting the tender passions and secret movements of the heart. Unfortunately, he did not yield sufficiently often to his natural impulse. After having produced " Venceslas," he tried, in " Cosroes," to imitate Corneille ; and his work was characterised by all the defects of imitators, excepting exaggeration of the manner of his model. " Cosroes " is a rather well-arranged tragedy, in which political interests are discussed with considerable wisdom, and in which the author has succeeded in representing, with sufficient interest, the various events of a revolution which deprives a king of his throne, and substitutes in his place that one of his sons whom he intended to rob of his legitimate rights, in order to bestow the crown upon a younger brother. But there is nothing in the piece to strike the imagination, and nothing to excite any strong curiosity. Siroes, the eldest son of Cosroes, sometimes yielding with grief to the necessities of his position and the advice of his adherents, who compel him to condemn his father and brother, and sometimes giving way to those natural feelings which he has had so much difficulty to overcome, is perhaps a very natural character ; but he does not possess sufficient ambition, or sufficient virtue, for the stage. The same may be said of Merdesanes, his brother ; who at first refuses the crown which Cosroes wishes to confer upon him, to the prejudice of his elder brother, but afterwards accepts it. There is nothing sufficiently emphatic or determinate in this tragedy to support its pretensions to revive the recollection of Corneille. The early scenes, however, between Siroes and his mother-in-law, may have suggested the idea of " Nicomède." [1]

After " Cosroes," " Florimonde " and " Don Lope de Cardonne," probably imitations from the Spanish, and which are remarkable only by the resemblance of the latter to " Venceslas," terminated the dramatic career of Rotrou. He had been married for some time to Marguerite Le Camus, was the father of three children, and probably feeling determined to introduce into his conduct a little more of the regularity required by his new position, he had bought the office of Lieutenant of the bailiwick of Dreux. Notwithstanding the exactitude with which it would appear that he discharged the duties of this post,

[1] " Nicomède" appeared in 1652, and " Cosroes " in 1648.

he was at Paris when he learned that Dreux was ravaged by a contagious disease, and that death had removed, or fear frightened away, the authorities whose business it was to maintain public order, and to strive to arrest the progress of the evil. He set out at once for the post of duty ; and at a time which called for the manifestation of the noble and excellent qualities of every lofty soul, he devoted himself, without hesitation or self-regard, to the performance of those duties which were required for the public welfare and care for every individual. In vain did his brother and friends urge him to provide for his own safety ; his only answer was that his presence was needed, and he terminates his letter with these words : " It is not that the peril in which I am placed is not very great, since at the moment at which I am writing the bells are tolling for the twenty-second person who has died to-day ; it will be my turn when it shall please God." These words, which may be regarded as a model of the simplicity and calmness of true courage, sustained by the conviction of duty, are the last which remain to us of Rotrou ; for he was attacked by the malady a few days afterwards, and died on the 27th of June, 1650, in the forty-first year of his age. [1]

[1] The death of Rotrou was proposed, in 1810, as the subject for the prize for poetry awarded by the French Academy ; and the prize was gained by M. Millevoye.

Thus perished, in the prime of his life, character, and talents, a man, who, if we may judge of him by the last act of his life, was destined to give a memorable example of virtues whose exercise had been only suspended by the impetuosity of youth ; and a poet, who, from the lofty flight he had just taken, might have been thought destined to discover new beauties in the art of song. All that remains of Rotrou gives us the idea of a man who was not strong enough to rise above his age, but who was worthy of a time capable of giving him better support. Rotrou is wanting in that invention which can produce, arrange, and direct the incidents of a great drama ; but it is not easy to assign limits to the splendid effects which he might have derived from the emotions of the heart and the movement of the passions. His style, though frequently obscure, unsuitable, and forced, sometimes receives from the sentiment by which it is animated a natural elegance, which a little more art and study might have rendered more familiar to him. In a word, though he makes us regret that he was not all that he might have been, Rotrou rises far above the common herd of his contemporaries, who could not but have been what they were.

PAUL SCARRON.

(1610—1660.)

—————◆—————

THERE are periods in history when a craving after pleasure is displayed with almost furious vehemence, although it proves to be nothing but a craving after dissipation. At such periods, diversions destitute of gaiety are abundant ; the noise of festivity is not accompanied by the sounds of joy : splendour must be combined with every pleasure to prove that it is a pleasure ; and those men who hasten in pursuit of enjoyments, surprised to find them so cold and empty, complain of the *ennui* connected with that agitation with which they cannot dispense.

It is especially in times of public misfortune that this moral infirmity exhibits itself. At such times, the soul, tormented by painful feelings, tries to rid itself of its own existence, and to dissipate, in momentary enjoyments, that strength which it could not employ without pain ; it issues continually out of itself, and goes begging the means of self-oblivion in every direction ; but it meets itself everywhere, and carries its sorrows wherever it goes. Pleasures enter without effort, and take up a permanent abode only where they are received by happiness ; when sought out by misfortune, they are either rejected or corrupted. Great calamities are almost invariably accompanied by dissoluteness of manners ; and excess of suffering or affright casts men into excessive indulgence in diversions ; but there is nothing to indicate that, at these fatal epochs, they have ever found joy in their amusements.

Joy, on the other hand, a taste rather than a craving for pleasure, a capacity for finding amusement everywhere, and a gaiety as natural as it is frolicsome, seem to be, at least for the wealthier classes, the appanage of certain periods, which, though not strictly speaking periods of happiness, afford the means and justify the hope of its attainment. These are times when there is a kind of youthfulness in the minds of men—an intoxication of life and strength—an activity which diffuses itself over all objects, because it meets with nothing which it deems worthy to occupy its entire attention. To minds thus disposed, the present moment is sufficient, for they devote themselves to it with all the energy of their faculties ; they may allow themselves to be carried away by every pleasure, for to them all pleasures are equally alluring ; even excesses are then endowed with a natural attractiveness, and a vein of originality, which will bring a smile to the countenance even of that wisdom which condemns them; and, like the follies of youth, they carry with them their own excuse and almost their seductiveness.

> " Tel fut le temps de la bonne Régence,"

the Regency of Anne of Austria, which Saint-Evremond so bitterly regretted :—

> " Temps où régnoit une heureuse abondance,
> Temps où la ville aussi bien que la cour
> Ne respiroient que les jeux et l'amour." [1]

A time when, as Bautru said, "*honnête homme* and *bonnes mœurs* were incompatible." [2] Morality was not, indeed, despised, but it was never thought of; no fear was felt of serious subjects, but they could never be treated with greater seriousness than the most frivolous matters; for frivolous matters were of

---

[1] *Saint-Evremond,* " Œuvres," vol. iii. p. 294.

[2] Ibid. p. 38. The *honnête homme* was then synonymous with " the member of fashionable society "; he was at once " the man of gallantry," and " the man of the world." This name implied a certain elegance of manners unattainable by any but those who moved in the highest circles. A good address, ready wit, and gentlemanly manners were indispensable requisites. " You do not pass in the world as a connoisseur of poetry," says Pascal, " if you do not put on the insignia of a poet, or as clever in mathematics unless you wear those of a mathematician. But your true *honnêtes gens* will have no insignia, and make no difference between the profession of a poet and that of an embroiderer. They are not called either poets or geometricians, but they are the judges of all such. You cannot guess their intentions; they will speak on any subject that may be mentioned when they enter. You cannot perceive that they possess one quality more than another, except the necessity of bringing it into use; but then you call to mind that it is equally important to their character that it should not be said of them that they speak well when no question of language is under discussion, and that it should be said that they do speak well when such a question is under debate." It was essential that the *honnête homme* should always be able to adapt himself to the tone of the society in which he might happen to be placed.

great importance in the eyes of people whose whole existence was spent in the pursuit of pleasure. Civil troubles occurred to interrupt the " games and love " in which their life was passed, but love continued still to be the great business even of those who aimed at reforming or overturning the State. It was love for the Duchess de Longueville that induced La Roche-foucauld to join the party of the Fronde ; and Cardinal de Retz, while as yet a mere coadjutor, made use of its powers to gain over to his side several ladies, who proved important auxiliaries in this children's war. The heroes of the Fronde, on their return from a skirmish with the troops of Mazarin, clothed in their armour, and adorned with their scarfs, hastened to present themselves to the ladies who filled the apart-ments of the Duchess de Longueville. The violins struck up within the house ; outside, in the public street, the trumpets resounded ; and Noirmoutier, in delight, pictured to himself Galatée and Lindamor besieged in Marcilli. [1] The Marshal d'Hocquincourt [2] promised Péronne to Mme. de Montbazon, " the fairest of the fair " ; [3] and men frequently had less reasonable motives than his for deciding on their course. Rouillac, brave and reckless, came to offer his services to the coadjutor, who was then at the

---

[1] Characters in " Astrée." See the " Memoirs of De Retz," vol. i. p. 213.

[2] Afterwards a Marshal of France, then Governor of Peronne.

[3] " Memoirs of de Retz," vol. i. p. 271.

height of his quarrels with the Prince ; Canillac, equally brave and reckless, came at the same time, with the same intentions ; but, on seeing Rouillac, he withdrew, saying, " It is not fair that the two greatest madcaps in the kingdom should both belong to the same party ; I shall go to the Hôtel Condé : " [1] and thither he went.   A whim was then a sufficient motive ; a joke furnished a peremptory argument ; men laughed at themselves almost as much as at their friends ; as far as raillery was concerned, neither party could be said to have the advantage ; and in those important cabals which alarmed the Court and caused the minister to tremble, it would, perhaps, have been difficult to find a dozen men whose chief object was not to amuse themselves with that which seemed so passionately to absorb their energies.

At this period lived Scarron. He had received from nature a mind and character well adapted to conform to the disposition of the times in which his life was passed ; and fortune seemed to have secured him a position of sufficient wealth and rank to enable him to yield without constraint to the tastes of his mind and the inclinations of his character.

Paul Scarron was born in 1610 or 1611. His father, Paul Scarron, was a councillor of the Parliament at Paris, a man of ancient family, [2] and possessing,

---

[1] " Memoirs of De Retz," vol. ii. p. 364.

[2] Originally of Moncallier, in Piedmont, where it had resided since the

it is said, an income of more than twenty thousand livres; a considerable fortune for that time, which his son might hope he would have to share only with two sisters, born of the same marriage. The second marriage of Councillor Scarron, however, diminished the expectations of his elder children, and his new wife did her best to nullify them altogether. She obtained such influence over the mind, property, and affairs of her negligent husband, that, if we are to believe Scarron, " when she was once very ill, and her husband feared he would be left a widower, he entreated her to leave him a pension of six hundred livres after her death." [1]   Young Scarron, though

thirteenth century. (See Moreri's Dictionary.) He was a relative of the Scarrons of Vaujour, one of whom, Jean Scarron, was appointed Provost of the merchants in 1664; another, Michel Scarron, a Councillor of State, married his daughter Catherine to the Maréchal d'Aumont. During the Regency of Anne of Austria, there lived a certain Pierre Scarron, an uncle or cousin of the poet, who is noticed in the memoirs of the time for the length of his beard, an ornament which a few grave personages then retained in opposition to the customs of the age. One day, a lackey said to him at table, " My lord, there is some dirt on the beard of your greatness." " Why don't you say," rejoined one of the company, " upon the greatness of your beard ?" (" Menagiana," vol. i. p. 284.) Molé, the keeper of the seals, who was remarkable for a singularity of the same kind, said, when he saw Pierre Scarron, " That casts my beard into the shade." (Ibid. p. 285.)

[1] " A deed or requisition, or whatever you please, on behalf of Paul Scarron, senior of the invalids of France, Anne Scarron, a poor widow, twice pillaged during the blockade, and Frances Scarron, who is ill-paid by her lodger—children, by the first marriage, of the late Master Paul Scarron, Councillor of the Parliament, all three very ill at ease, both in their persons and properties, defendants; against Charles Robin, lord of Sigoigne, husband of Madelaine Scarron, Daniel Boileau, lord of Plessis, husband of Claude Scarron, and Nicolas Scarron, children by his second marriage, all well and healthy, and rejoicing at the expense of others, appellants." *Scarron,* "Œuvres," vol. i. part 2, edit. 1737. This edition we shall always quote,

old enough to perceive the designs of his mother-in-law, was neither sufficiently patient nor sufficiently skilful in his treatment of the weakness of his father,— "the best man in the world," he says, "but not the best father to his children by his first marriage." Probably, Councillor Scarron was already disposed to feel displeased with his son, whose principal virtue was certainly not deference to opinions and tastes in which he did not coincide. "He has threatened a hundred times to disinherit his eldest son," says Scarron, "because he ventured to maintain that Malherbe wrote better verses than Ronsard ; and has predicted that he would never make his fortune, because he did not read his Bible, and tie up his breeches with points." [1]

Subjects of more serious quarrels, which arose from young Scarron's dislike of his mother-in-law, and the equally great aversion which she felt for himself, compelled his father to banish him for some time from the paternal residence. He spent two years at Charleville with one of his relations. Either because the tedium of exile had led him to reflect a little upon the necessity of patience, or because the age of

---

except in extracts from the "Roman Comique." This *Factum* was printed on the occasion of a lawsuit which he had, after his father's death, with his half brothers and sisters, and to which we shall presently refer.

[1] The fashion of tying the breeches to the doublet with tagged points preceded that of wearing trunk hose, but old men long retained the habit. Harpagon, in *Molière's* "Avare," was "trussed with points." Act ii. sc. 6.

enjoyment had rendered him careless of business,
Scarron, on his return to Paris, determined to allow
his father to waste in peace the fortune of his children ;
whilst, on his part, he plunged with equal tranquillity
into all those pursuits which render the possession of
fortune indispensable. At all events, it does not
appear that new differences had necessitated a fresh
separation, and forced the son to seek resources independently of his family.

He had adopted the ecclesiastical profession, but
without gaining the emoluments, or subjecting himself
to the discipline, of his new calling. The garb which
he wore was assumed merely as a means of saving himself from the necessity of choosing another occupation
less favourable to his tastes for idleness and dissipation. These tastes led him wherever amusement was
to be found, and he carried amusement whithersoever
he went. His method of diverting others was to
divert himself ; and he did not think that wit could be
useful for any other purpose. I do not know whether
his wit would have made his fortune at the Hôtel
de Rambouillet, for where Voiture reigned supreme,
Scarron might well have found the society tedious ;
but Ninon's parties, and all those societies in which
a taste for pleasure combined with a taste for wit, and
liberty of action was united to liberty of thought,
were the societies which Scarron frequented; and it is
by no means improbable that he frequented others in

still less conformity to ecclesiastical regularity. A journey which he made to Rome, when about twenty-four years of age, does not appear to have been dictated by more serious motives, or to have produced more serious results, than those which ordinarily characterised his conduct. The recollections which remain to us, in his Works, of the time of his youth, tell us only of the pleasures which he regretted, and the natural gratifications with which they supplied him. " When I reflect," he writes to M. de Marigny, " that I was strong enough until twenty-seven years of age to drink frequently in the German fashion, and that, if Heaven had left me the legs that once danced so elegantly, and the hands that could paint and play the lute so well, I might still lead a very happy, though perhaps rather obscure, life—I swear to you, my dear friend, that, if it were lawful for me to terminate my own existence, I would have poisoned myself long ago." [1]

At length Scarron was afflicted with those maladies which were destined to gain him a celebrity which he had never anticipated, and to devote to the service of the public a gaiety of mind which a poor invalid could no longer always employ in his own service. We possess no positive information regarding the origin of the strange infirmities which seem to have fallen

[1] *Scarron,* " Œuvres," vol. i. part 2, pp. 83, 84. See also his Portrait of himself at p. 20 of the same volume; and his " Epître à Pelisson," in vol. viii. p. 106.

upon him suddenly, and made him a cripple for the remainder of his life. Scarron himself speaks of them as unknown to his physicians.[1] The following anecdote is related by La Beaumelle, and has been repeated by all the compilers of anecdotes : " He had gone to spend the carnival at his canonicate of Mans. At Mans, as in most large provincial towns, the carnival ended by public masquerades which strongly resembled our fairs of Bezons. Abbé Scarron determined to join the maskers ; but under what disguise should he conceal himself? He had at once to redeem the eccentricity of his character and the dignity of his position, to respect the Church and do honour to burlesque. He covered every part of his body with honey, ripped open a feather-bed, jumped into it, and rolled about until he was completely covered with feathers. In this costume he paraded through the fair, and attracted universal attention. The women soon surrounded him ; some ran away, but others plucked him of his plumes, and soon the fine masker looked more like a canon than an American Indian. At this sight, the people collected

---

[1] " Mal dangereux puisqu'il est inconnu."

The line stands thus, at least, in the Amsterdam edition. The edition of 1737, which we generally follow, gives it thus, vol. viii. p. 54 :—

" Mal dangereux puisqu'il est si connu."

This last version is evidently erroneous, as well as contrary to the sense of the two following lines on poverty :—

" Et chose autant dangereuse tenue,
　Quoiqu'elle soit, mieux que mon mal, connue."

in crowds, and indignantly inveighed against so
scandalous an exhibition. At last Scarron got clear
of his persecutors, and fled, hotly pursued, dripping
with honey and water, and almost dead with fatigue.
When just at bay, he came to a bridge, jumped
heroically over the parapet, and hid himself among
the reeds on the banks of the river. Here his heat
subsided, a chilling cold pervaded his system, and
infused into his blood the seeds of the maladies which
afterwards afflicted him." [1]

A single word is sufficient to disprove the whole of
this story. Scarron did not obtain the canonry of
Mans until 1646 ; that is, until after he had been an
invalid for eight years, for his malady commenced in
1638.[2] At the time when he took possession of his
benefice, he had already lost the entire use of all his
limbs.[3] This benefice was the first and only prefer-

---

[1] "Mémoires de Maintenon," vol. i. pp. 118, 119. I may here observe,
once for all, that I shall only correct La Beaumelle when I think it absolutely indispensable to do so. To attempt to point out and disprove all
the absurd conjectures in which he has indulged, both in his Memoirs and
in his collection of Letters, would be to involve myself in discussions as
interminable as useless.

[2] The year of the birth of Louis XIV. In his " Typhon," he says :—

> " Et par maudite maladie,
> Dont ma face est toute enlaidie,
> Je suis persécuté dès-lors
> Que du très-adorable corps
> De notre Reine, que tant j'aime,
> Sortit Louis le quatorzième."

[3] In his Epistle to Mlle. d'Hautefort, he writes (vol. viii. p. 167) :—

> " Cependant notre pauvre corps
> Devient pitoyablement tors ;

ment that he ever received.[1]   It is true that, in his
youth, he had been at Mans on a visit to Mlle. de
Hautefort, whose estates were situated in the neighbourhood of that town ; but he speaks of this visit
only as of a time of happiness,[2] the remembrance of
which was not attended by any unpleasant circumstances.   Finally, the only authority for the truth of
this anecdote is La Beaumelle ; no allusion is made
to it either in Scarron's numerous works, which are
full of information regarding himself and his misfortunes, or in the particulars handed down to us
respecting him by Ménage and Segrais, his intimate
friends, or in the works of La Marnière[3] and
Chauffepié,[4] his biographers, who have most diligently
collected together all discoverable details relating to
his life.   Without going very far in search of singular

> Ma tête à gauche trop s'incline,
> Ce qui rabat bien de ma mine :
> De plus sur ma poitrine chet
> Mon menton touche à *mon brechet*."

The date of this Epistle, 1646, is proved by that of the *taxe des aisés* which
is mentioned in it.

[1] In another Epistle to Mlle. d'Hautefort during the early years of the
widowhood of Anne of Austria (1643), we find these lines :—

> " Mais j'en aurois été larron
> Si je jouissois d'abbaye,
> Car, hélas ! en jour de ma vie
> On ne m'a jamais rien donné,
> Quoique je sois ensoutané."

He had then been an invalid for five years.

[2] See the " Légende de Bourbon," written in 1641, in vol. viii. p. 10 of
his Works.

[3] See his Life of Scarron, at the beginning of his Works, edit. 1737.

[4] See the article on Scarron, in his " Dictionnaire historique et critique."

adventures to account for Scarron's malady, a
sufficient explanation will probably be found in the
ordinary adventures to which he so carelessly exposed
himself. [1]

But of whatever imprudent actions he might have
been guilty, his punishment was cruelly severe.
Irremediable pains successively seized upon all the
members of his body ; and he became contorted and
deformed in the strangest manner. He has left us
the following description of his appearance, when
between thirty and forty years old :—

"My sight is tolerably good, though my eyes are
large ; they are blue, and one is more deeply sunken
than the other, on the side on which I bend my head.
My nose is rather well formed. My teeth, formerly
square pearls, are now of the colour of wood, and
will soon be of the colour of slate ; I have lost one-
and-a-half on the right side, and two-and-a-half on
the left side, and two are not quite sound. My legs
and thighs first formed an obtuse angle, afterwards
an equilateral angle, and, at length, an acute one.
My thighs and body form another ; and my head,
always dropping on my breast, makes me not ill
represent a **Z**. I have got my arms shortened as
well as my legs ; and my fingers as well as my arms.

[2] In support of this opinion, see an epigram by Gilles Boileau, in vol. i.
part 2, p. 176 of Scarron's Works. It is only fair to say that this epigram,
which is full of odious invectives, cannot be received as authoritative in the
matter.

In a word, I am an abridgment of human miseries." [1]
In another place, he tells us that he is unable to use
his hands for any purpose whatever ; [2] and he frequently informs his correspondents that he is obliged
to employ one of his servants to write his letters. [3]
On one occasion, he was overwhelmed with grief at
not having been able to see Mme. de Villarceaux,
when she paid him a visit :—

"Car elle étoit à côté de sa chaise," [4]

and he could not turn his head round to look at her.
As for walking, it was entirely out of the question ; [5]
and he could hardly be seated in his padded chair
without suffering excruciating pain. [6] The slightest

[1] See the "Portrait de M. Scarron, fait par lui-même, et adressé au
lecteur qui ne m'a jamais vu," in vol. i., part 2, p. 20, of his Works.

[2] In a letter to the Countess de Fiesque (vol. viii. p. 123 of his Works)
he complains that a fly once settled on his nose, and he was unable to
drive it away because his servants had left the room.

"Pour mes mains, vous le savez bien,
Elles me servent moins que rien."

He was at this time able to write with them, but several passages in his
letters prove that he was frequently unable to use them at all.

[3] In his "Seconde Légende de Bourbon," vol. viii. p. 15, he says :—

"Mes mains, ou bien celles d'un autre,
Car point n'en a l'esclave vôtre,
Ou bien, s'il en pend à son bras,
Le pauvret ne s'en aide pas."

See also the "Epître à Pélisson," vol. viii. p. 107.

[4] "Epître à Mademoiselle de Lenville," vol. viii. p. 94.

[5] In the "Epître à l'Infante d'Escars," vol. viii. p. 100, he says :—

"Et même on dit, mais ce sont médisans,
Qu'on ne m'a vu marcher depuis trois ans."

[6] In the "Seconde Légende de Bourbon," vol. viii. p. 15, he says :—

"Comment y trouver repos
N'étant assis que sur des os ?"

movement put him to torture ; [1] he was able to sleep only by the aid of opium ; [2] and his emaciation was so great, that his body hardly possessed the consistency of a skeleton. [3]

Under these dreadful circumstances, Scarron still retained two sources of consolation,—his wit and his stomach. [4]   But if courage be necessary to make use of wit, money is still more necessary to supply the wants of the stomach ; and poverty formed the climax of Scarron's misfortunes.   Without a profession, and utterly incapable of earning his own livelihood, Scarron had no resource but the fortune of his father, who was still alive ; and it would appear that his mother-in-law, whose interest it was to confirm him in his carelessness rather than to

---

> Mais ici je me glorifie,
> Homme sans c . . . ne s'assit mie,
> Et moi pauvret je n'en ai point."

[1] "A single visit which he paid not long ago to the Chancellor gave him a great pain in the back, and caused him to say, '*Hélas !*' more than two thousand times, besides exclaiming, '*Je renie ma vie !*' and '*Maudit soit le procès !*' more than two hundred times apiece."   See the "Factum."

> [2] "Tant l'opium m'a hébêté,
> Dont j'use l'hiver et l'été,
> Afin que dessus ma carcasse
> Le sommeil parfois séjour fasse."

[3] See the "Vers adressés à Scarron sur son Virgile Travesti," vol. iv. p. 73 :—

> "Toi qui chantas jadis Typhon,
> Chétif de corps, d'âme sublime,
> Toi qui pèses moins qu'un chiffon."

[4] "The interior of my body is still so good that I drink all sorts of liquors, and eat all sorts of viands, with as little reserve as the greatest glutton."—"Letter to M. de Marigny," vol. i., part 2, p. 84.

arouse him to effort, had always allowed his wants to
be supplied in such a manner that he should have no
cause for complaint. But external circumstances
occurred to aggravate and disclose the disordered
state of his affairs. Richelieu, who was deeply
incensed against the Parliament for the opposition
which it continually offered to his measures, revenged
himself upon it from time to time by strokes of
authority which awed it into temporary submission.
On every manifestation of resistance, two or three
councillors were banished ; and their recall was
made to depend upon the obedience of their colleagues.
On one of these occasions, Scarron's father, animated,
as it would appear, by the example and eloquence of
the President Barillon, and the Councillors Salo and
Bitaux, [1] displayed so much zeal and vigour, that the
public bestowed upon him the nickname of " the
apostle." [2] He was banished, with those of his colleagues whose views he had maintained ; and shortly
afterwards, in 1641, the king having declared that
" he alone had the right to dispose of all the offices
of the Parliament," [3] they were deprived of their
emoluments, and continued in their banishment.

[1] In his "Requête au Cardinal de Richelieu," vol. viii. p. 54, he thus
inveighs against these gentlemen :—

> " O Barillon, Salo l'aîné, Bitaux,
> Votre parler nous cause de grands maux."

[2] See various letters, in Scarron's Works, vol. i., part 1, p. 169, and
vol. viii. pp. 53, 86, 90. [3] "Mézerai," vol. xii. p. 145.

This event completed the derangement of Councillor Scarron's affairs ;[1] and his wife, who remained at Paris, did not settle them to the advantage of her step-children, or indeed of her own sons and daughters. Avidity is a snare in which avarice is frequently caught. If we are to believe Scarron's stories about his mother-in-law, her fondness for gambling, and the losses which she experienced through having "lent out her money at exorbitant interest," did more than absorb the profits derived from her parsimonious house-keeping, which she carried so far as to "make the holes of her sugar-castor very small," that the sugar might pour out in less abundance. Scarron, who was busied in efforts to obtain the recall and restoration of his father, encouraged by a slight expression of the Cardinal's approval of the burlesque requisition which he had presented to him on the subject,[2] was beginning

[1] See the "Requête au Cardinal de Richelieu," vol. viii. p. 54 :—

> "Quatre ou cinq fois maudit soit la harangue
> Que langue fit, et dont punie est langue,
> Car je crois bien que depuis ce temps-là
> Fort peu de quoi mettre sur langue il a."

[2] The requisition ended with these lines :—

> "Fait à Paris, ce dernier jour d'Octobre,
> Par moi, Scarron, qui malgré moi suis sobre,
> L'an que l'on prit le fameux Perpignan,
> Et sans canon la ville de Sédan."

The Cardinal observed that the letter was dated pleasantly. Scarron, who was immediately informed of this saying, was led by it to entertain the highest hopes, and hastened to thank the Cardinal in an ode which is not sufficiently burlesque to cover its attempts at pomposity. He was so much

to entertain some hope of success, when Richelieu
died, at the end of 1642.   Councillor Scarron himself
died, it appears, in 1643, while still in disgrace and
exile at Loches ; and Paul Scarron and his two sisters
inherited, not the remnant of his father's fortune, but
the lawsuits brought against them, to deprive them
of it, by their mother-in-law, " Françoise de Plaix,
the most litigating woman in the world ;" and these
lawsuits were continued for several years after her
death, by the three children born of her marriage
with the Councillor.

Against this accumulation of evils, Scarron had
to contend with a body that was scarcely alive, an
acute, frivolous, and impetuous mind, and a soul
which had undergone no preparation for misfortune.
Scarron, therefore, felt no desire to maintain this
unequal conflict, and exerted all his talents to escape
from it.   A complete child, as regarded the change-
fulness and vivacity of his impressions, he yielded
unresistingly to pain when it became strong enough
to overcome him ; and as soon as it allowed him a
little relaxation, he abandoned himself with equal
thoroughness to the impulses of his gaiety and
wit.   In the excess of his misfortunes, or even in
the simplest disappointments of life, he declined recourse to none of the consolations of weakness.   He

flattered by this compliment that, long after the Cardinal's death, he
alludes to it in several parts of his works.   Among others, see the " Epitre
à Mlle. d'Hautefort," vol. viii. p. 166.

indulged in tears[1] as well as in the most violent
expressions of very harmless anger ;[2] and when his
sufferings became less intense, he laughingly ended
by forgetting them.   At such times, he could complain without falling into despondency, and frequently
amused himself by the vivacity of his complaints,
and the originality of the shapes assumed in his mind
by the idea of his sufferings.   " He was agreeable
and diverting in all things," says Segrais, " even in
his ill-humour and his anger, because the burlesque
side of everything invariably presented itself to his
mind, and he immediately expressed in words all that

---

[1] His singular propensity to weeping is noticed in several passages of his
Works.   He terminates a jocular letter to Mme. Tambonneau, because his
agony tortures him, he says :—

"Et le fait pleurer comme un veau."

Nothing so violent as an attack of rheumatism, however, was necessary to
call forth his tears; they were ready to flow, even when he was embarrassed by the interchange of compliments. "When I receive, or am obliged
to pay compliments," he says in a letter to M. de Vivonne, " I begin to
cry, and get rid of them in the most pitiable manner in the world ; " and
he again mentions this peculiarity in a letter to the Maréchal d'Albret. In
the " Seconde Légende de Bourbon," he thus describes an adventure with
a footman, who attempted to prevent him from entering a ball-room :—

"Un jour que j'entrois dans un bal,
Sans que je lui fisse aucun mal,
Sa main voulut ma gorge prendre,
Et la prit sans vouloir la rendre,
Comme si ma gorge eût été
Un bien dont il eût hérité ;
Enfin il ressentit les charmes
De deux yeux qui versent des larmes ;
Le cœur de caillou devint chair
De cet impitoyable archer,
Et j'entrai dedans l'assemblée,
Essuyant ma face mouillée."

[2] " All that I do under this new misfortune," he writes to M. de Marigny.

his imagination pourtrayed to him." [1]   That openness
of soul, the readiness of his wit to display its powers,
and that playfulness of imagination and humour,
which led Scarron so rapidly from idea to idea, and
from sentiment to sentiment, rendered society the
chief element of his existence, and made him the
life and soul of every society that he frequented.
" I call my valet a fool," he tells us, in his description
of himself, " and an instant afterwards I call him
' sir.' "   Among his friends, passing continually from
fits of the most amusing indignation to outbursts
of the gayest buffoonery, full of animation on
every subject, set in motion by a single word,
ever disposed to dispute but never to bitterness
of feeling, prone to maliciousness but devoid of
malignity, good-natured in disposition,[2] and most

in reference to an attack of gout, " and in the furious state of grief in which
I am plunged by my bad fortune, is that I swear, without boasting, as well
as any man in France. I am sometimes so furious that if all the devils
would come to carry me off, I think I should go half the way with them."

[1] "Segraisiana," p. 159.

[2] An anecdote related by Segrais would seem, however, to prove that he
could not always take a joke; but the trick which was played him was a
cruel one to a man in Scarron's condition. One of his friends, named
Madaillan, " wrote to him under the name of a young lady, pretending
that she was charmed with his wit, and that she desired nothing more
than to see him, but she could not make up her mind to call upon him.
After the interchange of several letters, the . pretended lady made an
appointment to meet him somewhere in the Faubourg Saint-Germain.
Scarron, who then lived in the Marais, did not fail to go to the place of
assignation; but he found no one. No sooner had he arrived at home
than he received a letter, in which the pretended lady made her excuses that
an unforeseen obstacle had prevented her from keeping her word. Two
or three other appointments were made with no better success. At length,

ingenuous in his self-consciousness,[1] Scarron was
one of those amiable creatures to whom we become
attached because they please us, whom we forgive
everything because we should never have the courage
to find fault with them, whom we love to see happy
because we share in their happiness, and whose
misfortunes interest us all the more because they
never appear to us under too painful an aspect.
When Scarron was no longer able to visit his friends,
his friends came to see him : friendship and taste
brought his first visitors ; curiosity and fashion
brought a still larger number ; and his house became
one of the chief rendezvous of that joyous, witty,
and frivolous crowd, who found sufficient pleasure
in change of occupation, and whose love of amusement was so great that, in their eyes, the power to
amuse became almost a title to respect.

Never did an invalid lead a more animated life ;
but the invalid was poor, and the pleasures which

having discovered Madaillan's trick, he never spoke of his conduct without
anger."—"Segraisiana," p. 155. It was for this "unknown lady" that
Scarron wrote the lines contained in vol. viii. p. 170 of his Works.

[1] His self-consciousness as an author was concealed just as little by
him as his other qualities. "When you paid him a visit," says Segrais,
"you had first to endure the perusal of all he had written since you
last saw him."—"Segraisiana," p. 158. He called this "trying on his
works." This mania in Scarron had the good effect of correcting another
author of the same bad habit. "I perceived," says Segrais, "that I was
bored to death when Scarron, who was my particular friend, and who
concealed nothing from me, opened his portfolio, and read me his verses."—
"Segraisiana," pp. 12, 13. From this time forth Segrais thought it would
not be right to read his own poems to any one, unless he were requested
to do so.

health procures are the only ones that cost nothing·
To a taste for neatness and elegance,[1] which was the
necessary result of his habits, Scarron united the
keenest relish for the only enjoyments which still
remained within his reach. He had retained, as he
says, a good stomach, and was somewhat of a
gourmand. His *gourmandise,* like all his movements,
was communicative, and Scarron would never have
consented to take a dull meal. His table was almost
always surrounded by friends of good humour and
good appetite. It is true that the freedom of
familiarity· had banished from these repasts all
affectation, ceremony, and *entremets*— a sort of
luxury then reserved for the wealthy alone.[2] Every

[1] " Although Scarron was not rich, he was nevertheless lodged very comfortably, and had a furniture of yellow damask, which, with its accompani-
ments, might well be worth five or six thousand livres." " Segraisiana,"
pp. 127, 128. " Scarron was very neat in his dress and furniture."
Ibid. p. 186.

[2] " A very rich man may eat *entremets,* paint his ceilings and alcoves,
enjoy a palace in the country and another in town, keep a handsome
equipage, introduce a duke into his family, and make his son a lord." *La
Bruyère,* " Caractères," vol. i. p. 229. Several passages in Scarron's own
works confirm this peculiarity in the habits of his time. See the " Epître
à Guillemette," vol. i., part 2, p. 26 ; and the " Epître à la Reine," vol. viii.
p. 150. An invitation to Mignard (vol. viii. p. 438), while it gives us a
tolerably exact idea of our poet's ordinary entertainments, informs us that
he did not carry luxury so far as *entremets :*—

> " Dimanche, Mignart, si tu veux,
> Nous mangerons un bon potage,
> Suivi d'un ragoût ou de deux,
> De rôti, dessert, et fromage.
> Nous boirons d'un vin excellent,
> Et contre le froid violent
> Nous aurons grand feu dans ma chambre ;
> Nous aurons des vins de liqueur,
> Des compotes avec de l'ambre,
> Et je serai de bonne humeur."

guest was well received who contributed a dish to the entertainment, [1] and many of his friends who were not present took pleasure in thus ministering to his enjoyment ; [2] but these presents served rather to increase the number of his guests than to diminish his expenditure.   His two sisters, who had been as badly treated as himself in the distribution of their father's property, [3] had come to add to the joyous disorder of his affairs, and to augment, it is said, the number of visitors to the house. [4]

[1] " D'Elbene and I," writes Scarron to M. de Vivonne, " are excellently well pleased with our *petits soupers* of contributed dishes." He says, in another place, that this M. d'Elbene came every day to share his supper with him. He was one of Scarron's greatest cronies, and appears to have been placed in a very similar position.   He was so overwhelmed with debt that he did not venture to leave his residence in the Luxembourg in the daytime ; but he cared very little about this confinement.   One of his creditors, meeting him one day walking in the garden with Ménage and Segrais, pulled him by the coat and inquired, " Sir, do you think I shall ever be paid ? " M. d'Elbene said, in a most obliging tone of voice, " Sir, I will think about it ; " and continued his walk without bestowing a thought on the subject. After he had taken two or three turns up and down, the creditor, thinking he had had time enough for reflection, stopped him again.   M. d'Elbene turned round, recognised him, and said very quietly, " Sir, I think not." The creditor, with equal quietness, made his bow and went off.   Madame d'Elbene was in the same predicament as her husband.   When they married they had nearly eighty lawsuits between them.   " Segraisiana," pp. 66-68.

[2] His letters to Mlle. d'Hautefort, Mlle. d'Escars, the Maréchal d'Albret, and other friends, are filled with thanks for presents of this kind.

[3] In his " Factum," he demands " if it is reasonable that the children of his father's second marriage should have coursing dogs and carriages, whilst Paul Scarron, who has no other property than his lawsuit, is over head and ears in debt, and has tired out all his friends ; Anne Scarron walks the streets on foot, with her head bent forward, and muddy up to her knees, a style of walking which she has inherited from her father ; and Frances Scarron, who is neater and more delicate, is too poor to ride in a chair, and spoils a vast quantity of pretty shoes."

[4] He used to say of his two sisters that " one was fond of wine, and the other of men." He used also to say that, in the Rue des Douze Portes, in

What resources had Scarron to maintain such a
mode of life ?　The first and surest means was to incur
debts, which never troubled him until the time came
for paying them ; but this always arrived so quickly,
that he was constantly obliged to devise other means
of subsistence.　Then, he did not spare his solicita-
tions, nor were his Court friends deficient in promises.
As he was an Abbé, or at least wore a cassock, the
most natural method of assisting him would have been
to give him a benefice ; but to what benefice was it
possible to appoint so unclerical an Abbé ?　He

which he resided, there were " a dozen prostitutes, counting his two sisters
only as one."　One of them, Frances, was very pretty, and had the Duke
de Trêmes for her lover.　She was kept by him, it appears, for a considerable time, and bore him a son, whom Scarron used to call his nephew.
When asked how he came by this nephew, he replied that he was a nephew
à la mode du Marais.　See the " Segraisiana," pp. 88, 157.　Segrais tells us,
somewhere, that Scarron's sisters were not married.　But then, why does
he call Anne Scarron a " poor widow," in his " Factum ?"　And if she was
a widow, why does he speak of her by her maiden name?　In the same
document, he says that Frances Scarron was " ill paid by her lodger."　It
does not appear that any of Councillor Scarron's elder children had any
houses to let.　Was the Duke de Trêmes this lodger?　This is not
incredible when we consider the times in which Scarron lived.　He afterwards quarrelled with one or both of his sisters.　Among his Works we
find a dedicatory epistle addressed to the " très-honnête et très-divertissante
chienne, dame Guillemette, petite levrette de ma sœur."　Ménage declares that,
at the time of this quarrel, Scarron reprinted his works, with this erratum,
instead of " chienne de ma sœur," read " ma chienne de sœur."　" Ménagiana,"
vol. iii. p. 66.　This was probably one of Scarron's jokes turned into a fact
by Ménage ; and a reference to the title is sufficient to prove that such an
erratum could not have been made.　Nothing, moreover, is more open to
doubt than what has been written about Scarron.　I do not here refer to
La Beaumelle alone, but to the statements of Segrais and Ménage, his intimate friends; even the documents based upon his works and the most
authentic facts of the time, are everywhere full of the most unaccountable
contradictions.　Some of these I shall point out; but many more must be
passed over in silence.

therefore applied for a very simple one—" so simple," he said, " that it was only necessary to believe in God to fulfil its duties." [1]   But even of this he was as yet scarcely deemed capable.

At length Mlle. d'Hautefort, the firm friend of his youth, who had returned to Court after the death of Louis XIII., [2] and was held in high favour by the Queen, inspired Her Majesty with a desire to see so fashionable an invalid. Scarron was carried to the Louvre " in his grey chair ; " and, after the first few moments of awkwardness, from which not even the vivacity of his wit could deliver him, and which was augmented by the consciousness of his strange appearance, he regained his senses and originality, and requested the Queen's permission to serve her in the capacity of her invalid. The Queen smiled ; and this was Scarron's appointment. He hoped by means of his title to obtain a lodging in the Louvre ; and urged his request in several pieces of verse, in which he informs Her Majesty that " her invalid fulfils—

" Sa charge avec intégrité." [3]

But this favour was not granted him. He received a gratuity of five hundred crowns, [4] which was

---

[1] " Ménagiana," vol. iii. p. 154.

[2] Louis XIII., who was once in love with her, had afterwards banished her.

[3] " Stances à la Reine," vol. viii. p. 304.

[4] According to the " Epître à Guillemette," it was M. de Schomberg who obtained this gratuity for him. This gentleman, who subsequently married Mlle. d'Hautefort, seems to have shared in her partiality for Scarron.

afterwards changed into a pension. [1] But in vain, to render his pension certain, did he request that it might be settled upon some benefice ; in vain, to obtain his demand, did he employ every tone, including even that of penitence, confessing that in his youth he had been—

" Un vrai vaisseau d'iniquité,"

or, to speak more naturally, and in his ordinary manner,—

" Un très-mauvais petit vilain ; " [2]

in vain did he promise cheerfully to endure his sufferings for the love of God ; devotion could not possibly be numbered among his means of obtaining a fortune. His best resource, the friendship of Mlle. d'Hautefort, at length obtained for him from M. de Lavardin, the Bishop of Mans, the little canonry in which he was installed in 1646.

To these means of subsistence, Scarron did not neglect to add the resources derived from a more abundant than laborious use of his pen. It does not appear that the idea of writing for publication

---

[1] It was the Commander de Souvré, according to the " Epître à Guillemette," who obtained the conversion of the gratuity into a pension. Scarron's different biographers suppose that this pension was granted in 1643. We are inclined to believe it was not granted until 1645. The matter will be placed beyond dispute if, as is asserted, it was granted by the protection of Cardinal Mazarin, to whom Scarron had appealed in a poem entitled " L'Estocade." Now, this poem necessarily belongs to 1645, as Scarron mentions in it that he had been ill for *seven* years. See vol. viii. p. 71 of his Works. Many other reasons might be adduced in support of this opinion, if it were worth discussion.

[2] " Epître à la Reine," vol. viii. p. 149.

ever occurred to him during his younger days, when he thought he could employ his time to better advantage ; and, with the exception of a few songs to Iris and Chloris, which are all above mediocrity, we possess no poem of his composition which does not belong to the time of his sufferings. " There is nothing," says the Abbé de Choisi, " which loosens the tongue so effectually as gout in the feet and hands ; " [1] and during the few solitary hours in which his tongue was compelled to remain idle, Scarron committed to paper, in rhymes which were less piquant than his conversation, whatever he had been unable to utter verbally.   These writings were originally intended only for the amusement of a select circle ; and some excessively familiar letters, a few occasional pieces, dashed off under the inspiration of the moment, as fast as his pen could write ; [2]

---

[1] *Choisi*, " Mémoires," pp. 45, 46.

[2] See the " Epître à l'Abbé d'Espagny," vol. viii. p. 175 :—

> " Foin ! rime sur rime m'engage
> A griffonner plus d'une page,
> Et ce n'étoit pas mon dessein
> De griffonner plus d'un dixain,
> Ou d'un douzain, que je ne mente ;
> Mais toujours la somme s'augmente,
> Et j'écrirois jusqu'à demain
> Si je ne retirois ma main."

It was thus that Scarron wrote verses. At one time he ends his letter because "he is going to bed;" and at another, because " it is late, and he is going to sup." He dates one letter from his chair in the chimney-corner—

> " Entre un épagneul et ma chatte,
> Qui vient de lui donner la patte."

He avails himself of every circumstance ; nothing comes amiss to him. It seems sometimes as if he had the privilege of saying in verse what was not worth saying in prose.

verses distinguished only by arbitrary rhymes from irregular prose, a natural gaiety which nothing could trammel or regulate, a sort of childishness which occasionally possessed the merit of simplicity, and a prattle which was often witty enough to conceal its frequently insignificant character, — were the first foundations of Scarron's literary renown ; and these credentials were more than sufficient to establish his reputation, even among men of letters. Segrais speaks of Scarron's verses as "very good ;" [1] and the following lines from his little poem of " Hero " were greatly admired :—

> " Avec l'émail de nos prairies,
> Quand on sait bien le façonner,
> On peut aussi bien couronner
> Qu'avec l'or et les pierreries."

" These lines," says Ménage, " are worth all the gold and jewels to which they allude." [2] The persons to whom Scarron addressed his effusions hastened to make them public, and this publicity led others to desire the honour of having something of the kind to show. The Count (afterwards Duke) de Saint-Aignan, who is mentioned in the " Légende de Bourbon," acknowledged the honour in a poetical epistle, in which he assured the " divine Scarron " that he had read the passage in which his name was mentioned " upon his knees." [3] A work of greater

[1] "Segraisiana," p. 12.   [2] " Ménagiana," vol. ii. p. 324.
[3] *Scarron,* " Œuvres," vol. viii. p. 117.

pretensions, the " Typhon," a poem in three cantos, appeared worthy of the attention of a less limited public, and Scarron had it printed in 1644.   Its success fully equalled his expectations ; and the " Typhon," though now unknown even in the provinces, to which Boileau banished its admirers,[1] was then considered as the type of that style of composition of which Scarron was regarded as the model.   Henceforward he might reckon among his surest sources of revenue the income derived from his Marquisate of Quinette, a nickname which he had bestowed on the profits arising from the sale of his works, from the name of the publisher to whom he sold them.   He diligently cultivated this fertile domain ; and the collection of his early poems, printed in 1645, and two series of tales imitated from the Spanish,[2] maintained that reputation which was beginning to be of real service to him.   Our stage, which was then open to all comers, also presented a fruitful source of income to a man who could compose

---

[1] " Mais de ce genre enfin la cour désabusée
     Dédaigna de ces vers l'extravagance aisée,
     Distingua le naïf du plat et du bouffon
     Et laissa la province admirer le *Typhon*."
              Boileau, " Art Poétique," lines 91—94.

[2] One of these tales, " La Précaution inutile," furnished Molière with the idea of the " Ecole des Femmes," and Sedaine with the subject of " La Gageure."   In the " Hypocrites," we find the substance of one of the principal scenes of " Tartuffe."   Did Molière borrow from Scarron, or from the Spanish author to whom Scarron himself was indebted ?   This question is not of sufficient interest to justify the researches which would be required for its solution.

a comedy in three weeks ; and the Spanish drama
furnished him with inexhaustible subjects, which it
cost him little trouble to remodel. There was no
obstacle in the taste of the age to the success of those
romantic intrigues which formed the substance of such
pieces, or of those extravagant buffooneries which
constituted their principal ornament ; and Scarron
had no pretensions to reform the public taste. At
length, in 1646, a journey to Mans, where a troop of
comedians were then performing, gave him the idea
of his " Roman Comique," "the only one of his works
which will go down to posterity," says Ménage ; [1] and
in 1648 appeared the first book of his " Virgile
Travesti," the name and some passages of which
have at least belied Ménage's statement, and the
prodigious success of which assured the triumph of
burlesque.

But of all the literary labours in which Scarron
was engaged, dedications were the most lucrative ;
and he was not sparing of them. " No one," says
Segrais, " has written more dedications than he has ;
but he dedicated in order to obtain money. M. de
Bellièvre sent him a hundred pistoles for a dedication
which he had addressed to him, and I took him fifty
from Mademoiselle, for a wicked comedy which he
had dedicated to her."[2] Princes, nobles, and even

[1] " Ménagiana," vol. iii. p. 291.
[2] The " Ecolier de Salamanque." " Segraisiana," p. 97.

private persons, took pleasure in deserving, by their liberality, the place assigned to them by Scarron in his works. All, however, did not attach the same price to the compliment ; and Scarron complained particularly of the French princes :—

> " Nos princes sont beaux et courtois,
> Doux en faits ainsi qu'en paroles ;
> Mais au diable si deux pistoles,
> Fût-on devant eux aux abois,
> Sortirent jamais de leurs doigts,
> Arbalètes à croquignoles ;
> Et l'auteur enragé, qui leur fait un sonnet,
> N'en tire qu'un coup de bonnet." [1]

Mazarin was not more liberal than the princes. Scarron had dedicated his "Typhon" to him ; but the prime minister had not inherited from his predecessor that taste for literature which, in a person of high rank, is ever akin to the love of glory. Mazarin, however, was either insensible to homage of this kind, or else he thought it amply recompensed by the pension which, according to all appearance, he had just obtained for Scarron. He therefore received the dedication as a mark of gratitude which was due to him, and with the cold kindness of a protector who thought the poet had no right to ask any further favours. Wounded in his self-love, as well as deceived in his hopes, Scarron, unfortunately, did not consider himself as under sufficient obligation to a man from whom he had nothing more to expect ;

---

[1] See the "Ode au Prince d'Orange," vol. viii. p. 273.

and, though compelled to leave, in his "Typhon,"
the invocation which formed a part of the work
itself, and the suppression of which would have been
too open an insult, he nevertheless suppressed the
sonnet containing the dedication, and supplied its
place by another, which was probably not printed
at that period, but which occurs in all the later
editions of his works. Even if Mazarin had been
aware of this, neither the offence nor the offender
then appeared worthy of his resentment ; but Scarron
soon found means for making himself more remarkable.

He was at the height of his burlesque reputation
when the troubles of the Fronde broke out. A man
who held a pension from the queen, with which he
could not dispense, naturally hesitated before declaring against the minister ; and therefore Scarron,
notwithstanding his ill-will, was at first *a Mazarin*.
But the difficulties of the Court probably suspended
the payment of his pension ; and the author of
" Typhon " then gave full vent to his feelings of
dislike. When cries of public indignation were
raised against *the Mazarin*, he laughingly added,
" I dedicated my ' Typhon ' to him, but he did not
condescend to look at it." To this motive for revenge were doubtless added a multitude of others
calculated to arouse the patriotism of such a man as
Scarron. The Fronde was the party of all good

company ; and the laughers, as usual, were in
opposition to authority. Scarron naturally ranged
himself on the gayest side ; and, surrounded as he
was by friends of the coadjutor or partisans of the
Prince, he was not the man to hold out long for
a party which was regarded as thoroughly ridiculous
in all those societies which constituted the amusement and occupation of his life. He therefore became
a Frondeur ; the "Mazarinade" was the fruit of
his conversion, and gained him enough honour among
his own party to counterbalance the injury it inflicted
on his fortune with the Court party, and doubtless
also on his reputation in the judgment of reasonable
people. The Cardinal, who cared little for ridicule
after he had braved hatred, carefully perused, and
formed an impartial opinion, it is said, of the literary
merit of the poetical lampoons with which his enemies
inundated Paris and the provinces. Had he read
the "Mazarinade" only as a man of taste, we might
forgive him the anger with which he was filled by
this revolting tissue of coarse and obscene insults,
devoid alike of wit and gaiety. But, more than
this, the blows thus brutally struck had touched him
on a sensitive point. In the splendour of his brilliant
fortune, Mazarin remembered with pain the humilia-
tions he had endured in consequence of the lowly
amours of his youth, which were thought all the more
ridiculous because his intentions had been perfectly

serious.[1] Though he listened quietly to all the infamous acts with which he was charged by the new
libel that had been brought under his notice, he
lost patience, it is said, at this passage, which reminded him of his youthful follies :—

> " L'amour de certaine fruitière
> Te causa maint coups d'étrivière,
> Quand le Cardinal Colonna
> De paroles te malmena,
> Et qu'à beau pied comme un bricone
> Tu te sauvas de Barcelone.
>   *   *   *
> Ton incroyable destinée,
> Par ce très-sortable hyménée
> De toi, prince des maquignons,
> Avec la vendeuse d'oignons,
> Eût été vouée en Espagne
> A revendre quelque châtagne."[2]

Although Scarron may for a moment have enjoyed
his triumph, he soon felt that such pleasures always
cost more than they are worth ; and the brief period
of glory which he gained by this slight victory over
the common enemy did not recompense him for the
loss of his pension, which, from that time forth,
ceased to be paid, and he was never able to obtain
its restoration. Peace was made : the powerful men
who had disturbed public tranquillity obtained either
pardon or new favours ; even their rebellion, the
dangers it had occasioned, and the fears it had
inspired, were titles which they did not even find it

---

[1] His love for a fruit-girl of Alcala, whom he wished to marry ; which
caused his dismissal by Cardinal Colonna, his first protector.

[2] *Scarron,* " Mazarinade," vol. ix. pp. 6, 7.

necessary to adduce in support of their claims to the consideration of the still frightened Court. But what hopes could be entertained by a man who had been imprudent enough to wound without possessing any means of making himself feared ? In vain did Scarron repent and pray, even confessing his fault, and beseeching its remission—

> " Par le malheur des temps, et surtout pour le mien,
> J'ai douté d'un mérite aussi pur que le sien ;"

he says in a sonnet in praise of the Cardinal, "for-merly the object of his unjust satire." It was, indeed, a small matter, after the "Mazarinade," simply to confess that he had entertained doubts regarding "so pure a merit ;" but, after having lost his pension, it was a great deal too much to praise the Cardinal "for not having deemed him worthy of his anger."[1] Scarron offended like a child in a capricious mood ; when the caprice was passed, he begged pardon like a child. His friends probably did not blame him for his change of tone, but the Court did not consider it a merit ; it forgot his faults only by forgetting the culprit, and its indifference was the only thing for which Scarron had to thank it.

The author of the "Mazarinade" continued, never-

---

[1] *Scarron*, "Œuvres," vol. iii. p. 418. He adds :—

> "Je confesse un péché que j'aurois pu celer,
> Mais le laissant douteux, je croirois lui voler
> La plus grande action qu'il ait jamais pu faire."

The force of abnegation could surely be carried no further.

theless, to enjoy most brilliant popularity, which
extended through all classes of society. We learn that
a clerk in Fouquet's office refused to render Scarron
a service because he had never " dedicated or given
any of his books to him,"—a piece of politeness
which had gained him the protection of another of the
clerks ; and, in the letter in which Scarron relates
this circumstance, he can boast at the same time
that " queens,[1] princesses, and all the persons of
condition in the kingdom, do him the honour to visit
him." [2] The Court had not yet extended its influence
over the opinions and tastes of those who were not
attached to it by personal, and so to speak, domestic
service ; to have displeased the Court was not a
reason for leaving it, even to those who were in most
habitual intercourse with it ; and a pension of sixteen hundred livres, bestowed on Scarron by Fouquet,
the superintendent of the finances and the favourite
of the Cardinal, soon supplied the place of that
which had been refused him by the queen.

It was, however, during the period of distress
which followed the suppression of his first pension,
that a new guest sought an asylum in the house of
Scarron, and was received with his ordinary cor-
diality. The choice was singular ; this guest was a
nun. A lady whom he had loved in his youth,

[1] The Queen of Sweden.
[2] *Scarron*, "Œuvres," vol. i. part 2, p. 133.

Céleste de Palaiseau, though insensible to his protestations of affection, had afterwards yielded to the
entreaties of a wealthy gentleman who had promised
to marry her, but who, finding himself rich enough
to dispense with the performance of his promise, had
redeemed himself from his engagement by the payment of forty thousand francs. With this sum,
Mlle. de Palaiseau had retired to the Convent of the
Conception, which had just been established at Paris ;
but the expenses of the convent proving greater than
the funds which it possessed, reduced the nuns to
bankruptcy, and obliged them to abandon their house
to their creditors, and to seek refuge, in couples,
wherever they could. In the position in which
Scarron was placed, Mlle. de Palaiseau thought she
might appeal to his generosity without causing
scandal or fearing a refusal ; and she therefore
reminded him of their former affection. Scarron
received her into his house with her companion, and
afterwards obtained for her the priory of Argenteuil.

But Scarron, though wretched enough to inspire
such confidence, nevertheless contemplated matri-
mony, and had been inspired with this idea by a
young and pretty girl. Whatever uncertainty may
prevail with regard to the adventures which led to
the marriage of Constant d'Aubigné, the father of
Mlle. d'Aubigné, and which afterwards drove his
family from Europe to America, and from America

to Europe, it is at least certain that his family were always under the pressure of misfortune, so as to be at length reduced to the lowest degree of misery. Under these circumstances, Scarron became acquainted with Mlle. d'Aubigné.   It is not known how they were first brought together. Segrais seems to ascribe their acquaintance to a project which Scarron had long entertained. The example of a Commandeur de Poincy, who had been cured of the gout by a voyage to Martinique, had awakened within him a strong desire to try the climate of America for his own complaint. " My dog of a destiny," he writes to Sarrasin, in a letter the date of which cannot now be ascertained, " will take me within a month to the West Indies.   I have invested a thousand crowns in the new Indian Company, which proposes to found a colony at the distance of three degrees from the Line, on the banks of the Orillana and Orinoco.[1] Farewell France ! farewell Paris ! farewell ye tigresses disguised as angels ! farewell Ménage, Sarrasin, and Chavigny !   I renounce burlesque poems, comic romances and comedies, to go to a

[1] Reconcile who can Scarron and Segrais upon a point on which both seem as if they ought to have been equally well-informed. Segrais says nothing about this Indian Company. " Scarron," he says, " intended to form a company, the direction of which he offered to me, seeing that I was then more prudent than men usually are at my age, for I was then only twenty-five or twenty-six years old; and as I was connected with nothing at that time, I was not averse to undertake the management, but several obstacles arose which prevented the execution of this fine project." —" Segraisiana," p. 126.

country where there will be no sham saints, no devout
blacklegs, no inquisition, no winter to murder me,
no inflammation to cripple me, and no war to make
me die of hunger." [1]   Scarron said farewell, but
never departed ; we do not know what hindered
him ; but his mind had long been filled with this
project, and he found it beneficial to talk about a
country into which his imagination incessantly transported him, with all the hopes of joy and health,
and which these hopes adorned for him with all the
colours of fairy-land.   At this period, as Segrais
informs us, Mlle. d'Aubigné, whom he always
mentions as Mme. de Maintenon, "who had just
returned from America with her mother, lived
opposite Scarron's house." [2]   Did she reside with her
mother ?   Segrais would seem to say so ; but then
what would become of the story told of the servitude
and oppression to which she was subjected by the
parsimonious relative who, it is said, had given her
a home ? [3]   On the other hand, if Mlle. d'Aubigné
were not living with her mother, what interest would
Scarron be likely to take in the acquaintance of a girl
of fourteen or fifteen, who was kept in such subjection
that she was hardly ever suffered to speak ?   However
this may be, Mlle. d'Aubigné visited Scarron ; she
appeared at one of his parties in "too short a frock," [4]

[1] *Scarron,* "Œuvres," vol. i. part 2, pp. 38, 39.   [2] "Segraisiana," p. 126.
[3] Mme. de Neuillant. See the various biographies of Scarron and
Mme. de Maintenon.   [4] *Scarron,* "Œuvres," vol. i. part 2, p. 54.

and, unable to endure this humiliation, she began to cry on entering the room. Scarron, as it appears, took little notice, at first, of the child, but his attention was ere long aroused by a letter which Mlle. d'Aubigné wrote to one of her friends, Mlle. de Saint-Hermant. This letter was shown, we know not for what reason, to Scarron, and it struck him all the more because it was totally unexpected; for, in. his opinion, it was a singular phenomenon that a " little girl," [1] who did not know how to enter a room, should be able to write such remarkably clever letters. He entered into a correspondence with her ; mutual confidence was soon established ; and Scarron was ignorant of none of the details of a position well calculated to augment the interest inspired by a young and beautiful person.[2] At length, as Segrais informs us, the wretched state of the affairs of both mother and daughter determined Scarron to ask Mlle. d'Aubigné in marriage, though

---

[1] *Scarron*, "Œuvres," vol. i. part 2, p. 54.

[2] In vol. i. part 2, p. 54, of his Works, we find a letter which does not mention the name of the person to whom it was addressed, but which was evidently written to Mlle. d'Aubigné, who was then ill in Poitou. This letter contains the following lines, which, at the present day, it would be thought somewhat strange to address to a girl of fifteen :—

" Tandis que, la cuisse étendue
Dans un lit toute nue,
Vous reposez votre corps blanc et gras
Entre deux sales draps."

He also expresses his fear that she does not receive " all the care that she ought to have," and his grief " at seeing you," he says, "as unfortunate as I am useless to you."

she was not more than fifteen years old.[1] Was this
unfortunate situation regarded by Scarron as a
motive of interest or as an encouragement ? Segrais
does not inform us. Was he influenced by the com-
passion which he felt for his pretty neighbour, or by
his desire to obtain a companion whose care might
alleviate his sufferings ? This is a question which it
would be difficult to decide; pity might have inspired
him with some other project than that of marriage,
in favour of a pretty girl of fifteen ; and reason
might have suggested a more experienced nurse.
" What a plague it is that I love you ! " he wrote to
her while she was absent in Poitou, during the
interval of two years which elapsed between the time
when he first made her acquaintance and the period
of his marriage, " and what a folly it is to love so
much ! Upon my soul, I am continually tempted to
start for Poitou, notwithstanding the cold weather.
Is not this sheer madness ? Ah ! come back, for
heaven's sake, come back, since I am fool enough to
take it into my head to regret absent beauties : I

[1] Segrais tells us ("Segraisiana," p. 126,) that the marriage took place
after two years; as to the year in which it occurred, Segrais says (p. 150.)
that it was in 1650, and (p. 157) in 1651. These variations are natural
enough in the recollections of an old man, not collected by himself, but
from what he had been heard to relate. This same Segrais tells us (p. 12,)
that he was born in 1625, and informs us (p. 160,) that he was born in 1624.
From these contradictions let us try to extract the truth. Suppose that
Segrais, born in 1624, was, as he tells us, twenty-five years old at the time
of the proposed voyage to America, this project would have been formed
in 1649, and the marriage would have taken place two years afterwards,
in 1651. This conjecture is at least probable.

ought to know myself better, and to consider that I have more than enough to make me a cripple from head to foot, without being troubled, in addition, by that devilish disorder which is called *impatience to see you;* this is indeed a cursed disease." It appears to me that, in the feeling which dictated this letter, there is something more than mere reason or kindness. Scarron doubtless had not entirely forgotten his youth ; his mind was more than ever filled with the idea of a voyage to America ; and it is impossible to say what hopes may not have passed through the head of the invalid. At length, Scarron married ; gave up the notion of going to America ; was not cured ; and probably renounced all hope but that of those momentary alleviations which formed the happiness of his existence, and all other pleasures but those which he might derive from the society of an amiable person. On the very day of his marriage, he said, speaking of his wife : " I shall not do her any follies, but I shall teach her a great many." [1] There is reason to believe that he kept his word on both points.

Of all persons, however, whom he could have chosen, Mme. Scarron was perhaps the least fitted for that kind of jokes which he did not fail to make at her expense ; [2] and she was also the only person

---

[1] "Segraisiana," p. 97.

[2] Segrais, talking with Scarron, soon after his marriage, inquired, whether seriously or not I cannot tell, what hopes and means he had of

capable of arresting, or at least moderating, his bad habits. "Before they had been married three years," says Segrais, "she had corrected him of a great many things."[1] But how, when only seventeen years old, at an age when virtue is so timid, and modesty is afraid even to intimate that it is offended,—how, with fewer means of persuasion, perhaps, than a woman usually possesses over her husband, did she so quickly attain to sufficient influence to overcome habits so deeply rooted? How came this influence to extend over all those visitors whom her husband had accustomed to such unrestrained freedom? Mme. de Caylus, to whom the fact had been confirmed by all the contemporaries of her aunt,[2] tells us with astonishment that this young person, "by her virtuous and modest manners, inspired so much respect that none of the young men who surrounded her ever ventured to utter any words of double meaning in her presence."[3] In the innocence and

---

obtaining a posterity. "Do you offer," said Scarron, laughingly, "to do me this pleasure? Maugin here will do me that service whenever I please." Maugin was his *valet-de-chambre*, and a very good fellow. "Maugin," continued Scarron, "will you not beget a child for my wife?" Maugin replied: "Yes, sir, if it please God." "This answer, which Maugin had to repeat more than a hundred times, made all those laugh who were accustomed to visit Scarron." "Segraisiana," p. 156. Perhaps Mme. Scarron had to laugh with the rest.

[1] "Segraisiana," p. 159.

[2] "I was not told these particulars by herself alone, but by my father, by the Marquis de Beuvron, and by many others, who lived in the house at the same time." "Souvenirs de Caylus," p. 8.

[3] Ibid. It is not easy to reconcile this statement with the account which Scarron himself gives of the tone of his visitors, in a letter to M. de Vivonne.

modesty of youth, there is something which all
hesitate to wound, for fear of sullying it lustre ; and
youth thus derives, from the enthusiasm peculiar to
it, an austere courage which sometimes astonishes
reason itself. Scarron's house, meanwhile, lost none
of its charms ; for, with the strict propriety of her
age, Mme. Scarron had introduced the refined
tastes of a mind well adapted to profit by all that
was so lavishly displayed around her. " Mme. de
Maintenon," says Segrais, " is indebted for her wit to
Scarron, and she knows it ; "[1] and Scarron, on his
part, freely acknowledged the fertility of the soil
which he had cultivated. " Mme. de Maintenon,
who was a lady of perfect wisdom," continues
Segrais, " rendered important services to Scarron ; for
he consulted her regarding his works, and profited
greatly by her corrections."[2]

The wife, however, who had acquired sufficient
influence over her husband to curb and regulate his
imagination to a considerable extent, was unable to
introduce into her household that orderly management which was required by the state of their
finances. Shortly after his marriage, Scarron had
lost the lawsuit which had been his plague for so
long a time. This is, at least, stated as a fact by the
" Muse de Loret ; "[3] but it is somewhat difficult to

[1] " Segraisiana," p. 99.   [2] Ibid. p. 127.
[3] A kind of literary gazette, in which nearly all the literary events

reconcile this assertion with another statement equally well authenticated, that about this time his relatives restored to him the property which he had made over to them as a gift.[1] Whatever this property may have been, it is probable that Scarron was never able to turn it to much account. Ménage tell us that " he possessed a house, which

of the time were recorded. In the number for June 9, 1653, we read:—

> " M. Scarron, esprit insigne,
> Et qui n'écrit aucune ligne,
> Du moins en qualité d'auteur,
> Qui ne plaise fort au lecteur,
> Avoit un procès d'importance
> Au premier parlement de France,
> Lequel il a perdu tout net;
> Plusieurs opinant du bonnet
> En faveur de sa belle-mère."

The gazetteer then compliments Scarron upon this circumstance, as delivering him from a very unpleasant dilemma:—

> " Car avec sa paralysie
> Ce seroit un mal plein d'excès
> Qu'une femme avec un procès."

One thing might lead us to doubt the testimony of the "Muse de Loret," and that is, that it speaks of Scarron's mother-in-law as alive, whereas Scarron, in his "Factum," five or six years before, mentions her as dead.

[1] In several passages in his Works he mentions this gift with regret. In his "Epître à M. Fourzeau," vol. viii. p. 132. he says:—

> " Et surtout le Seigneur vous garde
> D'être donataire entre vifs;"

and in his "Epître à Mgr. Rosteau," vol. viii. p. 234, he says:—

> " Tu sais comme on m'a guerdonné,
> Quand en sot j'ai mon bien donné."

This last letter is dated in 1648. Segrais tells us positively (p. 88): " When he married he had no property, for he had given the little he possessed to his relatives; but they returned it to him." The same Segrais tells us (p. 126,) that when Scarron asked Mlle. d'Aubigné in marriage, he said that " until they started for the Indies, they could live very comfortably on his small estate and his marquisate of Quinette."

he sold to M. Nublé for fourteen thousand francs.
M. Nublé, thinking it was worth more, gave him
sixteen thousand. Upon this, M. Scarron wrote to
me, begging me to call upon him. At first he told
me with great seriousness, as if he had been offended:
' M. Nublé has played me an unprecedented trick.
What do you think ? I sold him a house for fourteen thousand francs, and he has sent me sixteen
thousand. I repeat again, sir, this is contrary to all
custom ; and I have therefore requested you to call
upon me about it.' "[1] Segrais, who relates the same
anecdote, says that this house of Scarron's was
situated near Amboise, where all the property of
Councillor Scarron lay. Neither Segrais nor Ménage
fix the date of this circumstance ; but the natural
inference from their story is that Scarron still
possessed some property, and that he sold it ; from
which we may further conclude that he spent its
proceeds in his usual way. His expenditure and
embarrassments continued after his marriage just
as before it. His incessantly recurring wants were
insufficiently supplied even by the princely liberality of
Fouquet, whose taste for literature and whose natural
munificence had received an additional stimulus in
favour of Scarron from the recommendation of his
friend Pelisson, and the friendship of Madame
Fouquet, who was all the more sensible to the charms

---

[1] " Ménagiana," vol. iii. p. 291.

of Madame Scarron because she had nothing to fear
from the effect which they might produce upon her
husband.   We are told that a present of a thousand
crowns, sent to Scarron by the hands of Pelisson, were
of essential service—

> " Faire lever le siège ou le blocus
> Dont créanciers, gens de mauvais visage,
> D'esprit mauvais, de plus mauvais langage,
> Sourds à la plainte ainsi qu'à la raison,
> Troubloient souvent la paix de la maison." [1]

But the storm thus calmed was quickly followed by
other storms.   Scarron, in several letters, entreats
the support of Fouquet to obtain the concession of a
privilege which would " retrieve his position in the
world," and yield him an income of four or five
thousand livres.   " This is," he says, " the last hope
of my wife and myself." [2]   And so great was his
distress that, on one occasion when he thought his
request had been rejected, he wrote to his protector
that he had fallen ill of grief, and added : " If you
knew what we have to fear, and what will become of
us if this affair does not succeed, you would not be
astonished at the despair of M. de Vissins and myself,
if I may be allowed to speak of him in these terms.
Otherwise, all we have to do is to poison ourselves." [3]

---

[1] " Epître à Pelisson," vol. viii. p. 108.

[2] " Lettre au Surintendant," vol. i. part 2, p. 116.   The privilege was to
establish a company of porters at the gates of Paris.

[3] Ibid. p. 106.   These letters, as well as Scarron's various works, are so
carelessly arranged, even in the best editions, that the order of facts, which
might have been used to gain at least a presumption of the dates, is con-

The affair succeeded ; Scarron sold his privilege and bought it again ; and probably always made bad bargains. At another time, his letters inform us that he had promised, for six hundred pistoles, to use his influence with the Superintendent of the Finances in reference to an affair on which he had to decide ; and when a favourable decision had been given, Scarron applied to the Superintendent himself, in order to obtain from the parties interested the payment of the sum which they had promised, but now refused. The task of obtaining money occupied all that portion of his life which he did not employ in spending it.

Amid his embarrassments, misfortunes and gaiety, Scarron was fast approaching his end. His body, worn out by disease, could no longer continue the conflict it had maintained for twenty years. He knew that his death was at hand, and he contemplated its arrival with a tranquillity which was perhaps more astonishing than the vivacity of mind which he preserved to the last moment of his life. When Segrais was about to start for Bordeaux, whither the Court had proceeded on the occasion of the king's marriage, he called to take leave of Scarron. " I feel," said the latter, " that I shall soon die ; and my only regret is that I can leave no property to my

tinually transposed. For example, we find in a letter contained on p. 104, the continuation of an affair which is begun on p. 116. This M. de Vissins was apparently Scarron's partner in this business.

wife, who is a person of infinite merit, and whom I
have every imaginable reason to praise."[1]   Shortly
afterwards a fatal crisis increased his ordinary sufferings; he was attacked by a hiccough so violent that
his feeble frame seemed scarcely able to withstand
it.   "If I recover," he said, during an interval of
calmness, "I will write a tremendous satire upon
the hiccough."   "His friends," says Ménage, who
relates this circumstance, "expected he would
announce a totally different resolution."[2]   But
Scarron had now reached the last stage of the disease
which had tortured him so long; and he was soon
reduced to extremities.   "My children," he said to
his relatives and domestics, who stood weeping
around his bed, "you will never weep as much as
I have made you laugh."[3]   Segrais, on his return
from Bordeaux, saw nothing of Scarron; but, being
unaware of his death, he went to visit him.   "When
I arrived at his door," he says, "I saw them carrying
out of his house the chair on which he always used
to sit, and which had just been sold by auction."[4]

---

[1] "Segraisiana," p. 127.   [2] "Ménagiana," vol. iii. p. 290.

[3] "Ménagiana," vol. iii. p. 291.

[4] "Segraisiana," p. 150.   Segrais places Scarron's death in the month of
June, 1660; and the circumstance of his journey to attend the king's
marriage, which actually took place at that period, would not allow us to
suppose him mistaken, if, on the other hand, we did not find the same
news chronicled in the "Muse de Loret," under date of the 10th October.
We also possess a letter of Scarron's, dated September 5, 1660 (vol. i. part 2,
p. 160); but is this date correct?   He mentions in this letter that his affair
has just been signed, and we know of no other affair of his than the company of porters, which must have been arranged long before.   His letter to

So soon had the little that remained of this singular man, and even the remembrance of his habits, disappeared from that house which had so long been animated by his presence.

With Scarron perished in France that kind of poetry which he had so largely contributed to render popular. It is a fantastic style, devoid of rules and of fixed character, the whole secret of which consists in the art of employing falsehood with skill ; of substituting, for the true relations of objects, relations which are entirely contrary to their nature ; and of thus surprising the imagination with impressions exactly opposite to those which it expected to receive, amusing the mind by what it does not believe, and deriving pleasure from the very impropriety of the images presented to its notice. As the imitation of reality is never the object aimed at in burlesque composition, in judging of works of this kind we have no means of comparison derived from real objects, and are guided by none of those rules of taste which reason deduces from the nature of things. We

the Count de Vivonne, which has already been frequently quoted, bears the date of June 12, 1660, and this date cannot be contested, as the letter turns chiefly upon the king's marriage, and the journey to Bordeaux, which had already commenced. "I am continually growing worse," he says in this letter, "and I find myself advancing towards my end faster than I could wish." It is true that this letter is long, interspersed with prose and verse, and that it contains details which prove that no alteration had as yet been made in Scarron's mode of life; but his habits had been so long associated with his disease, that they may have continued unchanged until his death.

cannot even assign any determinate form to burlesque. For things which really exist, there is only one, or a few modes of existence ; but the number of modes in which they do not exist is incalculable. " The reverse of the truth," says Montaigne, " has a hundred thousand shapes and an indefinite field. A thousand routes lead astray from the centre, but one leads to it." [1] We may travesty in a thousand ways that which we can properly delineate in one shape only ; there may therefore be as many different kinds of burlesque as there are turns of mind and imagination applied to this kind of composition. Thus the burlesque of Scarron is by no means identical with that of Rabelais, and it is useless to inquire in what respects either of them may have been indebted to the Italian burlesque poets who were their contemporaries or predecessors ; for that which they have borrowed would be precisely that which would not be worth remarking in their works, the piquancy of which can consist only in their utterly unexpected originality. Rabelais was doubtless indebted to models for the gigantic subject of his work, but this is of very little importance ; had the subject been entirely his own invention, if this were his sole merit, Rabelais would have been entirely unknown at the present day. But when the subject was once given, the manner in which Rabelais

---

[1] *Montaigne*, " Essais," book i. chap. 9.

treated it, the points which he drew out of it, the
kind of relative truth which he imparted to the
details of a fantastic picture,—these belong to the
peculiar nature of his imagination, and constitute the
originality and charm of his work.

The subject of "Typhon" belongs still less to
Scarron, than his "Grand-Gousier," his "Gargantua,"
and his "Pantagruel" belong to Rabelais.   Scarron's
"Typhon"—

> "A qui cent bras longs comme gaules
> Sortoient de deux seules épaules,"

with his brothers Mimas, Enceladus, and others—

> "Qui certes ne lui cédoient guère
> Tant à déraciner les monts
> Qu'à passer ces rivières sans ponts,
> Mettre les plus hautes montagnes
> Au niveau des plates campagnes,
> Et de grands pins faire bâtons
> Qui n'étoient encore assez longs;"

all the details of the wondrous exploits of this race of
giants contain nothing which had not long ago been
far surpassed by the heroes of Rabelais, of the
"Gigantea,"[1] and of a host of other works of the
same kind.   But a new mode of bringing these
singular personages into action had presented itself
to the original imagination of Scarron ; although it is
not well suited to the subject which he had chosen
out of imitation, it is peculiarly his own ; it is
characteristic of the peculiar conformation of a mind

---

[1] An Italian burlesque poem, of the sixteenth century. See *Ginguené*,
"Histoire littéraire d'Italie," vol. v. p. 561.

which could see things only from a certain point of
view, and could describe them only as it saw them.
After having described these monstrous children of
earth, for what purposes will Scarron employ them?
What motive will rouse them to rebellion against the
gods, and kindle a war which will throw all Olympus
into confusion?   One Sunday, Typhon,

" Après avoir très-bien dîné,"

proposes to his brothers to have a game of skittles.
His proposal is accepted; but, while playing, Mimas
awkwardly hits him with a skittle on the ankle.
Typhon, in a rage, seizes upon both balls and skittles,
and hurls them through the skies with such vigour
that they penetrate into Heaven, and knock over the
table and break the glasses of Jupiter, who, being
rather more drunk than usual on that day, jumps up,

" Jure deux fois par l'Alcoran ;
C'étoit son serment ordinaire,"

and sends Mercury to earth to command the giants,
on pain of incurring his wrath and thunderbolts, to
send him, before the end of the week, a hundred
Venice glasses to repair the loss occasioned by the
overthrow of his sideboard.

From this specimen it is easy to perceive the
character of Scarron's burlesque.   All the pleasantry
which he can educe from it depends entirely upon
those common or puerile habits, and those petty and
vulgar incidents of which he composes his portraitures

of the marvellous personages whom he introduces into his productions. Mercury, on crossing Helicon, is regaled by the Muses with a " pot of cherries,"

> " Et du dedans d'un grand pâté,
> Qu'Apollon, leur Dieu tutélaire,
> Depuis peu leur avoit fait faire."

Being compelled to pass a night on earth, Mercury sleeps at the top of a tree, for fear of robbers ; and all that he obtains from the giants, in answer to his eloquent orations, is the *refrain* of a popular song, and the promise of a sound box on the ears if he talks any longer. War is declared, and Jupiter calls upon the Sun to sell him some of his exhalations for the manufacture of thunderbolts :—

> " Le soleil dit qu'il en avoit,
> Mais que déjà on lui devoit
> D'argent une somme assez bonne,
> Qu'au ciel on ne payoit personne."

He also complains that the last materials he supplied were only used—

> " A faire pétards et fusées ; "

but eventually he does not refuse his assistance. Jupiter appears armed for battle, mounted on his eagle, and holding—

> " Un grand tonnerre à son côté."

Mars passes his time in smoking tobacco and drinking beer :—

> " Et de vouloir l'en empêcher,
> C'étoit vouloir au sourd prêcher,
> Car il n'étoit pas amiable,
> Ains juroit Dieu comme un vrai diable."

Jupiter, on his side, calls Venus all the bad names that she deserves, and the tone of the other gods corresponds with that of the most powerful of them all. In a word, Scarron has travestied Olympus into a family of vulgar citizens.

Nothing, therefore, could have been less adapted to Scarron's turn of mind than the subject which he had chosen. As he was entirely destitute of that imaginative power which can forcibly depict the fantastic and extraordinary, and as he was, on the contrary, endowed with the faculty of vividly distinguishing all the details of a common and trivial truth, he has overloaded his personages with such details, although the position in which he has placed them would seem to destine them to surprise us rather by the singularity of their behaviour than by any other circumstance. It was not worth while to describe to us gods and giants, if he intended to make them act constantly like ordinary men, and never to recal our attention to the marvellous greatness of their nature, which is so well adapted to bring the littleness of their interests and actions into strong relief. Jupiter, disguised as Cassandra, would be amusing enough, if the Cassandra who is always present to our view did not make us ever forget the existence of the Jupiter.

Taking the nature of Scarron's talent into consideration, the idea of the " Virgile Travesti " must be

regarded as infinitely happier than that of the
" Typhon." It may have been furnished him by the
" Eneide Travestita " of Giovanni Battista Lalli, an
Italian poet, who may almost be called his contemporary ; [1] but " with the exception of the title,"
says Ménage, "the two works are entirely different."[2]
The choice of such a subject, moreover, was certainly
not very difficult ; but it was admirably adapted to
call forth Scarron's powers. Here he was not required
to create exalted personages, in order to render them
afterwards absurd and ridiculous. He found ready
made to his hand, noble lines which he might parody,
imposing recollections which he might load with
laughable details, splendid imagery which he might
travesty, and, throughout the work, a contrast
naturally existing between his subject and the
manner in which he was disposed to treat it. Virgil
always saved him at least half his trouble. We
might laugh to see a man who is endeavouring to
save something from his burning house, carefully
folding up :—

> " Six chemises, dont son pourpoint
> Fut trop juste de plus d'un point,"

and prudently ordering his son to carry off " the
snuffers ;" but the household economy thus ascribed
to the son of Venus and the lover of Dido, and these
details when related by a king to a queen in regard

[1] Lalli died in 1637.   [2] " Ménagiana," vol. i. p. 188.

to so great an event as the sack of Troy, acquire
a comic value which would not be possessed by
a meaner subject or humbler personages. The
remembrance which we retain of the despair and
lamentations of Dido imparts additional pleasantry
to the reproaches which, in the " Virgile Tra sti,"
she heaps upon Æneas, whom she finally calls a
"lackey," and threatens to pursue him after her
death,

" Pour lui faire partout *hou, hou !* "

All the piquancy possessed by the " Virgile
Travesti," is derived from contrasts of this kind, and
from that peculiar turn of Scarron's imagination,
which I have already noticed in my remarks on the
" Typhon," and which never represents any objects
to him except under their most common forms, and
accompanied by the most familiar details of ordinary
life. In his view the marvellous disappears, and the
extraordinary vanishes, to make room for that which
is of daily occurrence. He cannot add to the
monstrous any element of the grotesque ; and thus his
Harpies, with—

" Leurs pattes en chapon rôti,
Leur nez long, leur ventre aplâti,"

are not stranger figures than those of Virgil ; but,
when eating and spoiling the dinner of the Trojans,
they begin to sing "drinking songs," the Harpies,
transformed into a pack of drunkards at a public-
house, acquire a very amusing character.

A sort of childish naturalness mingles with the actions and feelings of all his personages ; thus when Æneas, in the midst of burning Troy, is desirous to avenge upon Helen the wrongs of his country, by freeing her for ever from—

" La peine de se plus moucher,"

Venus, his mother, appears suddenly to him, and stops him with a hard rap on the knuckles :—

" Ce coup, dit-il, dont ma main fut cinglée,
Et dont j'eus l'âme un peu troublée,
Me fit dire, en quoi j'eus grand tort,
Certain mot qui l'offensa fort.
Elle me dit, rouge au visage ;
' Vraiment je vous croyois plus sage ;
Fi, fi, je ne vous aime plus.'
—' Je suis de quatre doigts perclus,'
Lui dis-je : ' et qui diable ne jure
Alors qu'on reçoit telle injure ? '—
' Eh bien, ne jurez donc jamais,'
Dit-elle.—' Je vous le promets,'
Lui dis-je, ' et trève de houssine,
Car il n'est divin, ni divine
A qui, s'il m'en faisoit autant
Je ne le rendisse à l'instant.' "

Sometimes the opinions of the author himself are expressed with the most original simplicity ; thus, after having described the capture of Ganymede, and told how the youth's dog barked uselessly at the ravisher, he exclaims, with a burst of virtuous indignation :—

" Que le chien de Jean de Nivelle,
Auprès de ce mâtin de bien,
Est un abominable chien."

But, whether he speaks in the name of his cha-

racters, or in his own name, the ideas most familiar
to the habits of his own life are always brought into
greatest prominence by Scarron.   His Sibyl, in order
to appease Charon's indignation at being required to
admit a living man into his boat, enumerates the
good qualities of Æneas, saying that he was—

> "Point Mazarin, fort honnête homme."

And Æneas, in despair at seeing his ships on fire,
implores Jupiter to send a little of that rain which
he sometimes pours forth with such abundance,—

> "Alors qu'on s'en passeroit bien,
> Qu'un chapeau neuf ne dure rien."

No one is better able than Scarron to discern, in
an event, all the little circumstances which may enter
into it; thus when Æneas, notwithstanding the
advice of the Sibyl, draws his sword to disperse the
shades who flit about him on his entrance into
the infernal regions, the poet does not fail to make
him fall on his face, toppled over by the impetus of
a blow with which he had attempted to transfix a
Gorgon, whose fantastic body offered no resistance to
his thrust; and he then dilates on the bad temper of
Æneas,—

> " Jurant en chartier embourbé,"

and on the politeness with which the Sibyl offers him
her hand to help him up.   His pictures, on account
of the details of which they are composed, are always
characterised by a sort of trivial truthfulness, well

adapted to give piquancy and appropriateness to the
application which he makes of them to lofty objects.
But this truthfulness is sometimes devoid of interest ;
and these details are not always worthy of occupying attention, or capable of exciting laughter.   For
example, Scarron tells us that Æneas, being desirous
to honour with an offering of incense the shade
of his father, who has come to visit him, fails in his
attempt :—

> " Et remplit sa chambre de braise,
> Ayant donné contre une chaise ;"

a circumstance which, though not wanting in truthfulness, is utterly destitute of pleasantry.   And
circumstances of this kind are not of rare occurrence
in Scarron's works ; he never rejects any insignificant
details which may occur to his mind, and he often
unreasonably protracts most witless reflections,
through a series of namby-pamby verses which are
more prosaic than even prose would be permitted to
be.   Expressions frequently more trivial than original
strike us, more from their contrast to the object to
which they refer, than from their adaptation to the
image which the poet wishes to convey ; and finally,
his gaiety, though rarely indecent, too often reminds
us of that school-boy blackguardism which is inaccessible to disgust, and which is never embarrassed
by the feelings it may occasion.   Hence it is that the
" Virgile Travesti," some passages of which are

worthy to be quoted as models of truly original gaiety, cannot be read consecutively for a quarter of an hour, and that it leaves no impression on the memory but the recollection of a few lines, and the general impression of a buffoonery which often causes greater fatigue than amusement.

This is not the case in reference to the " Roman Comique." " Scarron's ' Roman Comique,' " says Segrais, " had not a dignified object, as I have told the author himself; for he amuses himself by criticising the actions of certain comedians, which is too mean an occupation for such a man as he is."[1] We are not aware of Scarron's reply to these observations of Segrais ; he probably defended his work, and most probably not on the best grounds ; for an author is seldom aware of his most effective means of defence. Scarron, however, had excellent reasons to adduce ; but Segrais was perhaps incapable of understanding them. At this period criticism did not exist, and no rules of taste had as yet been firmly established by reason, which is the true foundation of taste ; every one formed his opinions according to his own special turn of mind, and absolutely rejected whatever he was unable to appreciate. Segrais, whose imagination had spent all its life in *bergeries* and Court romances, was naturally somewhat insensible to the influence of that ingenuous truthfulness which presents itself to

[1] "Segraisiana," p. 194.

view, devoid even of the charms of a careful toilette. However—

> " S'il n'est pas de serpent, ni de monstre odieux
> Qui, par l'art incité, ne puisse plaire aux yeux, " [1]

with still greater reason, art will succeed in adapting to our delicate taste subjects whose only fault is that they are somewhat removed from those ideas of elegance to which we are accustomed.

The principal personages in Scarron's romance are not mean, although he has not made them all respectable. On our entrance into the town of Mans, in which the scene is laid, amidst the grotesque description of a troop of poor country actors *en déshabille*, the author at once inspires us with a favourable opinion of his hero, the actor Destin, " a young man as poor in clothes as he was rich in good looks," and whose rather irregular accoutrement does not destroy the impression produced by these first words of the author. This impression is kept up and strengthened by the conduct of the young man himself, whose noble sentiments, in so inferior and undignified a position, are explained by the education he had received, and the necessity which had compelled him to adopt his present mode of life. The decency preserved by his companions, L'Etoile, Angélique, and La Caverne, though a rare quality in strolling actresses, is nevertheless in strict accordance

[1] *Boileau*, " Art Poétique."

with the probability required in a romance, the chief
object of which is not to extol the virtue and sentiments of its heroines. This decency is maintained
in the midst of scenes of every kind, which occur
during the journey of the troop, whose adventures
in the town and neighbourhood of Mans constitute
the subject of the " Roman Comique." Some
characters, inferior to these at least in their sentiments, undertake the more comical adventures ;
and thus allow to the principal personages a dignity
which does not at first sight seem consistent with
their profession, and the sorry trim in which they
are presented.

We might inquire of Segrais in what respect this
profession and its attendant circumstances seem to him
to injure the proprieties of romance ; why romance,
any more than comedy, should be deprived of the
right of treating undignified subjects ; and in what
particulars the actions of a few comedians are more
low and vulgar than the household quarrels of a
woodman and his wife,[1] the knaveries of a valet,[2] or
the flatteries of an intriguing person who is desirous
to get money from a miser ?[3] Wherever talent is
placed in its right position, the subject is well
chosen ; and nowhere was Scarron's talent more
rightly placed than in the " Roman Comique ; " and

[1] See *Molière's* " Médecin malgré lui."
[2] See the " Fourberies de Scapin."
[3] See *Molière's* " L'Avare," and other pieces.

nowhere has it produced more complete effect.
These personages are not presented to us disfigured
in a fantastical manner in order to excite our mirth ;
they are exhibited to our view under the natural
forms of their condition, position, and character ;
they are laughable because they are ridiculous, and
not because an effort has been made to render them
absurd. Their pleasantry springs from their very
nature. There is something truly original in the
character of La Rancune, a misanthropic, envious, vain
scoundrel, whose imperturbable coolness has, nevertheless, gained for him a sort of superiority and
respect. The figure of Ragotin is ever the same,
—always equally merry in the various adventures
in which he is involved by his love or his foolishness.
The scenes in which these different actors appear are
varied ; the descriptions are vivid, animated, and
striking ; in a word, although the " Roman Comique"
is not marked by that force of observation, and that
fund of philosophical truth which place " Gil Blas "
in the first rank of productions of this kind, we
find it characterised at least by great fidelity in
the reproduction of external and laughable forms,
by consummate talent in their arrangement and
delineation, by an imagination most fruitful in the
invention of details, by a careful choice of circumstances, and by a measure of pleasantry which we
were not perhaps prepared to expect from the

author : in a word, we find in it all those qualities which can entitle it to high praise, not as a burlesque composition, but as its name indicates, as a really comic work.

I shall say nothing of Scarron's comedies—works which their complicated and uninteresting plots, their trivial and unnatural folly, and their strained burlesque, have consigned to that oblivion which they so richly deserve. If one of the *Jodelets* and *Dom Japhet d'Arménie* have sometimes re-appeared in our own days, it has only been by the aid of the talent of some clever actor, who has redeemed the tediousness of these ignoble caricatures, and disguised their excessive platitude by his excessive grotesqueness. Some of Scarron's " Nouvelles," Dedications and Letters, with his " Factum," and a very few short poems, are the sources to which we may still look for the piquant originality of that mind and character, the singular combination of which gained Scarron a reputation which, in his own times, was superior to that which his works deserved ; and which at the present day has fallen below that which his talent might have merited if, less spoilt by the taste of the age in which he lived and the fluency of the style in which he achieved such brilliant success, he had been compelled to cultivate to a greater extent those natural gifts which had been so abundantly lavished upon him.

APPENDIX.

APPENDIX A.—PAGE 141.

PIERRE CORNEILLE, THE FATHER,

AND THE LETTERS OF NOBILITY GRANTED TO HIS FAMILY BY LOUIS XIII., AND LOUIS XIV., IN 1637 AND 1669.

Extract from a Memoir read by M. Floquet at the Academy of Rouen, January 20, 1837.

THE readiness with which you have always received any new documents relative to the illustrious Corneille may, I think, assure me that a favourable reception will be given to a document which I have very recently discovered, even though it concerns, not the great poet himself, but his father—who, as you know, exercised at Rouen, for about thirty years, the functions of general overseer of waters and forests. This honourable post was not always without its perils; at that time, interminable wars, protracted famines, frequent interruptions of commercial and industrial operations, often reduced our province, and especially its capital, to a condition of misery such as we can in these times with difficulty imagine. The people, having neither food nor occupation, could scarcely be restrained from violation of order; seditious movements were not unfrequent, and it was even a fortunate circumstance when the famished multitude confined their turbulence to the forests which bordered on the town of Rouen. In the ancient registers of the Parliament continual allusion is made to the devastation of these forests, not by a few isolated individuals, but by numerous bands, almost always armed, who were the terror of the forest constabulary, whom they boldly faced and put to flight, and whom they some times even killed.

During the long administration of Corneille the father, in the reign of Louis XIII., nothing was more frequent than these scenes of pillage, and all the perseverance, all the intrepidity which the overseer of woods and forests could command were required in order to suppress them. To confine myself to one fact among the many others which are to be found in the registers of the Parliament of Normandy, we find that in the month of January, 1612, the elder Corneille resisted in person the armed bands who every day pillaged the forest of Roumare. [1] It is a singular fact that, out of twelve sergeants who had been previously appointed to guard the forests bordering on Rouen, eight had just been dismissed at a time when the robbers in these woods were continually being multiplied. Corneille the elder, however, followed by only four sergeants, and assisted by a substitute of the Procureur-General, went on horseback to the scene of these disorders. On the road to Bapaume he was met by a band of fifteen or twenty plunderers, armed with bill-hooks and hatchets. To the remonstrances of Corneille these desperate men answered roughly " that they were going to the forest and were dying with hunger and cold." Corneille, even though attended by so few followers, did not hesitate to order that some of the hatchets and implements with which these men were armed should be taken away from them. This, however, was not accomplished without some difficulty, and " it was suspected," says the register, " that a revolt was rising against him and his colleagues." A few moments after this, one of his four sergeants was maltreated by the advanced guard of another band, consisting of more than three hundred armed plunderers ; who, having descended from the forest of Roumare, laden with wood, took up their position in line along the avenues—"and there was danger," says the register, " lest they should fall upon Pierre Corneille and those who accompanied him." He hastened his return to Rouen, and reported to the Parliament the particulars of his adventure, which we have reproduced almost verbatim. This sovereign tribunal perceived what disastrous consequences would result from such disorders, " not only," say the king's servants, " in the

---

[1] " Registre secret du Parlement de Rouen." (Manuscript.) Jan. 7th, 1612.

injury caused to the forests, but in the disposition to revolt which would manifest itself whenever scarcity should arrive." Accordingly, acting according to the information supplied by Pierre Corneille, they took such measures as put a stop, at least for a time, to these popular movements. If we reflect on all the similar cases, so frequent during the reign of Louis XIII., when, during an administration of thirty years, the elder Corneille had thus to resist in person, and, it may be said, alone, the outbreaks of a people reduced to desperation by famine,—we shall feel how justly he merited the *lettres de noblesse* which were granted to him, and which we have only recently discovered, after the lengthened but fruitless searches which have been made at different times by those who were interested in the descendants of the great poet. Not that,—we would carefully assert this,—not that we are insensible to the fact that any nobility which is granted by royal charter must appear insignificant when compared with that higher nobility which the great Corneille has won for himself by his works and his genius. None can feel this more than we do ; yet, in our times, when so much and unwearied attention is given to curious investigations, when information concerning such men as Corneille is eagerly sought after, why should we slight the remembrance of a mark of honour which was conferred in acknowledgment of long and eminent services upon the father of this great man—a distinction, moreover, of which our great poet and his brother Thomas always availed themselves? This was sufficiently natural, doubtless, at a time when such titles could in certain places secure an honourable reception, which might, perhaps, have been denied to unadorned native talent,—and in an age which was so profusely supplied with luminaries, and had attained to so high a philosophical eminence, that the man of worth who was not somewhat graced by wealth or distinguished rank was sometimes rather at a discount. Accordingly, as sons of a *Le Pesant de Bois-Guilbert* (a name which, for a long time, has been an honourable one in that province, and is even still honoured there)—as sons of a conscientious and intrepid magistrate, ennobled on account of numerous services, and of no mean repute,—Pierre and Thomas Corneille (the one entitled Sieur de Damville, the other, Sieur de Lisle, and both of them squires), were received into distinguished circles, at first as gentlemen of a good family, and were afterwards doubtless sought for and entertained as poets and writers.

It is not for us to despise what these distinguished men did not disdain, and what besides was granted to their family at a time when the recent and remarkable success of the " Cid "—a success previously unprecedented in the annals of the theatre— might justly seem a supplement to the numerous titles of the father, and a seal to the royal grant of nobility which was to descend to his eldest son, the great poet. The " Cid," in fact, appeared in 1636, and in January, 1637, exactly two hundred years ago, Louis XIII. signed the *lettres de noblesse* which were granted by him to Pierre Corneille, father of the great Corneille. By an edict of January, 1634 (Article iv.), this monarch had promised " that for the future he would not grant any letters to confer nobility, *except for great and important considerations.*" These letters, therefore, which were granted in January, 1637, so soon after the publication of this edict, seem to possess an additional value :—

" Louis, par la grâce de Dieu, roi de France et de Navarre, à tous présent et à venir, salut.

" La Noblesse, fille de la Vertu, prend sa naissance, en tous estats bien policés, des actes généreux de ceux qui tesmoignent, au peril et pertes de leurs biens et incommodités de leurs per- sonnes, estre utiles au service de leur prince et de la chose publique ; ce qui a donné subject aux roys nos prédécesseurs et à nous de faire choix de ceux qui, par leur bons et louables effets, ont rendu preuve entière de leur fidélité, pour les eslever et mettre au rang des nobles, et, par ceste prérogative, rendre leurs vie et actions remarquables à la postérité. Ce qui doibt servir d'émulation aux autres, à ceste exemple, de s'acquérir de l'honneur et réputation, en espérance de pareille rescompence.

" Et d'autant que, par le tesmoignage de nos plus spéciaux serviteurs, nous sommes deuement informés que nostre amé et féal Pierre Corneille, issu de bonne et honorable race et famille, a toujours eu en bonne et singulière recommandation le bien de cest estat et le nostre en divers emplois qu'il a eus par nostre commandement et pour le bien de nostre service et du publiq, et particulièrement en l'exercice de l'office de maistre de nos eaues et forests, en la viconté de Rouen, durant plus de vingt ans, dont il s'est acquitté avec un extrême soing et fidélité, pour la conservation de nos dictes forests, et en plusieurs autres occasions où il s'est porté avec tel zèle et affection que ses services rendus et ceux que nous espérons de luy, à l'advenir, nous donnent subject de recongnoistre sa vertu et mérites, et les décorer de ce degré d'honneur, pour marque et mémoire à sa postérité.

" Sçavoir faisons que nous, pour ces causes et autres bonnes et justes considérations à ce nous mouvans, voulans le gratifier et favorablement traicter, avons le dict Corneille, de nos grâce spécialle, pleine puissance et authorité royalle, ses enfans et postérité, masles et femelles, naiz et à naistre en loyal mariage, annoblys et annoblissons, et du titre et qualité de noblesse décoré et décorons par les présentes signées de nostre main. Voulons et nous plaist qu'en tous actes et endroicts, tant en jugements que dehors, ils soient tenus et réputez pour nobles, et puissent porter le titre d'escuyer, jouyr et uzer de tous honneurs, privilléges et exemptions, franchises, prérogatives, prééminences dont jouissent et ont accoustumé jouyr les autres nobles de nostre royaume, extraicts de noble et ancienne race ; et comme tels, ils puissent acquérir tous fiefs possessions nobles, de quelques nature et qualité qu'ils soient, et d'iceux, ensemble de ceux qu'ils ont acquis et leur pourroient escheoir à l'advenir, jouyr et uzer tout ainsy que s'ils estoient nais et issus de noble et ancienne race, sans qu'ils soient ou puissent estre contraints en vuider leurs mains, ayant, d'habondant, au dict Corneille, et à sa postérité, de nostre plus ample grâce, permis et octroyé, permectons et octroyons qu'ils puissent doresnavant porter partout et en tous lieux que bon leur semblera, mesmes faire eslever par toutes et chacune leurs terres et seigneuries, leurs armoiries timbrées tels que nous leurs donnons et sont cy empreintés,[1] tout ainsi et en la mesme forme et manière que font et ont accoustumé faire les autres nobles de nostre dict royaume.

" Si donnons en mandement à nos amés et féaux conseillers les gens tenans nostre cour des aides à Rouen, et autres nos justiciers et officiers qu'il appartiendra, chacun endroit soy, que de nos présente grâce, don d'armes, et de tout le contenu ci-dessus ils facent,

---

[1] D'azur, à la fasce d'or, chargées de trois têtes de lion de gueule, et accompagnées de trois étoiles d'argent posées deux en chef et une en pointe. " Armorial général de France. Ville de Paris, folio 1066. Bibliothèque Royale."

souffrent et laissent jouyr et uzer pleinement, paisiblement et
perpétuellement le dit Corneille, ses dits enfans et postérité masles
et femelles, nais et à naistre en loial mariage, cessant et faisant
cesser tous troubles, et empeschemens au contraire. Car tel est
nostre plaisir, nonobstant quelsconques édicts, ordonnances, re-
vocquations, et reiglements à ce contraires, auxquels et à la
desrogatoire des desrogatoires y contenué, nous avons desrogé et
desrogeons par les dictes présentes. Et afin que ce soit chose ferme
et stable à toujours, nous avons faict mectre nostre scel aux dictes
présentes, sauf, en autres choses, notre droict, et l'autruy en toutes.

" Donné à Paris, au mois de Janvier, l'an de grâce mil six cent
trente-sept, et de nostre règne le vingt-septième. Signé, Louis." Et
sur le reply, "Par le roy, De Loménie," ung paraphe. Et à costé *visa*,
et scellé et las de soye rouge et verd du grand sceau de cire verde.

Et sur le djct reply est escript : " Registrées au registre de la
Court des Aides en Normandie, suivant l'arrest d'icelle du vingt-
quatrième jour de Mars, mil six cent trente-sept. Signé De
Lestoille," ung paraphe.

" Louis, by the grace of God, king of France and Navarre,
to all whom these presents may concern, greeting.

" Nobility, the daughter of Virtue, springs, in all states which
are wisely ruled, from the generous deeds of those who testify, at
the peril and loss of their property and the inconvenience of their
persons, that they are of value in the service of their prince and
of the commonwealth ; which has induced our royal predecessors
and ourself to make choice of those who, by their good and praiseworthy performances, have given full proof of their fidelity, in
order that we may elevate them and place them in the rank of
nobles, and by this distinction render their life and actions
remarkable to posterity, which also may serve to excite the
emulation of others who witness this example, to gain honour
and reputation in hope of a similar recompense.

" And forasmuch as that, by the testimony of our special
servants, we have been duly informed that our friend and liege
subject Pierre Corneille, sprung from good and honourable race
and family, has always had in good and singular consideration the
welfare of this state and of ourself in divers offices which he has
exercised by our commandment and for the welfare of our service

and of the public—and particularly in the exercise of the office of overseer of our woods and forests, in the viscounty of Rouen, during more than twenty years, in which he has fulfilled his charge with the greatest care and fidelity, for the preservation of our said forests—and on several other occasions when he has acted with such zeal and affection that his services already rendered and those which we hope to receive from him in the future, admonish us to recognise his virtue and deserts, and to decorate them with this badge of honour, as a mark and a memorial to his posterity.

"Be it known, therefore, that we, for these causes, and led to this by other good and just considerations, wishing to gratify him and treat him with due favour, have ennobled, and do ennoble, the said Corneille, his children and posterity, male and female, who have been or may be born to him and them in lawful marriage, by our special grace, full power, and royal authority; and have decorated, and do decorate them, with the title and quality of nobility by these presents signed with our hand. It is our will and pleasure, that in all acts and rights, as well in legal declarations as elsewhere, they should be held and reputed as nobles, and should bear the title of Esquire, enjoying and using all the honours, privileges, and exemptions, franchises, prerogatives, and pre-eminences which the other nobles of our kingdom, descended from noble and ancient families, enjoy and have been accustomed to enjoy; and, as such, that they may acquire all fiefs as possessed by nobles, of what nature and quality soever they may be; and may enjoy and use the aforesaid, together with those which they have acquired, or which may fall to them in future, in all respects as if they had been born in and descended from a noble and ancient race; so that they shall not, and cannot, be constrained to give up the same out of their hands, since we have permitted and granted, and do permit and grant fully, to the said Corneille and to his posterity, by our most ample grace, that they shall for the future bear, everywhere and in all places in which it may seem fit to them; and also cause to be placed in all and each of their lands and manors their arms, stamped as we have granted them, and as are here impressed X, entirely in the same form and manner as the other nobles of our said kingdom do, and have been accustomed to do.

" So we give in command to our beloved and trusty counsellor holding our Court of Aids at Rouen, and others our justiciaries and officers to whom it may belong, each in his place, that of our present grace, gift of arms, and all the contents hereof, they should cause, suffer, and allow to enjoy and use fully, peaceably, and perpetually, the said Corneille, his children and their posterity, male and female, born, and to be born, in lawful wedlock, ceasing, and causing to cease, all troubles and hindrances to the contrary.

" For such is our pleasure, notwithstanding whatsoever edicts, orders, counter-orders, and rules contrary to this, to which, and to the derogatory of the derogatories therein contained, we have derogated, and derogate, by these presents. And in order that this thing may be firm and secure for all future time, we have caused our seal to be put to these presents, saving, in other things, our right, and that of others, in all.

" Given at Paris, in the month of January, the year of grace one thousand six hundred and thirty-seven, and in the twenty-seventh year of our reign. (Signed) LOUIS." And on the back : " By the king, DE LOMENIE," a flourish. And on the side *visa*, and sealed and tied with red and green silk, with the great seal of green wax.

And on the said back is written : " Registered in the register of the Court of Aids in Normandy, according to the decree of this twenty-fourth day of March, one thousand six hundred and thirty-seven. (Signed) DE LESTOILLE," a flourish.

These letters of nobility were registered on the 27th of March, 1637, in the Chamber of Accounts of Normandy, and were renewed by Louis XIV. in May, 1669, in favour of Pierre and Thomas Corneille.

APPENDIX B.—PAGE 193.

LETTER OF CLAUDE SARRAU TO CORNEILLE,

REQUESTING HIM TO CELEBRATE THE MEMORY OF CARDINAL RICHELIEU,
WHO HAD JUST DIED.

CLAUDE SARRAU, councillor at the Parliament of Paris, and a celebrated scholar, wrote, on the 14th of December, 1642, to Pierre Corneille, then at Rouen, where he had made the acquaintance of Sarrau, who had lived there some time after 1640, during the interdiction of the Parliament of Normandy :—

" Scire imprimis desidero, utrùm tribus eximiis et divinis tuis dramatibus quartum adjungere mediteris. Sed, præsertim, excitandæ sunt illæ tuæ Divæ ut aliquod carmen te seque dignum pangant super *Magni Panis obitu.*

" ' Multis ille quidem flebilis occidit,'

nulli flebilior quam tibi, Cornelî. Ille tamen, volens, nolens, Apollinari laureâ caput tuum redimivisset, si perennasset diutiùs. Operum saltem tuorum insignem laudatorem amisisti. Sed non eget virtus tua ullius præconio ; quippe quæ per universum terrarum orbem,

" ' Quò sol exoritur, quò sol se gurgite mergit,'

latissimè simul, cum gloriâ tuâ diffusa, tot admiratores nacta est quot vivunt eruditi et candidi.

" In tanto igitur argumento silere te posse vix credam. Istud tamen omne fuerit tui arbitrii :

" ' Invito non si va in Parnasso.'

" Inaudivi nescio quid de aliquo tuo poëmate sacro, quod an affectum, an perfectum sit, quæso, rescribe. Vale, et me, ut facere te scio, diligere perge.

" Lutetiæ Parisiorum, idûs Decembris, 1642."

TRANSLATION.

" First of all, I wish to know whether, to your three excellent and divine dramas, you have any intention to add a fourth. But especially is it fitting that your muse should be excited to produce some poem, worthy of you and of herself, on the death of *Great Pan*. He has departed to the great sorrow of many,

" ' Multis ille quidem flebilis occidit,'

and none has more cause to regret him than yourself. For, whether willingly or otherwise, had he lived longer, he would have encircled your brow with Apollo's garland. You have lost an illustrious admirer of your works. But your merit does not require to be proclaimed by any one; for throughout the whole world—

> " ' Quò sol exoritur, quò sol se gurgite mergit,'

so widely has it been spread to your great glory, that wherever there are learned and honourable men, there have you admirers.

" I can scarcely believe that you will be able to keep silence under the inspiration of such a theme; your inclination, however, must decide this :

> " ' Invito non si va in Parnasso.'

" Rumours have reached me of some sacred poem of yours; write, I beg of you, to inform me whether it is finished, or you have made much progress with it. Farewell : continue to love me, as I know you do.

" *Claudii Sarravii Epistolæ*, Epist. 49 "

APPENDIX C.—PAGE 231.

THE POLITICAL SIDE TAKEN BY CORNEILLE DURING THE FRONDE.

Document communicated to the Academy of Rouen by M. Floquet, at the sitting of November 18, 1836.

As I was consulting, some time ago, a register of the Parliament of Normandy, I met all at once with the name of CORNEILLE, and was naturally led to inquire whether the individual alluded to was the great poet whose renown is so dear to us all. This register belongs to the period of the Fronde—the year 1650—and the name of CORNEILLE is found under the date of the 19th of February. A month before, the Princes of Condé and of Conti, and the Duke de Longueville, their brother-in-law, had been taken prisoners. The Queen-mother, Louis XIV.. then twelve years of age, Cardinal Mazarin, and all the Court had come to Rouen, from which place the Duchess de Longueville had fled on their approach, in order, at Dieppe, to attempt to gather together some who could shield her, in which, however, she did not succeed to any very great extent. The Court, which had come to Normandy in order to defeat the designs of this intrepid and restless princess, could not forget all that the Duke de Longueville and his partisans had done during the preceding year at Rouen and in the province,—their plottings, their rebellion, and their levying of men against the king, who was confined to, and almost besieged in, the Château of Saint-Germain. Accordingly, after having punished the Prince, they did not spare his instruments.

Without speaking in this place of the Marquis de Beuvron and of his lieutenant, La Fontaine-du-Pin, who were expelled from the Vieux-Palais, and of M. de Montenay, councillor to the Parliament, an ally of Longueville, who was deprived of his office as captain of the townsmen—and confining myself to that which constitutes the subject of this notice,—the place of Procureur-syndic of the Estates of Normandy was then filled by Baudry, one of the most skilled and eloquent advocates in the Rouen Parliament. He had filled this post for seventeen years to the satisfaction of his fellow-citizens, whose confidence he had gained by the unremitting zeal with which he defended their interests : but, being the advocate of the Duke de Longueville, and strongly attached to his person, as he had distinguished himself at Rouen, in 1649, among his most exalted partisans, he of course had to endure the severities and opposition of the Court. Accordingly, we find that Saintot, that master of the ceremonies who is so often mentioned in history, came to the palace on the 19th of February, with orders from the king. When introduced into the Grand Chamber, he saluted the Parliament, which (so the register informs us) returned his greeting, and begged him to be seated, —showing more civility in this, so far as that officer was concerned, than had been shown by the first President of the Parliament of Paris, who on one occasion, while in the seat of justice, impatient at seeing how Saintot busied and agitated himself, had answered to his profound and repeated salutations in the crushing words, " Saintot, the Court does not acknowledge your civilities." Saintot presented to the gentlemen of the Grand Chamber an official letter which had been sent by the king, the purport of which is as follows :—

" De par le Roy.

" Nos amez et féaux, ayant, pour des considérations importantes à notre service, destitué le Sieur Baudry de la charge de

Procureur des Estatz de Normandie, nous avons, en mesme temps, commis à icelle le Sieur de Corneille, pour l'exercer et en faire les fonctions jusques à ce qu'aux premiers Estatz il y soit pourveu. Sur quoy, nous vous avons bien voulu faire cette lettre, de l'advis de la Reyne Régente, nostre très-honorée dame et mère, pour vous en informer. Et n'estant la présente pour un autre subject, nous ne vous la ferons plus longue.

"Donné à Rouen, le dix-septième jour de Febvrier, 1650.

"Louis,

"De Loménie."

"Our friendly and loyal servants, having, for reasons importantly concerned with our service, deprived the Sieur Baudry of the post of Procureur of the Estates of Normandy, we have, at the same time, commissioned to the aforesaid office, the Sieur de Corneille, to exercise it and perform its functions until such time as provision may be made by the first Estates. To which end we have thought it well to send this letter, by the advice of the Queen Regent, our greatly honoured lady and mother, that you may be informed of the same. And not intending these presents to refer to any other subject, we shall not make them of greater length.

"Given at Rouen, this seventeenth day of February, 1650.

"Louis,

"De Loménie."

Who was this *Sieur de Corneille*, appointed by the king to the office of syndic of the Estates? The elder Corneille, special master of the waters and forests at Rouen, had died on the 12th of February, 1639; Thomas, brother to Pierre, then only twenty-five years old, could not, we should think, have been chosen to occupy such an important position. I am therefore inclined to believe that our great poet must be here mentioned; but where shall we find the proof of this? The official letter, sent on this occasion to the Town Council of Rouen, was a little more explicit; it is as follows :—

"Sa Majesté, ayant pour des considérations importantes à son service, destitué par son ordonnance de ce jourd'huy, le Sieur

Baudry de la charge de Procureur des Estats de Normandie, et *estant nécessaire de la remplir de quelque personne capable, et dont la fidélité et affection soit connue*, Sa dite Majesté a fait choix du Sieur de Corneille, lequel, par l'advis de la Reyne Régente, elle a commis et commet à la dite charge, au lieu et place du dit Sieur Baudry, pour doresnavant l'exercer et en faire les fonctions, jusques à la tenue des Estats prochains, et jusques à ce qu'il en soit autrement ordonné par Sa dite Majesté, laquelle mande et ordonne à tous qu'il appartiendra de reconnoistre le dit Sieur de Corneille, en la dite qualité de Procureur des dits Estats sans difficulté.

" Faits à Rouen, le quinzième jour de Febvrier, 1650.

" LOUIS,

" DE LOMÉNIE."

" His Majesty, having for reasons which importantly concern his service, deprived by his decree of this day, the Sieur Baudry of the office of Procureur of the Estates of Normandy, *and it being necessary to fill it with some fit person of known fidelity and affection*, His Majesty has, by the advice of the Queen Regent, made choice of the Sieur de Corneille, whom He has commissioned and appointed to the said office, in the place of the said Sieur Baudry, to exercise it for the future, and to perform its functions until the next meeting of the Estates, and until it shall be otherwise decreed by His Majesty, who commands and orders all whom it may concern to recognise the said Sieur de Corneille in the said quality of Procureur of the said Estates, without opposition.

" Done at Rouen, this fifteenth day of February, 1650.

" LOUIS,

" DE LOMÉNIE." [1]

But in all this there is nothing to prove that the author of the "Cid" is the Corneille alluded to, and I was just about to give up any further inquiry when chance presented what I had failed to discover by research.

In 1650 there was printed at Amsterdam a book, entitled, "A Special Apology for the Duke de Longueville; in which is shown the Services rendered to the State by himself and his House, as well in War as in Peace, with an Answer to the

---

[1] " Registres de l'Hôtel de Ville de Rouen."

calumnious Imputations of his Enemies, by *a Gentleman of Brittany* "[1] This book, which is seldom to be met with now, having fallen into my hands, and its first pages appearing to be curious, the interest which it might possess with reference to our province, of which the Duke de Longueville was for so long a time Governor, gave me a great desire to read it through; and this the more because, although the title attributed the work to a gentleman of Brittany, the book had all the appearance of having been written by a Norman, and one well informed on the affairs of the times. . I was very soon convinced that this was the case, and could quite assent to the affirmation of a pamphlet of the same period : " Ce Breton-là a veu plus souvent l'emboucheure de la Seine que celle de la Loire." " This gentleman of Brittany has seen the mouth of the Seine oftener than the mouth of the Loire."[2] But what was my delight in finding in this pamphlet the solution of the problem which had puzzled me for some time! After having ably defended the Duke de Longueville, and after having endeavoured to show the injustice of the harsh treatment to which that prince had been subjected, the apologist turns his attention to the instruments of the duke who had been involved in his disgrace; and, as might be supposed, the advocate Baudry is not forgotten.

" Their rage," says this gentleman of Brittany, " has fastened itself not only upon the person and relatives of the Duke de Longueville, 'but also upon his instruments, and even upon persons who were only in a distant manner dependent upon him: witness the case of the Sieur Baudry, the celebrated advocate of the Parliament of Normandy, who, after having been Syndic of the Estates for the space of seventeen years, after having been nominated by the people, and having obtained the highest respect in the province, as well as in the Council and the Parliament, was dismissed from his post, because he was valued by the Duke de Longueville, and because the Lieutenant-general Roques was not

[1] " Apologie particulière pour Monsieur le Duc de Longueville, où il est traité des Services que sa Maison et sa Personne ont rendus à l'Estat, tant pour la Guerre que pour la Paix, avec la Response aux Imputations calomnieuses de ses Ennemis, *par un Gentilhomme Breton.*"   4to. Amsterdam, 1650, pp. 136.

[2] Desadveu du libelle intitulé : " Apologie Particulière de M. le Duc de Longueville," etc., 1651.   4to. pp. 42.

able to forgive him the grave offence which he committed when he presented to the Town Council the letters of the bailiff in favour of his Highness, besides that the ministers owed a grudge against him for the harangue which he made on the subject of the reversion granted by the Queen to the Count de Dunois."[1]

So far we have the history of the advocate Baudry, which little concerns us : what follows will interest us more.

"The Sieur Baudry," continues the apologist, "has at least this consolation in his disgrace, that the protection of the people[2] has not been taken away from him for any other reason than because they wish to oppress the people with impunity, and that he has not failed in the duties of his post. In fact, *a successor has been appointed for him who knows very well how to make verses for the theatre* (the *Sieur Corneille, a noted dramatic poet,*—is here inserted in an explanatory paragraph in the margin), *but who, it is said, is sufficiently incapable of managing public business. In short, he must be an enemy of the people or he would not be a pensioner of Mazarin.*"

This gentleman of Brittany, it is plain, did not strike very hard, and it was really of the author of the "Cid" that he complained ; for, at that time, Thomas had only brought out two pieces for representation, "Les Engagements du Hasard," and "Le feint Astrologue." Pierre Corneille, on the other hand, reigned triumphant over the theatre ; only one Corneille was then known,— only one was known for a long time after,—and this was our poet, the author of "Cinna," of "Rodogune," and of "Les Horaces ;" and what other could there have been, especially in 1650, qualified to bear the designation of a *noted dramatic poet?*

It does not appear that these duties of Procureur-syndic, which were taken away from the advocate Baudry, to the so great displeasure of the friends of the Duke de Longueville, had been very ardently coveted by Pierre Corneille, who they say was invested with them to his great chagrin. The thoughts of the poet were occupied, for the time, only with his "Andromède" and "Don Sanche d'Aragon," and how could he in such a case turn his attention to the syndicate of our provincial Estates ? Only a short time

---

[1] "Apologie particulière," pp. 114, 115.

[2] This must mean,—the power of protecting the people. (Note by M. Floquet.)

before Michel Montaigne had found himself in a similar way most unexpectedly made Mayor of Bordeaux, and all the functionaries of Guyenne thereupon composed themselves to sleep as soon as they could, under the peaceful *régime* of a mayor who himself never kept watch at all. I will engage to say that Pierre Corneille had as little dreamt that he would be appointed to the post of Procureur-syndic ; that when he was invested with this dignity he troubled himself very little about it, and that as he had allowed it to come into his possession without experiencing any very lively gratification, so he saw it taken from him without regret, having kept it without making great efforts to fulfil its duties. Indeed, he only remained in this office for a short time. A year afterwards, the gates of the citadel of Hâvre were thrown open to release the three captive princes. The Duke de Longueville, gaining experience by misfortune, had promised that he would remain quiet for the future, and he kept his word. The Duchess de Longueville and the Prince of Condé spared no persuasions to induce him to engage in new intrigues, but their efforts were fruitless. After the prince had become thus submissive, how could he be refused the restoration of all the rights and all the powers of which he had been despoiled in consequence of his exploits in 1649 ? And yet how also could this prince be reinstated in his ancient power without retaining a grateful recollection of those faithful friends who had suffered with him and for him ? This the Court well understood, and the duke was allowed to restore to all his adherents the places of which they had been deprived. Accordingly, we find that the Marquis de Beuvron and La Fontain-du-Pin re-entered the Vieux-Palais ; we find that the Councillor Montenay reappeared at the head of his company of citizen guards ; and, lastly, on the 24th of March, 1651, M. Duhamel, the first Conseiller-échevin, brought to the Town Council an official letter of the 15th of March, which re-established M. Baudry in the post recently given to Corneille, and commanded all to recognise him in that capacity, just as if he had never been degraded.

This was then the end of Pierre Corneille's syndicate ; but he doubtless resigned it without overwhelming mortification. He was at that time concluding his " Nicomède," and probably conjecturing what effect would be produced at the theatre by that tone of irony and raillery which had hitherto been unknown to the legitimate drama: he was thinking much about Bithynia, and apparently little about Normandy and its Estates.

Perhaps this will be thought a very long narration of a very insignificant fact, which certainly adds nothing to the glory already won by Corneille; but not one of his biographers have had an opportunity of reading all those official documents which are buried in the registers of the Town Council and the Palace; and not one seems to have read the "Apologie" of the Duke de Longueville, which is such a curious commentary on those documents. My gratification may therefore well be pardoned at having found a new fact, however unimportant a one, respecting a great man concerning whom two centuries have had so much to relate.

Appendix D.—Page 256.

APPEARANCE OF PIERRE CORNEILLE

BEFORE THE LIEUTENANT OF POLICE, AT THE CHATELET, FOR CONTRAVENTION OF THE HIGHWAY REGULATIONS. (JULY, 1667.)

Letter, dated July 30, 1667, *to Madame* ——, *by Robinet.* (*Extracted from Loret's " Muse Historique."*)

" AVANT que d'achever ma lettre,
Je dois encore un mot y mettre
De ce qui se passe à Paris,
Et cela pourra bien réveiller les esprits.
La police est toujours exacte au dernier point;
Elle ne relâche point.
Jugez-en, s'il vous plaît, par ce que je vais dire:
Vous pourrez bien vous en sourire;
Mais vous en concluerez, et selon mon souhait,
Qu'il ne faut pas vrayement, que notre bourgeoisie
Nonchalamment oublie
De tenir son devant, matin et soir, fort net.
Vous connaissez assez l'aîné des deux Corneilles,
Qui pour vos chers plaisirs produit tant de merveilles!

Hé bien, cet homme là, malgre son Apollon,
Fut naguère cité devant cette police,
    Ainsi qu'un petit violon,
Et réduit, en un mot, à se trouver en lice,
    Pour quelques pailles seulement,
    Qu'un trop vigilant commissaire
    Rencontra fortuitement
    Tout devant sa porte cochère.
    Jugez un peu quel affront!
Corneille, en son cothurne, étoit au double mont
    Quand il fut cité de la sorte;
Et, de peur qu'une amende honnît tous ses lauriers,
    Prenant sa muse pour escorte,
Il vint, comme le vent, au lieu des plaidoyers.
    Mais il plaida si bien sa cause,
Soit en beaux vers ou franche prose,
Qu'en termes gracieux la police lui dit:
    ' *La paille tourne à votre gloire ;*
    Allez, grand Corneille, il suffit.'
Mais de la paille il faut vous raconter l'histoire,
    Afin que vous sachiez comment
Elle *étoit à sa gloire*, en cet événement:
Sachez donc qu'un des fils de ce grand personnage
Se mêle, comme lui, de cueiller des lauriers,
Mais de ceux qu'aiment les guerriers,
Et qu'on va moissonner au milieu du carnage.
Or, ce jeune cadet, *à Douay* faisant voir
Qu'il sait des mieux remplir le belliqueux devoir,
D'un mousquet espagnol, au talon, reçut niche,
Et niche qui le fit aller à cloche-pié ;
Si bien qu'en ce moment étant estropié,
Il fallut, quoi qu'il dît, sur le cas, cent fois, briche,
    Toute sa bravoure cesser,
    Et venir à Paris pour se faire panser.
Or ce fut un brancard qui, dans cette aventure
    Lui servit de voiture,
    Etant de paille bien garni :
    Et comme il entra chez son père.
    Il s'en fit un peu de litière.
    Voilà tout le récit fini,

Qui fait voir à la bourgeoisie
(Il est bon que je le redie),
Qu'il faut, comme par ci-devant,
Qu'elle ait soin de tenir toujours net son devant."

ON THE METRICAL TRANSLATION OF THE " IMITATION OF CHRIST."

BY CORNEILLE. (1651—1656.)

CORNEILLE began this work in 1651, and published the first twenty chapters of the first book at Rouen, towards the end of that year, about the same time that François de Harlay de Chanvallon, who became afterwards (in 1674) Archbishop of Paris, took possession of the archbishopric of Rouen. " As this prelate," says Corneille, in his Dedication to Pope Alexander VII. (Fabio Chigi, who was promoted to the Holy See on the 7th of April, 1655), " has marvellous talents enabling him to fulfil all the duties of so high a pastorate, and an indefatigable ardour in discharging them, I owe all the most radiant lights which have aided me in carrying out this undertaking to the vivid clearness of those weighty and eloquent instructions which he does not cease to impart to his flock, or to the secret and penetrating rays which his familiar conversation scatters continually for the benefit of those who have the happiness of being intimate with him. * * * In dedicating to him my work, I should have wished not so much to present to him a production of my own, as a restitution of his own proper wealth. But the kind feeling which this archbishop entertains for me has so far prepossessed him in my favour, as to lead him to think that, as this attempt of my pen might be useful to all Christians, so it ought to have a protector whose power extends itself over the whole Church ; and having regarded it as the first-fruits of the Christian Muse since he has filled the chair of Saint-Romain, he has believed that, offering it to your Holiness, was for him to offer in some sort the first-fruits of his diocese. His injunctions have put to silence the distrust which I justly entertained of my own feebleness ; and what without such recommendation would have been only a proof

of most outrageous presumption, has become a duty to me so soon
as I received it.   May I venture to confess that such a command
is grateful, while it is imperative ! "

Alexander VII. was himself a poet : he had in his youth composed some Latin poems, which were printed at the Louvre, in
1656, after his elevation, under the title of " Philomathi Musæ
Juveniles." Corneille read these poems, and admired them
exceedingly, especially those in which the poet has spoken of
death.   In 1656, also, Corneille finished and published the fifth
and last part of his translation of the " Imitation of Jesus Christ,"
of which the second, third, and fourth parts had appeared at Rouen
in 1652, 1653, and 1654.   "May I venture to confess," he
says, in his dedication to the Pope, " that I am delighted at
being able to take this opportunity of applauding our Muses, and
of thanking you on their account, for the time which you have
in former days spent in their society, among the great affairs
which claimed your attention when you performed the important
negotiations which the Sovereign Pontiffs, your predecessors,
entrusted to your prudence.   From the results of the time thus
spent they received this striking testimony, and this invincible
proof, that, not only are they adapted to the most exalted virtues
and to the loftiest positions, but that they even dispose the mind
thereto, and conduct the spirit which cultivates them thither, if it
makes a good use of them.   This is a truth which is conspicuous
everywhere in *this precious collection of Latin verses, in which
you have not aimed at any other designation than that of a Friend
to the Muses—and which that great prelate (Harlay de Chanvallon) has taken pleasure in bringing under my notice as early as
possible*.   He has made me read it, he has made me admire it,
with him ; and, to do you the justice which it is fitting should be
rendered, during the whole of this reading I could merely repeat
the eulogies which each verse drew from his lips.   But among so
many excellent things *nothing made at the time so strong an
impression on my mind—and no impression has been so enduring—
as those admirable thoughts on death* which you have scattered
so abundantly through the volume.   They brought to my mind
serious reflections how I must appear before God, and render to
Him an account of the talent with which he has blessed me.

" This led me to consider that it was not enough that I had so happily been able to purge our theatre from the grossnesses which had been, as it were, incorporated into it by preceding ages, and from the licentiousness which the last ages had allowed ;—that it ought not to content me that in their place a throne had been established for moral and political excellences, and even to some extent for Christian virtues ;—that it behoved me to carry my thoughts further, and bring all the ardour of my genius to some new trial of its energies, which should have no less aim than *the service of the great Master and the benefit of my neighbour.* This it is which has induced me to undertake the translation of this devout moral treatise, which, by the simplicity of its style, opens up a way for the fairest graces of poesy ; and, so far from increasing my own reputation, I seem to sacrifice to ˙the glory of the illustrious author all that I have myself been able to gain in this description of writing.

" After having experienced such happy results of the general obligation which is acknowledged to your Holiness by all the Muses, I should be the most ungrateful of men, did I not dedicate my work to him who was its primary originator. My conscience would bitterly and ever reproach me if I suffered such neglect. *   *   *   * "

The work was approved before its publication by two doctors of the Sorbonne, Robert Le Cornier de Sainte-Hélène, and Antoine Gaulde, vicars-general of M. de Harlay. On the cover of a copy which was given in 1831 to the public Library of Rouen, by M. Henri Barbet, Mayor of the town, the following words, in the handwriting of Corneille, are inscribed :—

" Pour le R. P. Dom Augustin Vincent, Chartreux, son très-humble serviteur et ancien ami,   CORNEILLE."

APPENDIX F.—PAGE 266.

PENSIONS AND GIFTS BESTOWED ON CORNEILLE

UNDER LOUIS XIII. AND LOUIS XIV.

That Corneille shared in the liberalities dispensed by Cardinal Richelieu there can be no doubt; but whether he received from the Cardinal a pension, at what time he received it, and what was its amount, we cannot accurately determine.

Mazarin also made gifts to Corneille, though doubtless with less munificence than Richelieu.

The dedication of " Cinna " to M. de Montauron, and several minor facts, prove that wealthy persons, financiers, and others, also bestowed upon Corneille splendid proofs of their admiration.

It was in consequence of the liberality of Fouquet that Corneille, in 1658, determined to continue to work for the theatre.

In 1662, Colbert, by the order of Louis XIV., employed Costar and Chapelain separately to draw up a list of learned men and literary characters who were deserving of royal favour. In the list drawn up by Costar we read :—

" CORNEILLE, the first dramatic poet in the world."

And in that drawn up by Chapelain :—

" CORNEILLE (Pierre) is a prodigy of genius and the ornament of the French theatre. He has learning and sense which, however, appear rather in the details of his pieces than in their general conception, the design being often faulty—so much so, that they would deserve to be classed only with commonplace productions were not this general artistic defect amply compensated by an excellence in particulars which imparts the greatest perfection of refinement to the execution of the parts. Separated from the theatre, it is impossible to say whether he would succeed in prose or verse composition, when acting on his own account ; for he has but small experience of the world, and sees but little that exists out of his own immediate sphere. His paraphrase translations of the ' Imitation of Jesus Christ ' are very beautiful productions, but are merely translations, requiring but little inventive genius."

Corneille, after this, received a pension from the king of two thousand livres.

He had indirectly obtained, in 1655, a gift, the exact value of which we cannot determine. On the 15th of April, 1645, Mathieu de Lampérière, his father-in-law, died while in possession of the office of special civil lieutenant to the presidial bailiwick of Gisors, established at Andelys. The vacant office fell to Pierre Corneille, by right of his wife, Marie de Lampérière, and as her share in the inheritance. Corneille (who had previously resigned the office of Royal Advocate at the Marble Table of the Palace, at Rouen), not desiring to exercise the functions of special civil lieutenant at Andelys, resigned his office in favour of Marin Duval, who was appointed to it by the king, and took the oaths of his office before the Parliament of Rouen, December the 2nd, 1651. The stipend belonging to the office, which fell due in this intermediate time (that is to say, during the time when the post became vacant, from April 15, 1645, to December 2, 1651, the day when the vacancy was filled up) would, according to ordinary usage, have fallen to the Treasury. But Louis XIV., on the 7th of September, 1655, signed letters patent, called *intermediate*, by virtue of which the whole of the stipends which had become due during the time in which the office was vacant were assigned to Pierre Corneille, to whom the king commanded them to be paid. These letters are addressed to the Chamber of Accounts at Rouen, enjoining them to grant and allow in account to Pierre Corneille, the said stipends and rights belonging to the said office—and this from April 15, 1645, up to December 2, 1651.

On the 27th of November, 1655, the Chamber of Accounts of Rouen, on occasion of the request presented to it by Pierre Corneille, Esquire, ordered, by an official declaration, the registration of these letters-patent, which exist in the " Mémoriaux de la Chambre des Comptes de Rouen,"[1] from whence M. Floquet has kindly extracted for me these particulars.

Between the year 1674—in which his son, who was a lieutenant of cavalry, died, having been killed at the siege of Graves— and the year 1683, in which Colbert died, we find that the following petition was addressed by Corneille, doubtless to Colbert. The exact date I have been unable to determine :—

" SIR,—In the misfortune which has happened to me, for the last four years, of having received no part of the gratuities by which His Majesty is accustomed to honour literary men, I cannot seek for assistance more justly and with better prospects of a favourable notice from any one than from you, to whom I am entirely indebted for the favours which I have already received.

---

[1] Vol. lxxiii. folio 219, " Archives de la Préfecture."

I myself never have, I know, merited this distinction ; but I have at least endeavoured to prove myself not altogether unworthy of it by the use which I have made of it. I have not applied it to my own personal necessities, but to keep two sons in the armies of His Majesty, of whom one was killed in service at the siege of Graves ; the other has now served for fourteen years, and is a captain of light cavalry.

" Therefore, sir, the withdrawal of this favour, to the enjoyment of which you have accustomed me, cannot but sensibly affect me in this last respect ; not in my domestic interests, although that were the sole advantage which I have received after fifty years of toil, but because this was an honourable mark of esteem which the king was graciously pleased to bestow for the talent which God has given me, and because this disgrace will very soon put me out of a position any longer to support my son in the service in which he has employed the greater part of my small property, that he might honourably fill the post which he there occupies. I dare hope, sir, that you will have the kindness to afford me your protection, and not to allow your own work to be destroyed. But, if I am so unfortunate as to be mistaken in entertaining this hope, and must remain excluded from the favours which I so highly prize, and which are so necessary to me, I only ask from you that you will do me the justice to believe that the continuance of this unhappy influence will not, in any way, weaken either my zeal for the service of the king, or the sentiments of grateful recollection which are due to you for your past kindness ; and that, until I breathe my last sigh, I shall feel it an honour to be, with all possible devotedness and respect,

"Your very humble, obedient, and obliged servant,

"CORNEILLE."

Through what causes Corneille had ceased to enjoy his pension of 2000 livres, we do not know. There is reason to believe that the pension was immediately restored to him : for we read in the margin of his petition these words, written, it would appear, by Colbert :—" Pension granted to literary men, and of which he has been deprived for four years." Nevertheless, after the death of Colbert, in September, 1683, and only a short time before his own death (October 1, 1684), Corneille was still in a state of great poverty. It was then that Boileau, nobly protesting against such a disgrace being offered to literature, informed Louis XIV. of the circumstance, and offered to give up his own pension in order that Corneille, in his declining health, might at least be able to procure the necessaries of existence. The king immediately sent to Corneille 200 louis, and commissioned La Chapelle, a relation of Boileau, to convey the money to him.

APPENDIX G.—PAGE 267.

ON THE MANUSCRIPT OF ACCOUNTS

FOR THE PARISH OF SAINT-SAVIOUR, AT ROUEN, KEPT AND PRESENTED
BY CORNEILLE, IN 1651 AND 1652.

THE learned and accomplished M. Delille discovered at Rouen, in 1840, a fact and a manuscript, which are full of interest, with reference to the life of Corneille. I will present his discovery here in the same terms in which he himself related it, in 1841, to the Academy of Rouen:—

" We know that Pierre Corneille was born at Rouen, in the Rue de la Pie, in the paternal mansion, and that this house was situated in the parish of Saint-Saviour, of which the Church, which occupied a part of the Vieux-Marché, has completely disappeared. Having had occasion to examine the registers of this parish, in the archives of the department, whither they were removed at the Revolution, I have been fortunate enough to find a proof that the family of Pierre Corneille and himself were not strangers to the administration of this parish, and that testimonies to this fact, written in their hand, remain in these registers. * * * In following the track of this illustrious name through one of these huge folio volumes, still covered with its ancient calf binding, which contains the account of the parish of Saint-Saviour from the year 1622 to the year 1653, inclusively, what was my surprise and joy at discovering in the accounts of 1651 and 1652 the writing of Corneille himself, filling thirty-three entire pages ! All this was in his own handwriting. It was a statement of the receipts and expenses of the parish, which Pierre Corneille presented, as

acting-treasurer, to his companions in office. The preamble
to this account, written like all the rest in his own handwriting,
is as follows :—

" ' Compte et estat de la recepte mise et despense que Pierre
Corneille, Escuyer, cy-devant avocat de Sa Majesté aux siéges
généraux de la Table de Marbre du Palais à Rouen, trésorier
en charge de la paroisse de Saint-Sauveur au dit Rouen, a faite
des rentes, revenues et deniers appartenants à la dicte Eglise, et ce
pour l'année commençant à Pasques, 1651, et finissant à pareil
jour, 1652, par luy présenté à Messieurs les curé et trésoriers de la
dicte paroisse, à ce que pour sa décharge il soit procédé à l'examen
du dict compte et clausion d'icelui.'

" 'Account and statement of receipts, disbursements, and expenses, which Pierre Corneille, Esquire, formerly advocate of His
Majesty at the General Sittings of the Marble Table of the Palace
at Rouen, acting-treasurer for the parish of Saint-Saviour in the
said Rouen, has made of the rents, revenues, and moneys
belonging to the said parish, for the year beginning at Easter,
1651, and ending on the same day of 1652, by him presented to
the incumbent and treasurers of the said parish, in order that
before his retirement the examination and closing of the said
account may be duly gone through.'

" Then follows the detailed account, first of the receipts, then of
the expenses, arranged in chapters in 182 articles, with the amounts
carried out in the margin, all written with much neatness, and
classed with singular regularity. * * * At the end of the
account presented by Pierre Corneille, there is inscribed in the
register, under the date of Monday, April 1, 1652, the confirmation of it which was given by the incumbent and treasurers
of the parish. This confirmation is signed by these gentlemen
and by Pierre Corneille himself.

" These thirty-three folio pages, entirely in the handwriting of
this great man, are, notwithstanding the small amount of interest
attaching to the matters treated of, an exceedingly valuable relic
for the town of Rouen. The handwriting of Corneille is exceedingly seldom to be met with. This was the same year in which
Corneille wrote his admirable tragedy of " Nicomède," and

perhaps the same pen which was employed in writing this parish account was also employed in the tragedy. There is no doubt that it was composed at Rouen.

" That Corneille made a prolonged sojourn in his native town is confirmed by these registers of Saint-Saviour, although the generally received opinion is opposed to this. His signature is to be found there in the years 1648, 1649, 1651, and 1652, which shows that he was then at Rouen. We find him there almost continually up to the year 1662, the period when his latest biographer, M. Taschereau, supposes he quitted Rouen and took up his residence in Paris. After the year 1662, his name does not again appear. * * *

" At the end of the account presented by Corneille to the treasurers of his parish, we read in the register, under the date of April 1, 1652, the following note :—

" ' There was given by the Sieur Corneille, to the treasury of the said parish, a black velvet pall, for which his mother contributed the sum of one hundred livres which she has given to the said treasury, in order that the said Sieur Corneille might have the privilege of availing himself of it for them and his family and domestics, without paying anything for it.'

" This gift proves that Corneille entertained at that time the intention of ending his days at Rouen. It was destined to be otherwise. The black velvet pall at the church of Saint-Saviour did not cover the remains of the great poet; Saint-Roch, at Paris, was to be the scene of his obsequies."

(Biographical note on Pierre Corneille, by M. A. Delille, in the " Précis des Travaux de l'Académie Royale de Rouen pour l'Année 1840," pp. 276—283.)

THE END.